Oliver Pfirrmann · Günter H. Walter
(Editors)

Small Firms and Entrepreneurship in Central and Eastern Europe

A Socio-Economic Perspective

With 22 Figures and 42 Tables

Physica-Verlag
A Springer-Verlag Company

Dr. Oliver Pfirrmann
Free University of Berlin
Department of Political and Social Science
Center of Research on Policy and Technology
Ihnestraße 53
14195 Berlin
Germany
opfirrmann@t-online.de
www.fu-berlin.de

Dr. Günter H. Walter
Fraunhofer Institute for Systems
and Innovation Research ISI
Breslauer Straße 48
76139 Karlsruhe
Germany
guenter.walter@isi.fgh.de
www.isi.fgh.de

ISSN 1431-9667
ISBN 3-7908-1467-9 Physica-Verlag Heidelberg New York

Cataloging-in-Publication Data applied for
Die Deutsche Bibliothek – CIP-Einheitsaufnahme
Pfirrmann, Oliver: Small firms and entrepreneurship in Central and Eastern Europe: a socio-economic perspective; with 42 tables / Oliver Pfirrmann; Günter H. Walter. – Heidelberg; New York: Physica-Verl., 2002
(Technology, innovation and policy; 14)
ISBN 3-7908-1467-9

Physica-Verlag Heidelberg New York
a member of BertelsmannSpringer Science+Business Media GmbH

Softcover design: Erich Kirchner, Heidelberg
SPIN 10862608 88/2202-5 4 3 2 1 0 – Printed on acid-free paper

TECHNOLOGY, INNOVATION and POLICY 14

Series of the Fraunhofer Institute
for Systems and Innovation Research ISI

TECHNOLOGY, INNOVATION and POLICY

Series of the Fraunhofer Institute
for Systems and Innovation Research ISI

Volume 1:
Kerstin Cuhls, Terutaka Kuwahara
Outlook for Japanese and German Future Technology
1994. ISBN 3-7908-0800-8

Volume 2:
Guido Reger, Stefan Kuhlmann
European Technology Policy in Germany
1995. ISBN 3-7908-0826-1

Volume 3:
Guido Reger, Ulrich Schmoch (Eds.)
Organisation of Science and Technology at the Watershed
1996. ISBN 3-7908-0910-1

Volume 4:
Oliver Pfirrmann, Udo Wupperfeld and Joshua Lerner
Venture Capital and New Technology Based Firms
1997. ISBN 3-7908-0968-3

Volume 5:
Knut Koschatzky (Ed.)
Technology-Based Firms in the Innovation Process
1997. ISBN 3-7908-1021-5

Volume 6:
Frieder Meyer-Krahmer (Ed.)
Innovation and Sustainable Development
1998. ISBN 3-7908-1038-X

Volume 7:
Ulrike Bross, Annamária Inzelt and Thomas Reiß
Bio-Technology Audit in Hungary
1998. ISBN 3-7908-1092-4

Volume 8:
Gunter Lay, Philip Shapira and Jürgen Wengel (Eds.)
Innovation in Production
1999. ISBN 3-7908-1140-8

Volume 9:
Frieder Meyer-Krahmer (Ed.)
Globalisation of R&D and Technology Markets
1999. ISBN 3-7908-1175-0

Volume 10:
Klaus Menrad et al.
Future Impacts of Biotechnology on Agriculture, Food Production and Food Processing
2000. ISBN 3-7908-1215-3

Volume 11:
Emmanuel Muller
Innovation Interactions between Knowledge-Intensive Business Services and Small and Medium-Sized Enterprises
2001. ISBN 3-7908-1362-1

Volume 12:
Knut Koschatzky, Marianne Kulicke and Andrea Zenker (Eds.)
Innovation Networks
2001. ISBN 3-7908-1382-6

Volume 13:
Kerstin Cuhls, Knut Blind and Hariolf Grupp
Innovations for our Future
2002. ISBN 3-7908-1434-2

Preface and Acknowledgement

Since the collapse of communist governments in Central and Eastern European Countries (CEECs), there has been a broad agreement among economists and policy makers regarding the essential elements of an effective programme of transition towards a market economy. Macroeconomic issues had been given highest priority on the agenda. These were: how to control inflation, to maintain reasonable balance in the government's budget and the trading account, to relax control over prices and international transactions, as well as the aspects of privatisation, de-monopolisation, and restructuring. However, the cardinal social and economic transformations that appeared in the context of this agenda have left many hopes and expectations unfulfilled. While the general aim of these transformations, to create economically developed democratic societies, has become visible in several, but not all, CEECs more and more structural and innovation problems have come into view. As a consequence, so-called 'top-down transformation' has been complemented by 'bottom-up transformation', i.e. by the generation and support of new enterprises.

In CEECs much hope is pinned on the emerging entrepreneurial small firm sector to carry these economies out of their current economic position, e.g. either to a comparable level, adequate to meet the standards of a reunifying Europe, or at least to an improved level, first and foremost out of their specific transformation crisis. Now that bottom-up transformation has been practised for several years, it is time to examine progress in the development of the small and medium sized enterprises (SMEs) sector on the CEECs so far.

With the support of the German Ministry of Education and Research and the Volkswagen-Foundation, a conference was held on November 17/18, 1999 in Karlsruhe. The conference, launched by Fraunhofer Institute for Systems and Innovation Research (Karlsruhe) and the Center of Research on Policy and Technology at Free University Berlin was organised as a forum for dissemination and discussion of the results of recently completed and ongoing research on SME and entrepreneurship in CEECs and related subjects. These are, for example: the factors supporting and hindering SME development, small-scale privatisation and 'spin-offs', the transfer of technology to small firms, research and development (R&D) and innovation in manufacturing, the elaboration of industry-related policies. The conference presented recent results of techno-economic research and practical experiences relating to small and entrepreneurial firms in East and West, and especially their role in the generating of necessary market turbulences, economic regeneration and restructuring in transformation countries. The majority of the following contributions stem from this conference, some of them were written especially for this volume. The editors would like to thank all contributors for their engagement in providing information either on their country or on specific aspects of small firms and entrepreneurship in CEECs.

This volume would not have been completed without the assistance of Mrs. Gabriele Küchlin and Mrs. Anne Ray, who helped the editors with the layout of the contributions and eliminated several errors both with regard to meaning and from a grammatical viewpoint. Their work was of the highest quality. The remaining errors, however, are within our responsibility. Besides this, we hope that some of the theses presented in the book can contribute to the discussion on the socio-economics of the transformation process in Central and Eastern Europe.

Berlin/Karlsruhe, October 2001

Oliver Pfirrmann Günter H. Walter

Contents Page

Introduction

Oliver Pfirrmann, Günter H. Walter

1 Background and Objectives

Interest in small firms and entrepreneurship has spread over the last two decades from the US and England to the rest of Europe, first Western and then Eastern Europe, as well as to the former Soviet Union. In CEECs much hope was and still is pinned on the emerging entrepreneurial small firm sector to carry these economies out of their current economic position, e.g. either to a comparable level, adequate to meet the standards of a reunifying Europe, or at least to an improved level, first and foremost out of theit specific transformation crisis.[1]

One of the central tasks for the revitalisation of Eastern European economies today is still the development of the manufacturing sector. Improving the performance of the manufacturing sector implies improving the myriad firms and economic agents within it. In both developing and developed economies, the SME sector is seen as an essential component of manufacturing.[2] While large firms have played an essential role in developing the frontiers of processes and technology and account for a major share of employment and value added, SMEs constitute the majority of firms, and account for a significantly large share of employment and value added. According to several analyses, SMEs in the manufacturing sector are also an important part of the system of technology production and assimilation (Acs/Audretsch 1990; Brock/Adams 1996; Harhoff et al. 1996; Piore/Sabel 1984).

During the last twenty years, Western countries have faced the difficult task of restructuring their economies. Realising at the same time that SMEs generate employ-

---

1 Here we follow the European Bank of Reconstruction and Development (EBRD) definition provided by Dyker/Radosevic (1999) in using the term CEEC to refer to Poland, The Czech Republic, Slovakia, Hungary, the Yugoslav successor states, Romania, Bulgaria and Albania. For our purposes it also includes the former Soviet Union as the Commonwealth of Independent States (CIS) and the Baltic countries. However, due to limitations of the conference this volume is not able to cover all of them; some are presented in detailed country studies, another group of countries is discussed in the overview articles.

2 For pragmatic reasons we treat the terms "small firms" and "SMEs" as synonymous.

ment and are at least able to cope with an inherent size disadvantage, these countries endeavoured to use SMEs as a vehicle to diminish the negative consequences of the process of structural change, resulting in a variety of policy measures to support SMEs (OECD 1996). Small firms have been seen and treated as part of, and integrated into, the domestic manufacturing system – a system which itself is then linked to similar systems in other nations. Examples have shown that in many instances SMEs are productively linked to the large-firm sector. The empirical evidence suggests that at times large and SMEs may complement each other, at other times and in certain sectors they may substitute for each other (Meyer-Krahmer 1989; Kinch 1987; Rothwell/Dodgson 1993). Consequently, from a policy-maker's viewpoint, SMEs need to be supported in fulfilling their role as suppliers, providers of jobs, innovators, and in their general role of agents of economic change.

The problems confronting Eastern Europe now are even greater than the obstacles existing during structural change in the past in Western countries, because many Eastern European nations systematically eliminated most of their small firms, and with them their entrepreneurial potential. Small firms and entrepreneurship were simply not compatible with state ownership and control. In contrast, large units and combines, for example in production, were much more compatible with centralised planning. The existence of large firms (influenced obliquely by the Western law of "economies of scale") derived as a generalisation of the politically forced concentration of production processes in countries like former East Germany, Czechoslovakia, Poland, Hungary and Russia. The virtual obliteration of small firms and entrepreneurship deprived CEECs of a key element for facilitating industrial restructuring and technological change (Acs/Audretsch 1993). However, with the beginning of the 1990s more or less all countries in the East experienced the decline of the "large is better" attitude, which shaped socialist and Western economies as well over many years of the twentieth century. The restructuring of the manufacturing sector in Eastern Europe was now strongly connected with the generation of technological entrepreneurship and small firms.

Indeed, from a late Schumpeterian perspective large enterprises were seen for a long time as the central engines of growth even by their ability to create more complex innovations. SMEs, in contrast, were regarded as lagging behind. At the least, because of their limited resources, their capacities tended to produce incremental innovation only or act as qualified suppliers for larger companies. However, as the following examples from Western industrialised countries demonstrate, SMEs are often forced to react flexibly to basic technological breakthroughs, for example in microelectronics or biotechnology (Walter 1998).

Firstly, at the appearance of basic innovations, SMEs undertake a wide range of further developments and adaptations in order to meet the concrete needs of their specific customers. Here, SMEs act as "spearheads" of technological change. The modification of complex innovations adapted to their resources is beneficial. From this point of view, application-oriented scientific and technological know-how is becoming increasingly significant for small enterprises. The more SMEs are able to take up and implement technological information with their in-house resources, the more they will be capable of picking up and further developing basic innovations as soon as they appear, and accelerating the diffusion of innovations as a whole.

Secondly, SMEs can take on, in some respects, a complementary function for large enterprises. Particularly in some fields of bio- or information and communication technologies they often have to co-operate with external partners. Within the framework of such innovation projects, SMEs are, however, frequently unable to scale up. For this purpose they require capacities of both staff and apparatus on a high scientific level, a qualitatively superior production of large quantities and adequate financial resources. Usually in fields of a new technology such preconditions are only available in large enterprises whose strength is to be found in process engineering and world-wide marketing. New products for large enterprises may therefore be generated if such companies take up and correspondingly further develop product innovations by SMEs. Large enterprises transfer new developments from the laboratory to the production scale and establishment on the market (Meyer-Krahmer 1989).

Thirdly, a collaboration of independent small and medium sized manufacturing companies using a highly developed infrastructure also opens up the opportunity of coping with innovative tasks, by substituting innovations of large enterprises (Kinch 1987). Thus manufacturers can rely for their production on considerable innovative resources, placed at their disposal by co-operating with a large number of such SMEs. With these resources coupled in an industrial network and distributed among many SMEs, they can be in a position to compete with, for example, the cash-rich automobile industries of other countries, which maintain subsidiary plants in the most varied branches for prefabrication and subsequent sectors. This specific "resource strength" usually also enables the companies to compete successfully on the international market and establish a strong position in the cost-effective procurement of (foreign) supplied parts if necessary.

While Western experience argues towards an innovative potential of SMEs, the question arises whether this also applies to SMEs in Central and Eastern Europe? Theories as well as empirical research on structural change have shown that new industrial sectors based on information and communication technology, new materials or biotechnology, mainly driven by the entrepreneurial spirit, force economic restructuring, which will possibly lead to a disappearance of outdated industries (Audretsch 1995; Florida/Kenney 1990; Welfens/Grack 1999). There is a small but growing body of evidence that beyond this process new industries emerge in the countries of Eastern Europe (Brezinski et al. 1998; Bitzer 1997; v. Hirschhausen 1996; Rabkin 1997). Whereas at the beginning of the transformation process the numerous publications provided less information on size-related and structural developments, compared to macroeconomic issues such as taxation and ownership legislation, fiscal policies, and financial institutions, one can say that the tendency has now changed. Despite several years of effort towards developing a macroeconomic framework, few countries have achieved quick success. It is often accepted that short-term effects are going to be negative (Johnson et al. 1999). Yet more and more structural and innovation problems are coming into view. These are: sector-specific developments in industry, the transfer of technology from research to industry, the concentration of foreign direct investments in agglomerations and a further decline of the peripheral regions and, last but not least, the question of how to mobilise entrepreneurial potential taking into account country-specific cultures, i.e. values, attitudes and beliefs. In some countries, like Poland for instance, so-called "top down transformation", i.e. stabilisation of the macroeconomy, coupled with institutional reforms, was followed by a "bottom-up transformation", i.e. the formation and support of new enterprises. As Berg and Blanchard mentioned early (1992, 28), "...the growth is mostly in very small firms mostly in non-tradables and mostly outside manufacturing". Yet, nearly after a decade several problems are still present. Even if a reasonable number of SMEs already exist in the private sector, most firms were and still are founded in non-manufacturing sectors like services or trade. The reasons behind this are, for instance, high risks attaching to procurement and distribution in the manufacturing sector, unstable economic framework conditions, and little support from institutions in overcoming obstacles to market entry – for instance an inadequate banking system. In addition, there are still the successors of the former large industrial units, now active as state-owned enterprises or privatised companies. As empirical evidence shows, their economic position is strongly based on previous economic activities under central planning.[3] In contrast, SMEs in Eastern Europe that build on technology and create innovations are confronted with considerable barriers to market entry and their role for economic development and restructuring seems to be a little-investigated phenomenon. One may argue that innovative activities in the small firm sector in Central and Eastern Europe are less often investigated because of the low level of relevance. In this we come to the fact that R&D, as well as complementary innovation in SMEs, are difficult to measure, which often leads to their being underestimated, also in industrialised countries of the Western hemisphere (Kleinknecht 1987; Kleinknecht/ Reijnen 1991). As one can see, however, several chapters in this volume refer to innovative activities in CEECs in various ways.

The aim of the book is to build on previous research that was generated within the context of small firms and entrepreneurship in transformation countries. Thus several lessons can be drawn from the existing literature:

1. Even though many countries in Central and Eastern Europe had systematically eliminated small firms and entrepreneurship, SMEs can be regarded as a vehicle

[3] For example, the energy companies Gazprom and Lukoil in Russia, or the newly privatised telecom companies in Poland and Hungary.

to cope with the (negative) impacts of structural change and to foster economic restructuring.

2. To take part in the process of international and technology competition Eastern Europe needs a manufacturing base, and as experience shows, many countries in Eastern Europe still lack competitive SMEs in manufacturing.

3. Evidence in the literature shows that especially the innovative activities of SMEs in the process of economic restructuring tend to be underestimated, even in the manufacturing sector.

Based on the early contributions edited by Abell and Köllermeier (1993), Acs and Audretsch (1993) as well as the edition by Brezinski and Fritsch (1996) this volume not only considers previous work, but also tries to shed light on an sector of industry that seems to emerge as a promising starting point when economic development is analysed. About ten years that have elapsed since market reforms were introduced in most post-socialist economies have not provided sufficient results to draw final conclusions about the role of small firms and entrepreneurship in the transformation process or identify all the major implications for further development. In any case it is time to sum up new research and to examine progress in the development of the SME sector in CEECs so far.

2 Issues

Entrepreneurial and small privately owned firms are obviously essential to the development of competitive market economies in CEECs. Of course, a microeconomically based or 'bottom-up' development strategy is inherently more difficult to follow instead of focusing on the establishment of macroeconomic framework conditions. In the various issues that have been discussed, references can be found to the generation and growth of SMEs in transformation economies (Brezinski et al. 1998; Dimitrov/Todorov 1996; Hauer et al. 1993; Johnson/ Loveman 1995; Lagemann 1995; Levitsky 1996; Sengenberger et al. 1991).[4]

There is some agreement that the majority of countries in Central and Eastern Europe are faced today with the very topics which the countries of the South of Europe faced thirty years ago, and still faces. These are in detail: how to diversify the firm size structure of an economy, how to mobilise endogenous resources, how to open up channels for technology based co-operation for new firms and small enterprises respectively, how to close the productivity gap looming between an economy in transition and the industrialised economies, while simultaneously closing

---

4 Here only a small fraction of the numerous publications on small firms and entrepreneurship in Central and Eastern Europe have been named. Even the so-called 'grey literature' from conferences and meetings is often not available officially. An overview of additional material is presented in Welter (1997).

the productivity and technology divide that has widened between a largely informal small-industry sector and a dominant, government-supported large-scale sector (Brunner 1993). An important difference can be seen in the large industrial complexes which had, and still have, to be restructured and may lead in some cases to SMEs that are larger in size and more keeping with SMEs in industrialised countries than in the Third World (Levitsky 1996). There are also new challenges Central and Eastern Europe industries have to cope with. It is assumed that following the path of industrial reintegration, for instance into a reunified Europe, CEECs will not be able to avoid the consequences of the internationalisation of production and of a global economy (Zysman/Schwartz 1998). But before getting deeply involved in a discussion of perspectives of the small firm sector and policy options for dealing with it, a stock-taking of the various aspects small firms and entrepreneurial activities in Central and Eastern Europe has to be achieved.

One of the book's central issues is therefore the identification of sectors of industry where SMEs do play an important role. At present it is obvious that the majority of SMEs operate outside the manufacturing sector. Instead of development and production, it is the distribution of goods and the provision of services which rank top in the CEECs small firm sector. Closely relating to this question is the discussion on the criteria used to detect relevant SMEs, for example employment creation, innovative activities or market share. While employment is undoubtedly an important issue in analysing the small firm sector, the determination of market shares within developing economies seems to be crucial. Most firms, even the new ones, have problems in delineating their markets; furthermore, often little – or doubtful – information is provided by official or non-official statistics (Brezinski/ Fritsch 1997).

Besides concerning itself with low innovation level activities within the small firm sector, it seems necessary for research to focus on the area of new technologies. As discussed in the past, innovations were often viewed as radical new developments and mainly identified with large enterprises. The specific significance of SMEs for an innovative economy appeared less important. However, taking into account the experience from Western industrialised countries outlined above, SMEs would appear to fulfil several different roles.

Thus from an innovation perspective the SME sector seems promising, due to the various roles of SMEs either as qualified suppliers to large enterprises, as 'spearheads' of technological change, or within industrial networks. The question that arises with regard to CEECs, apart from their number of innovative SMEs, is whether firms exist there which perform more than one role in enhancing the overall innovative activity of a CEECs economy.

By discussing sectors of significant small firm activity, questions come into view which regard the sources and origins of entrepreneurship. An obvious source was and still is privatisation. This approach has been used even in many CEECs to execute the necessary institutional change and re-animate competitive processes, in order to foster economic efficiency. The contribution of property rights theory has opened up the view for the beneficial effects and moved the focus away from static economic efficiency.[5] For example North (1992) stressed the role of well-defined and enforced property rights in spurring property owners to make investments that they would not otherwise have launched, for example in the case of expropriation. More generally speaking, if potential entrepreneurs are uncertain about the state's commitment to respecting ownership of constructions or land, for instance, they may invest only in projects involving short time horizons and requiring little fixed capital. Following this assumption, the distribution and acceptance of property rights within a transition economy may imply characteristics of a future economy, for example an economy that is based on exchange rather than production. In any case, however, privatisation can be a powerful instrument for promoting entrepreneurship. As Wright and Petrin (1991) pointed out this only holds good provided two conditions are satisfied – privatisation must give entrepreneurs the right to entrepreneurial profit, and must give them access to the resources needed to carry out their entrepreneurial functions. But are these functions always carried out according to economically based perceptions and decision-making?

Even within the context of privatisation, entrepreneurship is often equated with both private ownership and small business. The development of entrepreneurship in CEECs, however, faced several severe hindrances, with the entrenched and lingering logic of egalitarianism in the minds of the people being one of the biggest obstacles (Arzeni 1996). And because of the hostile environment in which entrepreneurs functioned in the pre-reform period, they tend to be viewed as "heroic" individuals. This overrated picture in turn may encourage the perception that entrepreneurial abilities are largely innate, and that private enterprise is both necessary and sufficient for unleashing these abilities (Tyson et al. 1994). Viewed from a bottom-up perspective, the relevance of personal and social characteristics cannot be denied. Properly speaking, under socialism dynamic entrepreneurship was locked in. Central planners reduced economic development to a set of technological relationships. They regarded industrialisation as a set of technological imperatives, and established engineers and technicians as the principal agents of change. Among the functions of the entrepreneur, only invention was considered desirable (Schimank 1995). As a consequence, psychological rewards and social status accrued to inventors and engineers, but not to the innovative entrepreneur who combined invention with other resources in establishing a new enterprise. This technological paradigm failed earlier than the breakdown of the political system. For example, Michael Gorbatschow called at the beginning of his period of office for an acceleration of scientific and technological progress; he never used the term innovation (Sitter 1995). And – although innovation gained secret acceptance – extensive production,

5 See the contribution of Audretsch in this volume.

the bureaucratic system and technocratic behaviour dominated the socialist economy, restricting the development of entrepreneurs interested in creating new ventures. Ageev et. al. (1995) also refer to a disadvantageous cultural background for Russian entrepreneurs, which had a substantial impact on the creation of the country's entrepreneurial sector, despite periods of promising entrepreneurial culture. This supports the thesis that tradition and social values within a society, and their impact on technical and managerial elites, seem to be another important issue in CEECs for the generation and development of an entrepreneurial potential.

There is no doubt that industries consisting of SMEs as well as large firms are closely linked to their economic environment. However, from a policy-maker's viewpoint a variety of reasonable approaches exist to detecting possible influencing factors, e.g. the infrastructure viewed from a material, technological and knowledge perspective. For example, an innovation-oriented infrastructure is a precondition for the competitiveness of a knowledge based economy. It is especially important to support the transfer of knowledge to application through technology transfer units, technology centres and parks and a modern research infrastructure. These different units should also be co-ordinated to form a national network for technology transfer and innovation promotion. Technology policy can support these efforts by designing the network, by partly financing start-up operations and equipment, and also by subsidising industrial R&D programmes and providing other innovation-oriented services within this network. If all the different R&D supporting institutions and programmes have worked together, addition synergy effects can be expected. This topic also prepares the way for the last issue, the question of elaborating strategic options for CEECs to move the industrial system from a lower to a higher level of activity by focusing on SMEs.

One political challenge for CEECs is still the ranking of tasks (Zecchini 1997). Whereas in the early phases of macroeconomic transformation it was argued that all major steps have to be launched simultaneously, the process of economic development has shown in several countries of Central and Eastern Europe that this strategy often expects too much from the central economic agents. Resistance that has to be overcome, institutional reforms that cause considerable short-term disruption and prove hard to sustain, are only some examples of reform difficulties (Johnson et al. 1999). Despite considerable progress in the process of macroeconomic stabilisation, most CEECs economies are far from being competitive in relation to Western market economies. A more differentiated view clearly shows that the transition from an economy with a large share of products with low skill intensity and relatively low value added, often mainly consisting of large monostructured, vertically organised firms with traditional technologies, to an economy with mixed structures of small and large firms in different sectors, using modern technologies etc. is a major developmental challenge. Not only does the existing structure of manufacturing have to be understood and potentials for change (for instance industrial elites as a motor of modernisation) identified, but account must also be taken of industrial traditions within a country, and policies to transform it must be put into operation. Policies should be target group-oriented and should use specific instruments to address the financial and other innovation-oriented support needs of producer firms, the institutions and support infrastructure, and the mechanisms of resource flows to manufacturing. Furthermore it must be expected that these policies will have to be timed and sequenced to sustain the innovative efforts of firms, while at the same time they have to address the pressing issue of present unemployment and also consider possible future unemployment challenges that may be caused by technology developments. But how are priorities settled, what are the relevant goals beyond economic modernisation, growth and employment, in what ways do the sub-systems of a transition economy (the techno-economic sub-system, the political/legal-administrative sub-system, and the socio-cultural sub-system) influence each other and, finally, with regard to the dramatic financial situation in CEECs, who pays for all this? The question of strategic development options, possibly of an adequate strategy, and especially the role that SMEs may play in this strategy, is central for governments for the creation of new economic opportunities in post-socialist countries.

To summarise, the central issues of this volume are:

1. The identification of industrial sectors in Central and Eastern Europe where SMEs do play an important role.
2. A description and investigation into selected factors influencing the economic environment of the small firm sector in the countries under investigation.
3. A discussion of strategic options for Central and Eastern European countries to move their industrial system from a lower to a higher level of activity by focusing on small firms and entrepreneurship, and the role policy already plays or may play in the various CEECs in this context.

3 Methodology and Composition of the Book

In November 1999, a conference organised by the Fraunhofer Institute for Systems and Innovation Research, Karlsruhe and the Center on Policy and Technology at the Free University Berlin was held to provide a forum for the dissemination and discussion of the results of recently finished and ongoing research on small firms and entrepreneurship in Central and Eastern Europe and related subjects. We discussed, from a methodological point of view, several possibilities to launch this conference focusing on an informational exchange and experiences gathered in a number of countries. According to a prevalent differentiation there are four different approaches to cross-national comparison (Acs/Audrestch 1993):

- direct cross-national comparisons,
- cross-national historical studies,
- cross-national, cross-market comparison,

- cross-national, cross-regional comparison.

We chose the concept of direct cross-national comparison for the conference as well as for the country studies, allowing each national contributor to embed his description of the SME sector in some historical considerations. Following the main thesis of the book, the review often allows some relevant explanations of how the small firm and entrepreneurial sector is able to perform in the way it does now. The main methodology applied here, however, is common to prior research in this area, and therefore offers the opportunity to build on results that have been generated before. The main unit of observation was standardised to the firm level, and the contributions were supposed to cover at least two of the issues mentioned above.

Largely in correspondence with the central issues, the book is structured into three main chapters. After the introductory part, the second chapter combines experience in countries in the Western hemisphere (Audretsch) and general questions on small firms and entrepreneurship (Heering/Pfirrmann and Kandil/Walter). Audretsch's paper seeks to document how and why small business plays a very different role in industrial organisation research today than it did some three decades ago. His argumentation goes beyond the view of small business emerging from a static framework: he prefers the view of small business emerging from a dynamic framework – in striking contrast to conventional ideas of the role and contribution of small business, and complementing what has been described in post-war industrial organisation literature. In their contributions Kandil and Walter, as well as Heering and Pfirrmann, outline two specific considerations that seem to be characteristic of the ongoing discussion about transformation in Central and Eastern Europe: the former argues mainly from a socio-economic background, discussing industrial modernisation based on a practical-oriented modernisation strategy which relies primarily on endogenous resources and is implemented by new technical and managerial elites, whereas the latter refers to a purely economic view. Heering and Pfirrmann suggest that the concept of property rights and ownership applied to CEECs economies is an excellent basis for explaining differences in performance and development. Whereas privatisation is only a necessary step, not a sufficient one, to ensure an efficiently functioning market system, they argue towards stable economic institutions and framework conditions. Of course, neither of these views claims to have the ultimate explanation for the sometimes unsatisfactory performance of the small firm sector within CEECs. A consideration of the obviously extremely different argumentation of both papers makes it clear that neither an exclusively economic nor a purely socio-cultural perspective is sufficient. Moreover, as the following contributions and even the final outlook demonstrate, a synthesis or a interdisciplinary view on small firms and entrepreneurship in Central and Eastern Europe is needed.

The third chapter presents case studies from Hungary (Welter), Poland (Matusiak), Romania (Piturescu), Russia (Kovaleva), Slovenia (Godina) and Yugoslavia (Kutlaca). They largely follow a common structure, beginning with a short description of the development of the SME sector during socialism (and in the case of Yugoslavia also in the pre-socialist era) and proceeding to a differentiated, i.e. structural view of the current state of SMEs. Information on legal and governmental aspects regarding SMEs development is intended to lead to a more or less comprehensive picture within each country included in the survey.

The fourth chapter, which discusses selected aspects of SMEs support institutions, co-operative arrangements and policy towards small firms and entrepreneurship, aims to present an overview of relevant issues that seem to be important within the business environment of SMEs. A first and closer look is dedicated to institutions and infrastructure that support innovation. Here the contribution of Radosevic/ Walter seeks to explain why the building of knowledge networks, learning mechanisms and social capital is extremely important, taking into account the limited and often poor resources for supporting SMEs. They, as well as the author of the following paper, Heering, consider a specific part of the infrastructure for new technology based firms: technology centres and science parks. This is a model which was developed in economies of the Western world and had been transferred and implemented in CEECs with the help of Western experts. While Heering's paper compares technology centres and science parks in Hungary, Poland and Russia, and questions their role for innovative SMEs, although not for entrepreneurship in general, Radosevic and Walter demonstrate that innovation centres, innovation agencies and other institutions that remain isolated from their environment cannot fulfil their specific role. Moreover, although they have to build on the linkages developed during their set-up, they also have to be assisted in developing new links. In this context Muller, Zenker and Dőry argue in their contribution that good opportunities exist on a regional level for linking economic actors together in networks through which the innovation potential can be better exploited or supported by policy measures. Their comparative analysis of three regions in Saxony (East Germany), Slovenia and West Transdanubia (Hungary) is based on the hypothesis that the nature and frequency of interaction between firms, knowledge-intensive suppliers, universities and research labs significantly influences regional development. The emphasis on the regional dimension of the transformation process in CEECs is complemented by the contribution of Steiner. He argues that, based on experience gained in the West, countries in transition have to strengthen the regional dimension of their economic policy and concentrate on SMEs support and firm foundation, and on creating an infrastructure (both material and non-material) for co-operative forms of entrepreneurship.

The fourth chapter ends with the presentation of achieving specific aspects in industrial innovation as a strategy for modernisation supported by technology and innovation policy (Walter). The final chapter briefly summarises the main findings and attempts to shed light on issues that cannot be consistently explained, by defining some of the areas in which further research is required. We hope that, by taking into account the overwhelming structural distortions that still exist in the post-socialist/post-communist economies, the following contributions will pave the way for more discussion and research.

Literature

Abell, D. F.; Köllermeier, T. (1993, Eds.): Dynamic Entrepreneurship in Central and Eastern Europe, The Hague: Delwel Publishers.

Acs, Z. J.; Audretsch, D. B. (1990): Innovation and Small Firms. Cambridge, MA: The MIT Press.

Acs, Z. J.; Audretsch, D. B. (1993, Eds.): Small firms and Entrepreneurship: an East-West perspective. Cambridge, MA: Cambridge University Press.

Ageev, A. I.; Gratchev M. V.; Hisrich, R. D. (1995): Entrepreneurship in the Soviet Union and Post Socialist Russia. Small Business Economics 7, pp. 365-376.

Arzeni, S. (1996): Entrepreneurship in Eastern Europe: A Critical View. In: Brezinski, H.; Fritsch, M. (Eds.): The Economic Impact of New Firms in Post-Socialist Countries. Cheltenham: Edward Elgar, pp. 52-58.

Audretsch, D. B. (1995): Innovation and Industry Evolution. Cambridge, MA: The MIT Press.

Beesley, M. E.; Hamilton R. T. (1984): Small Firms' Seedbed Role and the Concept of Turbulence. Journal of Industrial Economics, 33, pp. 217-232.

Berg, A.; Blanchard, O. J. (1992): Stabilization and Transition: Poland 1990-1991, MIT, mimeograph.

Bitzer, B. (1997): The Computer Industry in East and West: Do Eastern European Countries Need a Specific Science and Technology Policy? In: Deutsches Institut für Wirtschaftsforschung. Discussion Paper no. 148, Berlin.

Brezinski, H.; Fritsch, M. (1996, Eds.): The Economic Impact of New Firms in Post-Socialist Countries. Cheltenham: Edward Elgar.

Brezinski, H.; Fritsch, M. (1997, Eds.): The Emergence and Evolution of Markets, Cheltenham: Edward Elgar.

Brezinski, H.; Franck, E.; Fritsch, M. (1998, Eds.): The Microeconomics of Transformation and Growth. Cheltenham: Edward Elgar.

Brock, W. A.; Adams, D. S. (1996): The Economics of Small Business. New York: Holmes and Meier.

Brunner, H.-P. (1993): The Development Experience and Government Policies: Lessons for Eastern Europe? In: Acs, Z. J.; Audretsch, D. B. (Eds.): Small firms and Entrepreneurship: an East-West Perspective. Cambridge, MA: Cambridge University Press, pp. 208-226.

Dimitrov, M.; Todorov, K. (1996, Eds.): Industrial Organisation and Entrepreneurship in Transition Economies, Sofia.

Dyker, D. A.; Radosevic, S. (1999, Eds.): Innovation and Structural Change in Post-Socialist Countries: A Quantitative Approach. Dordrecht: Kluwer.

Florida, R.; Kenney, M. (1990): The Breakthrough Illusion: Corporate America's Failure to move from Innovation to Mass Production. New York: Basic Books.

Harhoff, D. et al. (1996): Innovationsaktivitäten kleiner und mittlerer Unternehmen. Baden-Baden: Nomos.

Hauer, A.; Kleinhenz, Th.; Schuttenbach, L.v. (1993): Der Mittelstand im Transformationsprozeß Ostdeutschlands und Osteuropas. Heidelberg: Physica

Hirschhausen, C.v. (1996): Arguments for a Post-socialist Horizontal Industrial Policy in Eastern Europe: experience from five years of enterprise reforms. In: Brezinski, H.; Fritsch, M. (Eds.): The Economic Impact of New Firms in Post-Socialist Countries. Cheltenham: Edward Elgar, pp. 37-55.

Johnson, S.; Loveman, G. (1995): Starting Over in Eastern Europe: Entrepreneurship and Economic Renewal. Boston: Harvard Business School Press.

Johnson, S.; MacMillan, J.; Woodruff, C. (1999): Entrepreneurs and the Ordering of Institutional Reform: Poland, Romania, Russia, the Slovak Republic and Ukraine compared. EBRD Working Paper no. 44, London.

Kinch, N. (1987): Emerging Strategies in a Network Context: The Volvo Case. Scandinavian Journal of Management Studies, May 1987.

Kleinknecht, A. (1987): Measuring R&D in Small Firms: How much are we missing. Journal of Industrial Economics 36, pp. 253-256.

Kleinknecht, A.; Reijnen, J.O.N. (1991): More Evidence on the Undercounting of Small Firm R&D. Research Policy 20, pp. 579-587.

Lagemann, B. (1995): Die Entwicklung mittelständischer Wirtschaftsstrukturen in den osteuropäischen Ländern 1990-1994: Eine Bestandsaufnahme. Berichte des BIOst, Nr. 29-1995, Bonn.

Levitsky, J. (1996, Ed.): Preface. In: Small Business in Transition Economies. London: Intermediate Technology Publications, VIII-XV.

Meyer-Krahmer, F. (1989): Der Einfluß staatlicher Technologiepolitik auf industrielle Innovation. Baden-Baden: Nomos.

North, D. C. (1992): Privatisation, Incentives, and Economic Performance. In: Siebert, H. (Ed.), Privatisation, Kiel: Institut für Weltwirtschaft, pp. 3-16.

OECD (1996, Ed.): Small Business in Transition Economies. Paris.

Piore, M.; Sabel, C. (1984): The Second Industrial Divide. New York: Basic Books.

Rabkin, M. (1997): Diffusion of New Technologies in the Post-Communist World. Dordrecht: Kluwer.

Rothwell, R.; Dodgson, M. (1993): Technology Based SMEs: Their Role in Industrial and Economic Change. In: Dodgson, M.; Rothwell, R. (Eds.) International Journal of Technology Management. Special edition.

Schimank, U. (1995): Die Transformation der Forschungssysteme der mittel- und osteuropäischen Länder: Gemeinsamkeiten von Problemlagen und Problembearbeitung. In: Mayntz, R.; Schimank, U.; Weingart, P. (Eds.): Transformation mittel- und osteuropäischer Wissenssysteme. Opladen: Westdeutscher Verlag, pp. 10-39.

Sengenberger, W.; Loveman, G.; Piore, M. (1991, Eds.): The Re-Emergence of Small Enterprise – Industrial Restructuring in Industrialised Countries. Geneva, International Labour Organisation.

Sitter, W. (1995): Perestroika und Innovation, Stuttgart: G. Fischer.

Tyson, L. D.; Petrin, T.; Wright, M. (1994): Promoting Entrepreneurship in Eastern Europe. Small Business Economics 6, pp. 165-184.

Walter, G. H. (1998): Industrial Innovations by Small and Medium Sized Enterprises. Asia Pacific Tech Monitor, 15. New Delhi, Jan./Febr. 1999, pp. 8-12.

Welfens, P. J. J.; Graack, C. (1999, Eds.): Technologieorientierte Unternehmensgründungen und Mittelstandspolitik in Europa. Heidelberg: Physica.

Welter, F. (1997): Small and Medium Enterprises in Central and Eastern Europe: Trends, Barriers and Solutions. RWI Papiere Nr. 51, Essen.

Wright, M.; Petrin, T. (1991): Management/Employee Buy-outs in Public Corporate Restructuring. In: Prokopenko, J.; Pavlin, I. (Eds.): Entrepreneurship Development in Public Enterprises. Geneva, International Labour Organisation and Ljubljana, International Center for Public Enterprises in Developing Countries, pp. 36-44.

Zecchini, S. (1997, Ed.): Lessons from the Economic Transition: Central and Eastern Europe in 1990s. Dordrecht: Kluwer.

Zysman, J.; Schwartz, A. (1998): Reunifying Europe in an Emerging World Economy: Economic Heterogeneity, New Industrial Options and Political Choices. Journal of Common Market Studies 36, pp. 405-429.

Small Firms and Entrepreneurship: The Western Experience

David B. Audretsch

1 Introduction

The role that small firms play in economics has evolved considerably since the second world war. This paper seeks to document how and why small business plays a very different role in industrial organisation research today than it did some three decades ago.

The most important development in the field of small business economics has been a shift in the framework for analysing small business. While there were always a few studies around analysing small business through a dynamic lens, a much more profound and comprehensive shift in the literature began in the later 1980s and early 1990s. The most salient characteristic feature of this literature was the introduction of a dynamic or evolutionary framework.

In the second section of this paper, the view of small business emerging from the static framework of the post-war industrial organisation is described. This view identifies small business as being sub-optimal in terms of scale of production. The resulting impact on performance is negative, in terms of productivity and wages. The policy implication is that, at least in terms of economic efficiency, small business exerts a drag on economic welfare.

In the third section of the paper, the view of small business emerging from the dynamic framework of the last decade is introduced. This view provides a striking contrast to the role and contribution of small business. When viewed through the lens of a dynamic framework, small businesses are seen as an agent of change. The empirical evidence supporting this dynamic view of small business is presented in the fourth section. The implications for public policy towards business are presented in the fifth section. In particular, we find that the role of public policy towards business has shifted from constraining the power of large corporations to enabling the creation and commercialisation of knowledge, particularly by small business. A summary and conclusions are provided in the final section.

2 The Static View

In linking entrepreneurship to economic growth, the obvious starting point is the theory of the firm. The field of economics that focuses the most on links between the organisation of firms in industries and the resulting economic performance has been industrial organisation. The ascendancy of industrial organisation in the post-war period as an important and valued field economics came from the recognition not only by scholars but also by policy makers that industrial organisation matters. The widespread fear vis-à-vis the Soviet Union pervasive throughout the United States at the end of the 1950s and early 1960s was not just that the Soviets might bury the Americans because they were the first into space with the launching of the Sputnik, but that the superior organisation of industry facilitated by centralised planning was generating greater rates of growth in the Soviet Union. After all, the nations of Eastern Europe, and the Soviet Union in particular, had a "luxury" inherent in their systems of centralised planning – a concentration of economic assets on a scale beyond anything imaginable in the West, where the commitment to democracy seemingly imposed a concomitant commitment to economic decentralisation.

Although there may have been considerable debate about what to do about the perceived Soviet threat some four decades ago, there was little doubt at that time that the manner in which enterprises and entire industries were organised mattered. And even more striking, when one reviews the literature of the day, there seemed to be near unanimity about the way in which industrial organisation mattered. It is no doubt an irony of history that a remarkably similar version of the giantism embedded in Soviet doctrine, fuelled by the writings of Marx and ultimately implemented by the iron fist of Stalin, was also prevalent throughout the West. This was the era of mass production when economies of scale seemed to be the decisive factor in dictating efficiency. This was the world so colourfully described by John Kenneth Galbraith (1956) in his theory of countervailing power, in which the power of big business was held in check by big labour and by big government.

It became the task of the industrial organisation scholars to sort out the issues involving this perceived trade-off between economic efficiency on the one hand and political and economic decentralisation on the other. The scholars of industrial organisation responded by producing a massive literature focusing on essentially three issues: (i) What are the economic gains to size and large-scale production? (ii) What are the economic welfare implications of having an oligopolistic market structure, i.e. is economic performance promoted or reduced in an industry with just a handful of large-scale firms? and (iii) Given the overwhelming evidence from (ii) that large-scale production resulting in economic concentration is associated with increased efficiency, what are the public policy implications?

A fundamental characteristic of the industrial organisation literature was not only that it was obsessed with the oligopoly question but that it was essentially static in nature. There was considerable concern about what to do about the existing firms and industrial structure, but little attention was paid to where they came from and where they were going. Oliver Williamson's classic 1968 article in the American Economic Review, "Economies as an Antitrust Defence: The Welfare Tradeoffs," became something of a final statement demonstrating this seemingly inevitable trade-off between the gains in productive efficiency that could be obtained through increased concentration and gains in terms of competition that could be achieved through decentralising economic policies, such as antitrust. But it did not seem possible to have both, certainly not in Williamson's completely static model.

One of the most striking findings emerging in this static view of industrial organisation is that small firms generally operate at a level of output that is too small to sufficiently exhaust scale economies, even when the standard definition of a small firm employing fewer than 500 employees is applied. A large number of studies found that because the minimum efficient scale (MES) of output, or the lowest level of output where the minimum average cost is attained, large-scale production is typically required to exhaust scale economies in manufacturing. Any enterprise or establishment that was smaller than required by the MES was branded as being suboptimal or inefficient, in that it produced at average costs in excess of more efficient larger firms. Weiss (Audretsch/Yamawaki 1991, xiv) assumed that "The term "suboptimal" capacity describes a condition in which some plants are too small to be efficient."

The importance of scale economies in the typical manufacturing industry relegated most small firms to being classified as suboptimal. For example, Weiss (1964) found that suboptimal plants accounted for about 52.8 per cent of industry value-off-shipments, Scherer (1973) found that 58.2 per cent of value-of-shipments emanated from the suboptimal plants in twelve industries, and Pratten (1971) identified the suboptimal scale establishments accounting for 47.9 per cent of industry shipments. After reviewing the literature on the extent of suboptimal firms, Weiss (in Audretsch/Yamawaki 1991, 403) concluded that, "In most industries the great majority of firms is suboptimal. In a typical industry there are, let's say, one hundred firms. Typically only about five to ten of them will be operating at the MES level of output, or anything like it."

What are the economic welfare implications? Weiss (1979, 1137) argued that the existence of small firms which are sub-optimal represented a loss in economic efficiency and therefore advocated any public policy which "...creates social gains in the form of less sub-optimal capacity." This actually translated into an ingenuous argument against market power, since empirical evidence suggested that the price umbrella provided by monopoly power encouraged the existence of suboptimal capacity firms. Weiss (1979) went so far as to argue that the largest inefficiency associated with market power was not the higher prices charged to consumers but rather that it facilitated the existence of suboptimal scale small firms.

Wages and productivity would be expected to reflect the degree to which small firms are less efficient than their larger counterparts. There is a large body of empirical evidence spanning a broad range of samples, time periods and even countries that has consistently found wages (and non-wage compensation as well) to be positively related to firm size. Probably the most cited study is that of Brown, Hamilton/Medoff (1990, pp 88-89), who conclude that, "Workers in large firms earn higher wages, and this fact cannot be explained completely by differences in labour quality industry, working conditions, or union status. Workers in large firms enjoy better benefits and greater security than their counterparts in small firms. When these factors are added together, it appears that workers in large firms do have a superior employment package."

Seen through the static lens provided through traditional industrial organisation and labour economics the economic welfare implications of the recent shift in economic activity away from large firms and towards small enterprises is unequivocal – overall economic welfare is decreased since productivity and wages will be lower in small than in large firms. As Weiss (1979) argued in terms of efficiency and Brown, Hamilton/Medoff (1990) in terms of employee compensation, the implication for public policy is to implement policies to shift economic activity away from small firms and towards larger enterprises.

3 The Dynamic View

Coase (1937) was awarded a Nobel Prize for explaining why a firm should exist. But why should more than one firm exist in an industry? One answer is provided by the traditional economics literature focusing on industrial organisation. An excess level of profitability induces entry into the industry. And this is why the entry of new firms is interesting and important – because the new firms provide an equilibrating function in the market, in that the levels of price and profit are restored to the competitive levels. The new firms are about business as usual – they simply equilibrate the market by providing more of it.

An alternative explanation for the entry of new firms was provided for by Audretsch (1995), who suggests that new firms are not founded to be smaller clones of the larger incumbents but rather to serve as agents of change through innovative activity.

The starting point for most theories of innovation is the firm. In such theories the firms are exogenous and their performance in generating technological change is endogenous. For example, in the most prevalent model found in the literature of technological change, the model of the knowledge production function, formalised by Zvi Griliches (1979), firms exist exogenously and then engage in the pursuit of new economic knowledge as an input into the process of generating innovative activity.

The most decisive input in the knowledge production function is new economic knowledge. And as Cohen/Klepper (1991 and 1992) conclude, the greatest source generating new economic knowledge is generally considered to be R&D. Certainly a large body of empirical work has found a strong and positive relationship between knowledge inputs, such as R&D, on the one hand, and innovative outputs on the other hand.

The knowledge production function has been found to hold most strongly at broader levels of aggregation. The most innovative countries are those with the greatest investments in R&D. Little innovative output is associated with less developed countries, which are characterised by a paucity of production of new economic knowledge. Similarly, the most innovative industries also tend to be characterised by considerable investments in R&D and new economic knowledge. Not only are industries such as computers, pharmaceuticals and instruments high in R&D inputs that generate new economic knowledge, but also in terms of innovative outputs (Audretsch 1995). By contrast, industries with little R&D, such as wood products, textiles and paper, also tend to produce only a negligible amount of innovative output. Thus, the knowledge production model linking knowledge generating inputs to outputs certainly holds at the more aggregated levels of economic activity.

Where the relationship becomes less compelling is at the disaggregated microeconomic level of the enterprise, establishment, or even line of business. For example, while Acs/Audretsch (1990) found that the simple correlation between R&D inputs and innovative output was 0.84 for four-digit standard industrial classification (SIC) manufacturing industries in the United States, it was only about half, 0.40, among the largest U.S. corporations.

The model of the knowledge production function becomes even less compelling in view of the recent wave of studies revealing that small enterprises serve as the engine of innovative activity in certain industries. These results are startling, because as Scherer (1991) observes, the bulk of industrial R&D is undertaken in the largest corporations; small enterprises account only for a minor share of R&D inputs. Thus the knowledge production function seemingly implies that, as the Schumpeterian Hypothesis predicts, innovative activity favours those organisations with access to knowledge-producing inputs – the large incumbent organisation. The more recent evidence identifying the strong innovative activity raises the question, "Where do new and small firms get the innovation producing inputs, that is, the knowledge?"

One answer, proposed by Audretsch (1995), is that, although the model of the knowledge production function may still be valid, the implicitly assumed unit of observation – at the level of the firm – may be less valid. The reason why the knowledge production function holds more closely for more aggregated degrees of observation may be that investment in R&D and other sources of new knowledge spills over for economic exploitation by third-party firms.

A large literature has emerged focusing on what has become known as the appropriability problem. The underlying issue revolves around how firms which invest in the creation of new economic knowledge can best appropriate the economic returns from that knowledge (Arrow 1962). Audretsch (1995) proposes shifting the unit of observation away from exogenously assumed firms to individuals – agents with endowments of new economic knowledge. As J. de V. Graaf (1957) observed nearly four decades ago: "When we try to construct a transformation function for society as a whole from those facing the individual firms comprising it, a fundamental difficulty confronts us. There is, from a welfare point of view, nothing special about the firms actually existing in an economy at a given moment of time. The firm is in no sense a "natural unit". Only the individual members of the economy can lay claim to that distinction. All are potential entrepreneurs. It seems, therefore, that the natural thing to do is to build up from the transformation function of men, rather than the firms, constituting an economy. If we are interested in eventual empirical determination, this is extremely inconvenient. But it has conceptual advantages. The ultimate repositories of technological knowledge in any society are the men comprising it, and it is just this knowledge which is effectively summarised in the form of a transformation function. In itself a firm possesses no knowledge. That which is available to it belongs to the men associated with it. Its production function is really built up in exactly the same way, and from the same basic ingredients, as society's."

But when the lens is shifted away from focusing upon the firm as the relevant unit of observation to individuals, the relevant question becomes: How can economic agents with a given endowment of new knowledge best appropriate the returns from that knowledge?

The appropriability problem confronting the individual may converge with that confronting the firm. Economic agents can and do work for firms, and even if they do not, they can potentially be employed by an incumbent firm. In fact, in a model of perfect information with no agency costs, any positive economies of scale or scope will ensure that the appropriability problems of the firm and individual converge. If an agent has an idea for doing something different than is currently being practised by the incumbent enterprises – both in terms of a new product or process and in terms of organisation – the idea, which can be termed as an innovation, will be presented to the incumbent enterprise. Because of the assumption of perfect knowledge, both the firm and the agent would agree upon the expected value of the innovation. But to the degree that any economies of scale or scope exist, the expected value of implementing the innovation within the incumbent enterprise will exceed that of taking the innovation outside of the incumbent firm to start a new enterprise.

Thus, the incumbent firm and the inventor of the idea would be expected to reach a bargain splitting the value added to the firm contributed by the innovation. The payment to the inventor – either in terms of a higher wage or some other means of remuneration – would be bounded between the expected value of the innovation if it implemented by the incumbent enterprise on the upper end, and by the return that the agent could expect to earn if he used it to launch a new enterprise on the lower end. Or, as Frank Knight (1921, 273) observed nearly eighty years ago: "The labourer asks what he thinks the entrepreneur will be able to pay, and in any case will not accept less than he can get from some other entrepreneur, or by turning entrepreneur himself. In the same way the entrepreneur offers to any labourer what he thinks he must in order to secure his services, and in any case not more than he thinks the labourer will actually be worth to him, keeping in mind what he can get by turning labourer himself."

Thus, each economic agent would choose how to best appropriate the value of his endowment of economic knowledge by comparing the wage he would earn if he remains employed by an incumbent enterprise, w, to the expected net present discounted value of the profits accruing from starting a new firm, π. If these two values are relatively close, the probability that he would choose to appropriate the value of his knowledge through an external mechanism such as starting a new firm, Pr(e), would be relatively low. On the other hand, as the gap between w and π becomes larger, the likelihood of an agent choosing to appropriate the value of his knowledge externally through starting a new enterprise becomes greater, or

$$\Pr(e) = f(\pi - w) \qquad (1)$$

This model analysing the decision of how best to appropriate the value of new economic knowledge confronting an individual economic agent seems useful when considering the actual decision to a new firm taken by entrepreneurs. For example, Chester Carlson started Xerox after his proposal to produce a (new) copy machine was rejected by Kodak. Kodak based its decision on the premise that the new copy machine would not earn very much money, and in any case, Kodak was in a different line of business – photography. It is perhaps no small irony that this same entrepreneurial start-up, Xerox, decades later turned down a proposal from Steven Jobs to produce and market a personal computer, because they did not think that a personal computer would sell, and, in any case, they were in a different line of business – copy machines (Carrol 1993). After seventeen other companies turned down Jobs for virtually identical reasons, including IBM and Hewlett Packard, Jobs resorted to starting his own company, Apple Computer.

Similarly, IBM turned down an offer from Bill Gates, the chance to buy ten per cent of Microsoft for a song in 1986, a missed opportunity that would cost $3 billion today. IBM reached its decision on the grounds that neither Gates nor any of his band of thirty some employees had anything approaching the credentials or personal characteristics required to work at IBM.

Divergences in beliefs with respect to the value of a new idea need not be restricted to what is formally known as a product or even a process innovation. Rather, the fact that economic agents choose to start a new firm due to divergences in the expected value of an idea applies to the sphere of managerial style and organisation as well. One of the most vivid examples involves Bob Noyce, who founded Intel. Noyce had been employed by Fairchild Semiconductor, which is credited with being the pioneering semiconductor firm. In 1957 Noyce and seven other engineers quit en masse from Shockley Semiconductor to form Fairchild Semiconductor, an enterprise that in turn is considered the start of what is today known as Silicon Valley. Although Fairchild Semiconductor had "possibly the most potent management and technical team ever assembled" (Gilder 1989, 89): "Noyce couldn't get Fairchild's eastern owners to accept the idea that stock options should be part of compensation for all employees, not just for management. He wanted to tie everyone, from janitors to bosses, into the overall success of the company...This management style still sets the standard for every computer, software, and semiconductor company in the Valley today... Every CEO still wants to think that the place is run the way Bob Noyce would have run it" (Cringley 1993, 39). That is, Noyce's vision of a firm excluded the dress codes, reserved parking places, closed offices, and executive dining rooms, along with the other trappings of status that were standard in virtually every hierarchical and bureaucratic U.S. corporation. But when he tried to impress this vision upon the owners of Fairchild Semiconductor, he was flatly rejected. The formation of Intel in 1968 was the ultimate result of the divergence in beliefs about how to organise and manage the firm.

The key development at Intel was the microprocessor. When long time IBM employee Ted Hoff approached IBM and later DEC with his new microprocessor in the late 1960s: "IBM and DEC decided there was no market. They could not imagine why anyone would need or want a small computer; if people wanted to use a computer, they could hook into time-sharing systems" (Palfreman/Swade 1991, 108).

The model proposed by Audretsch (1995) refocuses the unit of observation away from firms deciding whether to increase their output from a level of zero to some positive amount in a new industry, to individual agents in possession of new knowledge that, due to uncertainty, may or may not have some positive economic value. It is the uncertainty inherent in new economic knowledge, combined with asymmetries between the agent possessing that knowledge and the decision making vertical hierarchy of the incumbent organisation with respect to its expected value that potentially leads to a gap in the valuation of that knowledge between the agent and the decision making hierarchy.

How the economic agent chooses to appropriate the value of his knowledge, that is either within an incumbent firm or by starting or joining a new enterprise will be shaped by the knowledge conditions underlying the industry. Under the routinised technological regime the agent will tend to appropriate the value of his new ideas within the boundaries of incumbent firms. Thus, the propensity for new firms to be started should be relatively low in industries characterised by the routinised technological regime.

By contrast, under the entrepreneurial regime the agent will tend to appropriate the value of his new ideas outside of the boundaries of incumbent firms by starting a new enterprise. Thus, the propensity for new firms to enter should be relatively high in industries characterised by the entrepreneurial regime.

Audretsch (1995) suggests that divergences in the expected value regarding new knowledge will, under certain conditions, lead an agent to exercise what Albert O. Hirschman (1970) has termed as exit rather than voice, and depart from an incumbent enterprise to launch a new firm. But who is right, the departing agents or those agents remaining in the organisational decision making hierarchy who, by assigning the new idea a relatively low value, have effectively driven the agent with the potential innovation away? Ex post the answer may not be too difficult. But given the uncertainty inherent in new knowledge, the answer is anything but trivial a priori.

Thus, when a new firm is launched, its prospects are shrouded in uncertainty. If the new firm is built around a new idea, i.e., potential innovation, it is uncertain whether there is sufficient demand for the new idea or if some competitor will have the same or even a superior idea. Even if the new firm is formed to be an exact replica of a successful incumbent enterprise, it is uncertain whether sufficient demand for a new clone, or even for the existing incumbent, will prevail in the future. Tastes can change, and new ideas emerging from other firms will certainty influence those tastes.

Finally, an additional layer of uncertainty pervades a new enterprise. It is not known how competent the new firm really is, in terms of management, organisation, and workforce. At least incumbent enterprises know something about their underlying competencies from past experience. Which is to say that a new enterprise is burdened with uncertainty as to whether it can produce and market the intended product as well as sell it. In both cases the degree of uncertainty will typically exceed that confronting incumbent enterprises.

This initial condition of not just uncertainty, but greater degree of uncertainty vis-à-vis incumbent enterprises in the industry is captured in the theory of firm selection and industry evolution proposed by Boyan Jovanovic (1982). Jovanovic presents a model in which the new firms, which he terms entrepreneurs, face costs that are not only random but also differ across firms. A central feature of the model is that a new firm does not know what its cost function is, that is its relative efficiency, but rather discovers this through the process of learning from its actual post-entry performance. In particular, Jovanovic (1982) assumes that entrepreneurs are unsure about their ability to manage a new-firm start-up and therefore their prospects for success. Although entrepreneurs may launch a new firm based on a vague sense of expected post-entry performance, they only discover their true ability – in terms of managerial competence and of having based the firm on an idea that is viable on the market – once their business is established. Those entrepreneurs who discover that their ability exceeds their expectations expand the scale of their business, whereas those discovering that their post-entry performance is less than commensurate with their expectations will contact the scale of output and possibly exit from the industry. Thus, Jovanovic's model is a theory of noisy selection, where efficient firms grow and survive and inefficient firms decline and fail.

The role of learning in the selection process has been the subject of considerable debate. On the one hand is what has been referred to as the Larackian assumption that learning refers to adaptations made by the new enterprise. In this sense, those new firms that are the most flexible and adaptable will be the most successful in adjusting to whatever the demands of the market are. As Nelson/Winter (1982, 11) point out: "Many kinds of organisations commit resources to learning; organisations seek to copy the forms of their most successful competitors."

On the other hand is the interpretation that the role of learning is restricted to discovering if the firm has the right stuff in terms of the goods it is producing as well as the way they are being produced. Under this interpretation the new enterprise is not necessarily able to adapt or adjust to market conditions, but receives information based on its market performance with respect to its fitness in terms of meeting demand most efficiently vis-à-vis rivals. The theory of organisational ecology proposed by Hannan/Freeman (1989,) most pointedly adheres to the notion that, "We assume that individual organisations are characterised by relative inertia in structure." That is, firms learn not in the sense that they adjust their actions as reflected by their fundamental identity and purpose, but in the sense of their perception. What is then learned is whether or not the firm has the right stuff, but not how to change that stuff.

The theory of firm selection is particularly appealing in view of the rather startling size of most new firms. For example, the mean size of more than 11 000 new-firm start-ups in the manufacturing sector in the United States was found to be fewer than eight workers per firm (Audretsch 1995). While the MES varies substantially across industries, and even to some degree across various product classes within any given industry, the observed size of most new firms is sufficiently small to ensure that the bulk of new firms will be operating at a suboptimal scale of output. Why would an entrepreneur start a new firm that would immediately be confronted by scale disadvantages?

An implication of the theory of firm selection is that new firms may begin at a small, even suboptimal, scale of output, and then if merited by subsequent performance expand. Those new firms that are successful will grow, whereas those that are not successful will remain small and may ultimately be forced to exit from the industry if they are operating at a suboptimal scale of output.

Subsequent to entering an industry, an entrepreneur must decide whether to maintain its output expand, contract, or exit. Two different strands of literature have identified several major influences shaping the decision to exit an industry. The first, and most obvious strand of literature suggests that the probability of a business exiting will tend to increase as the gap between its level of output and the MES level of output increases. The second strand of literature points to the role that the technological environment plays in shaping the decision to exit. As Dosi (1988) and Arrow (1962) argue, an environment characterised by more frequent innovation may also be associated with a greater amount of uncertainty regarding not only the technical nature of the product but also the demand for that product. As technological uncertainty increases, particularly under the entrepreneurial regime, the likelihood that the business will be able to produce a viable product and ultimately be able to survive decreases.

An important implication of the dynamic process of firm selection and industry evolution is that new firms are more likely to be operating at a suboptimal scale of output if the underlying technological conditions are such that there is a greater chance of making an innovation, that is under the entrepreneurial regime. If new firms successfully learn and adapt, or are just plain lucky, they grow into viably sized enterprises. If not, they stagnate and may ultimately exit from the industry. This suggests, that entry and the start-up of new firms may not be greatly deterred in the presence of scale economies. As long as entrepreneurs perceive that there is some prospect for growth and ultimately survival, such entry will occur. Thus, in industries where the MES is high, it follows from the observed general small size of new-firm start-ups that the growth rate of the surviving firms would presumably be relatively high.

At the same time, those new firms not able to grow and attain the MES level of output would presumably be forced to exit from the industry, resulting in a relatively low likelihood of survival. In industries characterised by a low MES, neither the need for growth, nor the consequences of its absence are as severe, so that relatively lower growth rates but higher survival rates would be expected. Similarly, in industries where the probability of innovating is greater, more entrepreneurs may actually take a chance that they will succeed by growing into a viably sized enterprise. In such industries, one would expect that the growth of successful enterprises would be greater, but that the likelihood of survival would be correspondingly lower.

4 The Empirical Evidence

Not only was the large corporation thought to have superior productive efficiency, but conventional wisdom also held the large corporation to serve as the engine of technological change and innovative activity. After all, Schumpeter (1942, 106) concluded that, "What we have got to accept is that the large-scale establishment has come to be the most powerful engine of progress." A few years later, John Kenneth Galbraith (1956, 86) echoed Schumpeter's sentiment when he lamented: "There is no more pleasant fiction than that technological change is the product of the matchless ingenuity of the small man forced by competition to employ his wits to better his neighbour. Unhappily, it is a fiction."

Knowledge regarding both the determinants and the impact of technological change has been largely shaped by measurement. Measures of technological change have typically involved one of the three major aspects of the innovative process:

- a measure of inputs into the process, such as R&D expenditures, or the share of the labour force accounted for by employees involved in R&D activities,
- an intermediate output, such as the number of inventions that have been patented, or
- a direct measure of innovative output.

The earliest sources of data, R&D measured, indicated that virtually all of the innovative activity was undertaken by large corporations. As patent measures became available, the general qualitative conclusions did not change, although it became clear that small firms were more involved with patent activity than with R&D. The development of direct measures of innovative activity, such as data bases measuring new product and process introductions in the market, indicated something quite different. In a series of studies, Acs/Audretsch (1987, 1988 and 1990) found that while large firms in manufacturing introduced a slightly greater number of significant new innovations than small firms, small-firm employment was only about half as great as large-firm employment, yielding an average small-firm innovation rate in manufacturing of 0.309, compared to a large-firm innovation rate of 0.202. The relative innovative advantage of small and large firms was found to vary considerably across industries. In some industries, such as computers and process control instruments, small firms provide the engine of innovative activity. In other industries, such as pharmaceutical products and aircraft, large firms generate most of the innovative activity. Knowledge regarding both the determinants and the impact of technological change has been largely shaped by measurement.

Acs/Audretsch (1988 and 1990) concluded that some industries are more conducive to small-firm innovation while others foster the innovative activity of large corporations corresponds to the notion of distinct technological regimes – the routinised and entrepreneurial technological regimes.

Empirical evidence in support of the traditional model of entry, which focuses on the role of excess profits as the major incentive to enter, has been ambiguous at best, leading Geroski (1991, 282) to conclude: "Right from the start, scholars have had some trouble in reconciling the stories told about entry in standard textbooks with the substance of what they have found in their data. Very few have emerged from their work feeling that they have answered half as many questions as they have raised, much less that they have answered most of the interesting ones."

Perhaps one reason for this trouble is the inherently static model used to capture an inherently dynamic process. Manfred Neumann (1993) has criticised this traditional model of entry, as found in the individual country studies contained in Geroski/Schwalbach (1991), because they are predicated on the adoption of a basically static framework. It is assumed that start-ups enter a given market where they are facing incumbents which naturally try to fend off entry. Since the impact of entry on the performance of incumbents seems to be only slight, the question arises whether the costs of entry are worthwhile, given the high rate of exit associated with entry. Geroski appears to be rather sceptical about that. I submit that adopting a static framework is misleading. In fact, generally, an entrant can only hope to succeed if he employs either a new technology or offers a new product, or both. Just imitating incumbents is almost certainly doomed to failure. If the process of entry is looked upon from this perspective the high correlation between gross entry and exit reflects the inherent risks of innovating activities. Obviously it is rather difficult to break loose from the inherited mode of reasoning within the static framework. It is not without merit, to be sure, but it needs to be enlarged by putting it into a dynamic setting.

Still, one of the most startling results that has emerged in empirical studies is that entry by firms into an industry is apparently not substantially deterred or even deterred at all in capital-intensive industries in which scale economies play an important role (Audretsch 1995). While studies have generally produced considerable ambiguity concerning the impact of scale economies and other measures traditionally thought to represent a barrier to entry, Audretsch (1995) found conclusive evidence linking the technological regime to start-up activity. New-firm start-up activity tends to be substantially more prevalent under the entrepreneurial regime, or where small enterprises account for the bulk of the innovative activity, than under the routinised regime, or where the large incumbent enterprises account for most of the innovative activity. These findings are consistent with the view that differences in beliefs about the expected value of new ideas are not constant across industries but rather depend on the knowledge conditions inherent in the underlying technological regime.

Geroski/Audretsch (1995) point out that one of the major conclusions from studies about entry is that the process of entry does not end with entry itself. Rather, it is what happens to new firms subsequent to entering that sheds considerable light on industry dynamics. The early studies (Mansfield 1962; Hall 1987; Dunne Roberts/ Samuelson 1989; Audretsch 1991) established not only that the likelihood of a new entrant surviving is quite low, but that the likelihood of survival is positively related to firm size and age. More recently, a wave of studies have confirmed these findings for diverse countries, including Portugal (Mata, Portugal and Guimaraes 1994, and Mata 1994), Germany (Wagner 1994), and Canada (Baldwin/Gorecki 1991; Baldwin 1995; Baldwin/Rafiquzzaman 1995).

Audretsch (1991), Audretsch/Mahmood (1995) shifted the relevant question away from Why does the likelihood of survival vary systematically across firms? to Why does the propensity for firms to survive vary systematically across industries? The answer to this question suggests that what had previously been considered to pose a barrier to entry may, in fact, constitute not an entry barrier but rather a barrier to survival.

What has become known as Gibrat's Law, or the assumption that growth rates are invariant to firm size, has been subject to numerous empirical tests. Studies linking firm size and age to growth have also produced a number of stylised facts (Wagner 1992). For small and new firms there is substantial evidence suggesting that growth is negatively related to firm size and age (Hall 1987, Wagner 1992 and 1994, Mata 1993, Audretsch 1995). However, for larger firms, particularly those having attained the MES level of output, the evidence suggests that firm growth is unrelated to size and age.

Wagner (1994) has found that the industry environment plays an important role in shaping the amount of entrepreneurial activity in Germany.[1] Based on a longitudinal data base between 1979 and 1989, he finds that the start-up of new small firms tends to be greater in those industries experiencing high growth and which are highly concentrated. He finds that start-up activity is not significantly influenced by the importance of capital intensity and R&D in the industry. These non-significant statistical results are important because they suggest that entrepreneurs are not deterred from starting new firms even in industries which are capital intensive and where R&D plays an important role.

Harhoff/Stahl (1995) use a data base of around 11 000 firms in manufacturing, construction, trade, finance, and services to examine how the post-entry performance of German firms varies across different sectors, in terms of the likelihood of survival and growth. In particular, Harhoff and Stahl find evidence that the likelihood of

1 For an analysis of the five new Laender, see Steil (1997).

survival is positively related to firm size. In addition, firm growth is negatively related to firm size. In addition, the likelihood of survival and growth rates differ systematically across different sectors of the economy.

The results of Harhoff/Stahl (1995) are not consistent with those found in earlier studies, according to the careful survey by Joachim Wagner (1992). After reviewing the most important studies, Wagner (1996, 201) concludes that, "Studies using german data tend to show that firm size and firm growth are uncorrelated."

Wagner (1997) uses a large panel data base from the German Federal State of Lower Saxony to examine the link between firm size and the quality of jobs. In particular, he finds that small firms have the same propensity to offer high-quality jobs as do their larger counterparts, in terms of the duration of the job. This finding holds across different industries, both for high-technology sectors and for low-technology sectors.

Almus and Nerlinger (1998a and 1998b) also use a large panel data base to examine how the post-entry performance of new firms varies across sectors. In particular, they find that the growth rates of new firms tends to be greater in very high-tech industries than in high-tech industries and other manufacturing industries.

An important finding of Audretsch (1991 and 1995) and Audretsch/Mahmood (1995) is that although entry may still occur in industries characterised by a high degree of scale economies, the likelihood of survival is considerably less. People will start new firms in an attempt to appropriate the expected value of their new ideas, or potential innovations, particularly under the entrepreneurial regime. As entrepreneurs gain experience in the market they learn in at least two ways. First, they discover whether they possess the right stuff, in terms of producing goods and offering services for which sufficient demand exists, as well as whether they can produce that good more efficiently than their rivals. Second, they learn whether they can adapt to market conditions as well as to strategies engaged in by rival firms. In terms of the first type of learning, entrepreneurs who discover that they have a viable firm will tend to expand and ultimately survive. But what about those entrepreneurs who discover that they are either not efficient or not offering a product for which their is a viable demand? The answer is, it depends – on the extent of scale economies as well as on conditions of demand. The consequences of not being able to grow will depend, to a large degree, on the extent of scale economies. Thus, in markets with only negligible scale economies, firms have a considerably greater likelihood of survival. However, where scale economies play an important role the consequences of not growing are substantially more severe, as evidenced by a lower likelihood of survival.

What emerges from the new evolutionary theories and empirical evidence on the economic role of new and small firms is that markets are in motion, with a lot of new firms entering the industry and a lot of firms exiting out of the industry. But is this motion horizontal, in that the bulk of firms exiting are comprised of firms that had entered relatively recently, or vertical, in that a significant share of the exiting firms had been established incumbents that were displaced by younger firms? In trying to shed some light on this question, Audretsch (1995) proposes two different models of the evolutionary process of industries over time. Some industries can be best characterised by the model of the conical revolving door, where new businesses enter, but where there is a high propensity to subsequently exit from the market. Other industries may be better characterised by the metaphor of the forest, where incumbent establishments are displaced by new entrants. Which view is more applicable apparently depends on three major factors – the underlying technological conditions, scale economies, and demand. Where scale economies play an important role, the model of the revolving door seems to be more applicable. While the rather startling result discussed above that the start-up and entry of new businesses is apparently not deterred by the presence of high scale economies, a process of firm selection analogous to a revolving door ensures that only those establishments successful enough to grow will be able to survive beyond more than a few years. Thus the bulk of new entrants that are not so successful ultimately exit within a few years subsequent to entry.

There is at least some evidence also suggesting that the underlying technological regime influences the process of firm selection and therefore the type of firm with a higher propensity to exit. Under the entrepreneurial regime new entrants have a greater likelihood of making an innovation. Thus, they are less likely to decide to exit from the industry, even in the face of negative profits. By contrast, under the routinised regime the incumbent businesses tend to have the innovative advantage, so that a higher portion of exiting businesses tend to be new entrants. Thus, the model of the revolving door is more applicable under technological conditions consistent with the routinised regime, and the metaphor of the forest, where the new entrants displace the incumbents – is more applicable to the entrepreneurial regime.

Why is the general shape of the firm-size distribution not only strikingly similar across virtually every industry – that is, skewed with only a few large enterprises and numerous small ones – but has persisted with tenacity not only across developed countries but even over a long period of time? The evolutionary view of the process of industry evolution is that new firms typically start at a very small scale of output. They are motivated by the desire to appropriate the expected value of new economic knowledge. But, depending upon the extent of scale economies in the industry, the firm may not be able to remain viable indefinitely at its start-up size. Rather, if scale economies are anything other than negligible, the new firm is likely to have to grow to survival. The temporary survival of new firms is presumably supported through the deployment of a strategy of compensating factor differentials that enables the firm to discover whether or not it has a viable product.

The empirical evidence supports such an evolutionary view of the role of new firms in manufacturing, because the post-entry growth of firms that survive tends to be spurred by the extent to which there is a gap between the MES level of output and the size of the firm. However, the likelihood of any particular new firm surviving tends to decrease as this gap increases. Such new suboptimal scale firms are apparently engaged in the selection process. Only those firms offering a viable product that can be produced efficiently will grow and ultimately approach or attain the MES level of output. The remainder will stagnate, and depending upon the severity of the other selection mechanism – the extent of scale economies – may ultimately be forced to exit out of the industry. Thus, the persistence of an asymmetric firm-size distribution biased towards small-scale enterprise reflects the continuing process of the entry of new firms into industries and not necessarily the permanence of such small and sub-optimal enterprises over the long run. Although the skewed size distribution of firms persists with remarkable stability over long periods of time, a constant set of small and suboptimal scale firms does not appear to be responsible for this skewed distribution. Rather, by serving as agents of change, new firms provide an essential source of new ideas and experimentation that otherwise would remain untapped in the economy.

The literature linking SMEs to the regional environment focuses on two themes. The first addresses which type of regional environment best promotes SMEs activities. The second addresses how the presence of a vibrant entrepreneurial region influences subsequent growth. An example of the first type is Audretsch/Fritsch (1994), who examine the impact that location plays on entrepreneurial activity in (West) Germany. Using a data base derived from the social insurance statistics, which covers about 90 per cent of employment, they identify the birth rates of new start-ups for each of 75 distinct economic regions. These regions are distinguished on the basis of planning regions, or Raumordungsregionen. They find that, for the late 1980s, the birth rates of new firms are higher in regions experiencing low unemployment, which have a dense population, a high growth rate of population, a high share of skilled workers, and a strong presence of small businesses.[2]

Similarly, Pfirrmann (1994) has found that the innovative activity of small- and medium-sized firms in West Germany is shaped by regional factors. He uses a data base consisting of innovative small and medium-sized firms and finds that the innovative activity of small- and medium-sized enterprises tends to be greater in those regions where there is a strong presence of knowledge resources. However, his results also indicate that factors internal to the firm are more important for the innovation efforts of a small firm than is the regional environment.

---

2 For an extension of this study that controls specifically for the detailed disaggregated industry, see Audretsch and Fritsch (forthcoming).

An example of the second type of literature, which focuses on the impact of entrepreneurship on subsequent economic growth is Audretsch/Fritsch (1996) and Fritsch/Audretsch (1995), who analysed a database identifying new business start-ups and exits from the social insurance statistics in Germany to examine whether a greater degree of turbulence leads to greater economic growth, as suggested by Joseph Schumpeter in his pathbreaking 1911 treatise. These social insurance statistics are collected for individuals. Each record in the database identifies the establishment at which an individual is employed. The start-up of a new firm is recorded when a new establishment identification appears in the database, which generally indicates the birth of a new enterprise. While there is some evidence for the United States linking a greater degree of turbulence at the regional level to higher rates of growth for regions, Audretsch/Fritsch (1996) find that the opposite is true for Germany during the 1980s. In both the manufacturing and the service sectors, a high rate of turbulence in a region tends to lead to a lower and not a higher rate of growth. They attribute this negative relationship to the fact that the underlying components – the start-up and death rates – are both negatively related to subsequent economic growth. Those areas with higher start-up rates tend to experience lower growth rates in subsequent years. Most strikingly, the same is also true for the death rates. The German regions experiencing higher death rates also tend to experience lower growth rates in subsequent years.[3]

Audretsch/Fritsch (1996) conjecture that one possible explanation for the disparity in results between the United States and Germany may lie in the role that innovative activity, and therefore the ability of new firms to ultimately displace the incumbent enterprises, plays in new-firm start-ups. It may be that innovative activity does not play the same role for the German Mittelstand as it does for SMEs in the United States (Audretsch 1995). To the degree that this is true, it may be hold that regional growth emanates from SMEs only when they serve as agents of change through innovative activity.

5 The Public Policy Response

The policy response to this new view of the knowledge production function has been to shift away from targeting outputs to inputs. In particular, this involves the creation and commercialisation of knowledge. Examples include the promotion of joint R&D programs, education and training programs, and policies to encourage people to start new firms. As Saxenian (1985) points out: "Attracting high-tech has become the only development game of the 1980s." Justman (1995) and Justman/Teubel (1986) show how investment in infrastructure provide an important source of growth.

3 Similar evidence is provided by Fritsch (1997).

Policy efforts to address the most pressing contemporary economic problems have focused on enablement rather than constraint. Emphasis on enabling firms and individuals to create and commercialise new knowledge is not restricted to any single country or set of countries. Laura Tyson (1994), former chair of the Council of Economic Advisers in the Clinton Administration, recently emphasised the importance of government policies to promote entrepreneurship and new-firm start-ups in the former Soviet Union.

The provision of venture and informal capital to facilitate the creation and growth of new firms has replaced concern about the market power of existing ones in policy debates (Hughes 1997; Mason/Harrison 1997). The lack of finance capital for new ventures has been blamed for the inability of Germany and France to shift economic activity into new industries that generate high-wage employment. One of the most repeated phrases on the pages of the business news over the last few years has been "Put Bill Gates in Europe and it just wouldn't have worked out."[4]

Audretsch/Elston (1997) argue that something of a paradox has emerged with respect to the system of financing for the German Mittelstand, or SMEs in Germany. On the one hand, there is reason to believe that through the development of a finely layered system of institutions linking together financial institutions, governments, and private firms, that the system of finance in Germany serves as a model for providing funds to SMEs. Not only was the Mittelstand the backbone of the German Wirtschaftswunder, or economic miracle, and subsequent rise to economic power, but it also appears to have a played a more important role in German economic development than in either the United States or the United Kingdom.

On the other hand, while the German Mittelstand has provided the backbone for Germany's economic success, one aspect has been noticeably lacking in recent years – the emergence of small high-technology companies in the emerging industries such as software, biotechnology, and computers. The evidence suggests that the lack of entrepreneurial activity in high-technology industries is directly attributable to rigidities and constraints in providing liquidity and access to finance to new firms in new industries imposed by the very same system of finance in Germany.

There are two institutional features of the German financial system that sharply contrast to that practised in the United States and the United Kingdom, both of which may impact the extent to which small- and medium-sized enterprises are able to obtain access to finance (Vitols 1998; Deeg 1998). First, companies in Germany typically rely almost exclusively upon banks for external finance. The external

---

4 „Where's the Venture Capital?" Newsweek, 31 October, 1994, pp. 44. Similar sentiment was expressed by Joschka Fischer, parliamentary leader of the Green Party in Germany, who laments: „A company like Microsoft would never have a chance in Germany" („Those German Banks and Their Industrial Treasures"). The Economist, 21 January, 1994, pp. 77-78.

capital market remains relatively undeveloped in Germany. Second, not only do the banks represent the major financial intermediary supplying capital to firms, but they are also extensively represented on the supervisory board of companies.

This paradox explains the emergence of a fierce debate revolving around the viability of the system of finance with respect to the finance of the German Mittelstand. As the title of an article in Business Week observes, "Suddenly, Germans Love to Hate Their Banks."[5]

In the Audretsch/Elston (1994) study the extent of financial constraints is linked to firm investment behaviour through the lens of the Q theory of investment. The Q framework is based on the assumption that in the absence of capital market imperfections (and taxes), the value-maximising firm will continue to invest as long as the shadow price of a marginal unit of capital, Q, exceeds unity. One of the greatest impediments to measuring the impact of liquidity constraints on investment behaviour across firm size in Germany has been the lack of a reliable and comprehensive panel data set. Audretsch/Elston (1994) employ a data base consisting of a collection of financial reports of German firms quoted on the German stock exchange over a long period of time. The authors find no evidence that the institutional structure of finance in Germany has been able to avoid the impact of financing constraints. In particular, they find that the impact of financing constraints on investment behaviour tends to increase systematically as firm size decreases. Smaller enterprises tend to be more vulnerable to financing constraints than their larger counterparts, even under the German model of finance where the spread between the large- and small-firm lending rates is relatively low. Audretsch and Elston (1994) do, however, find evidence that the German model of finance was able to avoid financing constraints on German enterprises prior to the mid-1970s. A particularly striking feature of this era in West Germany was a relative abundance of cheap credit. This era, however, seems to coincide with the Wirtschaftswunder, or economic miracle, in Germany. Since the mid-1970s there is no evidence that German firms, and in particular the smaller enterprises, have been able to avoid finance constraints.
Haid/Weigand (1998) find that family-owned firms in Germany are not liquidity constrained in that they have sufficient access to finance. Based on a data base consisting of 109 reporting firms, they find that German family-owned firms may have better access to finance than do small-and medium-sized firms in the United States.

A different study, undertaken by Egeln, Licht/Steil (1997) finds that, in fact, small and young firms in high-tech industries in Germany do experience finance constraints. Forty-two per cent of firms which are less than five years old perceive that access to capital is "an important obstacle to innovation activity", while only 35 per

5 „Suddenly, Germans Love to Hate their Banks: Anger over Bank Control of Industry May Reshape the Economy". Business Week, 20 February 1995, pp. 42.

cent of firms older than 20 years experience a finance constraint. Similarly, only 2.2 per cent of firms with fewer than 50 employees received a credit rating of "excellent", while 41 per cent if firms with employment exceeding 1 000 received a credit rating of "excellent."

Weigand (1998) analyses an important longitudinal data base from the German Bundesbank (Deutsche Bundesbank 1992) consisting of 18 281 firms over the period 1978-1989. She finds that the share of internal finance by the large firms rose from about 26 per cent in 1978 to about 28 per cent in 1989. By contrast, the share total finance accounted for by internal finance by small firms decreased from about 22 per cent in 1978 to 18 per cent in 1989. Similarly, the share of total finance accounted for by internal finance in medium-sized enterprises fell from about 21 per cent in 1978 to 18 per cent in 1989. Weigand (1998) also shows that

- smaller firms tend to have longer-term relationships with financial institutions than their larger counterparts, and
- this has become more important over time.

Pfirrmann/Wupperfeld/Lerner (1997) undertook an exhaustive study comparing the venture capital in Germany with that in the United States. They identified three major differences in venture capital between the U.S. and Germany:

- the size and rate of growth of venture capital,
- the legal structure of venture capital funds, and
- the market structure of venture capital. In addition, they find that German venture capital managers typically do not specialise in certain high technology sectors or industries. Instead, they prefer a broad distribution of industries in their portfolios in order to minimise risk. While this German strategy of diversification serves to reduce risk it also reduces the ability of fund managers to accumulate expertise in any particular industry.

There is evidence that the amount of venture capital available to new-firm start-ups in high-technology industries is dramatically increasing. The amount of venture capital provided by direct-investment and venture capital programs sponsored by the Federal Ministry for Education, Science, Research and Technology (BMBF) has increased from about 10 million DM in 1989 to more than 458 million DM in 1997 (BMBF 1996). The BMBF has had a series of specific programs to promote German SMEs.

For example, indirect promotion of new technology-based firms (NTBFs) by the German federal government has risen from 45.9 million DM in 1991 to almost 82 million DM in 1993 (BMBF 1996).[6] Similarly, Sternberg (1996) has shown that a number of government-sponsored technology policies has triggered the start-up of new firms. The majority of the start-up programs are targeted towards eliminated particular bottlenecks in the development and financing of new firms. Sternberg (1990) examines the impact that 70 innovation centres have had on the development of technology-based small firms. He finds that the majority of the entrepreneurs find a number of advantages from locating at an innovation centre.[7] Becher/Wolff (1995) provide detailed evidence of the role and impact that government programs play in supporting R&D co-operation among German SMEs.

The Kreditanstalt für Wiederaufbau (KfW), or German Reconstruction Bank has been one of the most important institutions promoting SMEs in Germany. The KfW provides financial support for around 20 000 SMEs each year. Of these firms, 80 per cent have sales less than 10 million DM. The support of SMEs by the KfW resulted in the creation of nearly 150 000 jobs in 1992 and 40 000 jobs in 1995.

One of the most important conclusions of Feldman/Pfirrmann (1998, 14) is that "since biotechnology has only really begun to be competitive in Germany over the last five years, the financial infrastructure lacks the expertise to invest in promising biotech start-ups. Although venture capital exists, there appears to be a bias against investing in early stage ventures. Established German pharmaceuticals are more likely to invest in foreign biotech's, which are seen as more stable or profitable, than domestic biotech's." Perhaps in a response to bolster the fledgling biotechnology industry, the German government started a national initiative, Biotechnologie 2000, to support entrepreneurship in biotechnology. In addition, the BioRegio program was started, in which the German Laender compete for investment in local biotechnology firms. To participate, regions were required to develop a plan for research and commercialisation of biotechnology, with a special emphasis on co-operation between the universities and private industry. Feldman/Pfirrmann (1998) have concluded that, "without doubt the BioRegio competition fostered biotechnology activities not only in the so-called winner regions Aachen, Heidelberg and Munich, but also in other areas like Berlin/Brandenburg that have got no public support."

Audretsch/Feldman (1996) argue that industrial policies targeting the production and commercialisation of new economic knowledge will have a greater impact on particular regions and not diffuse rapidly across geographic space. They point out

---

6 The studies contained in Becher/Kuhlmann (1995) provide an excellent overview of the specific technology policy programs in Germany and their impact on SMEs. See in particular Kuntze/Hornschild (1995).

7 Additional analyses of German innovation centers can be found in Baranowski/Gross (1996). The advantages of locating within close regional proximity of knowledge sources in Germany is analyzed in Berger/Nerlinger (1997).

that knowledge spill 'overs are a key source of new knowledge generating innovative activity, but due to the tacit nature of that knowledge, knowledge flows tend to be geographically bounded. Although the cost of transmitting information has become invariant to distance, the cost of transmitting knowledge, and especially tacit knowledge, rises with distance. By creating regions of knowledge-based economic activities, government policies can generate highly concentrated innovative clusters.

As long as the major policy issue was restricting large, oligopolistic firms in command of considerable market power, a federal or national locus of control was appropriate. This is because the benefits and costs derived from that market power are asymmetric between the local region where the firm is located and the national market, where the firm sells its product. Not only was production concentrated in one or just several regions, but the workers along with the ancillary suppliers also tended to be located in the same regions. These workers as well as the community at large share the fruits accruing from monopoly power. Systematic empirical evidence (Weiss 1966) shows that wages are positively related to the degree of market power held by a firm, even after controlling for the degree of unionisation. Higher profits resulting from market power are shared by labour. Workers and firms in the region have the same interest.

As Olson (1982) shows, relatively small coalitions of economic agents benefiting from some collective action tend to prevail over a large group of dispersed economic agents each incurring a small cost from that action. The costs of organising and influencing policy are relatively low for the small coalition enjoying the benefits but large for the group of dispersed economic agents. Government policies to control large oligopolistic firms with substantial market power are not likely to be successful if implemented on the local level. Rather, as Olson (1982) predicts, a regional locus of policy towards business tends to result in the capture of policy by the coalition of local interests benefiting from that policy. Only by shifting the locus of policy away from the region to the national level can the capture of policy by special interest groups be minimised. This is because the negative effects of market power in the form of higher prices are spread throughout the national market while the benefits accruing from that power are locally concentrated.

Starting in the Carter Administration in the late 1970s and continuing into the Administrations of presidents Reagan, Bush and Clinton, antitrust has been deemphasised and a twenty year wave of deregulation has led to a downsizing and even closure of a number of the former regulatory agencies.

Many economists interpret the downsizing of the federal agencies charged with the regulation of business as the eclipse of government intervention. But to interpret the retreat of the federal government as the end of public intervention is to confuse the downsizing of government with a shifting of the locus of government policy away from the federal to the local level. The last decade has seen the emergence of a set of enabling policy initiatives at the local level. This new type of industrial policy is decentralised and regional in nature. As Sternberg (1996) emphasises in his review of successful technology policies in the four leading technological countries, the most important industrial policies in the last decades have been local, not national. They have occurred in locations such as Research Triangle (Link 1995), Austin, Texas and Cambridge (UK). Sternberg (1996) shows how the success of a number of different high-technology clusters spanning the four most technologically advanced countries is the direct result of enabling policies undertaken at the regional level.

Eisinger (1990) asks the question: "Do American States Do Industrial Policy?" in a 1990 article published in the British Journal of Political Science. Lowery/Gray (1990) confirm Eisinger's affirmative answer by analysing the impact of state industrial policy in the United States. They develop a new data set on gross state product and a new measure of state industrial policy activism. Their results suggest that the implementation of industrial policy at the state level tends to promote growth. For example, Feller (1997, 289) points out that "in theory and implementation, state technology development programs – as in Texas, Ohio, New York, New Jersey, and Pennsylvania – may be viewed as bands on a wide spectrum from basic research to product development, with the ends reflecting quite divergent state strategies." The Advanced Research Program in Texas has provided support for basic research and the strengthening of the university infrastructure, which played a central role in recruiting MCC and Sematech and developing a high-tech cluster around Austin. The Thomas Edison Centres in Ohio, the Advanced Technology Centres in New Jersey, and the Centres for Advanced Technology at Case Western Reserve University, Rutgers University and the University of Rochester have supported generic, precompetitive research. This support has generally provided diversified technology development involving a mix of activities encompassing generic research, applied research, and manufacturing modernisation through a broad spectrum of industrial collaborators spanning technology-intensive multinational corporations, regional manufactures and new-firm start-ups.

This shift in the locus of policy is the result of two factors. First, because the source of comparative advantage is knowledge, which tends to be localised in regional clusters, public policy requires an understanding of region-specific characteristics and idiosyncrasies. As Sternberg (1996) concludes, regional strengths provide the major source of innovative clusters. The second factor is that the motivation underlying government policy is now growth and the creation of (high-paying) jobs, largely through the creation of new firms. These new firms are typically small and pose no oligopolistic threat in national or international markets. There are no external costs imposed on consumers in the national economy in the form of higher prices as in the case of a large oligopolistic corporation in possession of market power. There is no reason that the promotion of local economies imposes a cost on consumers in the national economy, so that localised industrial policy is justified and does not result in any particular loss incurred by agents outside of the region.

6 Conclusion

While traditional theories suggest that entrepreneurship will retard economic growth, new theories suggest exactly the opposite – that entrepreneurship will stimulate and generate growth. The reason for these theoretical discrepancies lies in the context of the underlying theory. In the traditional theory, new knowledge plays no role; rather, static efficiency, determined largely by the ability to exhaust scale economies dictates growth. By contrast, the new theories are dynamic in nature and emphasise the role that knowledge plays. Because knowledge is inherently uncertain, asymmetric and associated with high costs of transactions, divergences emerge concerning the expected value of new ideas. Economic agents therefore have an incentive to leave an incumbent firm and start a new firm in an attempt to commercialise the perceived value of their knowledge. Entrepreneurship is the vehicle by which (the most radical) new ideas are sometimes implemented.

While this policy emphasis on small and new firms as engines of dynamic efficiency may seem startling after decades at looking to the corporate giants to bestow efficiency, it is anything but new. Before the country was even half a century old, Alexis de Tocqueville, in 1935, reported: "What astonishes me in the United States is not so much the marvellous grandeur of some undertakings as the innumerable multitude of small ones."

Literature

Acs, Z. J.; Audretsch, D. B. (1988): Innovation in Large and Small Firms: An Empirical Analysis. American Economic Review, 78 (4), September, pp. 678-690.

Acs, Z. J.; Audretsch, D. B. (1990): Innovation and Small Firms, Cambridge: MIT Press.

ADT (Arbeitsgemeinschaft Deutscher Technologie- und Gründerzentren e. V., Berlin) (1998): Ausgründungen technologieorientierter Unternehmen aus Hochschulen und außeruniversitären Forschungseinrichtungen. Report prepared for the Bundesministerium für Bildung und Forschung (BMBF).

Almus, M.; Nerlinger, E. (1998b): Growth Determinants of New Technology-Based Firms: Empirical Results for West-Germany. Unpublished manuscript, Centre for European Economic Research (ZEW), Mannheim, Germany.

Almus, M.; Nerlinger, E. (1998a): Beschäftigungsdynamik in jungen innovativen Unternehmen: Ergebnisse für West-Deutschland. ZEW Discussion Paper no. 98-09, Centre for European Economic Research (ZEW), Mannheim, Germany.

Arrow, K. J. (1962): Economic Welfare and the Allocation of Resources for Invention. In Nelson, R. R. (Ed.): The Rate and Direction of Inventive Activity Princeton. Princeton: University Press.

Audretsch, D. B. (1991): New Firm Survival and the Technological Regime. Review of Economics and Statistics, 73, no. 3, August, pp. 441-450.

Audretsch, D. B. (1995): Innovation and Industry Evolution. Cambridge: MIT Press.

Audretsch, D. B.; Elston, J. A. (forthcoming): Does Firm Size Matter? Evidence on the Impacts of Liquidity Constraints on Investment Behaviour in Germany. International Journal of Industrial Organisation.

Audretsch, D. B.; Elston, J. A. (1997): Financing the German Mittelstand. Small Business Economics, 9 (2), pp. 97-110.

Audretsch, D. B.; Feldman, M. P. (1996): R&D Spill 'overs and the Geography of Innovation and Production. American Economic Review, vol. 86, no. 3, June, pp. 630-640.

Audretsch, D. B.; Fritsch, M. (1993): Betriebliche Turbulenz und regionale Beschäftigungsdynamik. Discussion Paper 93/7, Bergakademie Freiberg.

Audretsch, D. B.; Fritsch, M. (1994): The Geography of Firm Births in Germany. Regional Studies, 28(4), pp. 359-365.

Audretsch, D. B.; Fritsch, M. (1996): Creative Destruction: Turbulence and Economic Growth in Germany. In: Helmstädter, E.; Perlman, M. (Eds.): Behavioural Norms, Technological Progress and Economic Dynamics. Ann Arbor: The University of Michigan Press, pp. 137-150.

Audretsch, D. B.; Fritsch, M. (forthcoming): The Geographic and Industry Components of New Firm Start-ups in Germany. Review of Industrial Organisation.

Audretsch, D. B.; Stephan, P. E. (1996): Company-Scientist Locational Links: The Case of Biotechnology. American Economic Review, vol. 86, no. 3, June, pp. 641-652.

Audretsch, D. B.; Thurik, R. (1999): Innovation, Industry Evolution and Employment. Cambridge: Cambridge University Press.

Audretsch, D. B.; Mahmood, T. (1995): New-Firm Survival: New Results Using a Hazard Function. Review of Economics and Statistics, vol. 77, no. 1, February, pp. 97-103.

Audretsch, D. B. (1995): Innovation and Industry Evolution. Cambridge: MIT Press.

Audretsch, D. B. (1999): Mittelstandspolitik, Neugründungen und die Standortkrise. In: Welfens, P. (Ed.): Economic Globalisation, Innovation Dynamics and Labour Markets. Heidelberg: Springer.

Baldwin, J. R. (1995): The Dynamics of Industrial Competition. Cambridge: Cambridge University Press.

Baldwin, J. R.; Rafiquzzaman, M. (1995): Selection versus Evolutionary Adaptation: Learning and Post-Entry Performance. International Journal of Industrial Organisation, vol. 13, no. 4, December, pp. 501-523.

Baldwin, J. R.; Gorecki, P. K. (1991): Entry, Exit, and Production Growth. In: Geroski, P.; Schwalbach, J. (Eds.): Entry and Market Contestability – An International Comparison. Oxford: Basil Blackwell.

Becher, G.; Wolff, H. (1995): Evaluation of the Promotion of R&D Cooperations of Small and Medium Sized Enterprises. In: Becher, G.; Kuhlmann, S. (Eds.): Evaluation of Technology Policy Programmes in Germany. Boston: Kluwer Academic Publishers, pp. 55-80.

Becher, G.; Kuhlmann, S. (1995, Eds.): Evaluation of Technology Policy Programmes in Germany. Boston: Kluwer Academic Publishers.

Beise, M.; Licht, G. (1996): Innovationsverhalten der deutschen Wirtschaft. Unpublished manuscript. Zentrum für Europäische Wirtschaftsforschung (ZEW), Mannheim, January.

Berger, G.; Nerlinger, E. (1997): Regionale Verteilung von Unternehmensgründungen in der Informationstechnik: Empirische Ergebnisse für Westdeutschland. In: Harhoff, D. (Ed.): Unternehmensgründungen: Empirische Analysen für die alten und neuen Bundesländer. Baden-Baden: Nomos, pp. 151-186.

Berger, J.; Domeyer, V.; Funder, M. (1990, Eds.): Kleinbetriebe im wirtschaftlichen Wandel. Berlin: Campus.

BMBF (Bundesministerium für Bildung und Forschung), (1996): Bundesbericht Forschung 1996, Bonn.

Bögenhold, D. (1985): Die neuen Selbständigen. New York: Springer.

Brown, Ch.; Hamilton, J.; Medoff, J. (1990): Employers Large and Small. Cambridge: Cambridge University Press.

Brüderl, J.; Preisendörfer, P. (1998): Network Support and the Success of Newly Founded Businesses. Small Business Economics, 10 (3), pp. 213-225.

Burgel, O.; Murray, G.; Fier, A.; Licht, G.; Nerlinger, E. (1998): The Internationalisation of Britisch and German Start-up Companies in High-Technology Industries. Unpublished manuscript. Centre for European Economic Research (ZEW), Mannheim, Germany.

Carrol, P. (1993): Big Blues: The Unmaking of IBM. New York: Crown Publishers.

Caves, R. E. (1998): Industrial Organisation and New Findings on the Turnover and Mobility of Firms. Journal of Economic Literature, vol. 36, no. 4, December, pp. 1947-1982.

Chandler, A. D. Jr. (1977): The Visible Hand: The Managerial Revolution in American Business. Cambridge: Harvard University Press.

Coase, R. H.(1937): The Nature of the Firm. Economica, vol. 4, no. 4, pp. 386-405.

Cringley, R. X. (1993): Accidental Empires. New York: Harper Business.

Deeg, R. (1998): What Makes German Banks Different? Small Business Economics, 10(2), pp. 93-101.

Dunne, T.; Roberts, M. J.; Samuelson, L. (1989): The Growth and Failure of U.S. Manufacturing Plants. Quarterly Journal of Economics, vol. 104, pp. 671-698.

Egeln, J.; Licht, G.; Steil, F. (1997): Firm Foundations and the Role of Financial Constraints. Small Business Economics, 9 (2), pp. 137-150.

Eisinger, P. (1990): Do the American States do Industrial Policy? British Journal of Political Science, 20, vol. 20, October, pp. 509-535.

Feldman, M. P.; Pfirrmann, O. (1998): Bio-Entrepreneurship in the U.S. and Germany. Unpublished manuscript.

Feller, I. (1997): Federal and State Government Roles in Science and Technology. Economic Development Quarterly, 11(4), pp. 283-296.

Fritsch, M.; Audretsch, D. B. (1995): Betriebliche Turbulenz und regionale Beschäftigungsdynamik. In: Semlinger, K.; Frick, B.: Betriebliche Modernisierung in personeller Erneuerung. Berlin: Edition sigma, pp. 59-74.

Fritsch, M. (1993): The Role of Small Firms in West Germany. In: Acs, Z. J.; Audretsch, D. B. (Eds.): Small Firms and Entrepreneurship: An East-West Perspective. Cambridge: Cambridge University Press, pp. 38-54.

Fritsch, M. (1997): New Firms and Regional Employment Change. Small Business Economics, 9(5), pp. 437-448.

Galbraith, J. K. (1956): American Capitalism. Boston: Houghton Mifflin.

Geroski, P. A. (1991): Some Data-Driven Reflections on the Entry Process. In: Georski, P.; Schwalbach, J. (Eds.): Entry and Market Contestability: An International Comparison. Oxford: Basil Blackwell, pp. 282-286.

Geroski, P. A. (1995): What do we know about Entry. International Journal of Industrial Organisation (Special Issue on The Post Entry Performance of Firms; Audretsch, D. B.; Mata, J. Eds.), vol. 13, no. 4, December, pp. 421-440.

Geroski, P. A.; Schwalbach, J. (1991, Eds.): Entry and Market Contestability: An International Comparison. Oxford, Basil Blackwell.

Graaf, J. de V. (1957): Theoretical Welfare Economics. Cambridge: Cambridge University Press.

Griliches, Z. (1979): Issues in Assessing the Contribution of R&D to Productivity Growth. Bell Journal of Economics, 10(Spring), pp. 92-116.

Hall, B. H. (1987): The Relationship Between Firm Size and Firm Growth in the U.S. Manufacturing Sector. Journal of Industrial Economics, 35 (June), pp. 583-605.

Hannan, M. T.; Freeman, J. (1989): Organisational Ecology Cambridge: Harvard University Press.

Harhoff, D. (1997, Ed.): Unternehmensgründungen: Empirische Analysen für die alten und neuen Bundesländer. Baden-Baden: Nomos.

Harhoff, D.; Steil, F. (1997): Die ZEW-Gründungspanels: Konzeptionelle Überlegungen und Analysepotential. In: Harhoff, D. (Ed.): Unternehmensgründungen: Empirische Analysen für die alten und neuen Bundesländer. Baden-Baden: Nomos, pp. 11-28.

Harhoff, D.; Licht, G. (1996): Innovationsaktivitäten kleiner und mittlerer Unternehmen. Baden-Baden: Nomos.

Harhoff, D.; Stahl, K. (1995): Unternehmens- und Beschäftigungsdynamik in Westdeutschland: Zum Einfluss von Haftungsregeln und Eigentümerstruktur. In: Oppenländer, K. H. (Ed.): Industrieökonomik und Finanzmärkte. ifo Studien, 41, pp.17-50.

Hirschman, A. O. (1970): Exit, Voice and Loyalty. Cambridge: Harvard University Press.

Hughes, A. (1997): Finance for SMEs: A U.K. Perspective. Small Business Economics, 9(2), April, pp. 151-166.

Ijiri, Y.; Simon, H. A. (1977): Skew Distributions and Sizes of Business Firms. Amsterdam: North Holland.

Jovanovic, B. (1982): Selection and Evolution of Industry. Econometrica, vol. 50, no. 2, pp. 649-670.

Justman, M.; Teubal, M. (1986): Innovation Policy in an Open Economy: A Normative Framework to Strategic and Tactical Issues. Research Policy, 15, pp. 121-138.

Justman, M. (1995): Infrastructure, Growth and the Two Dimensions of Industrial Policy. Review of Economic Studies, 62 (1), January, pp. 131-157.

Knight, F. H. (1921): Risk, Uncertainty and Profit. New York: Houghton Mifflin.

Kulicke, M. (1987): Technologieorientierte Unternehmen in der Bundesrepublik Deutschland: Eine empirische Untersuchung der Strukturbildungs- und Wachstumsphase von Neugründungen. Frankfurt: Peter Lang.

Kuntze, U.; Hornschild, K. (1995): Evaluation of the Promotion of R&D Activities in Small and Medium Sized Enterprises. In: Becher, G.; Kuhlmann, S. (1995, Eds.): Evaluation of Technology Policy Programmes in Germany. Boston: Kluwer Academic Publishers, pp. 33-54.

Licht, G.; Nerlinger, E. (1997): Junge innovative Unternehmen in Europa: Ein internationaler Vergleich. In: Harhoff, D. (1997, Ed.): Unternehmensgründungen: Empirische Analysen für die alten und neuen Bundesländer, Baden-Baden: Nomos, pp. 187-208.

Licht, G.; Nerlinger, E.; Berger, G. (1995): Germany: NTBF Literature Review. ZEW, Mannheim.

Link A. (1995): A Generosity of Spirit. Durham, NC: Duke University Press.

Loveman, G.; Sengenberger, W. (1991): The Re-emergence of Small-Scale Production: An International Comparison. Small Business Economics, 3(1), pp. 1-38.

Mansfield, E. (1962): Entry, Gibrat's Law, Innovation, and the Growth of Firms. American Economic Review, vol. 52, no. 5, pp. 1023-1051.

Manz, T. (1990): Innovationsprozesse in Klein- und Mittelbetrieben. Opladen: Westdeutscher Verlag.

Mata, J. (1994): Firm Growth During Infancy. Small Business Economics 6(1), pp. 27-40.

Mata, J.; Portugal, P. (1994): Life Duration of new Firms. Journal of Industrial Economics, 27 (3), pp. 227-246.

Mata, J.; Portugal, P.; Guimaraes, P. (1995): The Survival of New Plants: Start-Up Conditions and Post-Entry Evolution. International Journal of Industrial Organisation 13(4), December, pp. 459-482.

Meyer-Krahmer, F. (1993, Ed.): Innovationsökonomie und Technologiepolitik, Heidelberg: Physica-Verlag.

Moore, J. H. (1992): Measuring Soviet Economic Growth: Old Problems and New Complications. Journal of Institutional and Theoretical Economics, 148(1), pp. 72-92.

Nelson, R. R.; Winter, S. G. (1982): An Evolutionary Theory of Economic Change. Cambridge: Harvard University Press.

Nerlinger, E. (1998): Standorte und Entwicklung junger innovativer Unternehmen: Empirische Ergebnisse für West-Deutschland. Baden-Baden: Nomos.

Neumann, M. (1993): Review of Entry and Market Contestability: An International Comparison. International Journal of Industrial Organization, vol. 11, no. 4, pp. 593-594.

Palfreman, J.; Swade, D. (1991): The Dream Machine: Exploring the Computer Age. London: BBC Books.

Pfirrmann, O.; Wupperfeld, U.; Lerner, J. (1997): Venture Capital and New Technology Based Firms: A US-German Comparison. Berlin: Physica-Verlag.

Pfirrmann, O. (1994): The Geography of Innovation in Small and Medium-Sized Firms in West Germany. Small Business Economics, 6 (1), pp. 27-41.

Picot, A.; Laub, U. D.; Scheider, D. (1989): Innovative Unternehmensgründungen: Eine ökonomisch-empirische Analyse. Berlin: Springer.

Pratten, C. F. (1971): Economies of Scale in Manufacturing Industry. Cambridge: Cambridge University Press.

Saxenian, A. (1990): Regional Networks and the Resurgence of Silicon Valley. California Management Review, 33 (1), pp. 89-111.

Scherer, F. M. (1976): Industrial Structure, Scale Economies, and Worker Alienation. In: Robert T. M.; David Qualls P. (Eds.): Essays on Industrial Organisation in Honour of Joe S. Bain. Cambridge: Ballinger, pp. 105-122.

Scherer, F. M. (1991): Changing Perspectives on the Firm Size Problem. In: Acs, Z. J.; Audretsch, D. B. (Eds.): Innovation and Technological Change. An International Comparison. Ann Arbor: University of Michigan Press, pp. 24-38.

Schumpeter, J. A. (1911): Theorie der wirtschaftlichen Entwicklung. Eine Untersuchung über Unternehmergewinn, Kapital, Kredit, Zins und den Konjunkturzyklus. Berlin: Duncker und Humblot.

Schumpeter, J. A. (1942): Capitalism, Socialism and Democracy. New York: Harper and Row.

Schwalbach, J. (1989): Small Business in German Manufacturing. Small Business Economics, 1 (2), pp. 129-136.

Schwalbach, J. (1990): Small Business in German Manufacturing. In: Acs, Z. J.; Audretsch, D. B. (Eds.): The Economics of Small Firms: A European Challenge. Boston: Kluwer Academic Publisher, pp. 63-73.

Schwalbach, J. (1994): Small Business Dynamics in Europe. Small Business Economics, 6 (1), pp. 21-26.

Simon, H. A.; Bonini, Ch. P. (1958): The Size Distribution of Business Firms. American Economic Review, vol. 48, no. 4, pp. 607-617.

Steil, F. (1997): Unternehmensgründungen in Ostdeutschland. In: Harhoff, D. (Ed.): Unternehmensgründungen: Empirische Analysen für die alten und neuen Bundesländer. Baden-Baden: Nomos, pp. 29-72.

Sternberg, R. (1990): The Impact of Innovation Centres on Small Technology-Based Firms: The Example of the Federal Republic of Germany. Small Business Economics, 2 (2), pp. 105-118.

Sternberg, R. (1996): Technology Policies and the Growth of Regions: Evidence from Four Countries. Small Business Economics, 8 (2), pp. 75-86.

Stockmann, R.; Leicht, R. (1994): The Pattern of Changes in the Long-Term Development of Establishment Size. Small Business Economics, 6 (6), pp. 451-464.

Sutton, J. 1997): Gibrat's Legacy. Journal of Economic Literature, vol. 35, no. 1, pp. 40-59.

Tyson, L. d'Andrea; Petrin, T.; Rogers, H. (1994): Promoting Entrepreneurship in Eastern Europe. Small Business Economics, 6 (3), June, pp. 165-184.

Vitols, S. (1998): Are German Banks Different? Small Business Economics, 10 (2), pp. 79-91.

Wagner, J. 1992): Firm Size, Firm Growth, and Persistence of Chance: Testing Gibrat's Law with Establishment Data from Lower Saxony, 1978-1989. Small Business Economics, 4 (2), pp. 125-131.

Wagner, J. (1994): Small Firm Entry in Manufacturing Industries: Lower Saxony, 1979-1989. Small Business Economics, vol. 6, no. 3, pp. 211-224.

Wagner, J. (1992): Firm Size, Firm Growth, and Persistence of Chance: Testing Gibrat's Law with Establishment Data from Lower Saxony, 1978-1989. Small Business Economics, 4 (2), pp. 125-131.

Wagner, J. 1995a): Exports, Firm Size, and Firm Dynamics. Small Business Economics, 7 (1), pp. 29-40.

Wagner, J. 1995b): Firm Size and Job Creation in Germany. Small Business Economics, 7 (6), pp. 469-474.

Wagner, J. (1997): Firm Size and Job Quality: A Survey of the Evidence from Germany. Small Business Economics, 9 (5), pp. 411-425.

Weigand, C. (1998): Der Einfluss der Bankkreditvergabe auf den Unternehmenswettbewerb. Hamburg: Verlag Dr. Kovac.

Weigand, J. (1996): Innovationen, Wettbewerb und Konjunktur. Berlin: Duncker und Humblot.

Weiss, L. W. (1979): The Structure-Performance Paradigm and Antitrust. University of Pennsylvania Law Review, 127 (April), pp. 1104-1140.

Williamson, O. E. (1975): Markets and Hierarchies: Antitrust Analysis and Implications. New York: The Free Press.

Williamson, O. E. (1968): Economies as an Antitrust Defense: The Welfare Tradeoffs. American Economic Review, 58 (1), pp. 18-36.

Winter, S. G. (1984): Schumpeterian Competition in Alternative Technological Regimes. Journal of Economic Behaviour and Organisation, vol. 5, September-December, pp. 287-320.

Private Ownership and Markets: Limits to Privatisation in the Transition Process

Walter Heering, Oliver Pfirrmann

1 Introduction

An almost stereotypically repeated phrase in scientific literature as well as in political statements maintains that one of the essentials of a market economy lies in the existence of private ownership in general, and of the means of production in particular. Whereas for critiques of market society, private ownership is the very root of nearly all evils, proponents see it as an absolute prerequisite for individual freedom, human dignity and social justice, as is expressed for example in John Locke's famous sentence: "Where there is no [private] property there is no justice" (Hayek 1988, 34).[1] Whether this may hold in general or not, in any case it seems to be true that some private property is at least favourable for a person's privacy and individuality, and must thus be seen as a virtue in itself (Munzer 1990, 88 ff). Although not independent from the above-mentioned discourse, from an economic point of view private ownership of resources and goods provides a necessary condition for economic efficiency, meaning a state in which any resource and good in the economy finds its best (i.e. highest valued) use. It is for this reason that privatisation of state-owned enterprises, land, accommodation etc. has become a pivotal issue of political, social and economic transition in countries formerly under the control of Soviet-oriented communists. Great hopes have been placed in privatisation, not least with regard to stimulating an entrepreneurial potential. The target is clear and sensible enough, but the route, speed and results of this undertaking have hitherto nowhere been completely satisfactory, though there are, of course, significant differences in degree between countries. A closer look, in particular, raises doubts as to whether the results achieved justify focusing on privatisation as an important policy for promoting entrepreneurship. In this essay we shall look more closely at the concept of ownership to find out some of the reasons why privatisation in CEECs is so thorny a matter. We argue two main theses: first, whatever further reasons may (and

---

1 Note that the U. S. Constitution, in wording reminiscent of John Locke, uses the expression "life, liberty, or property" with respect to the "due process clause" in a sort of umbrella fashion, indicating their intimate connection (Munzer 1990, Richter 1993).

actually do) exist for the overall unsatisfactory state of transition after ten years, as well as for the large differentials in performance between the economies, the remaining deficiencies with regard to property rights and ownership, properly understood, are perfectly sufficient as an explanation. Second, while privatisation of state-owned enterprises is an important step towards a private ownership economy, it is not the only necessary step, and at any rate it is far from being sufficient to ensure an efficiently functioning market system. In Section 2 we introduce the concept of ownership, demonstrating its quite complex nature. In section 3 we argue that private ownership needs to be checked by competition in order to yield efficient market results. There are many conditions for competitive markets, but the most important is that the rules of the market game must be as clear as possible, must be reliable, and must be understood as well as accepted by market participants. The anonymity requirement for competitiveness is stressed and hence the necessity for a well-functioning monetary arrangement, an essential not often mentioned in this context. In section 4 privatisation in transition economies is compared to privatisation in Western countries, where we find quite a lot of fairly crucial differences. Our arguments suggest that experiences with Western privatisation are not very helpful as a guideline to the task in transitional economies. In section 5 we discuss several almost inevitable limitations to privatisation in CEECs, supporting both of our main theses. Finally, section 6 summarises and concludes with a plea for more patience concerning the historic project of transition.

2 The Concept of Ownership

"Ownership ... is a "meta-right" or "super-right" exercised over property rights" (Jasay 1991, 74), i.e. "rights to perform actions which involve the use and/or the alienation of a thing. Rights to act are prerogatives for performing some kinds of action according to the prevailing norms. If a right holder's set of permitted actions includes the right to alienate the thing, that is the power to revoke all existing property rights over the thing, he is the owner of that thing. This characterisation .. does [however] not imply that owners are absolute rulers over the thing they own. Their right to alienate a thing may be attenuated in various ways by contracts or by norms" (Haller 1998, 170). Several remarks on this definition are in order.

First, property rights are "rights to action", which must be protected by social norms to be effective. "The existence of effective property norms distinguishes property relations from mere possession" (Haller 1998, 169). Such norms may be established by law, agreement or convention. In philosophy and political theory it is still controversial how their emergence can be explained (Thomas Hobbes' problem), but, as a matter of fact, in modern societies it is one role ascribed to the state to enforce legal norms. In itself, however, this would hardly prove effective unless individuals themselves (at least as a majority) shared a mutual and tacit agreement to respect their property rights (Jasay 1991). This is the rationale of what may be called an "ownership culture". Moreover, individual awareness of property rights will also be necessary, since they have to be protected not only against other private agents but also against the state itself.

Second, ownership essentially rests on a technical possibility and on one basic legal principle, namely: the feasibility to exclude non-owners from the usage of the object in question and the property right to transfer property rights to the object, including full ownership, to others (Ryan 1987; Jasay 1991). Ownership therefore not only gives the right to use or abuse an object or to earn an income from it,[2] but also to enter into contracts with other actors concerning the transfer of property rights referring to the object in question. This right (or privilege[3]) to transfer property rights with regard to some object constitutes the ownership for that object; it is nothing else than the freedom to contract (Jasay 1991), lying at the core of a market system, where owners exchange property rights by mutually beneficial agreements. Where this freedom is excluded or severely limited, markets do not function at all or only very inefficiently. The socialist principle, quite consistent in itself, ultimately postulates "that individuals do not rightfully own either themselves or productive assets, only "society" does. ... It rejects contractual freedom because it has already rejected personal ownership" (Jasay 1991, 103).

Third, there may be and mostly are limits to the set of property rights, and in some cases property rights may even be almost completely abandoned. During the National Socialist regime in Germany, for instance, property rights of firms were severely restricted, although private ownership as such was seldom (and only for purely ideological reasons) denied. As long as both the two above-mentioned basic features apply, this does not destroy ownership, although its usage may be more or less restricted. The privilege of ownership, as any freedom, is always limited by property rights of others: "It is not an infringement of my ownership of this knife that I may not stick it in your chest. The law allows nobody to stick a knife in anyone's chest, but whatever anyone may lawfully do with any knife, I (and nobody else) may do with this one" (Ryan 1987, 227f).

---

2 A. M. Honoré's classical list of incidents of ownership includes rights "to possess, use, manage, and receive income; the powers to transfer, waive, exclude, and abandon; the liberties to consume or destroy; immunity from expropriation; the duty not to use harmfully; and liability for execution to satisfy a court judgement" (Munzer 1990, 22).

3 The term "right" is here used in a broad (and even somewhat loose) fashion; there are two important distinctions to be beard in mind: A right may be a claim, i.e. must have another person's obligation as its correlative. But rights in a broader sense imply the freedom to do something, which is rather a privilege or liberty, not a claim (Munzer 1990, Jasay 1991, both referring to Hohfeld's "Fundamental Legal Conceptions", published in 1919). The essential of ownership, as stated in the text, is in this strict sense a privilege, not a claim, and so are many property rights. While this distinction refers to the type of relation between actors which a right establishes, similar but not identical, we may distinguish rights with regard to the foundation of the relation. There are reciprocal rights originating by mutual agreement, and rights of decree defined simply by the absence of any sanction the user of the right may face (Hesse 1983).

Fourth, while the right to exclude others from the usage of an object follows from ownership in the above sense, exclusion may not always be feasible or worthwhile. If rivalry exists with regard to the usage of an object, in the sense that any additional user diminishes the benefits to the owner (which normally will be the case), the owner will be strongly inclined to exclude other users unless they are ready to compensate for his disadvantage associated with their usage of the same objects. Nevertheless, he will factually exclude only if the costs of excluding do not exceed the disadvantage otherwise incurred to him. If rivalry in usage and excludability in the above sense both apply, the object in question is called a "pure private good". It follows from the above, however, that exclusion will not take place with regard to an object for which no rivalry of usage exists (in which case the literature speaks of "pure public goods" (Haller 1998[4]). If to become the "owner" of such an object is only possible at a positive price (which need not be pecuniary), however, a free-riding problem will necessarily evolve. Any possible threat to exclude other users will not be credible, since it will be realised by non-owners that, once the object is acquired, the owner will have no incentive to exclude (given the positive cost of excluding). Thus, although there are several (possibly many) individuals who would like to use the object, nobody may actually acquire it, because he would have to bear all the costs while the benefits would fall to others as well. In general, if exclusion is not feasible, or is only feasible at a cost that does not make it worthwhile to the owner, there exists a positive externality, which thus is simply a problem of enforcing (or defining) property rights. On the other hand, a negative externality exists if other agents are not able to exclude effects of the usage of an object by its owner which negatively interfere with their own property rights. Well-defined property rights to an object therefore require excludability with regard to non-owners as well as includability with regard to its owner. The legitimate user of an object should not only exclusively benefit from the usage but should also be exclusively responsible for any harm this does to himself or other agents. Whereas the beneficial dimension of ownership is usually referred to (as the very term "property rights" suggests), its inevitable counterpart is not so often taken into account.

Fifth, almost all human activities, i.e. uses of goods and resources in the broad sense, have positive or negative external effects, sometimes even both. Not all of

---

[4] Even if feasible, non-rivalry implies that exclusion is in general not worthwhile. Non-rivalry would thus be necessary and sufficient for the definition of a public good. However, at least if taken literally, non-rivalry is theoretically but a limit case which will practically seldom (if ever) occur. To make it the decisive criterion for public goods is not reasonable, because the set of public goods may then turn out to be empty. Closer inspection of the matter reveals that non-excludability (and not non-rivalry) marks the true problematic nature of public goods (Molitor 1988, Jasay 1991). Those are therefore nothing but large positive externalities, that is objects the access to which can be denied to practically no individual within a community (possibly the nation). Given nation-wide access, in particular, there is the further problem that some members of the community may have no choice but to „consume the good“ (or emigrate), although they would prefer not to do so (as an example consider military defence). For those individuals the public „good“ in question is in effect a negative externality, i.e. a public „bad“.

those effects cause serious problems of market co-ordination, and in many cases, they effectively work through the market mechanism itself. In particular, property rights in general do not entail a fixed market value of a resource, but only its physical intactness. Use of one property right will often decrease or increase the value of others, in which case we speak of a "pecuniary externality". Obviously, this type of externality is a normal side-effect of a functioning market system. Nevertheless, in practice, there are many instances where public regulation (for right or wrong) has tried to mitigate the associated negative consequences for individual actors (Meyer 1983). Furthermore, even "physical" external effects do not matter that much, as long as those externalities are quantitatively and/or qualitatively insignificant and therefore tolerable (given costs of avoidance), cancel out over actors at least within some reasonable time period, or can be internalised by means of private contracts. Problems only arise where there are significant, asymmetric external effects which cannot be internalised because the costs of doing so are too high to render it worthwhile (Coase 1960). If ownership for all items were unambiguous and property rights perfectly executable, then there would, by definition, be no external effects: "Under hypothetically perfect private property rights none of my actions with my resources may affect the physical attributes of any other person's private property" (Alchian 1987, 232). Prohibitive transaction costs are the general reason why proper definition and/or enforcement of property rights is impossible, both for the owner of the object in question and for non-owners (Molitor 1988).

Sixth, ownership may be private, public or common; while both of the former concepts may in turn be differentiated into individual ownership and corporate ownership, common ownership is necessarily corporate. It is tied to a group of actors, and is acquired (lost) by individuals through entering (leaving) the group. Common ownership depends on effective exclusion of non-members, and on reliable internal rules regulating usage by members (Richter 1993; Haller 1998). Since no automatic relation exists between individual costs and benefits of usage, a free-riding problem is always virulent. Each member has an incentive to minimise his personal contribution to excluding non-owners and/or to maximise his personal benefit from usage. As a rule, the larger the group, the more urgent the problem, because monitoring and sanctioning become more difficult. Moreover, transforming property rights to all things in the whole world into "common ownership", would factually negate ownership itself. Property rights from which nobody is excluded cannot constitute ownership in any meaningful sense (Jasay 1991).[5] Common ownership should not be confused with public ownership, which is tied to political institutions, not to persons as private and common ownership are. While private ownership gives rights to persons, public ownership gives rights to political functions. These rights thus depend on legitimate political power. Public ownership also has to be distinguished

---

5 For these reasons, "people's ownership" ("Volkseigentum" in German), typical a formulation in socialist constitutions, is a self-contradictory term. Internally it means annulment of ownership altogether, while externally it is simply redundant.

from ownership of public goods. Public goods are often privately owned or supplied (Jasay 1991), while public ownership in most practical cases refers to private goods, as even the shortest inspection of items owned by any state very easily reveals (Haller 1998). Experience suggests that functional responsibility as defined by public ownership does not, as a rule, imply the same unambiguous incentive structure as personal responsibility defined by private ownership: "The moral significance of private property ... (lies in) the threefold identity of the person responsible for choices, the one bearing their costs and the one benefiting from them, (which) is severed when property is collectively owned" (Jasay 1991, 78). Although corporate private ownership somewhat relaxes the identity by separating decision from control, this principal-agent-arrangement, known as "corporate governance", is completely different in nature from the one involved in public ownership. Since there seem to be only a few exceptional cases of "real" public goods which cannot be thought of as being privatised in any appreciable sense of the word, liberals will opt, in case of doubt, for private ownership (Jasay 1991).

3 Private Ownership and the Market

Private ownership, in the sense of the general concept discussed in the previous section, obviously has not merely a strong economic connotation; it is also a guarantee for civil freedom, personal responsibility and individual self-determination, and as such is a prerequisite for any liberal society. However, it is clear that the freedom of one individual must be limited by the freedom of others; freedom, like ownership, cannot be absolute. This aspect becomes even more relevant when we look at private ownership from the viewpoint of economics, where it is interpreted as a functional concept rather than a virtue in itself, and in any case not as a fetish.[6] It is private ownership on which the efficiency of a market system is supposed to rest. Therefore, private ownership derives economic legitimacy from its role in improving the welfare of society as a whole. It is not the benefit an owner draws from the use of his property right, but the benefits he creates for others, which gives private ownership its economic and social foundation.

In this sense, "ownership obliges", as the German Constitution says. This obligation, however, is not in itself legally enforceable, nor should it be so (contrary to what some social romantics demand); the fulfilment of the obligation must be conceived as a positive side-effect of an owner's effort to increase his personal welfare.

6 The discussion under economists surrounding the "principle of restitution" in the German Unification Treaty of 1990 may serve to illustrate the point: even the bulk of consistent proponents of a market economy were quite critical to the principle, since it was expected to undermine private investment activity in the former GDR. There seems to be some ambiguity between the political dimension and the economic dimension of private ownership. However, from a broader perspective, the consistency and reliability of the legal system and its effects on economic performance must be taken into account (for a defence of the "principle of restitution" as a sensible principle in the German case see Heering 2000).

Although similar, this side-effect is not an externality in the sense defined above. Rather it implies that the benefit from co-operation with others is fairly shared and not expropriated by one actor alone; in this sense it may even be interpreted as the avoidance of a negative externality, which the trading partners of some actor would otherwise bear. While trade as a co-operative activity is a positive-sum game in which all gains are internalised by the partners involved, the distribution of a given co-operation rent is, nevertheless, a zero-sum game. But if social benefits cannot be, and (in a liberal society at least) are not, directly imposed, it must be "the rules of the game" which create them. It is the environment which ought to force the owner to produce the socially beneficial side-effect. This, of course, is the general idea of competition. Without competition, private ownership would not be able to create the welfare effects known from the history of market societies; quite to the contrary, the overall welfare effects might often even be damaging. As Walter Eucken put it: "Private ownership of the means of production needs control by competition" (Eucken 1952, 275, transl. by authors). While incentives of private ownership are in themselves an important element of competition, private ownership as such does not automatically lead to competition. Obviously, any private owner has an interest in escaping from a competitive environment, because this will allow him to monopolise co-operation rents. This in itself must have negative effects on the willingness of others to co-operate, i.e. it will decrease the potential for mutually advantageous trading transactions. Competition, that is to say, must be external to the constitution of markets (Eucken 1952):

Firstly, while it is a straightforward consequence of the freedom of contract that transactors must have the sole competence to settle on any price for their goods and services they may come to agree upon, it is an important aspect of competition to limit the impact of individual traders on market prices. In microeconomics, competition (more precisely "perfect competition") is captured by the feature that no single actor nor any coalition can influence market prices to his or its benefit ("price-taking behaviour"). In the idealised Arrow-Debreu-model it can be shown that only under such conditions does the market system generate all those beautiful results entailed in the well-known theorems of welfare economics, and in particular the Pareto-efficiency of market allocation. Competition in this sense obviously requires that there are (at least potentially) many traders on both sides of the markets, since only the existence of sufficient alternative trading opportunities can diminish the influence of any individual trader. This, in turn, implies that all sort of barriers to entry must be absent, which means that any actor must essentially have the same chance to enter a market and to make his deals with any other. No legal, institutional or personal discrimination exists against some (group of) actors. Moreover, no actor should be hindered by lack of "liquidity" from entering a market or, inversely, be forced to quit the market. If capital markets worked perfectly, then anybody "owning" wealth in the sense of having a positive present value of expected future income flows would be able to borrow up to this limit. In reality, this condition is extremely awkward, because of uncertainty as well as asymmetric information with regard to individual income expectations. In practice, lenders will normally insist on collateral, which may not be available to every actor. Furthermore, the Arrow-Debreu-model does not explicitly account for transaction costs. This may not really matter, since transaction costs per se do not disturb efficiency properly defined. However, there are two empirical features with frequently far-reaching consequences: on the one hand, transaction costs will normally display a heavy fixed component which may lead to non-convexities and therefore to monopolisation or to non-existent markets. On the other hand, transaction costs tend to be specific to individual actors and/or goods and may thus prove to be a source of market discrimination.

Secondly, besides these empirical deviations from the ideal of perfect competition, there are more fundamental problems, which sometimes even give rise to dilemmas (Platteau 1994a). For example, it is often maintained that the Arrow-Debreu-model only generates "static efficiency", while what is really demanded is "dynamic efficiency" (North 1992). One reason for this may be seen in the fact that inventions, because of their information-generating character, imply a public-goods problem, which can call for a deviation from the state of perfect competition. This factor may legitimate barriers to entry in the form of patents, permitting the inventor a temporary legal monopoly to amortise his research costs, a measure which, however, creates its own difficulties (Eucken 1952). Moreover, because of uncertainties and asymmetric information concerning goods and services offered on markets, the anonymity condition implicit in the absence of any personal discrimination between transactors is often not sensible. Competition between different suppliers of basically homogeneous goods and services (in the sense of being near substitutes for one another) will therefore generally not simply involve prices but also qualities of goods and services. Transparency of market conditions (a further precondition for competition) must then obviously entail not only information on prices as in the standard model, but actually implies questions such as: "Who supplies what, at what quality and price?" Customers must thus be able to identify specific suppliers, and in such a context, firms will compete by way of building up a favourable reputation and trying to bind customers, that is by creating discriminating systems.[7] There are many other similar points of apparent contradiction. Thus it seems that several trade-offs exist between different dimensions of the functionality of markets. Among other things, these trade-offs are a source of many market institutions which

---

7 In particular, Friedrich von Hayek, who generally opposed the standard concept of competition, interpreting the latter essentially as a "discovery process", has emphasised this dimension quite early: "Especially remarkable in this connection is the explicit and complete exclusion from the theory of perfect competition of all personal relationships between the parties. In actual life the fact that our inadequate knowledge of the available commodities or services is made up for by our experience with the persons or firms supplying them – that competition is in a large measure competition for reputation or good will – is one of the most important facts which enables us to solve our daily problems. The function of competition is here precisely to teach us who will serve us well" (Hayek 1948, 96 f).

act as media to balance such antagonistic requirements. As a matter of fact, economic research on these institutions as well as on underlying trade-offs is only just beginning (North 1990).

Thirdly, free entry to markets, which despite the above-mentioned qualifications certainly remains one of basic elements of any competitive system, must necessarily be complemented by freedom to leave the market. In particular, firms must have the flexibility to adapt their level of operation and costs to actual market conditions, even if this implies quitting the market altogether. If this adaptability is restricted (for example by employment protection laws) then the competitive mechanism may be seriously disturbed. Not least, the threat of enforced market exit by bankruptcy for firms which do not meet the market demand cannot then legitimately be executed. Without this threat, however, ownership, as has been explained in the former section, would only be half-baked; gains would be privately acquired, whereas losses would be socialised.

Fourthly and most importantly, the rules of the market game must be as clear as possible, reliable, and understood as well as accepted by all (or at least most) market participants. The essential point here is the distinction between the "choice of rules" and the "choice within rules" (Brennan/Buchanan 1985). While the latter can in case of doubt be left to individual actors, the former implies a public choice, which should not be taken by market participants themselves. Typically it is the role of the state to set, monitor and enforce the rules. This refers specifically to the "regulatory policy" of the community, but must obviously also have consequences for a "process-oriented policy" of the government; in particular, the latter must be consistent with the former, and should not change unforeseeably. A particularly difficult, but nevertheless necessary, part of the regulatory task consists in monitoring adherence to the rules of competition themselves, as selfish actors will always be tempted to evade those rules. Furthermore, it is not always clearly realised that the monetary system too falls within the realm of "rules of the game", to be chosen by an impartial instance. Money is basically an instrument by which individual actors within a large, anonymous market society are forced into their respective budget constraints.[8] To be acceptable, money must be essentially "neutral", meaning that its use in transactions as such should not induce unanticipated redistribution's of wealth. In practice, this requirement possibly amounts to the demand for a value-stable money. In developed market economies the established monetary system is usually of a dual nature; a central bank defining the unit of account is

8 If individuals were completely trustworthy (as in the fabulous Arrow-Debreu-world), there would exist no problem in balancing the goods and services any actor hands out to others with the goods and services he receives from others in return, and thus there would be no need for money. Because in a competitive society this condition is not reflected in fact, most beneficial transactions would not be incentive-feasible unless specific media had been developed to solve the strategic dilemmas. One basic medium of this type is money (Heering 1999a; for some arguments relating money to competitive markets see Heering 1999b).

complemented by decentralised provision of money (denominated in the unit of account) by private banks. Whether this arrangement is an optimal one is still controversial.

This analytical background suggests that existing and, by and large, well-functioning markets in modern Western societies are a grandiose cultural achievement which cannot easily be copied, at any rate not in short term. To be sure, there are several technical details a government can and should in fact implement to support emergence, but the foregoing makes it clear that competitive markets rest upon many facets, in part still unexplained, which cannot be produced deliberately. For example, trust in the political and institutional system and some form of business morality play an important role in nearly all market operations; how the development of these cultural element can be fostered is still unclear: "To function effectively, at least in a long-term perspective, the market requires the society to be structured in a way that ensures the widespread prevalence of abstract and impersonal relationships among agents as well as the pervasive influence of norms of generalised morality. ...It must be admitted at the same time that, if an external agency can suddenly establish market-supporting institutions (private property rights, laws of contract, money and so on), it cannot likewise create the social conditions required to make them work effectively by a simple act of will. ... Even a strong ideology of generalised morality diffused by the state has little chance to take root if it falls on a social terrain unable to understand it or unwilling to grant the state the role of a norm supplier" (Platteau 1994b, 795).

4 Privatisation in East and West

The twentieth century has been characterised by an increase of state intervention and engagement in the economy (Wagner's Law), a trend which has been particularly marked after World War II. In the last two decades of the century, however, a remarkable reversal took place, culminating in the dramatic collapse of Communism in the early nineties. However, the decade before already saw a strong tendency towards privatisation and deregulation all across the world (Bishop/Kay 1992). In particular, the UK during the eighties pursued the most extensive privatisation programme ever seen at that time, while in the USA (which had never had a significant state sector) the focus was on deregulation. The reason in both cases was a strong shift in the intellectual and political climate towards a realisation that market failures, at best, are a necessary but not a sufficient condition for state intervention; it is generally not assured that the problem at hand can be solved better and/or at lower cost by authority than by the market, and, additionally, government intervention creates its own failures which may even be more severe than the failures of the market process that intervention seeks to counter.

Privatisation, of course, means transferring property rights from public to private ownership. The transfer may be executed by sale at market value, by sale at some discount, or even by (free) give-away (or a combination of these three variants), depending not least on the objectives. In Western countries several objectives of privatisation have been launched (Bishop/Kay 1992; Donges 1992), including the reduction of the governmental share in the economy, broadening the distribution of productive wealth, levying of revenues to improve the government's budget, and, last but not least, improving economic efficiency. Undoubtedly the by and large positive effects, particularly with regard to efficiency, have had an important influence on transition debates in CEECs. However, privatisation in East and West can only be compared to a very limited degree, either quantitatively or qualitatively, for several reasons (Wijnbergen 1998).

First, there is great difference with regard to the scope of privatisation. Before privatisation the public sector in Great Britain accounted for 10 per cent of GNP, 8 per cent of employment and 17 per cent of capital; in 1989, for example, the corresponding Polish figures were 82 per cent of GNP, 68 per cent of employment and 81 per cent of capital (Iwanek 1992). It must obviously matter whether it is some single enterprises, or a complete economy, that are to be sold to private owners (Inotai 1992). Apart from technical and logistic problems, there are economic effects in the latter case which are absent in the former (Sinn/Sinn 1991). Moreover, there are political (and strategic) dimensions: economy-wide privatisation must start and proceed as quick as possible if the programme is to remain credible, and it must be applied simultaneously to all sectors of the economy to fulfil standards of fairness which are necessary for public acceptance. But these different demands may not fit together very well, leading to delay or non-optimal results, or a mixture of both. The experiences of the German Treuhandanstalt (the body set up to administer property relations in the former GDR) would seem to provide a good example illustrating this dilemma (Hax 1992).

Second, the quantitative dimension also reveals a crucial difference in the objectives of privatisation. In market economies, state-owned enterprises (SOEs) are working by and large within a competitive environment. They may be inefficient for well-known reasons, but not necessarily so, and in any case the degree of wastage of resources in this context is presumably much lower than it was under central planning regimes in Eastern Europe (Inotai 1992). To what degree such inefficiencies make a change in ownership really necessary is debatable. In particular, there is evidence that it may be competition rather than private ownership which accounts for the positive results of Western privatisation (Bishop/Kay 1992; Meyer 1983). In any case, it was not to be expected that privatisation would have a dramatic impact on the performance of the economy as a whole. In contrast, privatisation in CEECs is seen as one of the main instruments for improving the performance of the whole economy (Iwanek 1992), both from a microeconomic and macroeconomic perspective: the industrial legacy from Socialism consists of huge, essentially autarkic

SOEs which often had, and still have, a monopolistic market position. Privatisation is conceived as a powerful instrument to transform this structure into a competitive, market-oriented one (Broadman/Recanatini 2000; Hirschler 2000). Even more importantly, the principle task in former socialist countries is to establish a private ownership economy, and for this priority privatisation is indispensable. This strategic decision must not be confused with the secondary question of what concrete shape these economies will take; in particular, in all market economies there is a state sector, which varies significantly across countries, and each transition country, in the end, will have to find its appropriate ownership structure. Generally, the scope of privatisation objectives in transition countries has been much broader than in Western countries (Inotai 1992).

Third, there are differences with regard to the preconditions for privatisation. Whereas in Western countries there are well-developed capital markets which are able to smooth the change in ownership, and also a sufficient domestic stock of private means to be swapped for privatised companies, both these elements are missing in the transition countries. Additionally, there is a problem of valuation of the assets: none of the Western standard procedures can be applied satisfactorily (Iwanek 1992). Janusz Lewandowski, a member of the Polish parliament, once summarised these difficulties with grim humour: "Our privatisation amounts to selling unclaimed property of unknown value to people lacking any money" (Wentzel 1995, 147, transl. by authors). Obviously, these preconditions have strongly restricted the choice of privatisation variants.

Fourth and most importantly, there are wealth effects of privatisation in CEECs which are absent in the Western experience. Privatisation in a well-established market economy is basically an asset exchange in the portfolios of the government and private wealth owners. That is, it does not, in principle at least, affect the given distribution of wealth. We say "in principle", since this is not altogether correct; there are always some formal or (mostly) informal privileges (of employees as well as of managers), which are lost or at least are at risk through privatisation. Nevertheless, the situation is completely different in former socialist countries, where privatisation is an important factor in establishing an initial endowment of wealth. The formal taking over of the whole "people's ownership" by the state (by a simple juridical transcription of the factual status formerly existing) has resolved the issue formally, but surely not materially (Engerer 1996). Since the assignment of initial endowments to individuals or corporations is obviously dependent on the procedure of privatisation, the hot debates surrounding this theme, and the ambiguity and inconsistent timing of the policy strategies of most Eastern governments, are easily understandable (Bönker 1995).

Fifth, as Mancur Olson has remarked, the meaning of "privatisation" also differs markedly under the two sets of circumstances. In Western countries the term has relatively clear implications which are absent in transition countries, where legal and conventional guaranties of ownership are seriously in doubt (Olson 1992). Privatisation in the West occurs within a well-developed, relatively stable and broadly accepted legal and institutional framework, while this has first to be established in the East.

Taken together, these arguments, in our opinion at least, demonstrate convincingly that the context and content of privatisation in West and East are too different to draw too heavily on Western experiences when designing Eastern privatisation policies (Furubotn 1992; Engerer 1996). This does not mean that privatisation in these countries is the wrong path. From a systemic perspective the only alternative would be to close down all SOEs at once, hoping for a quick development of a new, genuine private economy (Kornai 2000). Such a radical step, however, would not be politically feasible, and may not even be economically reasonable. On the other hand, it is completely beside the point to argue that Western experiences suggest that enhancing competition for SOEs could do the job as well as (or even better than) changing ownership, and that privatisation for transition may therefore seem less urgent than usually claimed. Firstly, in all CEECs there will in the end remain a set of enterprises for which the ownership of the state will factually be preserved. It will be a political decision as to which enterprises this may apply to, and what to do with them. To decide and declare this beforehand would obviously be a serious strategic failure. Secondly, the primary argument in favour of preserving state ownership of large enterprises in transition countries is to avoid unemployment resulting from mass lay-offs by private owners. However, if public firms are to act competitively, they too will have no choice but to reduce their staff. The argument therefore rests on the tacit premise that private owners would dismiss employees even if this were not necessary, an absurd assumption. Thirdly, the very problem is exactly how to enhance market competition in basically non-competitive societies. Since it is the task of government to set the rules for this competitive game, not merely logic but all experiences suggest that it would be a fatal strategic flaw for the state itself to remain one of the main players. Fourthly, while competition and ownership may formally be seen as two distinct elements in fostering efficiency, private ownership seems to be just as important a factor in generating competition (Donges 1992; Grubel 1992) as is competition in controlling private ownership. All in all, for CEECs economies privatisation seems to be much more urgent even than in Western countries, but unfortunately also much more difficult (Iwanek 1992).

5 Limits to Privatisation in Transition Economies

Macroeconomic stabilisation and privatisation were the two key issues in the first phase of transforming formerly communist countries from planned economies into market economies. While the former task was rightly undertaken at a very early stage in the process and has meanwhile, by and large, been fairly successfully accomplished, the fulfilment of the latter remains precarious in more than one respect.

This fact poses two interrelated questions. The first is: why has the privatisation process as such not been very satisfying, at any rate in terms of the time required and the quantitative results? In 1998 the private sector's contribution to GDP was 80 per cent (45 per cent) in Hungary, 75 per cent in the Czech (30 per cent) and Slovak Republics (25 per cent), 70 per cent in Estonia (50 per cent), Lithuania (40 per cent) and Russia (20 per cent), 65 per cent (50 per cent) in Poland, 60 per cent in Latvia (50 per cent) and Romania (35 per cent), 55 per cent in Croatia (45 per cent), Slovenia (45 per cent) and the Ukraine (30 per cent), and 50 per cent (40 per cent) in Bulgaria (Raiser 1999, Wyplosz 2000). Although these are very rough figures, which include newly established private enterprises as well (contributions of the latter to total GDP are reported in parenthesis), they also reflect successes and failures of privatisation policies such as share auctions, individual sales of shares or complete enterprises, employee or management buyouts (EBOs/MBOs), and voucher or share distribution. The second is: why has privatisation not fulfilled the hopes which were associated with it? We try to give several tentative answers.

Firstly, starting off transition with liberalisation and macroeconomic stabilisation has certainly been the right choice (Kornai 2000; Wyplosz 2000). Whether we look at the transition challenge from a "Big Bang" or a more gradualist approach, there must at any rate be some sort of sequencing between the different steps: in an unstable environment resulting partly from the first measures of liberalisation, and partly from "paralysing" interactions between the vanishing old regime and the still weakly-developed new arrangement, an attempt to privatise a significant part of an economy would be a hopeless – and presumably also counterproductive – activism; corresponding results of early trials in Russia clearly warn against this track (Dabrowski 1996; Gomulka 2000). Depending on the speed and success of stabilisation policies, there will therefore almost inevitably be some delay in privatisation.

Secondly, privatisation in itself, at any rate under the conditions found in transition countries, is an extremely complex and complicated problem which needs time, even if the target is clear and uncontroversial and is to be reached within the minimum time schedule. If state-owned enterprises are to be sold, appropriate assets must be defined (which, in practical terms, means splitting up large companies into saleable fragments) and evaluated (a task for which practically no sensible guideline exists). New owners must be found and reasonable prices must be negotiated. All this must be settled by agents appointed – or licensed – by the government, who as a rule are inexperienced and, in any case, cannot seriously know where future market opportunities may lie; in general, they have proved overly optimistic with regard to the market value of their assets, thus setting a severe restriction on bargaining processes. Moreover, public and/or officials' opposition to negative price sales have frequently made it impossible to sell enterprises to outsiders (Wijnbergen 1998). Depending on the privatisation procedure, the concrete performance of steps may, of course, differ (for an overview of different variants of privatisation see Leipold 1992 and Schmieding 1992; practice and experiences are summarised in

Havrylyshyn/McGettigan 1999). Mass privatisation by vouchers or the like, for example, does not necessarily require a prior solution to all of the above-mentioned tasks, but it is questionable whether such delay will really turn out to be an advantage in the end (Honkkila 2000; Kornai 2000; Lainela 2000).[9] Large firms in particular, if not privatised to solid outsiders, often still face three intertwined problems: lack of external funds, so that they still depend on governmental support; remaining internal power of the management, often from the old elite; and lasting control by the state which provides subsidies, regulatory favours and/or tax arrears (Pistor/Raiser/Gelfer 2000).

Thirdly, not only is privatisation a technically difficult issue, it is also politically a most sensitive one, at least in the given context. After all, there is the general paradox that the state itself must design and organise the process of denationalisation (Iwanek 1992; Hurwicz 1992). During the first period of initially optimistic expectations concerning sale revenues, there may be a simple fiscal interest of the government in privatisation; however, as more realistic figures emerge, this interest will tend to dry up. The task therefore requires a strong, firm government, able to undertake the necessary steps to make the process irreversible even by its potential successors. If this cannot be established in the first period of the transition, during which the "political window of opportunity" is normally wide open, a great chance will be lost; subsequently the issue will necessarily become more and more difficult to set up (Dabrowski 1996). Almost inevitably, discrepancies between actual progress and over-optimistic prognoses must increase impatience on the part of the public, who may then tend to fall back on former ideologies and support the political opponents of privatisation. Moreover, as has been noted in the preceding section, privatisation in transition economies is mainly about the assigning of initial property rights ("initial endowments") to individuals. Even if this initial distribution were to turn out to be neutral with regard to final allocation (which seems to be true only if we abstract from transaction costs), it would still necessarily determine the initial welfare positions of individual actors. Therefore there may be a serious contradiction between allocative efficiency and equity or justice. As Willem Buiter recently remarked, "there is no elegant, efficient, and fair solution to this problem. We cannot undo history's earlier throw of the dice. Probably the best we can hope for is that ... (subsequent development) will gradually diminish the significance of the initial distribution of property rights" (Buiter 2000, 25). Distributional measures will very often be possible only if potential losers are appropriately compensated, and sometimes privatisation is even perceived as "theft" by the public (Csaba 2000). Furthermore, even if its impact on privatisation may be disastrous (virtually

9 Recent empirical findings seem, however, to suggest that privatization funds, created in connection with mass privatisation in some countries, do not perform as badly as was guessed on a priori grounds (Frydman/Gray/Hessel/Rapaczynski 1997). In particular, in the absence of well-functioning capital markets and restrictions to foreign investors, those investment funds may actually perform at least better than firms privatised to insiders (Estrin/Nuti/Uvalic 2000).

breakneck), government must take seriously the fear of "sell-out" that is virulent in many of the countries. It is not astonishing that the issue of privatisation has been hotly debated not only for economic, but also for political and social reasons (Kirchner 1992; Furubotn 1992).

Fourthly, the technical act of privatisation does not, in general, establish proper ownership (Engerer 1996). We have seen above how sophisticated the concept of ownership really is; taking into account the environment in transition countries as well as the fact that in most cases real property rights have to be established, sometimes for the very first time, and at the least following a long period of absence, it cannot come as a surprise that this aim comes up against all sort of difficulties. Among other things, it seems doubtful whether a majority of people in CEECs are able to understand the deep moral implications of ownership; we would not even dare to bet on this being true in developed Western countries. The point here is not that understanding as such is a necessary precondition for the concept to work, but rather that fundamental misunderstanding may well be a reason for non-acceptance, and this is presumably very important. Furthermore, we have to consider disposal rights as well as liabilities. There seems to be practically no country in which the former are not restricted by one or several of the following factors: prohibition of the resale of property rights in general or to specific groups of actors (foreign investors, for instance); exclusion of full ownership concerning parts of the objects (land, for example); burdens inherited from the past (financial debts; ecological burdens); conditions for employment and/or investment; co-determination by employees or governmental administrations; guidelines for prices and/or wages and so forth. To be sure, some of these factors are present in Western countries too, but in CEECs they are much more massive and are in any case applied in completely different circumstances. At least as important are limits to liabilities, appearing among other forms as enduring "soft" budget constraints for former state-owned enterprises (large enterprises in particular), and inconsistent application (if at all) of bankruptcy principles. Finally, there is the question concerning the reliability of property rights. There is overwhelming evidence of fears on the part of the relevant business actors relating to many aspects, which can be shown to have significant negative impacts on economic engagement, in particular on static as well as dynamic efficiency (Brunetti/Kisunko/Weder 1997b, Johnson/McMillan/Woodruff 1999a, 1999b; Buiter 2000). Moreover, it is not so much the formal existence of laws which seems to be relevant. Whereas – on paper – improvements in the law, for instance on the protection of shareholders' or creditors' rights, in most transition countries during the last ten years have been quite impressive (on average they seem even to outstrip developed Western countries), deep uncertainties remain with regard to the factual enforcement of the law, with the degree of uncertainty varying very widely between different CEECs. According to an index of legal effectiveness on a scale from 1 to 10, for example, the Commonwealth of Independent States (CIS) countries showed an average value of about 3 in 1998, while the CEECs figure at 7 (Pistor/Raiser/ Gelfer 2000).[10]

Fifthly, it is generally unlikely that markets in transition countries will be sufficiently developed to execute the necessary control of the use of ownership. There are serious deficits in almost all the aspects discussed in section 3 above (Broadman/Recanatini 2000). Certainly, most of those frictions do exist in Western economies too, but in CEECs economies they appear to a much higher degree and in a much more cumulative fashion. Moreover, Western societies have had much more time to develop appropriate institutions to remedy these defects; in some cases at least, these institutions cannot be simply imported. Thus transaction costs are generally significantly higher in transitions economies; in particular, the costs of entering markets are substantial, due not least to widespread corruption in administrations and the frequent existence of mafia-like criminal activities (Raiser 1997; Johnson/Kaufmann/McMillan/Woodruff 1999).[11] Further, still-existing networks between governmental officials and managers of large firms (even if formally privatised) lead to the preservation of monopoly positions and to discrimination against newly-founded firms, a problem which seems especially severe for SMEs (Wentzel 1995).[12] While capital markets often do not perform with optimum efficiency even in developed economies, the degree of inefficiency in CEECs is of a quite different quality. Not only is there a shortage of domestic financial wealth, but there are also higher and often incalculable risks as well as a lack of suitable private assets that might serve as collateral.[13] Moreover, some of the measures taken over from Western banking systems (especially from the USA) seem not to fit in very well with the overall environment of CEECs (Wijnbergen 1998). Finally, although most countries have implemented a dual banking system following the Western model, much remains to be done in this respect (Wentzel 1995; Wijnbergen 1998).

---

10 In our general definition of CEECs the CIS countries are included.

11 Corruption, under the conditions of transition at least, has two dimensions, one relatively passive ("administrative corruption", where private actors are extorted by officials to make given rules work) and the other more active ("state capture", implying that private actors collude with officials or politicians in the formation of the rules of the game. Interestingly, there seems to be no necessary relation between the levels of the two phenomena. In effect, state capture seems low in countries where civil liberties are basically still absent (such as Belarus and Uzbekistan) as well as in countries where these rights are already fairly well developed (as in the Czech Republic, Estonia, Hungary, Lithuania, Poland and Slovenia), but high in countries with a middle level of civil rights, such as Russia, Ukraine, Croatia, Georgia etc. (Hellman/Jones/Kaufmann 2000).

12 Meanwhile nearly all CEECs (beginning with Hungary and Poland as early as 1990) have adopted competition laws; but problems with implementation and effectiveness remain in all cases although differing in degree (Dutz/Vagliasindi 1999; Broadman/Recanatini 2000).

13 Whether lack of collaterals is in fact a major restriction, is unclear; there are indications that it may be primarily the demand-side of capital markets which is shortest, in particular, because of uncertainties of property rights (Johnson/McMillan/Woodruff 1999a; 1999b). However, uncertainties of property rights obviously work on both sides of the capital market (Pistor/Raiser/Gelfer 2000).

And while the efforts towards macroeconomic stabilisation have proved quite successful in reducing inflation substantially, mostly to two-digit and sometimes even to one-digit rates (Wyplosz 2000), it remains a striking fact that in nearly all countries a significant part of transactions is still executed by barter and other non-monetary arrangements. The shares of barter transactions differ widely, being highest in Croatia and Slovenia (presumably as a consequence of the war), but being only slightly lower in Moldova, the Ukraine, Russia and Belarus; on the other hand, their importance is generally much less in the CEECs (in particular in Hungary, where it seems negligible), but even there barter still persists (Carlin/Fries/ Schaffer/Seabright 2000). Whatever the reasons for the phenomenon, and newer empirical findings suggest that for the individual economic actors there may be good reasons indeed (Commander/Dolinskaya/ Mumssen 2000; Guriev/Kvassov 2000), its presence is a clear indication for the persistence of limited trading networks, and thus for the fact that anonymous, non-discriminating markets, which can only work using money as the dominant medium of exchange and means of payment, are still not sufficiently developed. Money, to recall the argument of preceding sections, is above all a medium to enforce a tight budget constraint on indivi-dual actors. Taking all these facts into account, the extreme variety of present income and wealth distribution in transition societies is not that astonishing; it follows, that is to say, not from the adoption of the market economy as such, but rather from its malfunctioning. It seems true to some extent that such frictions arise as almost inevitable side-effects during the first phase of market emergence (Brezinski/Fritsch 1997), and it is equally true that the potentially high incomes to be earned under those conditions themselves tend to set up the mechanism for overcoming the teething troubles. This process can only work, however, if the underlying institutional obstacles are removed. It is in these areas that the most urgent policy tasks for the CEECs in the near future do lie.

Sixthly, in a market economy it is the entrepreneur who has the functional role of detecting and exploiting existing potentials for market gains. In effect, these opportunities seem to be plentiful in CEECs. It is often doubted, however, that these countries are able for themselves to generate the necessary entrepreneurial capabilities (Tyson/Petrin/Rogers 1994). For our purpose some general remarks on this difficult question may suffice: above all, privatisation per se does not solve the entrepreneurial problem. This, of course, depends on the chosen privatisation variant, and thus on the type of owner, but the average performance of domestically privatised firms is rather bad. They often tend to engage in passive restructuring activities (especially MBOs and even more EBOs), not facing as offensively as required the real entrepreneurial task of designing new goods and services which will be able to meet the market test (Frydman/Gray/Hessel/Rapaczynski 1997, Gomulka 2000). Much of the real dynamics of the newly-established economies must therefore come from newly-founded firms, which on average seem to perform significantly better than spin-offs from SOEs (Johnson/McMillan/Woodruff 1999b). This is a crucial point which does not seem to be realised very often (Kornai 2000). The way in which the figures for the numbers of small private firms have shot up like mushrooms in most transition countries following liberalisation is quite impressive (see the contribution of Heering, in this volume), and casts some doubt upon the fears concerning a scarcity of entrepreneurial abilities in those societies. It seems more likely that at present these human resources are just badly allocated. There are fairly obvious and much-cited funding problems to explain the fact that new firms are most often established in trade and service sectors, where capital requirements are relatively low. But equally plausible seems to be the conjecture that it is primarily the deep mistrust towards political and other institutions which lead to engagements in rather short-term, low-risk activities (Iwanek 1992). Without progress in the security of property rights as well as in other elements of the legal and institutional system, there is little hope of improvement.

In summary, confronting the theoretical requirements of ownership and functioning markets with the empirical conditions found in CEECs economies, the overall unsatisfactory performance is as understandable as are the meanwhile quite significant differences between the countries. Apart from material shortages in all areas, which need time and resources to be remedied, one of the most relevant factors (maybe the most important factor) seems to be the reliability of the rules of the game; lack of trust concerning the new political and institutional system apparently emerges as the pivotal element of the whole transition process (Raiser 1997; 1999). The following table, which has been compiled from material of a world-wide business survey in 69 countries performed by the World Bank between August 1996 and January 1997 is quite instructive. It compares the caveats concerning relevant institutional aspects reported by private firms from the Commonwealth of Independent States (CIS), Central and Eastern Europe Countries including the Baltic States (CEECs) and Developed Countries (DC). Interestingly, the significant differences displayed in the data correspond to the relative weights of the genuinely private sector in transition economies involving newly-established firms, whose average contribution to GDP amounts to slightly more than 20 per cent in the CIS countries but more than 40 per cent in the CEECs (Raiser 1999). On this aggregate level, moreover, these figures also correspond to the performance of GDP as a percentage of its level in 1989, amounting to 56 per cent for the CIS and 95 per cent for CEECs countries (Stern 1998).

Table 5-1: Institutional obstacles to business in transition and developed countries*

Issue	CIS	CEE	DC
1. Unpredictability of the law and politics	78	67	33
2. Predictability increased within last 5 (10) Years	20	29	18
3. Lack of credibility of governmental announcements	66	55	30
4. Fear of retroactive changes of regulations	68	48	23
5. Political instability because of governmental change:			
a. Constitutional change (Elections)	74	69	40
b. Unconstitutional change (Coups)	66	38	20
6. Theft and crime as business costs	87	81	55
7. Mistrust of state protection of personal security and private property	77	80	51
8. Unpredictability of judiciary	79	70	41
9. Additional payments for administrative services (bribes)	65	44	14
10. Time spent in negotiation with officials on laws and regulations:			
a. Less than 5% of senior management's time	20	33	59
b. 25% and more of senior management's time	27	11	2
11. Poor efficiency of governmental provision of services:			
a. General	73	61	30
b. Customs	77	61	28
c. Condition of roads	84	60	27
d. Mail delivery	69	38	30
e. Public health care	84	64	30
f. Power outages (once a week or more often)	29	13	1
g. Waiting time of 6 months or more for a public telephone line	34	38	3

*) The Survey was implemented in August 1996 - January 1997. The answers for issues 1 to 9 and 11 were scaled from 1 (very good) to 6 (very bad). Per centages given above are the percentages of firms answering 4 to 6 to the issues in the Survey. CIS = Commonwealth of Independent States; CEECs = Central and Eastern Europe Countries (including the Baltic's); DC = Developed Countries.

Source: Brunetti/Kisunko/Weder 1997a

6 Conclusions

We have come a long way from the first statement of our main theses at the beginning, and it is time to sum up. Having shown that private ownership is a complex subject, it does not come as a great surprise that its establishment in CEECs economies is still far from complete. Moreover, while private ownership is certainly a necessary condition for a functioning market economy, it is in itself by no means a sufficient condition for efficiency. Private ownership has to be accompanied by competitiveness of the economy, and the remaining large deficiencies in this regard constitute a second impediment to the efficient working of the economic system in transitional countries. Furthermore, while privatisation of state own enterprises is an important step in implementing a private ownership economy, it is again not a sufficient condition, because it does not in itself solve either of the two above-mentioned problems. In addition, privatisation may not be the most effective way to stimulate entrepreneurial activities. Entrepreneurship may be scarce in transition economies simply because of the imperfect framework conditions for market operations; thus, reducing market impediments should activate a sufficient potential of entrepreneurs. To be sure, in emerging and imperfectly working markets, such as can be found in CEECs, there are all sorts of potential gains to be made, but to direct these incentives into a non-zero-sum welfare-generating process requires a reliable system of rules, acceptable to the majority of private actors because it is in their own interest to follow the rules if others follow them too. The implementation of a productive order of this kind is still incomplete in all transition societies, and in many of them it has not even started yet.

Harold Demsetz wrote in 1991: "Solving the privatisation problem is the only real hope for these economies. Stabilisation problems come and go, and so do their solutions, in both West and East. It is the ownership problem, and its solution, that makes the basic difference. Long delay in this matter will inevitably saddle the populations of Eastern Europe with continuing poverty and bureaucracy. This is more likely to undermine the hopes that fuel the current drive towards capitalism than are the reversible flaws that may arise from quickly moving to private ownership" (cit. in Lal 1992, 186). We still regard this early statement as essentially right; privatisation is clearly a necessary condition for the success of the transition process. But privatisation is far from being sufficient. As long as the more fundamental institutional conditions for a functioning market economy remain in a deficient stadium, privatisation will not be able to fulfil the hopes placed in it. It is quite reasonable that many observers more recently have turned their interest towards these issues. But even so, one has to realise that the development of such a framework obviously needs much more time than has hitherto been envisaged. Essentially, what seems in order is a much greater degree of patience.

Literature

Alchian: A. A. (1987): Property Rights; Reprinted in: Eatwell, J.; Milgate, M.; Newman, P. (Eds.): The New Palgrave: The Invisible Hand. London and Basingstoke Macmillan, pp. 232-238.

Bishop, M. R.; Kay, J. (1992): Privatisation in Western Economies. In: Siebert H. (Ed.): Privatisation. Symposium in Honour of Herbert Giersch. Tübingen: Mohr-Siebeck, pp. 193-209.

Bönker, F. (1995): The Dog that did not Bark? Politische Restriktionen und ökonomische Reformen in den Visegrád-Ländern. In: Wollmann, H.; Wiesenthal, H.; Bönker, F. (Eds.): Transformation sozialistischer Gesellschaften: Am Ende des Anfangs. Opladen: Westdeutscher Verlag, pp. 180-206.

Brennan, G.; Buchanan, J. M. (1985): The Reason of Rules. Constitutional Political Economy; Reprinted as: The Collected Writings of James M. Buchanan, vol. 10. Indianapolis: Liberty Fund.

Brezinski, H.; Fritsch, M. (1997): Spot-markets, Hierarchies, Networks, and the Problem of Economic Transition. In: Brezinski, H.; Fritsch, M. (Eds.): The Emergence and Evolution of Markets. Cheltenham – Lyme: Edward Elgar, pp. 7-19.

Broadman, H. G.; Recanatini, F. (2000): Seeds of Corruption. Do Market Institutions Matter? World Bank Policy Research Working Papers no. 2368, June 2000.

Brunetti, A.; Kisunko, G.; Weder, B. (1997a): Institutional Obstacles for Doing Business. Data Description and Methodology of a Worldwide Private Sector Survey. World Bank Policy Research Working Papers no. 1759, April 1997.

Brunetti, A.; Kisunko, G.; Weder, B. (1997b): Institutions in Transition. Reliability of Rules and Economic Performance in Former Socialist Countries. World Bank Policy Research Working Papers no. 1809, August 1997.

Buiter, W. H. (2000): Challenges of the Second Transition Decade in Russia. Transition Newsletter, vol. 11, no. 5, August-September-October 2000, pp. 24-26.

Carlin, W.; Fries, S.; Schaffer, M.; Seabright, P. (2000): Barter and Non-monetary Transactions in Transition Economies: Evidence from a Cross-country Survey. EBRD Working Paper no. 50, European Bank for Reconstruction and Development, June 2000.

Coase, R. H. (1960): The Problem of Social Cost. Journal of Law and Economics, 3, pp. 1-44.

Commander, S.; Dolinskaya, I.; Mumssen, C. (2000): Determinants of Barter in Russia: An Empirical Analysis. IMF Working Paper 00/155, International Monetary Fund, October 2000.

Csaba, L. (2000): A Decade of Transformation: Russia and Hungary Compared. Transition Newsletter, vol. 11, no. 3-4, May-June-July 2000, pp. 22-25.

Dabrowski, M. (1996): Different Strategies of Transition to a Market Economy: How do they work in Practice? World Bank Policy Research Working Papers no. 1579, March 1996.

Donges, J. B. (1992): Comment on Matthew R. Bishop and John Kay, "Privatisation in Western Economies". In: Siebert, H. (Ed.): Privatisation. Symposium in Honour of Herbert Giersch. Tübingen: Mohr-Siebeck, pp. 210-213.

Dutz, M. A.; Vagliasindi, M. (1999): Competition Policy Implementation in Transition Economies: An Empirical Assessment. EBRD Working Paper no. 47, European Bank for Reconstruction and Development, December 1999.

Engerer, H. (1996): Privateigentum, Privatisierung und Transformation. Vierteljahrshefte zur Wirtschaftsforschung. Schwerpunktheft Systemtransformation; 65. Jg., pp. 14-29.

Estrin, S.; Nuti, D. M.; Uvalic, M. (2000): The Impact of Investment Funds on Corporate Governance in Mass Privatisation Schemes: Czech Republic, Poland and Slovenia. MOCT-MOST: Economic Policy in Transitional Economies, vol. 10, pp. 1-26.

Eucken, W. (1952): Grundsätze der Wirtschaftspolitik; 6. Auflage: Tübingen: Mohr-Siebeck.

Frydman, R.; Gray, C.; Hessel, M.; Rapaczynski, A. (1997): Private Ownership and Corporate Performance: Evidence from Transition Economies. EBRD Working Paper no. 26, European Bank for Reconstruction and Development, October 1997.

Furubotn, E. G. (1992): Eastern European Reconstruction Problems: Some General Observations. Journal of Institutional and Theoretical Economics, vol. 148, pp. 201-206.

Gomulka, S. (2000): Ten Years in Retrospect: Secrets of Succeefil Macroeconomic Policies. Transition Newsletter, vol. 11, no. 5, August-September-October 2000, pp. 16-19.

Grubel, H. G. (1992): Comment on Matthew R. Bishop and John Kay, "Privatisation in Western Economies" In: Siebert, H. (Ed.): Privatisation. Symposium in Honour of Herbert Giersch. Tübingen: Mohr-Siebeck, pp. 193-209.

Guriev, S.; Kvassov, D. (2000): Concentrated Market Feeds Barter in Russia: A New Explanation for the Spread of Nonmonetary Transactions. Transition Newsletter, vol. 11, no. 5, August-September-October 2000, p. 30.

Haller, M. (1998): Private, Public, and Common Ownership. In: Analyse und Kritik, vol. 20, pp. 166-183.

Havrylyshyn, O.; McGettigan, D. (1999): Privatisation in Transition Countries: A Sampling of the Literature. IMF Working Paper no. 99/6, International Monetary Fund. January 1999.

Hax, H. (1992): Privatisation Agencies: The Treuhand Approach. In: Siebert, H. (Ed.): Privatisation. Symposium in Honour of Herbert Giersch. Tübingen: Mohr-Siebeck, pp. 143-159.

Hayek, F. A. (1948): The Meaning of Competition. In: Individualism and Economic Order. Chicago, pp. 92-106.

Hayek, F. A. (1988): The Fatal Conceit. The Errors of Socialism. The Collected Works of Friedrich August Hayek, vol. 1; Paperback Edition. London: Routledge.

Heering, W. (1999a): Privateigentum, Vertrauen und Geld. Überlegungen zur Genese von Zahlungsmitteln in Marktökonomien oder: Wie man in Berlin, Bremen und anderswo über Geld denkt! In: Betz, K.; Roy, T. (Eds.): Privateigentum und Geld. Kontroversen um den Ansatz von Heinsohn und Steiger. Marburg: Metropolis, pp. 99-143.

Heering, W. (1999b): Erneut gelesen: Frank Hahns Kritik an einer Walrasianischen Fundierung der Geldtheorie. Zugleich eine Retrospektive auf einige Aspekte des Projektes "Mikrofundierung der Makroökonomik". apt-papers 2/99, Freie Universität Berlin/Arbeitsstelle Politik und Technik, Dezember 1999.

Heering, W. (2000): Zur Politischen Ökonomie der deutschen Währungsunion. Ein Rückblick auf die umstrittene Entscheidung vor zehn Jahren. In: ZdF – Zeitschrift des Forschungsverbundes SED-Staat, Nr. 9/2000. Freie Universität Berlin, pp. 81-98.

Hellman, J. S.; Jones, G.; Kaufmann, D. (2000): "Seize the State, Seize the Day". State Capture, Corruption, and Influence in Transition. World Bank Policy Research Working Papers no. 2444, September 2000.

Hesse, G. (1983): Zur Erklärung der Änderung von Handlungsrechten mit Hilfe ökonomischer Theorie. In: Schüller, A. (Ed.): Property Rights und ökonomische Theorie. München: Vahlen, pp. 79-109.

Hirschler, R. (2000): Ten Years Transition: Recalling the Events of a Historic Decade with World Bank Chief Economist Nicholas Stern. Transition Newsletter, vol. 11, no. 5, August-September-October 2000, pp. 1-4.

Honkkila, J. (2000): New Wave of Privatisation in Russia? The Policy Choices. Transition Newsletter, vol. 11, no. 1, February 2000, p. 10.

Hurwicz, L. (1992): Some Issues in the Transformation of Ownership Institutions in Poland: Comment. Journal of Institutional and Theoretical Economics, 148, pp. 66-68.

Inotai, A. (1992): Experiences with Privatisation in East Central Europe. In: Siebert H. (Ed.): Privatisation. Symposium in Honour of Herbert Giersch. Tübingen: Mohr-Siebeck, pp. 163-182.

Iwanek, M. (1992): Some Issues in the Transformation of Ownership Institutions in Poland. Journal of Institutional and Theoretical Economics, 148, pp. 52-65.

Jasay de, A. (1991): Choice, Contract, Consent: A Restatement of Liberalism. Hobart paperback, 30. London: Institute of Economic Affairs.

Johnson, S.; Kaufmann, D.; McMillan, J.; Woodruff, C. (1999): Why do Firms Hide? Bribes and Unofficial Activity after Communism. EBRD Working Paper no. 42, European Bank for Reconstruction and Development, October 1999.

Johnson, S.; McMillan, J.; Woodruff, C. (1999a): Property Rights, Finance and Entrepreneurship. EBRD Working Paper no. 43, European Bank for Reconstruction and Development, October 1999.

Johnson, S.; McMillan, J.; Woodruff, C. (1999b): Entrepreneurs and the Ordering of Institutional Reform: Poland, Romania, Russia, the Slovak Republic and Ukraine Compared. EBRD Working Paper no. 44, European Bank for Reconstruction and Development, October 1999.

Kirchner, C. (1992): Privatisation Plans of Central and Eastern European States. Journal of Institutional and Theoretical Economics, 148, pp. 4-19.

Kornai, J. (2000): The Road to a Free Economy – Ten Years After. Transition Newsletter, vol. 11, no. 2, April 2000, pp. 3-5.

Lainela, S. (2000): Baltic Privatisation Compared – Most Industrial Enterprises Privatised. Transition Newsletter, vol. 11, no. 1, February 2000, p. 9.

Lal, D. (1992): Comment on András Inotai, "Experiences with Privatisation in East Central Europe". In: Siebert, H. (Ed.): Privatisation. Symposium in Honour of Herbert Giersch. Tübingen: Mohr-Siebeck, pp.186-189.

Leipold, H. (1992): Das Eigentumsproblem in der Transformationspolitik. In: Leipold, H. (Ed.): Privatisierungskonzepte im Systemwandel; Arbeitsberichte zum Systemvergleich Nr. 16, Forschungsstelle zum Vergleich wirtschaftlicher Lenkungssysteme/Philipps-Universität Marburg. Juni 1992, pp. 1-26.

Meyer, W. (1983): Entwicklung und Bedeutung des Property Rights-Ansatzes in der Nationalökonomie. In: Schüller, A. (Ed.): Property Rights und ökonomische Theorie. München: Vahlen, pp. 1-44.

Molitor, B. (1988): Wirtschaftspolitik. München – Wien: Vahlen.

Munzer, S. R. (1990): A Theory of Property. Cambridge: Cambridge University Press.

North, D. (1991): Institutions, Institutional Change and Economic Performance. Cambridge: Cambridge University Press.

North, D. (1992): Privatisation, Incentives, and Economic Performance. In: Siebert, H. (Ed.): Privatisation. Symposium in Honour of Herbert Giersch. Tübingen: Mohr-Siebeck, pp. 3-16.

Olson, M. (1992): The Hidden Path to a Successful Economy. In: Clague, C. K.; Rausser, G. C. (Eds.): The Emergence of Market Economies in Eastern Europe. Cambridge/Mass. – Oxford: Blackwell, pp. 55-75.

Pistor, K.; Raiser, M.; Gelfer, S. (2000): Law and Finance in Transition Economies. EBRD Working Paper no. 48, European Bank for Reconstruction and Development, February 2000.

Platteau, J.-P. (1994a): Behind the Market Stage where real Societies Exist – Part I: The Role of Public and Private Order Institutions. Journal of Development Studies, 30, pp. 531-577.

Platteau, J.-P. (1994b): Behind the Market Stage where real Societies Exist – Part II: The Role of Moral Norms. Journal of Development Studies, 30, pp. 753-817.

Raiser, M. (1997): Informational Institutions, Social Capital and Economic Transition: Reflection on a Neglected Dimension. EBRD Working Paper no. 25, European Bank for Reconstruction and Development, August 1997.

Raiser, M. (1999): Trust in Transition. EBRD Working Paper no. 39, European Bank for Reconstruction and Development, April 1999.

Richter, R. (1993): Ökonomische Theorie des Privateigentums: Thema und Variationen. In: Jahrbuch für Sozialwissenschaft, Bd. 44, pp. 311-347.

Ryan A. (1987): Property; Reprinted in: Eatwell, J.; Milgate, M.; Newman, P. (Eds.): The New Palgrave: The Invisible Hand. London and Basingstoke: Macmillan, pp. 227-231.

Schmieding, H. (1992): Alternative Approaches to Privatisation: Some Notes on the Debate. In: Siebert, H. (Ed.): Privatisation. Symposium in Honour of Herbert Giersch. Tübingen: Mohr-Siebeck, pp. 97-108.

Sinn, G.; Sinn, H.-W. (1991): Kaltstart. Volkswirtschaftliche Aspekte der deutschen Vereinigung. Tübingen: Mohr-Siebeck.

Stern, N. (1998): The Future of the Economic Transition. EBRD Working Paper no. 30, European Bank for Reconstruction and Development, July 1998.

Tyson, L. d' A.; Petrin, T.; Rogers, H. (1994): Promoting Entrepreneurship in Eastern Europe. Small Business Economics, 6, pp. 165-184.

Wentzel, D. (1995): Geldordnung und Systemtransformation. Ein Beitrag zur ökonomischen Theorie der Geldverfassung. Stuttgart - Jena - New York: G. Fischer.

Wijnbergen, v. S. (1998): Bank Restructuring and Enterprise Reform. EBRD Working Paper no. 29, European Bank for Reconstruction and Development, February 1998.

Wyplosz, C. (2000): Ten Years of Transformation: Macroeconomic Lessons. World Bank Policy Research Working Papers no. 2288, February 2000.

Industrial Modernisation in Post-Socialist Economies: Primary Endogenous and Elites Oriented Modernisation as a Socio-Economically Oriented Strategic Concept

Fuad Kandil, Günter H. Walter

1 Introduction

Following the collapse of communist rule in Central and Eastern Europe which was accelerated not least by serious deficits in the socialist economic system, the people there looked to a new beginning under the sign of a market oriented economic system. They hoped for the release of economic potentials which were definitely present but had previously been prevented from developing; under the conditions of a market economy, they expected to find the incentives which were necessary to strengthen the motivation to perform, and to benefit individual subjects and societal groups. Confidence was placed in the idea that the mass of the people in the former east block would necessarily experience more prosperity if the transition from a socialistic economic system to a free market economy could be successfully brought about.

Almost ten years on, the great expectations are still awaiting concrete fulfilment. In the meantime, an awareness has grown up among large sections of the population and among political and economic elites that the process of transition and the economic prosperity associated with it cannot be realised as smoothly or as easily as was initially believed. In most CEECs the "socialist legacy" and the starting conditions determined by it have set clear limits to a rapid transition in many ways. Above all, it has been necessary to recognise that the social structural and socio-cultural framework conditions which form the "data corollary" of economic activity have to be adapted to the desired economic change, if this is to be supported on a carefully constructed basis.

The countries of Western Europe, too, which basically have a strong interest in the continued development of CEECs' economies and are therefore also willing to provide assistance to a certain extent, have repeatedly found it necessary to rethink or redevelop their previous concepts over the past few years in order to spur the transition process in a sustainable way.

This is also true for the institutions and research establishments in Western countries that have been concerned with this process and have attempted right from the start to support economic development in Central and Eastern Europe in both word and deed. They have been primarily concerned with aspects of industrial modernisation of the economies of post-socialist states. Research is done on mechanisms and on initiatives to help the necessary technological and economic innovations in CEECs towards a breakthrough on a broad front (e.g. by building up innovative networks and innovation systems) and to initiate appropriate impulses which can result in a qualitative change in the national economy as a whole.

2 A Strategy for Industrial Modernisation

In the course of time, a strategic viewpoint has gradually crystallised out here, based on the relevant experiences of the past few years.[1] One of the main tenets of this concept is to make use of the resources, both material and non-material, which are available on the spot, developing them further and enhancing their efficiency. Industrial modernisation of CEEC economies following this concept is realistically based on the idea that the resources of these economies are limited, as are the resources of the Western European countries providing assistance for them. This approach is here called "PREEM". The abbreviation stands for a concept, according to which industrial modernisation can be characterised as a modernisation strategy which is predominantly primary, is based on endogenous resources and is implemented by local industrial elites dominating as driving forces of the process of modernisation. Modernisation of this kind

- is realised mainly through the efforts of the CEECs themselves (foreign support is given only as "help towards self-help", i.e. it takes the form of consulting, information procurement, management assistance and "coaching"),
- relies largely on mobilising and co-ordinating the existing resources of industry and science within CEECs (for instance by implementing an innovation and technology policy to support the building up of networks and innovation systems),
- concentrates on selected players (industrial elites) as the drivers and real carriers of the modernisation process.

---

1 The outlined approach was developed and confirmed during several projects carried out by Fraunhofer Institute for Systems and Innovation Research (Fraunhofer ISI) from 1993-2001 for the German Federal Ministry for Education and Research (BMBF) and for the European Commission, addressing innovation activities in CEECs such as: Belarus, Croatia, Czech Republic, Hungary, Poland and Slovenia.

In short: a concept of this kind can therefore be characterised as primary, endogenous and elite-oriented modernisation – "PREEM". In the following paragraphs these three characteristics are presented and described in more detail.

2.1 Primary Modernisation

The "primary" character of the industrial modernisation concept is emphasised here as a main characteristic, in the sense that the successful process of industrial modernisation is activated mainly and primarily by the autonomous efforts of the CEECs themselves, and is regarded by them as their own concern, for which they themselves bear the responsibility. Experience with development aid in the Third World has repeatedly shown that it is essential to adopt an attitude of this kind if external support, or assistance as such, is to bear fruit at all. It is not necessary to consider extreme cases such as those described by Erler (1985). It is, however, a cause for alarm when accusations of this kind are made from time to time in connection with obvious setbacks to the new economic beginnings of CEECs – setbacks which in many cases have led to the annulling of potentials that were – previously – effective! Here we are not so much concerned with pointing out existing structurally-caused conflicts in interests between the economies of "contributing" and "receiving" countries, although these do also influence the nature of the support given. We are talking about the "receiving" side itself, the "home front" as such or, in other words, the intra-societal socio-economic context of the economy to be modernised and its socio-cultural framework conditions. It is this "internal front" which needs to be mobilised. Potential actors at all levels need to be activated and motivated to recognise unexploited resources and existing potentials for development, make use of them and develop them further, so that the help provided does not lead to these potentials becoming "paralysed", as so often happens. This is especially relevant since support coming from an economically much stronger partner, such as Western states generally appear, has the danger that a passive attitude will gradually spread among the receivers, ultimately causing them to sit back in the role of spectators and expect the stronger partner to perform miracles, e.g. in form of a "great leap forward" towards the realisation of unrealistic modernisation goals. This is an attitude which especially needs to be overcome in order to allow the necessary indigenous impulses and primary development potentials to unfold. These alone can provide a sustainable base for the desired transition and for building up a viable market economy.

Of course, additional implications also underpin the description of "primary" applied to the strategic concept outlined here. It is not just that politico-economic elites as well as broader strata of the population perceive "industrial modernisation" as a goal to be striven for, necessary to survival. Such an aim is, to some extent, anchored primarily in subjective awareness and is not "secondarily" imparted. Rather, it corresponds to CEECs' primary needs to improve living conditions, and their conviction that "PREEM" is the only way, with no alternative – a course

CEECs are prepared to take, and which they can support by making use of the possibilities open to them. Thus it is important to create a degree of consensus in society regarding the needs which an industrial modernisation of this kind seeks to fulfil and the potentials it has to exploit, and to reach a consensus on the ranking of these needs. Above all, a consensus must take into account the opinions that predominate within the countries. This is extremely important, not least in order to reinforce the fundamental viewpoint, essential to the "primary" character of the strategic concept mentioned here, that the whole undertaking is a project to be realised out of one's own strength and for one's own welfare. Accepted in this context, help from the outside can only constitute a welcome complement to one's own efforts, but cannot diminish one's own responsibility.[2]

This also holds an important message for Western institutions. In all aid projects, and indeed in economic co-operation with CEECs in general, it is essential that support should be offered in a way which does not work contrary to the self-awareness mentioned here, or weaken it in any way. Of course this makes high demands on the social and intercultural competence of the experts involved on the side of Western support in implementing a co-operation of this kind. There is certainly an urgent need here for a high degree of sensitiveness, and especially for "empathy", that is, the ability to put oneself in someone else's position, an ability which can usually only be cultivated through long experience in context with one's "counterpart" on the spot. This is not the appropriate place for a more detailed discussion of the concomitant sociological and socio-psychological aspects. However, one conclusion holds good under all circumstances: if the "primary" modernisation concept outlined here is taken seriously enough, assistance – of whatever kind – must be oriented towards creating, in the truest sense of the word, a "co-operative partnership" resting on the collaboration of equal partners. It must provide CEECs with a model for the necessary mobilisation of endogenous resources, for the co-operation of actors from economy, policy and science within the country itself. The (potentially) disadvantaged "counter-partner" has to be positively encouraged at all times to confidently voice his particular interests and articulate them openly. The much-quoted and often stereotypically used phrase of "help towards self-help" remains an empty formula if the "self" it refers to is not taken really seriously in the help process, and if the encouraging of "self"-esteem tends to be undermined in the actual co-operation process.

---

2 In this connection it is appropriate to recall the model of industrialisation referred to in Senghaas' typology as "associative development", which has many affinities with the concept presented here; it denotes an industrialisation strategy which has led to great success in some East Asian threshold countries such as South Korea and Taiwan through successful association with the free market structure of the global economy (Senghaas/Menzel 1986).

2.2 Endogenous Modernisation

The endogenous nature of an industrial modernisation is complementary to the primary character of the favoured strategic concept described above, thus combining autonomy with an endogenous orientation. The one cannot be envisaged without the other. The characterisation as "endogenous" stands for a situation-oriented industrial modernisation strategy with a pragmatic approach relying, of necessity, on the country's own locally available "endogenous" resources and existing initiatives. It involves not only mobilising previously unexploited resources, but also developing them further in order to make more efficient use of them in an autonomous modernisation.

In post-socialist countries, as in Third World countries (Walter 1992), it is not unusual for the exploitation of many resources to be incomplete and their optimal use is still seldom. Besides entrepreneurial potentials, a prominent example of this is furnished by the substantial existing research and development (R&D) resources in universities research institutes and higher education establishments in CEECs, even if these capacities vary greatly from one CEEC to another and in some cases have been reduced over the last few years. Although building up and maintaining an R&D system of this kind absorbs substantial amounts of the limited capital available, the existing know-how is seldom put to use in improving industrial innovation capability and production, or solving the various techno-economic problems which beset many industrial firms. There is simply no functioning networking in existence between the costly R&D system and domestic industry. This is one of the main reasons why Western countries should emphatically support all measures in CEECs that are aimed at promoting technology transfer between the local science system and domestic industry. It is self-evident that these activities have to cover all necessary fields of technologies and will not always represent the newest techno-economic solutions. Nevertheless, it should be stated with emphasis that the "spin-off-effects" of such a procedure in terms of triggering techno-industrial learning processes are considerable. By contrast, such spin-off effects are not found in most cases where high tech solutions are simply taken over from abroad. Moreover, the latter type of relations exact a high price and require much "servicing".

Anticipated endogenous industrial modernisation, however, also aims at the effective use and further development of existing resources of all kinds, whether or not they are – as in this example – techno-scientific, institutional or industrial. Of course, techno-industrial modernisation which is committed to an orientation of this kind must give priority, depending on the possibilities, to existing resources as an input for the industrial process. The overriding aim is to build up an economy with functioning innovation oriented networks whatever their level of definition (local, regional and/or national). These networks have to be in a position to hold their own as active members of larger supra-regional and international networks (both the inevitable networks and the desirable ones), and to make optimal use of these networks and their positive effects to further the development of its own economic potential.

Unlike most so-called developing countries, a large number of CEECs can look back on a fairly long industrial tradition. In this respect, too, an endogenous industrial modernisation concept must make use of existing industrial tradition and build on it judiciously – which, however, does not imply simply staying with tradition. The main significant circumstance arising from a tradition is that industrial modernisation can rely on the support of long-standing specialist experience and a relatively widespread understanding of industrial processes, and also – at least to a certain extent – on entrepreneurial behaviour in general. In countries that lack any sort of industrial tradition, the absence of this understanding is often an impediment. Of course, the existing industry and research in CEECs need to be renewed in many ways, and industrial structures per se need to be reconsidered and adapted to the market situation. This is precisely the approach for a techno-economic modernisation strategy which aims to develop existing potentials further, deploy them more effectively and adapt them to changed conditions.

Thus, it will not be possible to preserve to their full extent the old "East Block" markets established for so long in the previously more-or-less functioning networks. However, an endogenously-oriented industrial modernisation strategy is aware of opportunities to exploit the industrial strengths and economic advantages arising in one form or another from previous industrial tradition, and cannot simply jettison them in favour of a completely new industrial orientation (Scheinacker 1997; Löhnig 1996). A new orientation of industry and the economy in the long run can only be based on the old, building on it gradually and circumspectly, since re-orientation processes of this kind are associated with many risks. However in the post-socialist countries it is not possible to base all activities in every domain on previous traditions. For instance, although to a certain extent better exploitation, more effective structuring and further development of existing institutions is possible and appears promising in the domain of science (scientific academies and universities), realisation of these tenets is much more difficult in the case of old economic institutions, whose main task used to be the central control and steering of the economy under a centrally planned system. A concept that is predominantly primary and is based on endogenous resources relies on decentral, indirect influencing of economic activity, on economically effective mechanisms, and also on the structuring of society through so-called techno-industrial elites, i.e. fast growing and innovative enterprises, in co-operation with R&D institutes (Schweickart 1996; Wollmann 1995).

In conclusion, it only remains to point out that an essential prerequisite for the success of "PREEM" as an "endogenous" modernisation concept – at least in long term – is the support of a functioning and robust material and non-material infrastructure. The non-material infrastructure needs to include not only a workable administration and an equally workable bureaucratic apparatus, but also a certain degree of legal certainty and sufficient political and social stability. These conditions are implicit assumptions in the "data corollary" of a viable economy. This makes it all the more important to conclude with a reminder that the infrastructure referred to here as "non-material" is no less important than the "material" infrastructure for the success of "PREEM".

2.3 Local Industrial Elites as Predominant Carriers of Modernisation

In CEECs, dissolution of the "planning elites" of the socialist era has taken place or still has to take place. New elites are needed. They could be defined as "practitioner" elites (management or innovator elites) in the different societal groups. Against the background of futures challenges policy, and especially research and technology policy, these elites have to organise a move away from the attitude of giving policy support exclusively to science; they need to follow a much more practice-oriented support for innovation. In industry and research there seems to be an urgent need for a change of attitude towards more open, co-operative behaviour. A precondition for this change is to encourage, convince and qualify the well-trained young people in CEECs to take over responsibilities, and to overcome the obstacles arising out of traditional attitudes and the socialistic legacy.

Firms that provide such working conditions (e.g. young technology-based companies, innovative enterprises, firms with R&D co-operations etc.) could themselves be regarded as elites – industrial elites. This category includes especially small and medium sized enterprises (SMEs): in view of their specific structure (short decision times, no hierarchies, flexibility, close contacts to the market, quick reactions to market needs etc.) and they provide good working conditions for elites. Growing, innovative SMEs especially are therefore to be seen as the main target group. Experience has shown that a healthy core of fast growing innovative SMEs could induce growth in other enterprises and modernisation in a whole country (Koschatzky et al. 1996), especially in the form of networks.

2.4 Modernisation as a Way for CEECs to Catch Up

For CEECs in transition, "PREEM" could offer a way to catch up, to converge into a "club" of healthy economies and to reduce disparities with Western countries as well as disparities between the different transition economies themselves and their regions. "PREEM" must enforce CEECs to master technologies in a way which enables them to achieve high levels of productivity and also in a way for which they possess sufficient human capital.

Under competitive conditions, advantages such as low costs, availability of personnel etc. are always considered to be decisive factors for entrepreneurs. If technologies and productivities in CEECs get closer to those in the west, then the countries, both individually and as a whole, will become more attractive. In the long run this will lead to higher incomes, hence to convergence.

Theory explains positive development endogenously: knowledge, human factors and financial capital become the engine of growth in the transition countries (Steiner/Walter 2000). If human capital is available, international trade can act as a transmission mechanism for technical knowledge in order to initiate a convergent process of growth between technologically unequal trading partners. Under these conditions the relation between economic growth and international trade is not simply a mirror of different national factor endowments: convergence takes place via the transmission of technical knowledge and improved access to technology. This distinction has decisive significance: it is not only "we are trading with each other", but "we are participating in your knowledge". Becoming more integrated in this sense implies an improvement in the transmission mechanism and membership of a "convergence club" (Tomann 1999).

It is important to emphasise that catching up is possible according to this approach (Jacobsen 1999). However, access to knowledge has to be a conscious result of entrepreneurial activity and it must hold a chance for the diffusion of knowledge and imitative behaviour.

Two arguments are important in this context. First: it is not so much a macroeconomic perspective that dominates the process, i.e. the decisive units are not states or national economies, but entities connected to each other via networks. The second argument is even more important in this context: the process of catching up is not deterministic; it is the result of entrepreneurial activity, especially with regard to knowledge creation, technological innovation and imitation, but also with regard to finding and creating new markets and new forms of organisation.

3 "PREEM" and the Role of the West

"PREEM" (primary endogenous elite modernisation) is based on the CEECs' own efforts. These efforts need to be seen by these countries as a possibility to meet existing demand. An appropriate procedure for Western countries participating in this process is to install a partnership-based co-operation and a dialogue between themselves and CEECs with clear advantages on both sides, to ensure that modernisation is performed primarily by the CEECs themselves. Western partners have to try to act as moderators in the structuring of modernisation processes in CEECs – very actively, yet with restraint. This moderation contributes its own ideas and experience to the processes, but does not attempt to dictate the results. The object of this approach is to achieve a consensus about strategies and procedures for installing or improving (network) relations between actors, as a precondition to establishing an innovation system. Usually, once these consensual aspects have been dealt with, solutions of concrete problems may be discussed and elaborated. The Western partners have to direct their efforts towards extending the horizons of their partners, taking into consideration their various different formal or informal power structures, resource possibilities and value differences. "PREEM" seems possible because usually in CEECs the actors – both powerful and less powerful – are generally interested in achieving solutions in the long term and contributing their own efforts. "PREEM" has to be based on free interchange and co-operation between actors within CEECs, and between CEECs and their Western partners, setting the interests and needs of the individual groups on a common footing and developing these common interests within networks to generate dynamics. For techno-economically focused modernisation to take place, co-operation initiatives between existing resources in research and industry seem to be an essential core activity to accelerate these processes for building up an innovation system. By providing "help towards self-help", Western countries can support the realisation of these efforts e.g. through an adequate research, technology and innovation policy. This is made possible by the provision of analytical, planning, conceptualisation and implementation tools for politicians in CEECs, such as new methods of analysis and evaluation, by the transfer of expert knowledge, training and advice and policy consultancy (Walter/Bross 1997).

In Western countries special schemes supporting CEECs in "PREEM" are needed, especially in the field of policy consultancy. These efforts, known as transitional assistance schemes, should be based on empirical and theoretical know-how and should be flexible enough to be adapted to the transitional context of individual CEECs. They need to be directed towards growth potentials in innovative industries (industrial elites) and towards the identified bottlenecks of innovation systems in CEECs (e.g. weak co-operation between R&D and industry). The way for Western support to achieve this is to integrate and support existing structures (endogenous resources) and especially initiatives in creating co-operation between science and industry and, later, integrating them into networks. Western partners must also make sure to draw attention specifically to the support capabilities and positive attitudes of their partners regarding self-organisation.

Western partners contribute to "PREEM" only by counselling that is strongly based on the initiatives, capabilities and creativity of partners in CEECs. In this way the take-over of responsibility at an early phase of co-operation is possible and the independence of CEECs actors is guaranteed. This is important in order for "PREEM" to be successful. The complex constellations of societal framework conditions in these countries – especially in technology and economy, policy and administration and in culture – mean that a co-operation between CEECs and the west has to be essentially exploratory. This implies that time, content and staffing requirements of the activities have to be flexibly adapted to changing conditions.

Such transitional assistance of Western countries for CEECs aims to stimulate, in consensus with the partners, modernisation processes based on the existing strengths of these countries, rather than giving (one-sided) policy recommendations whose mode of realisation remains an open question. It is a precondition that the decision-making and implementation activities should lie within the CEECs themselves. This requires strong adequate autonomous motivation in these countries based on a societal consensus and commitment to a mode of realisation by "small steps". A gradual, interactive procedure of this kind enables learning effects to take place and allows for a flexible demand orientation. But there are prerequisites which need to be fulfilled: governmental structures in CEECs – usually on a national and regional level – must already be strong and developed and willing to take over themselves the political responsibility for the individual steps, at least to a certain extent right from the beginning of the co-operation. They must also be able to provide, at least partly, the relevant services and funds. This means that policy-makers must be convinced of the success of "PREEM" and equipped with all relevant information to make necessary decisions concerning these procedures. Therefore well-developed and well developing CEECs such as the European Union access countries would constitute good candidates for "PREEM" to start with. On the one hand, the favourable overall economic development in these countries is a positive precondition and they can be considered as models for other CEECs. Another factor in favour of catching up by this approach is seen in the fact that the gap between the access countries and the west is relatively small.

Transitional assistance needs to be focused on efforts to activate communicative aspects, especially the free interchange of information between the different local actors and the west, in order to widen the horizons of both sides. Support activities need to focus not only on techno-economic aspects such as technology transfer between R&D and industry, but also need to take societal aspects into consideration.

3.1 Analysis and Communication

Transitional assistance from Western countries should begin with an analysis phase, (especially analysis of the existing endogenous resources), the collection of existing information and a compact descriptive profile of the country concerned. Innovation indicators (Bross 2000) are used to define the endogenous resources and capabilities of the CEECs and to characterise types of organisational entities according to their capability in co-operation and innovation, with a view to later proposals for policy measures for the different target groups. Especially relevant indicators are the growth in numbers of employees, turnover and exports. The data on which this profile is based should be collected from available national (e.g. Statistics Authorities) and international sources such as the OECD or the World Bank then interpreted in the areas of policy, industry and science. The profile serves as a basis for a more detailed inventory of the initial situation, elaborated jointly by the partners in the west and in CEECs. This profile should take into consideration the existing structures and initiatives in economy, policy and science. Adequate instruments need to be used to identify such structures and initiatives and to define the role the country could play in global competition. Information needs to be collected from experts in the different domains.

From a communicative viewpoint, and in view of the need to identify the "practitioner elites" within different societal groups, it is a good idea to hold some kind of meetings at an early stage for a discussion between the west and CEEC actors from policy, industry and science, on the aims of the co-operation and the steps for modernisation to be taken subsequently. Such meetings can also serve as an opportunity for presenting a brief outline and a first transfer of basic information from the west to CEECs.

Of especial interest are modern Western strategies for structural changes which are based on the implementation of new technologies supported by policy. The meetings also create an opportunity for the first exchanges of experience among actors, which lead to personal contacts and are very helpful for future co-operation and the formation of a broader consensus on procedures which have to be executed by the CEECs themselves. To record and evaluate the situation, discussions between the west and CEEC experts in the areas relevant to innovation need to be held with actors in ministries, universities and research institutes, enterprises, chambers of industry and commerce, banks and industrial associations, but direct contact is also necessary with representatives of typical firms that are in some way representative of existing industry in the relevant CEEC. Events, where first proposals in the form of conceptual approaches for improvements are presented to actors in the country and an intensive discussion with them takes place, serve as an orientation and an opportunity for consensual evaluation of the initial situation. If the proposals meet with broader acceptance in CEECs, they could be followed by specialist meetings. In order to create a broader understanding and reach a more general consensus, the results of discussions should be documented and passed on to interested parties.

3.2 Conceptual Approaches

To prepare the conceptual phase, foresight and other schemes can be used to provide methodological tools that will enable politicians in CEECs to select and define areas of present or future importance (priorities) of the country (Grupp 1997). As there is always a lack of finance in CEECs, concepts for technology and innovation policies are considered which have low capital requirements combined with high mobilisation effects on human capital and private innovation financing capital. Such policies use target group industrial elite-oriented measures to focus the available – usually low – budgets on subjects that foster dynamic development and structural changes. Another important condition lies in the mobilisation of capital, possibly to be realised by non-financial activities such as consultancy, co-ordination etc. In order to be able to administer such a policy, non-governmental agencies which are integrated into innovative networks usually play an important role (Walter 1999). The conceptual phase consists in elaborating concepts to solve concrete problems, e.g. concerning the activation or mobilisation of technology transfer between industry and science (Poland), or supporting the building up of a venture capital market (Czech Republic).

Since policy is seen as one of the key activities in "PREEM", some kind of a policy dialogue on research, technology and innovation should be initiated between policy-makers and experts from the west and from the CEECs. These specialists could elaborate concepts consisting of appropriate suggestions for policy to play an active role in modernisation, in view of the CEECs specific current situation and taking into account already-existing structures, initiatives and efforts as endogenous resources. Another important aspect to be considered is the demands of individuals and the various societal groups. Joint elaboration of suitable policy concepts should follow, aiming to

- improve the innovative capability of industry in co-operation with the country's research sectors, thus creating dynamic effects for development, and
- install network oriented diffusion (imitations) of innovations in order to achieve broader economic success for the country as a whole.

Since in CEECs personnel with the necessary qualifications are only available to a limited extent and for particular tasks, great importance must be given to the focusing and organisational concentration of know-how, possible associated synergy effects and "short cuts". Compared with these aspects, possible conflicts of interest between the participating actors and their various spheres of competence should appear secondary. In order to achieve an overall modernisation, the actors have to become interactive at a very early stage in "PREEM".

3.3 Implementation

The implementation phase of the transitional assistance scheme to CEECs consists of building up and establishing technology transfer institutions and providing information transfer and training (e.g. workshops in innovation project organisation and administration of public R&D support). Another possibility is the preparation and initiation of pilot and demonstration projects, which was considered in connection with the Slovenian Innovation Agency (SIA) and the technology transfer activities in Poland (see below). These pilot and demonstration projects are defined so as to be in some way representative of existing structures and the problems of large groups, e.g. of firms when generating innovations in co-operation with R&D institutes. Also, there should be a possibility for actors involved in this kind of project to engage in additional activities, e.g. for scientists to publish, for companies to take part in specific fairs in order to achieve publicity.

The implementation phase requires binding commitments. This phase, involving the institutional realisation of measures for improvement, is decisive for the success of transitional assistance as a whole: here the experience gained can be visibly concretised and may lead to improvements.

Transitional assistance given by Western industrialised nations thus needs to be competent in specialist fields and able to hold its own against short-term, day-to-day problems.

To sum up, the approach for transitional help consists in

- a preparatory analysis and communication phase to identify endogenous resources and "practitioner elites", creating the necessary preconditions for a joint approach,
- a partnership elaboration of policy concepts,
- implementation procedures.

It is very clear that these complex tasks of transitional assistance for "PREEM" from the west to CEECs will be characterised by numerous, parallel tasks with different time horizons, fluctuating determinant parameters and changing contact partners, frequent changes of situation and limited endogenous resources for action. This constellation in the CEECs overlays a basic structure with a multitude of personal dependencies, resulting in low flexibility and mobility. Thus, there is a necessity for a long-term, integrated approach in transitional assistance, with gradual realisation in successive steps and the possibility of correction; and there is also a need for relationships of interchange, the use of changing procedures and powers of improvisation.

4 Case Studies of Implementing "PREEM"

The analysis and communication phase in Slovenia[3] started with a preparatory evaluation of the situation based on existing information (e.g. studies, statistics). Taking account of this evaluation, additional data relating to policy, economy, science and spatial structure were collected and interpreted. This analysis later served as a basis for the extensive "inventory" of the country's initial situation and to structure first discussions with Slovenian actors.

In order to establish personal contacts an introductory workshop was organised, in which possible first work steps and Western networking approaches (especially in the field of co-operation between industry and science) were presented to Slove-

3 Most of the activities described in this chapter relate to Slovenia.

nia's main actors in policy, science and the economy. In addition, Western innovation systems and especially the "promotion landscape" in the area of innovation policy were sketched. Also at this workshop a first exchange of experiences between the Western and local experts took place and – helpful for further co-operation – personal contacts were established. The workshop was followed by a study tour for the Western experts and interviews with Slovenian ministries, universities and research institutes, enterprises, chambers of industry and crafts, banks and industrial associations. The next step relied upon on a screening of industry, science and policy in Slovenia in order to identify areas and potentials to be integrated into the "PREEM". Already at this time a preliminary characterisation of industrial enterprises as utilisers of the technologies provided by research institutes was developed, leading to a typification of firms according to their co-operative potential, and a definition of target groups to be supported by innovation and technology policy (Komac/Krawczynski 1994). This procedure of the systematic typification of firms has been further developed in Slovenia (Bross 2000) and Hungary (see chapter "Selected Aspects of Small Firms Environment and Policy", Muller, Zenker, Dőry).

The resultant screening and overview of the situation in Slovenia served as an orientation for further steps. This assessment of Slovenia revealed the following picture of the situation there, similar in many ways to the situation in other CEECs such as the Czech Republic, Hungary and Poland: basic and applied research and development were concentrated within specialist institutes in the public sector. In general, there was not much co-operation between science and industry. Companies received only little public R&D support. The majority of firms conducted little R&D or market-oriented product planning, and were still sticking to their traditional products and market areas. Technology information and consulting, as mediators of technology transfer between science (as technology provider) and firms (as technology utilisers), needed to be improved. Further deficits arose from the limited or non-existent supply of innovation financing and management consulting.

Policy in Slovenia was science based. Innovation policy in Slovenia (but also in Hungary and the Czech Republic), only existed in a rather embryonic stage. Innovation networks needed to be further developed. Special efforts had to be made to ensure that such a modernisation concept would be accepted within the country itself and supported by all relevant social groups. Certain potentials were seen for R&D and industry to act as technology providers and utilisers. Because of Slovenia's knowledge based past, its unique geographical location, its existing network in the Balkan states and other CEECs, possibilities were also seen for Slovenia to play a distinctive (niche) role in global competition, e.g. as market suppliers of high tech products in small quantities.

Proposals were discussed, and led to a broad consensus to continue the co-operation between Slovenia and Germany, especially in order to improve the planning, management and evaluation capabilities of policy makers and administration. A bilateral research, technology and innovation policy dialogue between Slovenia and Germany was started in Slovenia in 1993/1994, thus enabling the Slovenian side right from the beginning of the co-operation to be engaged in all relevant activities and to play an active part in using the results of this dialogue in their daily work.

However, before beginning with this dialogue, Slovenia wished to proceed with an additional and intermediate step: expert workshops should be organised on areas with the biggest problems and information deficits. These areas were: technology transfer between science and industry; information and documentation; innovation management in enterprises; innovation financing by public and private institutions; and regional technology and innovation promotion. Slovenian experts and practitioners were invited and, together with lecturers from other countries, pointed out the problems and possible solutions. The aim of the workshops, which involved about 200 participants in all, was an intensive discussion and consensus on measures for improvement in specific areas, and the indication of possibilities for realisation. The lectures and the results of discussions were summarised in reports and distributed, especially to about 800 "multipliers" within the country. These reports were positively received.

Parallel to the expert workshops, the policy dialogue began between politicians and experts from Slovenia and Germany. This kind of dialogue was a good possibility for the German and other Western partners to participate in the setting-up, adaptation, modification etc. of research, technology and innovation policy measures, and to be accepted by socially relevant groups. Policy analysis tools and concepts, but also steps for implementation, were elaborated and started as the core activities of a modernisation strategy.

4.1 The Analysis and Communication Phase of Transitional Help: New Tools for Policy Makers

Foresight is defined as a systematic attempt to look into the long-term future of science, technology economy and society, in order to identify the priority areas of research with a strategic interest and the emergence of generic technologies likely to yield the greatest economic and social benefits. The main objective in Slovenia (as before for Hungary) was to identify, within the set of emerging technologies and societal subjects, those specific ones which, on the basis of indications and perceptions of the different societal groups, appeared relevant for the country; which might, in other words, be defined as "key technologies or key societal subjects" for a successful innovative overall development. The results of such foresights are used by policy bodies on different levels (national, regional and local), mainly as an instrument to define priorities for future policy and needs.

Slovenia and Hungary learned about foresight methods and instruments, and are now able to use them for their activities. This applies particularly to advising on the analysis and interpretation of data, bringing in additional data and methods, and their interlinking. The question of what data and what methods to consider for individual instances was addressed together with the Hungarian and the Slovenian side. Moreover, international foresight data were made available and were used to evaluate the results of a national foresight process in an international context. In this way, Hungarian and Slovenian foresights did not only gain a reflection of the countries' own situation, but also enabled them to position themselves in an international context and make a comparison with other countries.

Another important tool for policy makers was the development of a system of indicators for the analysis of innovation potentials in Slovenia and Hungary. In general, the generation of indicators of this kind makes it possible to complement traditional statistical methods by the combination of different data sources and their parallel use. The aim was also to derive innovation policy recommendations. The activities consisted in collecting data in Slovenia and Hungary with emphasis on technology transfer between science and industry, concerning the innovation and co-operation activities of firms, the innovation-related infrastructure and the institutional framework conditions. The indicators developed were used to typify firms as target groups for innovation promotion according to their potentials to act as industrial elites, to generate dynamics for structural change and to become integrated into innovative networks. This enables modernisation efforts to be reinforced by public support. The resulting typology grouped firms with similar characteristics, whereas firms with divergent characteristics were assigned to other "clusters". Indicators were also used as an instrument to typify locations and characterise different contexts with regard to networking between innovation potentials and the socio-economic system as a whole (e.g. when implementing infrastructure improvements). Thus, the typology or classification of actors concentrated on specific signs, focusing on the needs of each group of firms and serving as a basis for consultancy to firms and as an input for policy. In the implementation phase of transitional aid, pilot or demonstration projects could be defined for the different types of firms.

A typification was performed intuitively in Slovenia in 1993, (e.g. identifying high tech firms, enterprises with sophisticated and conventional technologies, small manufacturing companies and so-called "extended workbenches" of international firms) and later on more systematically in Hungary. It was also necessary, to characterise scientific institutions and to determine their suitability and potential for co-operation with enterprises. With respect to providers of services, it was important to find out how they could act as intermediaries between industry and science.

4.2 The Conceptual Phase of Transitional Help – the Case of the Czech Republic and Poland

In free market economies in the West, the financing instrument of venture capital has increasingly gained importance in the last few years. Venture capital is understood as money brought into firms as equity or in an equivalent form. Since an investment of this kind may carry a high risk, it is generally linked with rights of control etc. Innovative enterprises use venture capital to finance their development work right up to the point when the product is mature for the market, for market entry, production preparation and production start-up. State promotion programmes in policy can offer incentives in order to stimulate the supply of venture capital to innovative areas that are important and relevant for the national economy. The main promotion instruments are re-financing and taking over investment risk. In many Western countries, the promotion of economically important fields by improving the availability of venture capital is a cost-effective instrument for supporting innovation, while at the same time fostering the expansion of a market for innovation financing. Especially industrial elites – meaning innovative firms in CEECs – require large volumes of equity capital and loan capital in order to be able to compete in the market place by producing innovative products. Building up a market for venture capital – if necessary with the assistance of the government – can help to meet the need for risk-bearing capital.

This was the background for assisting these activities in the Czech Republic. A summary was provided of German experiences during the past decades with the promotion and stimulation of venture capital as an instrument of policy and innovation financing. This overview included experiences of helpful and restrictive framework conditions, as well as an assessment of concrete promotion instruments. The current status and the existing starting conditions for establishing a venture capital market were identified and concrete suggestions for measures and ways to proceed were elaborated. These suggestions were then discussed with the venture capital companies, enterprises and institutions addressed as target groups, or playing a role in the realisation of such actions. Detailed explanations were given and adaptations to specific situations were made (Bross/Walter 1998).

As already shown, transfer between science and the economy is one of the most important efforts for modernisation of CEECs, but until now the promotion programmes of scientific institutions frequently follow a "supply-oriented" or a "technology push" approach. Thus they have only a limited impact and often encounter acceptance problems on the part of industry. The concept of "Mobilised or Activated Technology Transfer for Poland" attempts to avoid the weaknesses of this technology transfer model by adopting a demand-oriented approach (Steiner/Walter 2000). A neutral technology transfer team identifies a possible demand for technology in firms (usually by a personal visit) and, together with the enterprise, clarifies whether an academic establishment would come into question as a technology provider, and if so, which one. If interest is shown, the team mediates possibilities for a co-operation between science and the enterprise in the form of a joint project etc.

In Poland a short screening of the situation served to deduce the specific demand that could be met by technology transfer. Industry clusters were identified (e.g. industries in the areas of high tech, conventional technologies, skilled craft production). Each group required specific transfer projects (e.g. projects tended to take the form of pre-competitive joint projects for high tech firms, contract research for conventional technologies, licensing in the initiation of new technological industries, etc.). Pilot or demonstration projects have been prepared involving different types of firms and these will be carried out in co-operation with various organisations.

4.3 The Implementation Phase of Transitional Help: Seminars –, Agencies and Pilot Projects

In general young and qualified people in CEECs are seen as potential groups to start with activities to manage structural changes and to overcome obstacles resulting from the socialistic legacy. Therefore in Slovenia a seminar was held on how the work of administrators in public institutions can best support and influence R&D. While examining the perspective of perception and communication, participants discovered patterns which determine their behaviour. When experiencing and thinking about different work situations in their everyday life, it was essential for them to recognise their own especial strengths. Their behavioural repertoire was extended to involve more responsibilities and enlarge the possibilities for making autonomous decisions, i.e. to act as administrative elites in modernisation.

As there is also a lack of existing knowledge of project planning, project description, and project evaluation capabilities in industry and science in CEECs, the objective of several seminars in Slovenia was to impart the fundamentals of project planning, management and canvassing in a practice-oriented way. This enabled the participants to understand and manage innovation projects from a practical viewpoint in the context of their work in science, trade and industry, and policy. Seminars were organised in different regions of Slovenia so that needs in this field could be covered regionally close to demand. Not only Slovenians, but also young scientists from other CEECs (Poland, Russia, Yugoslavia, Croatia, Hungary and the Czech Republic) participated.

To ensure success of technology policy measures the idea was to establish agencies in CEECs e.g. Slovenian Innovation Agency (SIA) as the leader of an integrated nation-wide network of mobilisation and co-ordination of endogenous resources for innovation. The tasks and services of the SIA were to be based on customers' demands, also taking into account already existing Slovenian institutions and efforts by the country's ministries to support industrial innovation. The SIA was designed to fulfil administrative and other tasks in the public support of innovation on the one hand, and to work for industry and other private bodies on the other. A public-private financing model was implemented in order to ensure that the SIA would have a high degree of experience and closeness to practical solutions for enterprises. This mixed budget for the SIA was seen as a precondition for the support by the west. The SIA provides a primary platform for translating Slovenian policy into practice with regard to innovation and technology transfer, especially as it relates to innovative firms. Intermediary structures already in place are addressed, such as existing technology centres, industrial organisations, chambers of commerce and handicraft. Another very important task for the SIA is to facilitate the co-funding of innovative projects by banks and special funds. Since the need for innovation and technology transfer can only be partially met by Slovenian R&D structures, a role for the SIA in relation to international technology providers was considered. After some delays due to missing legal prerequisites, a new law for science and technology is envisaged that will also provide a good legal base for agencies such as the SIA (Walter/Bross 1998; Kalin 1999).

Implementation of policy concepts by pilot- and demonstrations projects for "PREEM" have to represent a particular interrelationship between private firms, policy and service infrastructure, they have to elaborate co-operative strategies for industry and science, and they must mobilise endogenous resources in order to secure or gain innovative competitiveness. The pilot and demonstration projects have to be typical of a large number of firms and their efforts to develop different strategies. These strategies rely on: specific strengths of these types of firms, co-operative approaches, and innovation support by public bodies.

Representativeness of the results obtained must be regarded with some caution because of the individuality of the cases. But because of the insights they provide, pilot and demonstration projects are suitable for both investigations and training, and are a well proven method for implementing innovation-supportive instruments and programmes.

Just as different types of enterprises in CEECs can be characterised by indicators, typical R&D or innovation projects can be correspondingly used to demonstrate specific strategies to be developed for different clusters, e.g. for

- high tech enterprises: joint R&D between firms and institutes for strategic basic research or for applied research in the field of precompetitive R&D (possibly supported by public R&D programmes),
- "sophisticated conventional technology" enterprises: projects for the development of additional products to ensure survival on existing markets (possibly supported by public innovation programmes),
- conventional technology enterprises: efforts towards a cost-reducing modernisation of production by integrating modern equipment and training,

- small-scale manufacturing enterprises: qualification measures as suppliers for companies with high tech or conventional technologies (management and network training; implementation of certification),
- "extended workbenches" of foreign large enterprises: activities for the development of the firm's own products.

Because of delays during the setting-up and installation of the SIA in Slovenia, realisation of the pilot and demonstration projects in this country has not yet taken place; however, Poland is also preparing activities of this kind as a follow-up to the elaboration of concepts for mobilising technology transfer (Walukiewicz 2000).

5 Conclusion

The success of "PREEM" relies on CEECs' own often individual efforts, knowledge and capabilities to meet real needs of individuals and societal groups. Actors in "PREEM" must address existing problems even if there are differences between their values and societal power, and they must co-operate within networks. Practitioner elites in industry, science and policy contribute to "PREEM" by their creativity and entrepreneurial behaviour to ensure the necessary dynamics for structural changes. Western partners of CEECs should try to

- enable CEEC actors especially in policy to manage modernisation processes by providing them with analytical, conceptual and implementation tools, and should train them in using and handling these instruments,
- support CEECs' policy makers in the identification, mobilisation and co-ordination of existing (endogenous) resources, especially human capital and innovation financing capital,
- rely on present and future elites in CEECs who are able and willing to manage structural changes, e.g. so that groups of network-oriented firms can co-operate adequately with the science sector in innovation and R&D. These firms could then be themselves regarded as institutional industrial elites.

To ensure broader societal acceptance, public events should be organised by CEECs and their Western partners in order to have the necessary publicity. Besides these activities, specific target groups should be addressed by demonstration and pilot projects in order to initiate imitative actions by these groups.

The necessary co-operation of actors in CEECs within innovative networks is seen as a good possibility to generate and realise innovations based on endogenous resources in industry and science. Historically developed, often very different and until now rather independent from each other, the societal institutions will have to collaborate if CEECs want to succeed in "PREEM". The necessary processes are difficult to realise and need a long time. The elaboration and implementation of concepts is difficult, because this is only possible if attitudes change. "PREEM" must have goals which are not inherently conflicting, and there should be no situations in which some actors have only advantages and others only disadvantages. Co-operation between the west and CEECs has to make sure that there are sufficient occasions between the partners to have enough communication and interaction on a personal level.

Literature

Balcerowicz, L. (1994): Common Fallacies in the Debate on the Transition to a Market Economy. Economic Policy, pp. 18-50.

Best, H.; Becker, U. (1997, Eds.): Elites in Transition. Elite Research in Central and Eastern Europe. Opladen: Leske + Budrich.

Bross, U. (2000): Innovationsnetzwerke in Transformationsländern. Heidelberg: Physica.

Bross, U.; Koschatzky, K.; Stanovnik, P. (1999): Development and Innovation Potential in the Slovene Manufacturing Industry. Working Paper Regionalforschung Nr.16. Fraunhofer ISI Karlsruhe.

Bross, U.; Walter, G. H. (1998): Development Prospects of the Czech Venture Capital Market: Assessment and Starting Points for Policy Measures. Fraunhofer IRB Verlag.

Bundesinstitut für ostwissenschaftliche und internationale Studien (1997, Ed.): Der Osten Europas im Prozess der Differenzierung – Fortschritte und Misserfolge der Transformation. München/Wien: Carl Hauser.

Dahm, H.; Assen, I. (1996, Eds.): Geschichte der philosophischen Traditionen Osteuropas. Darmstadt: Wissenschaftliche Buchgesellschaft.

Erler, B. (1985): Tödliche Hilfe. Freiburg: Dreisam.

Fogel, D. S. (1995): Firm Behavior in Emerging Market Economies. Cases from the Private and Public Sectors in Central and Eastern Europe. Aldershot: Avebury.

Grupp, H. (1997): Foresight and its Benefits for Policy and Society. In: Pejovnik, S.; Komac, M. (Eds.): FORUM BLED – From the Global to the Roots – Learning: The Treasure within. Ljubljana.

Hatschikjan, M.; Troebst, S. (1999, Eds.): Südosteuropa. Gesellschaft, Politik, Wirtschaft Kultur. Ein Handbuch. München: C. H. Beck.

Heilmann, S, (2000): Die Politik der Wirtschaftreformen in Russland und China. Hamburg: Institut für Asienkunde.

Herden, R. (1992): Technologieorientierte Außenbeziehungen im betrieblichen Innovationsmanagement. Heidelberg: Physica.

Hodenius, B.; Schmidt, G. (1996, Eds.): Transformationsprozess in Mittelost-Europa. Soziologische Revue, Sonderheft 4, München: Oldenbourg.

Jakobeit, C.; Alparslan (1993, Eds.): Gesamteuropa. Analysen, Probleme und Entwicklungsperspektiven. Bonn: Bundeszentrale für politische Bildung.

Jacobsen, A. (1999): Zentralosteuropäische Wachstumsperspektiven im Handel mit der Europäischen Gemeinschaft. Aachen: Shaker.

Kalin, T. (1999): Future Institutional Changes in Research Environment in Slovenia: For Better or for Worse. Paper presented on the 4th Semmering Science & Technology Forum: Institutional Changes: Efficiency and Effectiveness; The Interdisciplinary Centre for Comparative Research in the Social Sciences. Vienna, 3-5 December 1999.

Komac, M.; Krawczynski, J. (1994, Eds.): Conceptual Approaches to the Support of Industrial Research and Development in Slovenia. Forschungszentrum Jülich.

Koschatzky, K.; Frenkel, A.; Walter, G. H.; Shefer, D. (1996): Regional Concentration and Dynamics of Fast Growing Industries in Germany and Israel. In: Koschatzky, K.; Shefer, D. (Eds.): Spatial Diffusion of Industrial Innovation and Regional Development. Annual Report on Completion of the Second Year of Research under Support of the German-Israel Foundation Grant for 1996, Haifa and Karlsruhe.

Löhnig, C. (1996): Systemtransformation: Aspekte der wirtschaftlichen Umstrukturierung in den Reformstaaten Osteuropas und der ehemaligen Sowjetunion. Weiden: Eurotrans.

Meske, W.; Mosonsi-Fried, J.; Etzkowitz, H.; Nesvetailov, G. (1998): Transforming Science and Technology System – the Endless Transition. Amsterdam/ Berlin/Oxford/Tokyo/Washington, D.C.: IOS Press.

Olson, M. (2000): Power and Prosperity: Outgrowing Communist and Capitalist Dictatorships. New York: Basic Books.

Ott, R. (1995, Ed.): Der Riese erwacht. Osteuropa nach 1989. Facetten aus Gesellschaft, Politik und Medien. Frankfurt/Main: Institut für Medienentwicklung und Kommunikation der Frankfurter Allgemeinen Zeitung.

Senghaas, D.; Menzel, U. (1986): Europas Entwicklung und die Dritte Welt. Frankfurt/Main: Suhrkamp.

Scheinacker, B. D. (1997): Transformation des Wirtschaftssystems in den mittel- und osteuropäischen Ländern. Berlin: Duncker Humblot.

Schweickart, K. (1995, Ed.): Systemtransformation in Osteuropa. Herausforderungen an Unternehmen beim Übergang der Planwirtschaft in die Marktwirtschaft. Stuttgart: Schäffer-Pöschel.

Steiner, M.; Walter, G. H. (2000): Activated Technology Transfer of Theoretical Foundations, Models and Instruments. Presented on the International Conference on "Technology Transfer for Economic Development: Experience for Countries in Transition". 19.-20.6.2000, Zagreb.

Tomann, H. (1999): Die Osterweiterung der Europäischen Union aus ökonomischer Sicht, Volkswirtschaftliche Reihe Nr. 1999/28, Freie Universität Berlin.

Walter, G. H. (1999): Innovation Agencies: Their Role in Science, Technology and Innovation Policy. In: Pejovnik, S.; Komac, M. (Eds.): FORUM BLED, Science and Technology Investment. Priority in the Development Strategy of the Nation, Ljubljana: Ministry of Science and Technology.

Walter, G. H.; Bross, U. (1997): The Adaptation of German Experiences to Building Up Innovation Networks in Central and Eastern Europe. In: Koschatzky, K. (Ed.): Technology-Based Firms in the Innovation-Process. Management, Financing and Regional Networks, Heidelberg: Physica.

Walter, G. H.; Bross, U. (1998): Promoting Technology Development in Slovenia by International Co-operation. In: Kobal, E.; Štiblar-Martinčič (Eds.): Pospeševanje tehnološkega razvoja Slovenije, Ljubljana.

Walter, G. H. (1992): Integration einheimischer Hochschulen in die Modernisierung der Dritten Welt. Karlsruhe: Rufdruck Druck- und Verlagsgesellschaft.

Walukiewicz, S. (2000): Adapting Mobilised Technology Transfer to Polish Conditions. Presentation at the Polish-German-Workshop: "Mobilising Technology Transfer (MTT) in Poland". Warsaw 22./23.9.2000, mimeograph.

Weidenfels, W. (1995, Ed.): Demokratie und Marktwirtschaft für Osteuropa. Gütersloh: Bertelsmann Stiftung.

Weidenfels, W. (1997, Ed.): Neue Ostpolitik – Strategie für eine gesamteuropäische Entwicklung. Gütersloh: Bertelsmann Stiftung.

Weiss, H.; Reinprecht, Chr. (1998): Demokratischer Patriotismus oder etnischer Nationalismaus in Ost-Mitteleuropa. Wien/Köln/Weimar: Böhlau.

Wollmann, H. (1995, Ed.): Transformation sozialistischer Gesellschaften am Ende des Anfanges. Opladen: Westdeutscher Verlag.

Zorn, Hans van (1996): The Future of Industry in Central and Eastern Europe. Aldershot: Avebury.

Entrepreneurship and Innovativeness of Small and Medium-Sized Enterprises (SMEs) in Poland

Krzysztof B. Matusiak

1 Development of the SMEs Sector

Democratic upheaval and transformation of the economic system in Poland brought about a rapid growth of interest in self-employment and business activity. At the beginning of the 1990s the net number of new private enterprises increased by over two million. They made a significant contribution to overcoming economic stagnation, transformation of the economic structure and to Poland attaining an economic growth over 5 per cent rate. It should be noted here that the Polish economy, unlike economies of other CEECs, was characterised by a broad margin of freedom left for private business activity throughout the entire period of real socialism. Over 80 per cent of arable lands, a large part of the retail trade, the building sector and services were privately owned. Of course, business activity was run by private entities on a relatively small scale due to legal-administrative barriers and it could be carried only in fields that were not reserved for the public sector. Doctrinal barriers to market entries were removed gradually in the 1980s.[1] As a result of this, the number of private firms rose by almost 200 000 (from 375 000 to 572 000), while the size of the work force doubled (reaching 1 290 000 in 1988). Measures taken in that period provided an impetus for building a market economy started by the "Balcerowicz Programme". Removal of remaining legal and administrative barriers to business start-ups in 1989 released a true "explosion of entrepreneurship". Transformation of the economic system gave the proverbial "green light" for small and medium-sized private enterprises which had been handicapped in the previous period. In 1989 alone, the number of business units rose by 50 per cent, and by the end of 1991 had risen by a total of 162 per cent compared to pre-1989 figures. The average annual growth rate in the number of firms was around 20-40 per cent, decreasing gradually till 1994. The dynamic process of setting up new firms was due to the following factors:

1 A crucial role for the development of private business activity was played by the Business Activity Act of 28th December 1988 (Official Gazette 1988 no. 41, item 324), which gave equal rights to the public and the private sectors.

- liberalisation of business start-up conditions;
- removal of restrictions for private firms in many fields previously reserved for the public sector;
- processes of privatisation and restructuring of public enterprises and entire sectors of industry;
- bankruptcy proceedings in public enterprises;
- the threat of unemployment or deterioration of living standards faced by inhabitants in rural areas;
- re-privatisation of small businesses nationalised in the late 1940s and the early 1950s with infringement of law;
- the socio-political climate encouraging active involvement in transformations of the economic system.

The growth trend was interrupted in 1995, when the number of firms dropped by about 10 per cent for the only time in the entire decade. Many businesses were closed down shortly after overcoming the depression and achieving 5 per cent economic growth rate. The following four main causes of this situation should be distinguished:

1) market stabilisation of businesses initiated 3 to 4 years before;
2) adoption of legislative solutions disadvantageous to small businesses;
3) improvement in the labour market situation, bringing the alternative of better employment;
4) fears of the economic policy pursued by the Left-wing government.

However, the situation soon stabilised and the number of business units has been growing at the rate of about 10 per cent annually since 1996. The number of new businesses in Poland has been growing on average by 400 000-500 000 in recent years (460 000 in 1998), and this trend has been accompanied by the liquidation of 150 000-250 000 of existing units (241 000 in 1998). A continuous increase in the number of business units reaching over ten percentage points has been recorded recently, with the exception of 1995. Over three-quarters of entities active today did not exist ten years ago. Development of the private sector in Poland can be divided into three phases (Piasecki 1997):

- An early phase of entrepreneurial development – initiated at the beginning of the 1980s, which was an effect of attempts to reform the centrally planned economy. Measures taken at that time aimed at checking the intensifying socio-economic crisis. Certain barriers to market entries were eliminated gradually, which paved the way for a quantitative increase in the number of small firms.

- The period of entrepreneurship explosion – covering the first years following the democratic upheaval in 1989. This was a phase when administrative restrictions were eliminated and a new socio-political climate appeared, releasing among thousands of Poles the "spirit of entrepreneurship" which had been suppressed throughout the entire time of the centrally planned economy. Liberalisation of the economy and low entry barriers to many markets created desirable conditions and extraordinary opportunities for so-called "arbitrageur" entrepreneurship.
- A phase of market self-regulation – starting from 1992 as a result of the gradual exhaustion of simple growth reserves of new firms and the intensification of competition in most markets. Growth in the number of new business units slowed down and the number of business failures increased.

The need for entering a fourth phase characterised by an increase of innovativeness and technological orientation of the firms has been pointed out for a few years now. Without increasing the quality level of the products and the modernity of technologies, and without the development of innovation capabilities, domestic SMEs have few chances for further growth and adjustment to the demands of the common European market. The extensive resources of "explosive" entrepreneurial development in Poland are becoming exhausted. As a consequence, new potential businessmen as well as managers from small and medium sized firms face the new challenge of building up innovation capabilities within their enterprises.

In the first half of 1999 the number of entities having the right to engage in business activity exceeded 2.8 million (GUS 1999a). About 83 per cent of all registered business units are sole traders. They are characterised by a very low level of activity in the area of trade and service, and they are of self-employment character, which does not create workplaces for hired workers. Commercial partnerships constitute approximately 5 per cent of all economic entities. Statistically, an overall average of 3.9 persons is employed in each Polish enterprise, the average number of employees per unit being 1.7 in the private sector and 76.6 in state-owned businesses. These numbers differ from analogous data for the European Union, and point to the organisational weakness of domestic firms (Polska Fundacja 1998).

Figure 1-1: Structure of entities having the right to engage in business activity in the first half of 1999

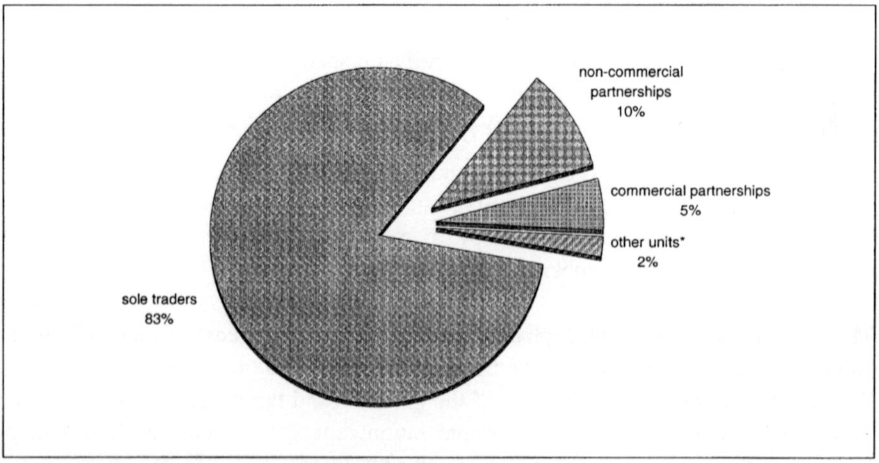

* – state-owned enterprises, co-operatives, foundations, associations, etc.

Source: Own calculations based on – Zmiany strukturalne grup podmiotów gospodarki narodowej w I pólroczu 1999 r., GUS, 1999a, pp. 16-17.

It appears that only 65 per cent of all registered businesses (outside agriculture, forestry, fisheries, and financial intermediary services) were really operating at the end of 1998.[2] Among such active firms, 99 per cent were small firms with less than 50 employees (1 709 292), and 92 per cent of these were micro-firms with less than 5 employees. There were 13,322 medium sized enterprises (0.8 per cent) and 3 457 large enterprises.

Irrespective of the growing number of SMEs, a steadily growing economic role of this sector can be also observed. In 1998 SMEs generated 48.1 per cent of Poland´s GDP (as compared to 45.3 per cent in 1997) – of which small firms accounted for 38.5 per cent and medium-sized firms for 9.6 per cent. In the same year, large enterprises generated 23 per cent of the GDP. This means that the share of SMEs in the GDP rose by 18 per cent compared to 1995. Almost 55 per cent of value added in the economy is created in the SMEs sector. Analysing only the sector of private enterprises (i.e. not including state-owned enterprises) this share amounts to 67.7 per cent. SMEs predominate in generating income in trade and repairs (94.4 per cent), services for real estate and firms (91.9 per cent), and financial services (89.9

2 The difference between the number of registered business units and those running business activity is a result of shortcomings of the statistical system. Correction covers mainly cases of registered units which did not start business activity (the so-called "sleepy heads") or which suspended such activity but did not report this to registration organs.

per cent). Their share in construction, hotels and restaurants reaches 80 per cent. In manufacturing activity SMEs generated about 45 per cent, and in transport and telecommunication 39 per cent of all value added. The lowest share of SMEs in value added (mainly for technological reasons) is traditionally observed in electrical energy, water and gas supply (12.6 per cent) and mining and quarrying (6.1 per cent).

Figure 1-2: **Structure of SMEs in main sectors of the economy (excluding agriculture) at the end of 1998**

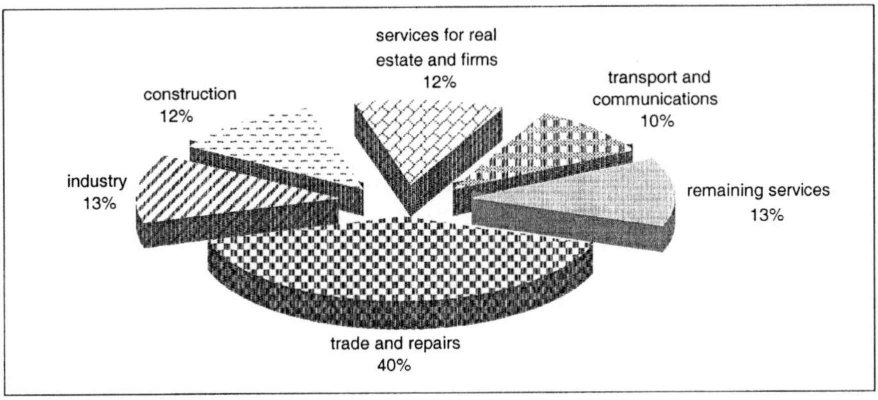

Source: Raport o stanie sektora malych i srednich przedsiebiorstw w latach 1998-1999, Polska Fundacja Promocji i Rozwoju Malych i Srednich Przedsiebiorstw, Warszawa 2000 p. 29.

From among 11.4 million persons employed in the national economy at the end of 1998 (excluding agriculture, forestry, and fishing), 7 million (62.5 per cent) worked in SMEs, of which 25.9 per cent worked in micro-firms, 21.4 per cent in other small firms (from 6 to 50 employees), and 17.8 per cent in medium-sized enterprises. SMEs account for about 44.2 per cent of all investment outlays in the sector of all enterprises (i.e. including state-owned enterprises) and 61.5 per cent in the private sector (i.e. not including state-owned enterprises). SMEs play an important role in international trade accounting for 48.1 per cent of total exports and 63.2 per cent of imports.

The distribution of the SMEs sector within Poland is quite uneven. 25 per cent of active small and medium-sized enterprises are concentrated in 6 per cent of the country's territory, and the next 25 per cent in 17 per cent of the country's territory. This means that over half of all SMEs are located on one quarter of Poland's territory. Concentration around large urban agglomerations and in regions with well-developed and differentiated industries – Krakow, Gdansk, Katowice, Lodz,

Poznan, Szczecin, and Warsaw – is clearly visible. Besides the Warsaw agglomeration, the area with the most dynamic start-up processes extends from Gdansk through Bydgoszcz, Poznan, Wroclaw to Opole.[3] These regions are characterised by a higher than average level of GDP per capita as well as higher innovativeness and efficiency of activity. High share of foreign investments, a high ratio of privatisation, and a low rate of unemployment are other characteristic features of the regions mentioned (Zienkowski 1998). Also worthy of note is the growing activity of SMEs in some border areas (Szczecin and Zielona Góra in the west, and Bialystok in the east) which benefit from trans-border trade.

2 Polish Entrepreneurs in the Light of Empirical Research

International comparisons point to a high readiness among Poles to run businesses. Over 79.9 per cent of Poles prefer running their own businesses to being employees in other enterprises. The next ranks in this hierarchy are taken by the Portuguese (73.3 per cent), Americans (70.8 per cent) and Swiss (64.5 per cent). In the Central East European countries the highest interest in self-employment was in Slovenia (63.3 per cent), Bulgaria (54.4 per cent), Hungary and in Russia (33.2 per cent).[4] Entrepreneurship and interest in individual economic activity is one of the basic sources supporting transformation and construction of the market economy in Poland.

Questionnaire surveys carried out in the Department of Economics, University of Lodz have yielded the following characteristics of entrepreneurs and the problems they come across during the first year of running their firm.[5] Business activity is undertaken primarily by men (66.4 per cent) aged 35-40 with higher education (42 per cent, of which 49 per cent possess technical education and 31 per cent economic) and secondary professional education (22 per cent). 57 per cent of entrepreneurs worked at state-owned enterprises earlier (for 13 years on average) frequently holding management positions. The number of persons setting up businesses directly after completing secondary schools or a short schooling in a private firm is tending to increase.

---

3 This area was a Polish west border before the II World War.

4 Empirical research conducted in 1998 in 23 countries on a sample of 25 thousand people by David Blanchflower (Dartmouth College and NBER, US) and Andrew Oswald (Wartwick University, UK), Measuring Latent Entrepreneurship Across Nations, December 1999, (from:) Raport o stanie sektora malych i srednich przedsiebiorstw w latach 1998-1999, Polska Fundacja Promocji i Rozwoju Malych i Srednich Przedsiebiorstw, Warszawa 2000, pp.80-82.

5 Surveys within the project: "Start into private business" were carried out in mid-1999 on a random sample of 320 entrepreneurs who had started business activity for the first time after 1989. The present material is the first publication of survey findings. The choice of entrepreneurs for the sample was determined by the structure of the SME sector according two kinds of activity, location of a firm (urban agglomeration, small town or rural areas) as well as the rates of starts up of new businesses in particular years.

Figure 2-1: Motives for business start-up *

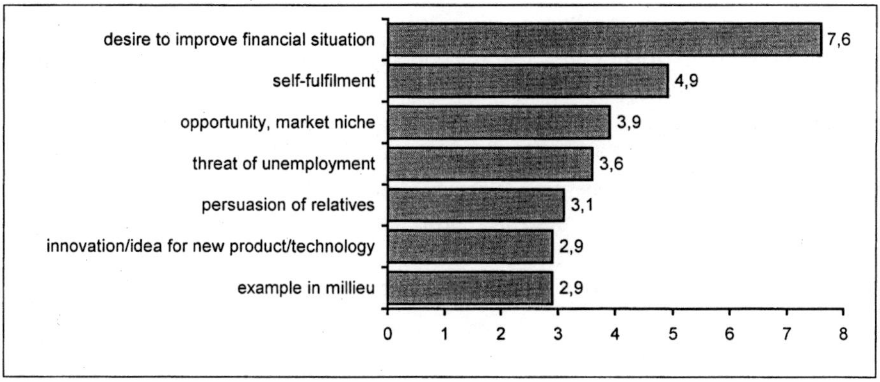

* – individual characteristics were assessed on a scale from 1 to 10.

Source: Own calculations based on empirical research (N= 350).

Among the motives for setting up a firm, a dominant position is held by the desire to improve one's financial situation, the need for self-fulfilment and the threat of redundancy. In 30 per cent of cases the main reason was the family tradition of running business activity.

Figure 2-2: Sources of experience and background for running business activity

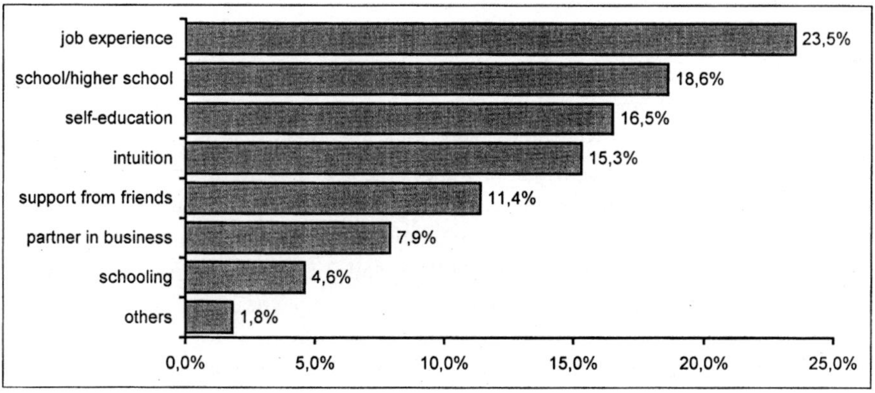

Source: Own calculations based on empirical research (N= 350).

A crucial role at the time of starting up business activity is played by personal contacts and experience from previous jobs, as well as education, complemented by self-education based on business literature. An important role is played by intuitive actions (15 per cent of entrepreneurs), not supported by professional skills. Support from friends, family or partners(s) in business at the preliminary stage of activity has a basic importance for almost every fifth entrepreneur. It appears that training courses in the field of entrepreneurship conducted by training centres, high schools or chambers of trade and commerce are of small importance in preparing a person for independent business activity. The majority of Polish entrepreneurs are not sufficiently critical where their professional skills, or the preparation for conducting economic activity, are concerned. It can be concluded that they attach low importance to their own and their employees' professional training.

Figure 2-3: Source finance for business start-up

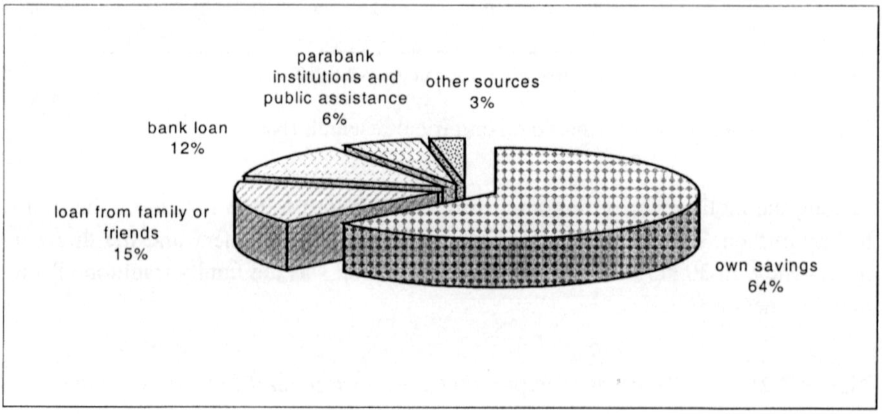

Source: Own calculations based on empirical research (N= 350).

The finance for business start-ups comes in 63.5 per cent of cases from own savings supplemented in 15.4 per cent of cases by a loan from family or friends. Preferential loans provided by specialised quasi-bank loan-guarantee institutions and government agencies and funds (e.g. Labour Fund, Agency of Agriculture Modernisation and Restructuring) constitute on average 6.3 per cent of the finance needed to start up a business. The cost of one job in a newly set up business reaches on average around 8 000 zloty (from 30 zl to 60 000 zl) and it is lower in trade and service business and much higher in manufacturing.

Over 72 per cent of sales in the first year of activity are on the local (54 per cent) or regional markets. Attempts to sell on foreign markets are undertaken by single firms. On average 14.5 per cent of sales during the first year of activity are made in the informal sector. Simultaneously, a large part of business units (about 50 per cent) try to operate in accordance with tax regulations. However, every fourth new firm does not register over 25 per cent of its sales.

Figure 2-4: Fields creating most difficulties for entrepreneurs in the initial period of the firm's operation *

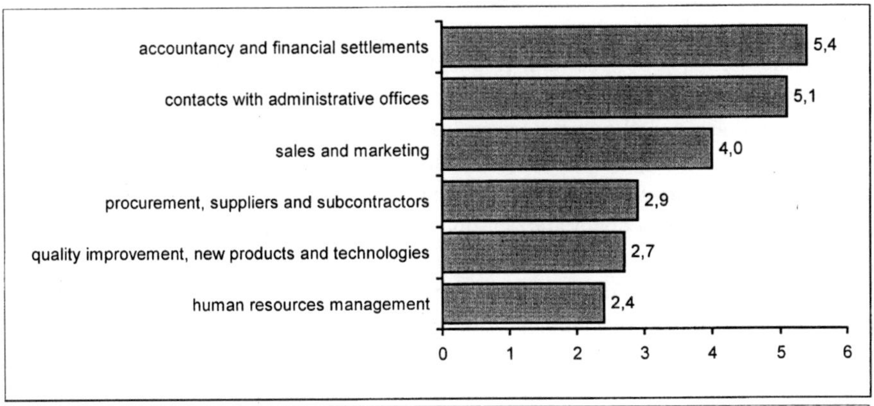

* – individual characteristics were assessed on the scale from 1 to 10.

Source: Own calculations based on empirical research (N=350).

The main problems for entrepreneurial beginners lie in the area of accounting and finance. The second important source of problems in running economic activity are contacts with public offices as the main problem area of firm activity. New entrepreneurs appear to have the biggest difficulties with accounting, financial settlements and contacts with administrative offices.

Figure 2-5: Main growth barriers for firms *

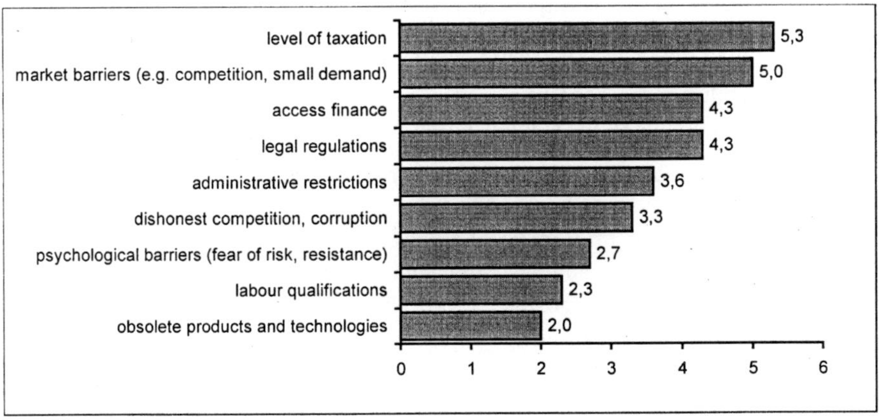

* – individual characteristics were assessed on a scale from 1 to 10.

Source: Own calculations based on empirical research (N = 350).

According to beginning entrepreneurs, the main growth barriers of firms arc limited demand for the goods and services offered, the level of taxation[6] as well as legal rules and administrative limitations (licences, concessions).

Despite numerous problems, and frequently also disappointments connected with business start-ups, only 5.5 per cent of entrepreneurs would give up the accepted path if they knew exactly what barriers they would come across. Every tenth entrepreneur would try to get a better professional background for running a business, and 8.6 per cent would look for "a partner with money" and experience. Every fourth firm was closed down after an (average) 26 months of operation, which was due primarily to difficulties with selling its products or services and with shortages of finance. Other major reasons for closing down a business were difficulties connected with collecting receivables from customers and problems with finding employees.

In the course of running a business 64 per cent of entrepreneurs used different forms of counselling received mainly from friends and family or business partner. Assistance provided by business support institutions and representative organisations is of marginal importance. The assistance obtained concerned primarily the main problems with which start-up entrepreneurs have to cope – revenue board control and finance management, sales and marketing, and preparation of a business plan.

Entrepreneurs point to a number of issues within the responsibility of the government and legislative authorities, the solving of which would improve the 'entrepreneurship climate' in the economy. Their expectations and proposals refer mainly to:

- the simplification of procedures for running small businesses;
- the introduction of tax incentives for investments;
- a reduction of the interest rate and easier access to finance for small firms;
- greater stability of the economic system, reduction of legal regulations and more efficient functioning of the administration;
- reduction of the socio-economic welfare burdens carried by firms.

As regards expectations from the local authorities, these concern, first of all, more efficient operation of the administration and improvement of the infrastructure. Further expectations of entrepreneurs regard the necessity for supporting the development of innovation and business support centres, and the development of interregional and international contacts.

---

6 This barrier should be treated with a certain distance, as in the majority of countries complaining of high taxes is very popular among private entrepreneurs.

3 Innovativeness of Small and Medium Sized Enterprises

According to statistical data and research findings, Polish SMEs propensity to innovation is quite low. For example, the latest questionnaire surveys carried out by the Central Statistical Office (GUS) in Polish manufacturing firms show that 37.6 per cent of all firms introduced at least one innovation in the years 1994-1996.[7] Public enterprises (52 per cent) and domestic firms appear to be more innovative. Only 28 per cent of enterprises with foreign capital are involved in R&D activity or stated their intention to commence R&D in the coming years. The propensity to innovate rises significantly with firm size. Only 16 per cent of firms with 6 to 50 employees introduced an innovation in the period analysed, as compared with 88 per cent of large enterprises with over 2 000 employees. Innovations that were made mainly concerned small changes in products and more infrequently in technological processes. Small firms implemented innovations half as frequently as medium ones, and the latter half as frequently as large firms (Zienkowski 1998). The most innovative firms are in traditional manufacturing branches: the production of coke, petroleum (where 78.6 per cent of firms introduced an innovation); chemical products (73.3 per cent); electrical equipment and machinery (63.8 per cent). The extent to which small and medium-sized enterprises conduct and finance their own R&D activity is negligible. Computer assisted manufacturing, designing or quality control are sporadically used. When assessing the low propensity to innovation of Polish SMEs, it is necessary to point to three issues:

- Transformation of the economic system created exceptional opportunities for the development of entrepreneurship. Liberalisation of the economy, removal of entry barriers and privatisation opened up for small businesses large areas of the market which had been previously been reserved for the public sector. This allowed a dynamic development of hundreds of thousands of firms without the necessity of looking for new products or technologies. These extensive development opportunities became gradually exhausted, and for several years now an increasingly great awareness of the necessity to reach for innovations has been observed among entrepreneurs. The necessity for technological modernisation is perceived most strongly in the oldest and the youngest firms.
- The "petrified", non-restructured sector of science and research does not perceive opportunities lying in the development of co-operation with SMEs. The technological market just emerging is one of main sources of new products and technologies for small firms. There is felt to be a shortage of professional institutions dealing with the transfer and commercialisation of technology and operating at the intersection of science and economy, e.g. technological agencies or incubators.

---

[7] The survey was carried out according to methodological recommendations of the European Union contained in the Oslo Manual. For more information see: Nauka i technika w 1997 roku (Science and Technique in 1997), GUS 1999b (Central Statistical Office), (in Polish).

- A lack of technology policy both at national and regional levels, and the lack of a system of innovation support, especially with regard to SMEs. Reformers in Poland assumed that innovativeness in the economy would improve automatically together with liberalisation and privatisation processes. Looking back now, it is obvious that these mechanisms of "innovation induction" did not act.

Despite many quantitative effects, the development of entrepreneurship was in fact arbitrage-related and arose with the transformation of the economy, privatisation and liberalisation, without the necessity for undertaking innovative activities. Empirical research conducted in the Institute of Economics at the University of Lodz[8] indicates that the Polish entrepreneurs compete by their still relatively cheap workforce and their ability to find market niches, not by quality of products or innovativeness. A network of small and medium entities able to co-operate with large domestic and foreign firms is still lacking. Among the sources of innovations in the firms there are indicated ideas and personal engagement of the owners, participation in fairs and exhibitions, and contacts with clients.

Figure 3-1: Main sources of innovations in small and medium sized firms *

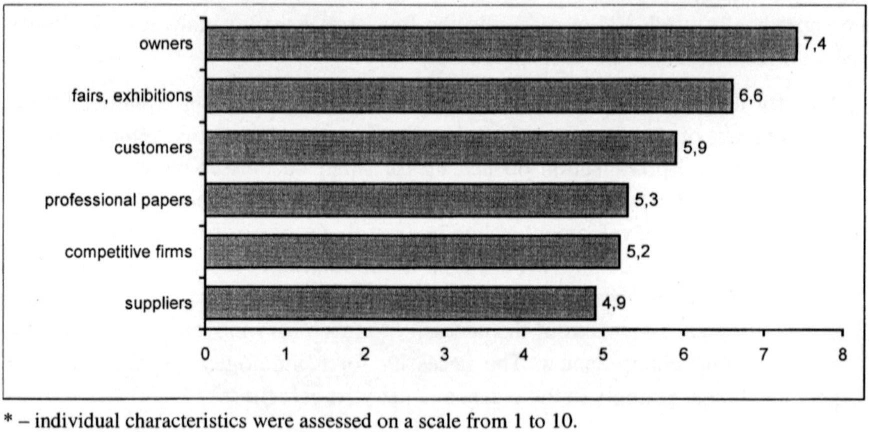

* – individual characteristics were assessed on a scale from 1 to 10.

Source: Own calculations based on empirical research (N = 102).

Scientific-research institutions, technology transfer centres, patent officers, incubators and technology centres are of marginal importance as sources of innovations.

8 The paper presents results of empirical research conducted on the sample of 100 innovative enterprises in the first half of 2000 in the framework of the Scientific Research Committee program "Determinants of creation and development of innovative firms" as well as previous research from the years 1994 and 1997.

The most important were higher education establishments (2.9 points) which gave the SMEs access to expertises, reports and analyses, enabled them to gain scientific information and provided advisory activity and training. The main problems with co-operation were as follows: costs too high; lack of information about scientific institutions, their offers and possibilities of transfer; limited possibilities of adaptation of offered solutions in the firms. Marginal co-operation with the institutions mentioned above concerns employee training, partner searches, assistance in developing a new product/technology. The main barriers to co-operation are: lack of information about activities and offers of the institutions, doubtful advantages of the co-operation and too high costs.

Implementation of innovative projects in the firms is based on the purchase of machinery and equipment as well as whole technology lines (39.3 per cent of expenditure). 23.1 per cent of resources are used for R&D and design activity (two thirds of these activities are internal, i.e. take place within the firms). A relatively large share of expenditure (13.6 per cent) is on marketing and promotion of the new products. Innovative activity is mainly based on the firm's own resources, while bank credits and leasing are of supplementary character. The main objectives of innovations are: to improve the main products, to introduce a new assortment of products, to improve product quality, and to increase the firm's market share.

Figure 3-2: Structure of expenditure on innovation

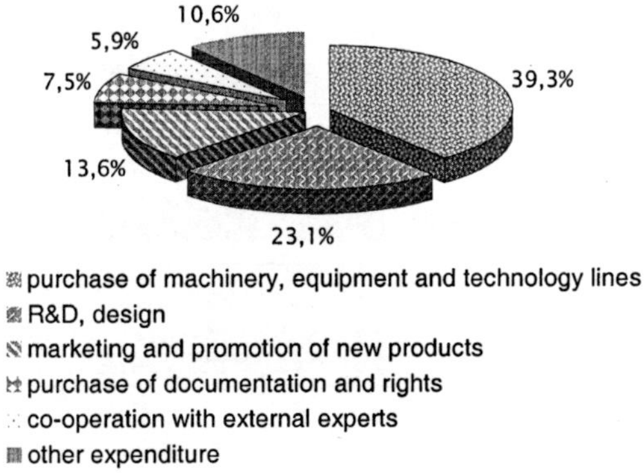

Source: Own calculations based on empirical research (N = 102).

Entrepreneurs point to the following main barriers to firms' development: governmental policy and tax levels, market barriers (competition, low demand) as well as limited access to external sources of financing.

Figure 3-3: Main growth barriers for firms *

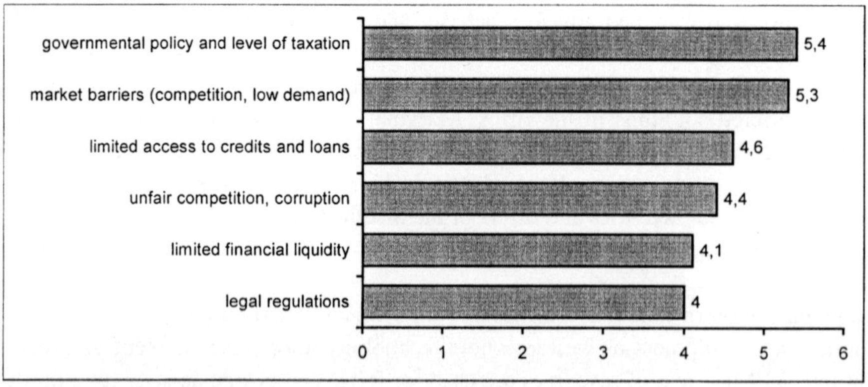

* – individual characteristics were assessed on a scale from 1 to 10.

Source: Own calculations based on empirical research (N = 102).

Entrepreneurs would like the government to create incentives for investment, lowering interest rates and simplifying the regulations on the running of businesses. As to the local authorities, they should raise standards of administration, improve the infrastructure, attract new firms and support the development of business centres.

Figure 3-4: What should the government do to support innovative firms? *

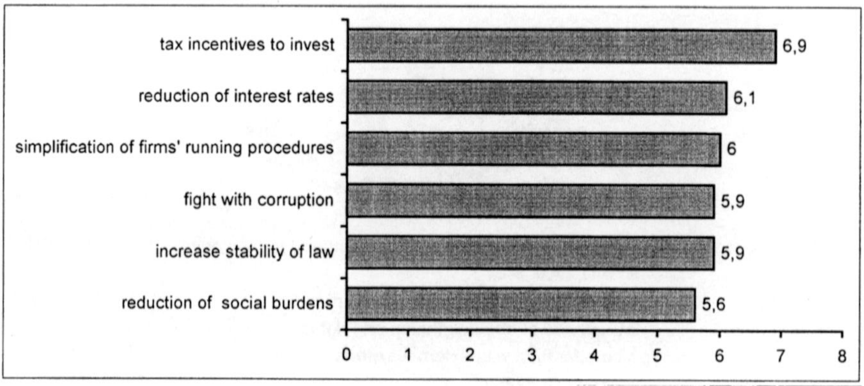

* – individual characteristics were assessed on a scale from 1 to 10

Source: Own calculations based on empirical research (N = 102).

Long years of experience in industrially developed countries have shown that SMEs need assistance in technology transfer, assessment of the market, technology applications, promotion and access to information. Regional innovation and business support systems are a response to such requirements. Each invention opens new technical opportunities; however, it is difficult to determine immediately the economic benefits it may bring. It is here that the process of technology commercialisation begins; this consists in a careful study of the advantages offered by a new product or technology, comparing them with alternatives available on the market, evaluating the size of the potential market, indispensable investment outlays, costs of production and distribution. Direct participants in technology transfer are frequently unable to answer themselves particular questions connected with assessing the effectiveness of an innovation project. Simultaneously, time is one of main determinants of future success. Hence, institutionalised systems of technology transfer and commercialisation have been being developed in most economically developed countries for over twenty years. Such a system is based on independent entities dealing in a professional manner with intermediary services between the sector of science and research and business practice. Entities dealing with technology transfer have been set up at universities, R&D institutions, business associations, and trade unions. Various tasks in this field are being accomplished by commercially oriented consulting firms, non-profit foundations and associations (Matusiak 1998). In Poland this infrastructure is at the preliminary stage of organisation. There is a shortage of strong local and regional institutions, a lack of mechanisms for financing their activity, and a lack of practical experience in how to organise technology transfer effectively.

4 The High-Technology Small Firm

A new category of economic units – small high-technology firms – appeared in the United States at the turn of the 'seventies and in Western Europe in the 'eighties. Such firms are defined as developing, manufacturing and selling goods and services which embody a significant element of contemporary science. As units characterised by a high propensity to innovation and entrepreneurship, they realise the conversion of science into new technologies, undertaking their commercialisation in the market (Oakey et al. 1998; Grudzewski et al. 1997). The high-technology small firm is an embodiment of the Schumpeterian entrepreneur-innovator, who in his function of a Newcomer is the main driving force of economic development. Support provided by innovation policy for high-technology small firms is associated with expectations that the development of these firms will lead to rapid new job creation and build a bridge between sciences – financed from the budget – and industry. Fulfilment of these expectations is determined, however, by the development level of the funding of high risk ventures by the capital market; by the business environment, the government's procurement policy, co-operation programmes between universities and small firms, social acceptance of innovations, and so on (Roberts 1994). Support for the development of small high-tech firms has become a basic component of economic policy in many countries (Sweden, Israel, Taiwan) and regions – such as Silicon Valley or Orange County in California, the Greater Boston Area in Massachusetts, or Baden-Württemberg in Germany.

In Poland, the economic power of such entities was perceived in the mid-'eighties. Looking for a model suitable for the conditions of the centrally planned economy, in 1985-1989 innovative firms were established in the form of innovation-application units benefiting from financial and tax preferences guaranteed by law. These units were established as experimental units in research centres, universities and institutes of the Polish Academy of Sciences, and in the form of non-commercial partnerships and limited liability companies in the environment of large enterprises. Their main goal was to tap scientific research in R&D activity, which could be transferred to enterprises. The Act on Innovation-Application Units was a great novelty in the 'eighties, but it became a source of "economic pathology", contributing more to benefiting from financial/tax preferences than to technology transfer into business practice.

Liberalisation and transformation of the economic system created a favourable climate for undertaking business activity along market economy principles by persons connected with scientific milieus. Surveys started at the University of Lodz in 1997 enabled the identification of high-technology small firms in Polish conditions in the 1990s.[9] According to an estimate made with the help of experts, about 600 to 700 small firms with a technological orientation are operating in Poland at the present time. These are mainly spin-off firms having their origins in universities (43.7 per cent), followed by entities deriving from research centres and the R&D and technical departments of enterprises (23.6 per cent each).

Most high-technology firms (85 per cent) operate in large agglomerations. These agglomerations include cities with their surrounding areas (above 500 000 inhabitants) and are characterised by the presence of universities, R&D centres and large companies with their own R&D departments. Moreover, areas where agglomera-

---

9 The studies were carried out by Department of Economics and they were commissioned by the Scientific Research Committee. They were an attempt to: (Stawasz 1998)

- identify the size of this specific group of business units in the Polish economy;
- identify their main strengths, weaknesses and risks, finding their expression primarily in growth barriers and priorities determined both by the character of a firm's resources, characteristics of its owner and conditions created by the environment in which firms operate;
- identify the degree and character of innovation propensity of these firms, and sources and barriers to innovation;
- determine the needs of firms in terms of assistance and support, including both central and regional (local) support;
- present conclusions which can be useful for government and regional policy of support for the sector of technology-based firms in Poland.

Surveys included the owners and managers of 55 small technology-based firms located in different parts of Poland. The sample was selected with help of experts from different business and technical milieus dealing professionally with modern technology transfer and commercialisation, or with technical counselling in industry, as well as from business promotion offices.

tions are located have a better developed business infrastructure, a bigger pool of qualified potential employees etc. than peripheral areas.

The most popular organisational-legal form in which these firms operate (54.5 per cent) is as a limited liability company, followed by non-commercial partnerships (23.7 per cent) and sole traders (18.2 per cent). Dormant equity holdings are very seldom. Firms owned by several active partners predominate, with the number of owners averaging 2.8 persons. Every fourth firm (23.6 per cent) has one owner. However, unlike the SMEs sector as a whole, the high-technology firms analysed are not "family businesses". This is the case in only 21.8 per cent of firms, whereas the share of "traditional" manufacturing SMEs is much bigger, exceeding 65 per cent (Piasecki et al. 1996).

High-technology firms are generally not very old; the average age in December 1996 was 5.3 years. Over half of these firms (50.9 per cent) were set up in the years 1992-1995, as compared to 38.2 per cent between 1988 and 1991. The smallest share of high-technology firms were established before 1988 (10.1 per cent). According to research findings, the most dynamic development of technological entrepreneurship occurred in the years 1991-1995, when 63.6 per cent of these firms were set up; thus this development took place after the period of fundamental economic transformations. It should be noted here that accelerated development of technological entrepreneurship in Poland took place later than the development of the whole SMEs sector, which was most dynamic in the years 1988-1991. The fairly small number of high-technology firms operating so far, and their more dynamic development in the first half of the 1990s, may indicate that technological entrepreneurship is only in its initial phase in Poland and that a phase of "explosion of technological entrepreneurship" is still before us.

Nearly 91 per cent of the owners of the small high-technology firms in the survey are men. Almost two-thirds of firm owners were involved in R&D activity in their parent organisations, and only about 13 per cent state that they are skilled in such fields as: selling/marketing, business economics and finance or economic law. For most respondents it is their first business, which they run alongside their scientific or research activity. Launching business activity is an attempt to take on a new challenge and achieve self-fulfilment, by persons around 40 years old, possessing sufficient experience and theoretical knowledge which they would like to transfer to the market following the transformations in the economy. Surveys have revealed their strong emotional attachment to the firm, and their unwillingness to take on credits or engage in strategic alliances which carry a risk that they may lose control over their firm. According to interviewers, over half the owners (59 per cent) resemble scientists in their personal characteristics and behaviour, and 41 per cent are typified as entrepreneurs who perceive their firm and business activity from the viewpoint of the market.

The main motives inducing people to set up their own firms were self-fulfilment, independence and autonomy, and a desire to obtain a higher income. These motives were stated by over half the firm owners interviewed. Much smaller share of respondents would point at family tradition, imitation of other entrepreneurs, or threat of unemployment. It should be noted, however, that by far the most important motive driving people to setting up their own firms operating in high technology field was self-fulfilment (for 60 per cent of such firms it was the main motive). Much lower rank was given to a desire to ensure independence and autonomy (a little over one-third of firms). These motives are significantly different from those indicated by traditional entrepreneurs (compare figure 2-1). This points to strong separateness of this category of high-tech entrepreneurs.

Analysis of the distribution of answers concerning motives for setting up a firm according to the period in which it was set up, yields quite interesting information. It reveals that motives tend to vary over time. For persons setting up their own firms in the period before economic transformation (1981-1987) and during its initial phase (1988-1991) the main motive was a desire for self-fulfilment, satisfaction of their own creative aspirations (over 80 per cent of firms), as well as gaining independence (over 70 per cent of firms). During the later period (1992-1995), when the setting up of firms with a technological orientation was accelerated, the main motives were equally a desire to gain independence and a desire to improve one's living standard, as well as self-fulfilment (over 60 per cent of firms). Much greater importance was also attached to imitating other entrepreneurs (29 per cent of firms) and – as a novelty – fear of unemployment (11 per cent of firms).

The main source of initial capital for high-technology small firms was owners' own savings. This was given as the most important source by over 78 per cent of firms, and for 45.5 per cent of firms own savings were the only source of capital. Bank credits and loans (16.4 per cent of firms) and capital from an earlier firm (12.7 per cent of firms) were somewhat less important. Such forms of initial capital as subsidies, quasi-bank loans and capital investment practically do not exist. Polish entrepreneurs do not know about such issues as seed or venture capital, as they simply do not exist in Poland.

Growth of sales in high-technology small firms was analysed for the years 1995-1996, which was a period when the Polish economy had already overcome the economic crisis from the late 'eighties and the early 'nineties and was entering the phase of growth, while at the same time symptoms of the acceleration of technological entrepreneurship could be observed. During this period the vast majority of firms analysed (91.3 per cent) recorded real growth of sales in compared to 1994. The average growth of real sales (for growth firms) was very high and reached 87 per cent. It should be noted here that major variations in growth of sales were recorded: from 5 per cent to 260 per cent. External determinants of sales growth were revealed in sectoral variations. The most favourable conditions for sales growth seem to have appeared in the biotechnology, chemistry and pharmaceuticals sectors (growth of 120 per cent), and in informatics and telecommunications (growth of 103 per cent). By contrast, the smallest sales growth was recorded by electronic and electro-engineering firms (growth of 53 per cent).

Figure 4-1: Motives behind setting up small technology-based firms *

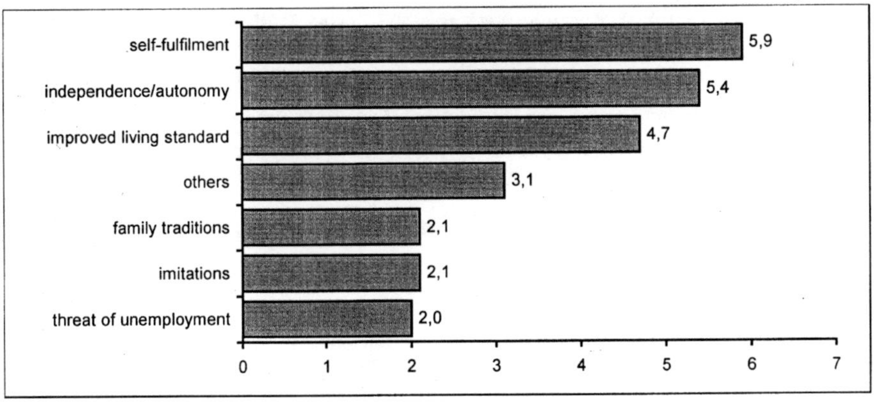

*– individual characteristics were assessed on a scale from 1 to 10

Source: Own calculations based on empirical research (N = 55).

The most important source of finance for investments made by the high-technology small firms analysed was profit generated by these firms. Almost 75 per cent of firms relied on this source of finance, and for 30 per cent it was the only source of finance for investments. The average share of investment financed from the firm's own profit amounted to 53.9 per cent of all investments made by these firms. The second important source of finance for investment is the owner's own savings, which may mean that high-technology firms also use their owners' own capital. A smaller role was played by bank loans, purchases on instalment plan or leasing. Worthy of note is the insignificant share of capital investment as a source for financing the growth of such firms.

The share of persons with a higher education background working in small technology-based firms is high, exceeding 52 per cent of the total workforce. This share is almost five times higher than in the Polish small business as a whole (Zienkowski 1998). It is comparable with the level of education in high-technology small firms in western countries, where the index surpasses 50 per cent (Oakey 1995).

The share of expenditure on research and development activity including research, design, laboratory, construction and other work is also quite high. The average share of these types of expenditure in the total turnover of the analysed firms is 17.2

per cent, and the median is 13 per cent. In the sample analysed, firms predominate in which the share of expenditure on R&D ranges between 10 per cent and 14 per cent, followed by firms allocating less than 10 per cent of their turnover for this purpose and those spending between 15 per cent and 19 per cent. About 13 per cent of firms made bigger outlays (over 25 per cent of turnover). The share of expenditure on R&D in the total turnover of high-technology firms – similarly to the share of employees with higher education – is negatively correlated with firm size. In micro-firms (1-5 employees) this index reaches 22 per cent, while in those with 6-20 employees it exceeds 17 per cent, and in firms with 21-100 employees it amounts to only 12.4 per cent. The biggest and, simultaneously, the oldest firms seem to be less dynamic and less innovative. The most innovative firms in this respect are those whose owners come from universities (22 per cent).

Figure 4-2: Types of innovations introduced by the analysed firms in the years 1993-1996

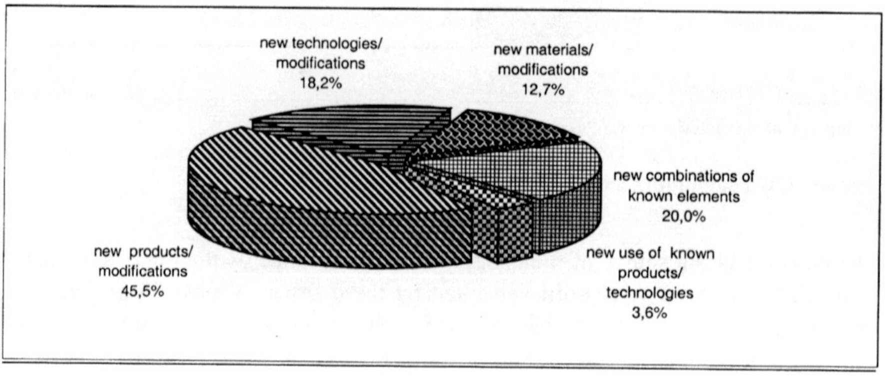

Source: Own calculations based on empirical research (N = 55).

All in all, the analysed firms were exploiting 174 technical innovations, which means that statistically 3.2 active innovations were exploited by one firm. These firms own 51 patents and 9 licences. Most firms have innovations (on average 2 to 3), which could be covered by legal protection, but their owners do not embark upon any procedures connected with this. Among the main reasons for such a situation the respondents listed: a too long preparatory period and complicated procedures, unfamiliarity with patent law, and high costs of patent protection. Some technical innovations were protected by law, but they could hardly be considered innovative even for these firms. This may be a testimony of apparent activities prompted by tax regulations, which allow bigger deductions for copyrights. A prevailing lack of interest in the protection of intellectual property can be observed.

Most firms (over 75 per cent) have introduced product, technological or material innovations. Product novelties predominate (45.5 per cent of firms), followed by new combinations of known elements and technological innovations. The share of new or modified materials and new applications of a known product or technology is quite small.

The high-technology firms analysed are characterised by a high intensity of changes. Over 70 per cent of firms steadily and constantly introduced innovations in their product range, technologies or materials over the years 1993-1996. The remaining 30 per cent introduced innovations sporadically and with varying intensity whenever such needs appeared.

Almost all firms analysed (96.4 per cent) use computer technologies (internal) in their activities, for production, design, sales, administration, and so on. The share of firms having access to external computer networks (e.g., internet, e-mail) is smaller although still fairly large (67.3 per cent). The above situation points to a high standard of modernity of equipment used by these firms, which allows them to introduce modern management methods and make effective use of diverse sources of scientific and technical information. It should be noted, however, that most of these firms did not have their own terminals linking them with external networks, but were using networks in a rather informal way through other institutions in which their owners had previously worked.

The analysed high-technology firms are involved in R&D activity, which is most frequently not separated organisationally (e.g. research units in departments of production, marketing, firm's office, etc.). This is the case in about 75 per cent of these firms. In 25 per cent of them R&D activity is conducted by separate organisational units such as departments of design, technology, research, and so on.

The firms under analysis assessed negatively the government's activity in the field of creating favourable conditions for their development. The ranking of particular factors showed that their most important problems were connected with the level of taxation and the protection of intellectual property. The main expectations of most analysed firms regarding government policy concerned the principles of running business activity (simplification and stability of regulations) and investment and R&D activity. Relatively smaller needs are stated by the firms in such fields as: easier access to information and consulting services in the sphere of technology and science, and improvement of the business infrastructure.

Figure 4-3: Main fields of government policy and regulations posing problems for firms *

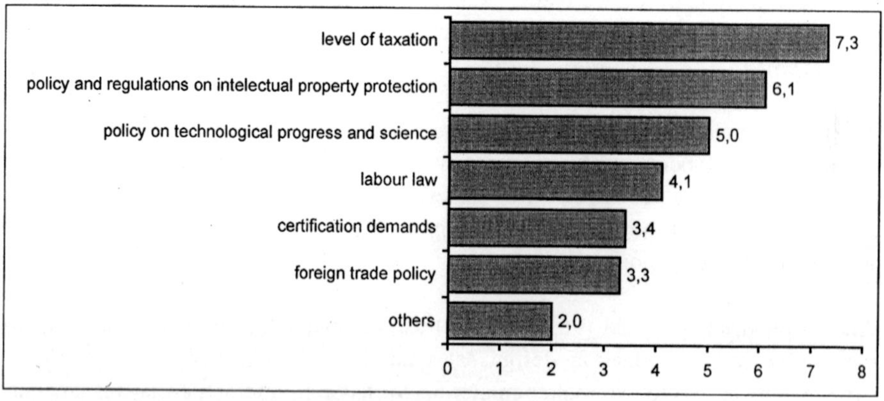

*– individual characteristics were assessed on a scale from 1 to 10

Source: Own calculations based on empirical research (N = 55).

As regards firms' expectations from local authorities, these were dominated by problems concerning their environment: promotion of inter-regional and international contacts, improvement of the local infrastructure, and support for the development of innovation and business support centres. According to 60-70 per cent of the analysed firms, these are the most important measures lying within the competencies of the local authorities which could help firms. Of smaller importance are local training programmes and the development of education and business services. It is noteworthy that small technology-based firms expect more involvement from the local authorities in seeking new business partners for them, and also in developing the local institutional infrastructure supporting entrepreneurship and technology transfer. Problems connected with the search for partners in business were considered by these firms to be among the most important problems which they cannot cope with by them selves.

5 Governmental Policy and Structure of the System of Entrepreneurship Support

Development of the sector of small and medium sized enterprises is of a spontaneous and uncontrolled character. Despite many declarations, the Polish government does very little to support this development. The lack of a cohesive, complementary entrepreneurial policy is clearly apparent. Governmental and ministerial programmes are strongly limited by technical and financial possibilities.[10] Industrial policy focuses on privatisation and restructuring traditional branches of industry. It should be underlined, however, that a perceptible increase of interest in entrepreneurship and the SMEs sector can be observed amongst the government and the Parliament. There is a growing consciousness that economic chances for Poland in the European Union are mainly based on a dynamic and competitive SMEs sector, not on the "dinosaurs" of the post-socialist economy (coal mining and metallurgy). The basis for governmental activities relating to the SMEs sector is constituted by two programmes elaborated in 1995 and 1999:

- "Small and medium sized enterprises in the national economy (1995)". The first document in Poland defining the policy towards small and medium sized enterprises till 1997. In the framework of the programme:
  - A lot of legislative initiatives were undertaken facilitating SMEs operations, including the act on economic activity, banking law;
  - the National Fund of Credit Guarantees was created (based on the budgetary sources) which is intended to facilitate SMEs access to bank credits (the activity of several years fructified in the granting of about 100 guarantees !!!);
  - the Polish Foundation for Promotion and Development of Small and Medium enterprises was created, which co-ordinates foreign support for the Polish SMEs. Among other activities, the Foundation has started to create the Domestic System of Services (DSS) in the form of local networks supporting SMEs in the range of information, advisory, training and financial services. The network consists of 130 business support centres;
  - the Agency of Technique and Technology was created, which aims at supporting technology transfer and facilitating the access of SMEs to new technologies. However, the activity of the Agency is strongly limited by insufficient financial resources.
- "Directions of governmental activity towards small and medium enterprises till 2002" (1999). This programme assumes creation of conditions for the broadest use of the development potential of the SMEs sector. The highest priority is given to activities aimed at increasing competitiveness, increasing exports and investment expenditure in the SMEs sector.

  Entrepreneurship in the widest sense was perceived by the Ministry of Labour and Social Policy as one of the ways of actively fighting unemployment. Financial (preferential loans) and training support was organised for the unemployed interested in starting up their own business. Also the Ministry of Agriculture has

---

[10] The attitude to this issue is especially apparent in the statement of the Minister of the Economy following governmental acceptance of the document "Assumptions of the governmental policy towards small and medium enterprises for the years 1998-2001" (...):"the government does not have money for an active policy towards SMEs, and documents such as "Assumptions..." are an indication of the good will of the ministry". See Nowe Zycie Gospodarcze 1998, no. 23, p. 10.

started to implement programmes of entrepreneurship support in rural regions, covering training, consulting and financial support for people starting their own businesses.

The development of local initiatives aiming at the creation of various non-profit business centres (mainly thanks to support from the European Union, the World Bank and western countries) should be considered as a success. At present there are operating in Poland (Matusiak et al. 1999):

- 49 business incubators and technology centres, that have enabled the creation and development of over 2 000 new firms, creating over 10 000 work places;
- 23 centres for technology transfer and information, offering assistance in the area of technology transfer;
- 147 training-advisory centres, that trained and offered consultations to over 300 thousand persons;
- 51 quasi-bank loan and guarantee funds that enabled creation and development of over 3 500 of small firms;
- one technology park, and two others are at the advanced stage of organisation and implementation.

The range of actions by the institutions mentioned is still too narrow compared to the firms' needs. There are no mechanisms of financial support from governmental and regional programmes of entrepreneurship support.

6 Summing Up

Owing to the introduction of democratic rules, entrepreneurship and small and medium-sized enterprises are becoming a basis for processes of transformation of the economy as well as Polish society. Continuous strengthening of market economy rules and changes in ownership structure have been observed, to the benefit of the private sector. Small and medium-sized enterprises are the most dynamically developing sector of the Polish economy. From a marginal role in the centrally planned economy at the end of the eighties, after ten years of transformation they today generate 65 per cent of the value added of all enterprises, provide jobs for 61 per cent of labour force and finance 41 per cent of all investments in the economy.

Despite significant effects of a quantitative nature, however, the major part of the development of entrepreneurship was arbitrage-related and resulted from the transformation of the economy, privatisation and liberalisation, without any necessity for becoming involved in innovation projects. The Polish entrepreneur can still compete with relatively cheap labour and an ability to fill in market niches, rather than through product quality and a propensity to innovation. A network of small and medium entities able to co-operate with large domestic and foreign enterprises has not been developed as yet. Meanwhile, it can be more and more easily seen that the "transformation potential" has been slowly eroded for several years now. To achieve success in the market, potential entrepreneurs and small and medium-sized domestic firms have to strive, to an increasing degree, for innovations and new technological solutions. The need for innovations in Polish firms is intensifying now in view of the requirements posed by the Single European Market and globalisation processes. Problems connected with the adaptation of Polish producers to EU norms and standards can already be seen in integration processes today. There is a danger that a big part of small firms will be producing omitting EU standards, which will eliminate a possibility of selling their products in the EU internal market. Both the government and regional authorities should support start-up processes in business as well as support activity of hitherto existing firms.

High-technology small firms are a new, rare, although quite dynamic phenomenon in Poland, they represent the economy's modern segment. Their main problem is a relative isolation, meagre resources and, in particular, finance, small experience. Polish garage entrepreneurs operate – unlike their counterparts in highly developed countries – in isolation, without indispensable financial, organisational and logistic support, and definite systemic preferences (grants, loans, investment reliefs etc.). Deficit of high risk funds at different stages of financing an innovation project is felt most acutely. The market of finance for innovation projects, especially as regards initial phases of technology development and commercialisation (seed and start-up capital) practically does not exist. What is meant here are different types of funds and programmes of financing, the shortage of which is felt very strongly by innovative firms and institutions supporting innovations and technology transfer. All attempts should be made to create more favourable conditions and tax and legal preferences for establishing of various types of domestic institutions and programmes of financing early phases of innovation projects. Wide participation of public finance, including budgetary and regional funds, in financing these projects should be considered advisable. Absence of support system for technological entrepreneurship limits strongly setting up and development of new innovative business units. It is urgently necessary to give a much stronger pro-innovation edge to economic-financial solutions serving SMEs.

Literature

Grudzewski, W. M.; Hejduk, I. K. (1997): Akademicka przedsiebiorczosc zródlem rozwoju nowoczesnej techniki i technologii, "Ekonomika i Organizacja Przedsiebiorstwa", no 9/10.

GUS (1999a, Ed.): Zmiany strukturalne grup podmiotów gospodarki narodowej w I pólroczu., Warszawa.

GUS (1999b, Ed.): Nauka i technika w 1997 roku, Warszawa.

Matusiak, K. B. (1998): Nowe tendencje we wspieraniu innowacji, przedsiebiorczosci i transferu technologii. In: Matusiak, K. B.; Stawasz E. (Eds.): Przedsiebiorczosc i transfer technologii. Polska perspektywa, Lódz/Zyrardówm.

Matusiak, K. B., Niesiolowski, T. (1999): Osrodki innowacji i przedsiebiorczosci. SOOIPP-Raport 2000, MPiPS, Warszawa.

Oakey, R. (1995): High-Technology New Firms: Variable Barriers to Growth. London: PCP.

Oakey, R.; Rothwell, R.; Cooper, S. (1988): The Management of Innovation in High-Technology Small Firms. London: Pinter Publishers Limited.

Piasecki, B. (1997): Przedsiebiorczosc i mala firma. Teoria i praktyka. Uniwersytet Lódzki, Lódz.

Piasecki, B.; Rogut, A.; Smallbone, D. (1996): Mocne i slabe strony malych i srednich przedsiebiorstw produkcyjnych w Polsce w 1995 roku oraz rekomendacje dla polityki. USAID, GEMINI-PEDS Project, Lódz, Londyn.

Polska F. (1998, Ed.): Warunki prowadzenia dzialalnosci gospodarczej przez MSP w Polsce i krajach Unii Europejskiej, Promocji i Rozwoju Malych i Srednich Przedsiebiorstw. Warszawa.

Roberts, E. B. (1991): Entrepreneurs in High Technology. New York: Oxford University Press.

Rothwell, R. (1994): The changing Nature of the Innovation Process: Implications for SMEs. In: Oakey, R. (Ed.): New technology-based firms in the 1990s, London: PCP, pp. 224-242.

Stawasz, E. (1998): Mala firma technologiczna na polskim rynku. In: Matusiak, K. B.; Stawasz E. (Eds.): Przedsiebiorczosc i transfer technologii. Polska perspektywa, Lódz/Zyrardówm.

Zienkowski L. (1998, Ed.): Stan rozwój sektora malych i srednich przedsiebiorstw w latach 1994-1996. Polska Fundacja Promocji i Rozwoju Malych i Srednich Przedsiebiorstw, Warszawa.

Small Businesses in Russia

Natalia Kovaleva

1 History of Small Enterprises in Modern Russia

The small business is considered as necessary in modern Russia and is claimed to be one of the priorities of a state policy oriented towards the development of favourable conditions for private initiative by Russian citizens. A competitive market economy cannot develop without small businesses.

The process of formation of Russian small businesses can be divided into several stages (Blinov 1998):

- In the 1970s the first ways for an alternative economic activity appeared outside the state planned system. This brought about the necessity to legalise this activity. Thus, in 1978 the State Law "On the individual labour activity of citizens of the USSR" was adopted in order to regulate the activity of individual enterprises. At that time the first specific soviet enterprises appeared, such as seasonal construction teams, gold-digging co-operatives (so called "artels"), youth centres for creative technical activity etc. These soon became transformed into different commercial entities.
- Ten years later about 200 000 people had joined business activity. In 1988 the State Law "On co-operation in the USSR" legalised small business. The number of co-operatives increased. Nevertheless they did not play any significant role in the Russian economy because as a rule they were parts of state enterprises and were organisationally attached to the state enterprises. Small state enterprises existed in this country but their role in the economy was very limited.
- In 1990 a new impetus was given to the development of small businesses. The Decree of the government of the Russian Federation regarding special measures on the establishing and development of small enterprises was adopted; one of its main features was the introduction of privileges for small enterprises. In the same year the State Law of the Russian Federation "On enterprises and business activity" was issued. According to this law, business activity was defined as independent activity by persons or their teams with the aim of gaining a profit.

However, although these efforts to reform the Russian economy did provide some opportunities for the formation of small businesses, they were nevertheless inefficient because the overall state planning system was preserved.

The year 1992 can be considered as a starting point for the most recent stage of small business formation in Russia. This year was associated with the beginning of active privatisation processes in the field of services and trade. Although the process was slowed down by the lack of money in the hands of employers, the lack of credits, the reduction of solvent demand from the population, and also by the destructive effects of state policy with regard to taxes and prices, the number of such enterprises rapidly increased. For several years Russia lived in the conditions of a "wild market". It was time to accumulate the starting capital.

By the beginning of 1995 the main features of the market system started to emerge more efficiently. The state began to pay more attention to the development of small business. The Federal Law "On the state support of small business in the Russian Federation" was issued. According to this law, a small business is a commercial organisation in which

- the authorised capital includes a contribution not exceeding 25 per cent from the Russian Federation, subjects of the Russian Federation, public and religious organisations (associations), charitable or other foundations,
- the share owned by one or several legal persons that are not small business does not exceed 25 per cent and
- the average number of the personnel in the year under consideration does not exceed: 100 persons in industry, construction and transport; 60 persons in agriculture and R&D sphere; 50 persons in wholesale trade; 30 persons in retail trade and consumer services; 50 persons in other branches or fields of activity.

Natural persons who are acting in this sphere without setting up an enterprise are also regarded as small businesses.

By this time the economy of small enterprises had assumed a certain importance, giving rise to the need for a reliable overview of their activity. The statistical observation of small enterprises was organised.

2 The Relevance of Small Businesses Today

Since 1996, a regular statistical survey of the activity of small enterprises has been conducted in Russia. This period is, of course, rather short to derive serious conclusions. In any case the statistics have recorded the initial period of small business development and formed a basis for further observation.

According to the data of the State Statistical Committee (Russian Statistical Yearbook 1999) from 1997 to 1999, the number of small enterprises increased slightly during that period, from 841 737 to 868 008. In 1998 the process practically stopped. At the beginning of 1999 the number of active small enterprises in Russia was only 0.8 per cent more than one year previously and only 3.1 per cent higher than at the beginning of 1997 (table 2-1).

Table 2-1: Small enterprises by branches, beginning of year

	Total number			Structure (in %)		
	1997	1998	1999	1997	1998	1999
Total	**841 737**	**861 063**	**868 008**	**100**	**100**	**100**
Manufacturing	131 878	134 810	136 117	15.7	15.6	15.7
Agriculture	10 879	11 899	13 759	1.3	1.4	1.6
Construction	137 970	142 087	137 511	16.4	16.5	15.8
Transport	17 506	18 588	18 570	2.1	2.2	2.1
Communication	2 865	2 733	3 213	0.3	0.3	0.4
Trade and public catering	359 357	372 836	386 110	42.7	43.3	44.5
Wholesale trade of products for production & technical use	14 593	14 268	13 214	1.7	1.7	1.5
Information & computation services	6 167	6 355	5 201	0.7	0.7	0.6
Real estate operations	3 859	4 625	5 865	0.5	0.5	0.7
Commercial activities providing operation of the market	35 919	35 955	35 244	4.3	4.2	4.0
Other activities in the field of material production	17 397	17 236	18 890	2.1	2.0	2.2
Housing	2 797	3 949	5 062	0.3	0.5	0.6
Consumer services	10 190	11 252	9 159	1.2	1.3	1.0
Health care	11 008	15 385	17 239	1.3	1.8	2.0
Education	6 655	6 956	6 668	0.8	0.8	0.8
Culture and arts	6 488	7 948	8 114	0.8	0.9	0.9
Science and science services	46 710	43 818	38 812	5.5	5.1	4.5
Finance, credit, insurance etc.	10 773	7 839	7 494	1.3	0.9	0.9
Miscellaneous	8 726	2 524	1 766	1.0	0.2	0.2

Source: Russian Statistical Yearbook (1999, p. 280).

The situation is characterised by different growth rates in the number of small enterprises representing various branches (table 2-2). An increase can be seen housing (81.0 per cent), health care (56.6 per cent), real estate operations (52.0 per cent), agriculture (26.5 per cent), communications (12.1 per cent), trade and public catering (7.4 per cent), and manufacturing (3.2 per cent). A decrease is observed in more or less all other branches. These include the sectors of "science and science ser-vices" and "finance, credit, insurance etc.", both of which show considerable decrease rates (16.9 per cent and 30.4 per cent respectively).

Table 2-2: Growth rate of number of small enterprises: 1997-1999 (in per cent)

	1998 relative to 1997 (in per cent)	**1999 relative to 1998** (in per cent)	**1999 relative to 1997** (in per cent)
Total	**102.3**	**100.8**	**103.1**
Manufacturing	102.2	101.0	103.2
Agriculture	109.4	115.6	126.5
Construction	103.0	96.8	99.7
Transport	106.2	99.9	106.1
Communication	95.4	117.6	112.1
Trade and public catering	103.8	103.6	107.4
Wholesale trade of products for production & technical use	97.8	92.6	90.6
Information & computation services	103.0	81.8	84.3
Real estate operations	119.8	126.8	152.0
Commercial activities providing operation of the market	100.1	98.0	98.1
Other activities in the field of material production	99.1	109.6	108.6
Housing	141.2	128.2	181.0
Consumer services	110.4	81.4	89.9
Health care	139.8	112.1	156.6
Education	104.5	95.9	100.2
Culture and arts	122.5	102.1	125.1
Science and science services	93.8	88.6	83.1
Finance, credit, insurance etc.	72.8	95.6	69.6

Source: Russian Statistical Yearbook (1999, p. 280).

These trends gave rise to some changes in the distribution of small enterprises by branches of industry (table 2-1). The main tendencies in this respect are connected with the expansion of the share of trade and public catering (from 42.7 per cent to 44.5 per cent of all small enterprises) and the reduction of the shares of construction (from 16.4 to 15.8 per cent), commercial activities providing operation of the market (from 4.3 to 4.0 per cent), science and science services (from 5.5 to 4.5 per cent). At the same time the "leaders" remained the same and thus in 1998 the most numerous branches were trade and public catering (386 110 small enterprises), construction (137 511), manufacturing (136 117), science and science services (38 812), and commercial activity providing operation of the market (35 244). The situation is different in such branches as communication, housing, information & computation services, real estate operations, education, culture and arts, finance, credit, insurance etc., and consumer services (in 1999 none of these branches had a share exceeding one per cent).

Table 2-3: Small enterprises by economic regions, beginning of year

	Total number			Structure (in percent)		
	1997	1998	1999	1997	1998	1999
Total	**841 737**	**861 063**	**868 008**	**100**	**100**	**100**
Northern	18 739	17 476	20 703	2.2	2.0	2.4
North-Western	104 624	118 524	129 259	12.4	13.8	14.9
of which St.-Petersburg	89 656	102 717	111 754	10.7	11.9	12.9
Central	271 008	267 610	266 056	32.2	31.1	30.7
of which Moscow	183 508	181 340	175 163	21.8	21.1	20.2
Volga-Vyatka	26 373	27 729	27 207	3.1	3.2	3.1
Central Black-Earth	22 970	22 668	26 168	2.7	2.6	3.0
Volga	73 340	72 927	78 034	8.7	8.5	9.0
North-Caucasian	69 418	83 977	79 484	8.2	9.8	9.2
Ural	74 753	81 863	85 565	8.9	9.5	9.9
West-Siberian	90 632	88 850	75 687	10.8	10.3	8.7
East-Siberian	44 503	37 047	35 597	5.3	4.3	4.1
Far-Eastern	39 247	35 746	35 077	4.7	4.2	4.0
Kaliningrad Region	6 130	6 646	9 171	0.7	0.8	1.1

Source: Russian Statistical Yearbook (1999, pp. 281-282).

The majority of small enterprises (89.6 per cent) are private property and only 10.4 per cent represent a mixed form of property. The share of completely private enterprises exceeds 90 per cent in such branches as construction, trade and public catering, housing and only in one – finance, credit, insurance etc. – it is lower than 50 per cent. A high degree of regional differentiation can be observed in the formation of small enterprise networks (table 2-3). By the beginning of 1999, about one third of the total number of small enterprises (30.7 per cent) were located in the Central Region (about two thirds of these being in Moscow) and 14.5 per cent were in the North Western region (most of these in St.-Petersburg). Other centres for small business are the Volga, North Caucasian, Ural and West Siberian regions (the corresponding indicator for each of these four regions is nearly 10 per cent). All the other economic regions have individual shares less than half this size.

Regarding the number of small enterprises (table 2-4), in 1998 a growth tendency was maintained in the North-Western region (13.3 per cent growth rate in 1997 and 9.1 per cent in 1998), the Ural region (9.5 and 4.5 per cent respectively) and the Kaliningrad region (8.4 and 38.0 per cent respectively). In some regions (Northern, Central Black-Earth) following a decrease in 1997/98, a small increase was observed in the next year. All other regions displayed an opposite tendency, the lowest growth indicators being in the East-Siberian (decrease by 16.8 and 3.9 per cent respectively) and Far-East (decrease by 8.9 and 1.9 per cent respectively) economic regions. Also among these "declining" regions are the "leaders" – the Central Region and Moscow.

Table 2-4: Growth rate of small enterprises by economic regions (in per cent)

	1998 relative to 1997 (in per cent)	**1999 relative to 1998** (in per cent)	**1999 relative to 1997** (in per cent)
Total	**102.3**	**100.8**	**103.1**
Northern	93.3	118.5	110.5
North-Western	113.3	109.1	123.5
of which St.-Petersburg	114.6	108.8	124.6
Central	98.7	99.4	98.2
of which Moscow	98.8	96.6	95.5
Volga-Vyatka	105.1	98.1	103.2
Central Black-Earth	98.7	115.4	113.9
Volga	99.4	107.0	106.4
North-Caucasian	121.0	94.6	114.5
Ural	109.5	104.5	114.5
West-Siberian	98.0	85.2	83.5
East-Siberian	83.2	96.1	80.0
Far-Eastern	91.1	98.1	89.4
Kaliningrad Region	108.4	138.0	149.6

Source: Russian Statistical Yearbook (1999, pp. 281-282).

In 1998, the total number of employees in small enterprises (excluding those occupied as combined or contract employees) constituted 6 207 800 persons, that is 12 per cent of all employed persons in Russia. In some branches, however, the share of small business employees in total employment is relatively high. In addition to this figure, 717 900 persons were occupied in "combined" jobs in small enterprises and 475 700 persons were occupied as contract workers. Thus small business provided employment in one form or another for more than 7 million people.

Table 2-5: Structure of employees in small enterprises by branches, 1998 (in per cent)

	Main personnel	Combined job-holders	Contract workers
Total	**100**	**100**	**100**
Manufacturing	21.9	17.9	19.9
Agriculture	2.2	0.8	0.9
Construction	21.7	18.0	26.6
Transport	2.9	2.2	2.9
Communication	0.4	0.7	0.7
Trade and public catering	35.5	32.4	19.0
Wholesale trade of products for production & technical use	1.5	1.2	1.2
Information & computation services	0.4	0.6	0.5
Real estate operations	0.4	0.6	1.0
Commercial activity providing operation of the market	3.1	4.5	3.4
Other activities in the field of material production	2.7	2.4	5.6
Housing	0.4	0.6	1.4
Consumer services	1.0	1.8	0.4
Health care	1.6	2.7	3.3
Education	0.7	2.0	0.9
Culture and the arts	0.6	1.3	0.8
Science and science services	2.4	9.5	10.2
Finance, credit, insurance etc.	0.6	0.7	1.1

Source: Russian Statistical Yearbook (1999, pp. 281-282).

With respect to the structure of "small business" employment by branches, the top positions in 1998 were gained by trade and public catering (35.5 per cent of all "small business" employment), manufacturing (21.9 per cent) and construction (21.7 per cent) (table 2-5). In all other branches the percentage share was 3 per cent or less. During 1998, total employment in small businesses decreased by 4.7 per cent. The most serious decrease occurred in such branches as housing, science & science services, and transport, while only two branches – commercial activity providing operation of the market and trade and public catering – showed positive dynamics.

Nearly 30 per cent of employees work in small enterprises in the Central Region (nearly 20 per cent in Moscow). Other regions where employment in small businesses is relatively high are the North-Western, North-Caucasian, East-Siberian, Ural and Volga regions (around 10 per cent).

Production output from the main activities of small enterprises amounted to 231.8 billion roubles in 1998. Its structure by branches of the economy is shown in table 2-6. The main input from small businesses into the economy in 1998 was made by such branches as construction, trade and public catering, and manufacturing.

Table 2-6: Shares of production output from the main activities of small enterprises, by sectors of the economy, 1998 (in per cent)

	1998
Total	**100**
Manufacturing	24.2
Transport	3.5
Construction	26.1
Trade and public catering	26.1
Commercial activities providing operation of the market	3.0
Science & science services	3.5
Others	13.6

Source: Mazurova (1999, p. 5).

The total investment expenditure of small business constituted 22.5 billion roubles in 1998. The leaders were trade and public catering, manufacturing, construction (table 2-7).

During 1998 changes took place in the branch structure of investment expenditure in small enterprises: in 1997, investments in the construction sector ranked first, constituting 41 per cent of all investment expenditure by small enterprises; in 1998, trade and public catering was the leading sector in this respect.

Table 2-7: Investment expenditure of small enterprises, by sectors of the economy

	1998	
	Mln roubles	**Percentage of total**
Total	**22 541,9**	**100**
Manufacturing	3 938,7	17.5
Agriculture	208,2	0.9
Transport	238,8	1.1
Construction	5 911,6	26.2
Trade and public catering	8 608,8	38.2
Commercial activities providing operation of the market	731,9	3.2
Housing	415,3	1.8
Science & science services	686,3	3.0

Source: Mazurova (1999, p. 5).

3 Public Support for Small Businesses

Governments in practically all developed countries provide small businesses with strong economic and social support. The necessity for such support is recognised in Russia as well. Some steps have been taken in this respect. However, as happens very often in Russia, the gap between the formal declaration of economic and social responsibility of the state and the real situation is very wide. Due to the lack of necessary financial support, as well as the lack of efficient co-ordination between the action of different executors of concrete measures, and also due to mistakes in organisational issues, the Second Federal Programme for the support of small businesses for 1996–1997 was not fulfilled. According to official data, only half of the 81 measures laid down in the programme were fulfilled; one quarter were partially fulfilled and almost the same number of items were not fulfilled. At the end of the 1990's a recent draft of the Third Programme of state support for small businesses was being considered at the State Duma (Vilenskiy 1999). The implementation of regional programmes is somewhat better. This is explained by the high interest of regional and local authorities in the development of local small businesses as a means of smoothing out acute economic and social problems.

In Russia a certain system of state support for small businesses has emerged. In June 1995 the main co-ordinating body – The State Committee of the Russian Federation for the Support and Development of Small Business – was established. Despite this system, the major part of respective problems is resolved on a regional level. Attached to local executive bodies, various councils, co-ordinating committees, working groups were also created. There exist about 60 foundations for small business support which work as independent organisations and have the status of legal entities.

More than ten oblates (regional administrative units) and republics have adopted corresponding local legislative and regulatory documents. These are: Karelia, Chuvashia, Komy, Mordovia, Irkutsk, Moscow and Moscow oblate, Leningrad oblate, Kirov oblate, and others (Blinov 1998). In many of these, however, it has not been possible to realise the perspective ideas formulated in the relevant documents, because of the lack of corresponding mechanisms. At the same time there are also positive examples. In some places regional tax benefits and other privileges for small enterprises have been adopted.

Small enterprises receive other kind of support aimed at giving their target groups access to technological, financial, labour and information resources. Regional and municipal infrastructures of small businesses support agencies are being formed. Activities primarily take the form of developing business incubators and specialised consultation institutions. A system of training and refresher courses has been organised for the managerial personnel of small businesses. While relying upon support to some extent, small enterprises are encouraged to try to solve their problems on their own, by uniting to form various unions and associations capable of dealing with some general tasks, including the information and legal support of small enterprises.

The elaboration of republic, oblate and local programmes is of great importance. Their realisation facilitates the shaping of relevant economic, organisational, financial and – to some extent – social conditions. This enables a market infrastructure of small business to be formed. Small businesses can be directed towards the solution of the most urgent current regional problems, their business share can be expanded through the privatisation of local property, and an economic mechanism can be created for the regulation of business activity.

It is necessary to say some words about the significance of mortgage banks, tender centres, insurance, deposit, investment companies in the formation of the financial and investment resources of small business. These companies can have a great input into the development of small enterprises. They have been organised under ministries and departments in different branches of the economy. There are special leasing companies oriented towards the support of small business. Taking into account the results of leasing activity in small businesses, the government supports such activities. In 1996, 120 billion roubles were made available to small enterprises using leasing services.

State financial support for small business is provided within the framework of "Garartija" (i.e. guaranty), a programme that expands the access of small enterprises (especially those operating in priority branches) to financial resources, creating opportunities for the accumulation of starting capital and for more effective use of the money accumulated by the various foundations which work with small enterprises.

It is clear now that the effectiveness of the system of state support for small enterprises is ensured by the activity of special centres that provide informational and analytical services. Central to this is the Chamber of Commerce and Industry, which has its network of regional branch offices and its own infrastructure in Russia and abroad. The offices give substantial support to small enterprises. Support covers registration, information and analytical, legal and consulting services, including protecting the interests of Russian businesses abroad. The Chamber has its own network of training and business centres, business schools, consulting centres and audit offices, i.e. all the infrastructure market components that are required for small business.

4 Innovative Activity in Small Business

The results of the survey conducted for the whole of Russia in 1995 by the Centre for Science Research and Statistics (Gokhberg/Kuznetsova 1997), showed that only 5.6 per cent of Russian enterprises were engaged in innovative activity at that time. As a rule, the greatest capacity for innovations was shown by large enterprises with a relatively stable financial position and diversified economic activities. Nearly half of the innovating enterprises had more than 1 000 employees and 40 per cent had a workforce between 200 and 1 000. Insofar as small enterprises were taken into account, the share of small innovative enterprises was considerably lower. Nearly 90 per cent of R&D firms in the survey were classified as large or medium-sized (among them 60 per cent as large) and only 12.1 per cent as small enterprises (1.7 per cent with less than 49 employees; 2.7 per cent with 50 – 99 employees and 7.7 per cent with a workforce of 100 –199; table 4-1).

The innovative activity of small enterprises is well illustrated by the results of a special survey conducted in December 1998 – January 1999 in the Resource Centre for Small Business (Alimova et al. 1999) in order to analyse the situation and main trends in the development of innovative processes. The total number of enterprises in the survey was 153. The sectoral distribution showed 108 firms representing various industrial activities: 17 construction firms, 52 science & science service enterprises, 21 information and computation service enterprises. In some cases firms stated that they belonged to more than one branch of industry, giving rise to multiple entries. In addition, twenty-five company heads were interviewed and 282 persons took part in the questionnaire survey.

Table 4-1: Distribution of innovative enterprises by size 1995 (in per cent)

Number of employees	Enterprises engaging in innovative activity – Total	Innovatively active R&D enterprises
Below 49	1.7	1.7
50-99	4.2	2.7
100-199	11.8	7.7
200-499	19.6	15.2
500-999	16.3	15.3
1 000-4 999	35.1	41.2
5 000-9 999	7.3	10.1
10 000 and more	4.0	6.1

Source: Gokhberg/Kuznetsova (1997, p. 18).

The survey defined innovative activity as a process oriented towards implementation of the results of R&D work or other S&T achievements in a new or improved product or in a new or improved technological process, realised in practice. Two thirds of the enterprises in the survey engaged in innovative activity. The main motives for the innovative activity of small enterprises were identified. They were: increased competitiveness, improvements to production quality, assimilation of new markets, expansion of the market segment, extending product range.

This demonstrates the emergence of a new mentality in the small business environment, i.e. right from the beginning the creation and selection of the innovative ideas is aimed at satisfying market demand. However, there are other specific difficulties that have to be overcome in the process of establishing a small enterprise. The results of the survey showed that the "number one problem" here is to attract the financial resources necessary to complete the research work. The second group of problems covers aspects such as poor marketing support of the innovative project and lack of equipment. The third complex includes problems associated with the search for specific information, copyright protection, lack of contacts with potential suppliers, testing and certification of production, and lack of premises. All problems mentioned above are production related. However, there are also problems of a different nature stipulated by the necessity to exploit market conditions as fast as possible. It was discovered that the necessity for market-oriented behaviour by enterprises makes managers of small enterprises focus more attention on other managerial problems.

At the present time 76 per cent of the 282 leaders in the survey realise that they do have managerial problems. The most serious of these problems are associated with: strategic planning of the activity of the enterprise, analysis and identification of hidden problems, analysis and assessment of the environment, planning of current activities (table 4-2). The origin of the difficulties indicated in the survey is to be found in the instability and uncertainty of economic development.

Table 4-2: Main managerial problems: viewpoint of the managers of small enterprises (as a percentage of the total number of responses; multiple occurence)

Managerial problem	Distribution of answers
Strategic planning of the activity of the enterprise	40
Analysis and identification of hidden problems	27
Analysis and assessment of the environment	23
Planning of current activities	21
Creation of an effective system for the control of task realisation	16
Formation of the innovation support system	14
Personnel management	14
Organisation of effective stock-tacking	12
Formation of new management structure	7
Analysis of results of the enterprise's activity	6

Source: Alimova et al. (1999, p.20).

It is interesting that there is a strong correlation between managerial problems and the activity of the enterprise: the better the results of the enterprise's activities, the larger the number of managers who specifically mention managerial problems. This shows that good results of the enterprise's innovative activity push them into activities in the managerial domain.

75 per cent of respondents identified the most difficult fields of managerial activity for the leaders of small enterprises (table 4-3). Finance, commerce and market behaviour are top of the list.

About 70 per cent of the respondents recognise the necessity for using new managerial methods, the so-called managerial innovations, in different spheres of their enterprises' activity. At the same time they point out various factors which prevent this. The main ones are the lack of financial resources, time and information about effective managerial innovations.

Table 4-3: The most difficult fields of management, from the viewpoint of leaders of small enterprises (as a percentage of total number of responses; multiple occurence)

The field of management	Distribution of answers
Finance	42
Commerce	34
Market behaviour	34
Formation of an effective management system	15
Management of innovations	11
Management of production activity	10
Management of personnel	9
Management of material & technical resources of the enterprise	8

Source: Alimova et al. (1999, p.21).

5 Small Enterprises in the R&D Sphere – an Outlook

The dynamics of small business in the R&D sphere are illustrated by the data in table 5-1.

Table 5-1: Small R&D business in Russia

	Number of enterprises, (in thousands)	Main personnel, (in thousands)	Combined job-holders (in thousands)	Contract workers (in thousands)
1996	46,7	161,7	79,1	226,2
1997	43,8	174,3	85,6	249,3
1998	38,8	146,3	68,5	48,3

Source: Science in Russia (1999, p.14).

In 1998, 38,8 thousand of small enterprises were operating in the sector of R&D; this constituted 4.5 per cent of the total number of small enterprises in Russia at that time. Most of them (82 per cent) were completely privately owned. 146,3 thousand persons were fully employed in small R&D enterprises. In addition 68,5 thousand employees performed combined jobs and 48,3 thousand persons were contract employees. It is necessary to underline that all these indicators demonstrate a declining trend. The economic crisis of August 1998 undermined the development of small businesses in the R&D sector. Their production output in 1998 (compared to 1997) decreased by 13.6 per cent, and the investment expenditure by 3.5 per cent (Mazurova 1999).

The optimal effectiveness of the work of small enterprises is determined by innovative technological activity which is not linked with the solution of fundamental problems and does not depend on complex co-operations. The main factors that favour the increase of innovative activity are the following: qualified personnel, strong motivation to engage in innovation activities, a good understanding of the market situation and the ability to deal with changes. At the same time poor management, tax burdens, a lack of efficient business services for small enterprises, and – particularly for small businesses in R&D – a lack of technological infrastructure, hamper the innovative activity of small enterprises.

Taking into consideration the important role played by small R&D enterprises in strengthening the innovative process, and their huge innovative potential, it is precisely enterprises of this kind which require special state support. Of great importance is the integration of small enterprises into stronger framework structures. The forms such integration takes may be very different. The "pluses" of this idea lie in the formation of guaranteed markets for small enterprises. An extensive network of technoparks, business-incubators and other innovation structures can also promote the development of small business. Here such enterprises can receive support from expert resources, can be given assistance in selecting innovative offers, R&D projects and programmes oriented towards the creation and implementation of new equipment and technologies, can be helped to estimate the risks connected with the implementation of such offers; they can receive support in carrying out research work and transferring its results to industry. Besides, such structures support small enterprises in the field of R&D by proving them with operating premises and equipment. They provide legal, financial, marketing, economic and other business services and assist in the commercial protection of intellectual property. In Russia, positive examples of innovative structures and activities of this kind do exist. The necessity now is to disseminate them actively. Here it is the role of federal government, as well as the governments of the Russian regions, to foster the dissemination of innovation structures by appropriate legislation.

Literature

Alimova, T.; Afanas'eva, T.; Pudenko, T.; Sapsay, B. (1999): Innovative Processes in Small Businesses. Voprosy Statistiki 8, pp. 7-42 (in Russian).

Blinov, A. (1998): The State Support of Small Businesses in the Russian Regions. Business 11-12, 14-15 (in Russian).

Gokhberg, L.; Kuznetsova, I. (1997): Technological Innovations in Russia. Moscow. Centre for Science Research and Statistics – CSRS (in Russian).

Mazurova, G. (1999): Small Enterprises in Russia: 1998, Voprosy Statistiki. 8, pp. 3-7 (in Russian).

Russian Statistical Yearbook (1999). Moscow. Goscomstat (in Russian).

Science in Russia (1999): Statistical Yearbook. Moscow. CSRS (in Russian).

Vilenskiy, A. (1999): Financial Support for Small Businesses. Economist 9, pp. 88-90 (in Russian).

Small and Medium Sized Enterprises in Hungary

Friederike Welter

1 Introduction

One of the important issues facing CEECs in the transformation from centrally planned to market economies is the need to develop SMEs. The potential role of SMEs includes generating employment and thereby possibly absorbing labour surpluses which result from economic restructuring, contributing to the development of a competitive economy with diversified structures, and being a source of innovation. Data for the European Union (EU) illustrates the important contribution of SMEs: They account for 99 per cent of all enterprises, 66 per cent of employment and turnover. In Central and Eastern Europe rapid progress with transformation was accompanied in most countries by a rapidly evolving private sector including SMEs due to privatisation and the formation of new firms.

The article will concentrate on the development of SMEs and their structures as well as on the institutional and policy framework in Hungary. The first part looks at private entrepreneurship and SMEs under socialism whilst the second part describes the "origin" of Hungarian entrepreneurs after socialism. Part three deals with SME development, part four with the structure of the SME sector and its contribution to the national economy during the 1990s. Part five analyses the institutional framework and SME policies of the Hungarian government. Part six summarises the findings and considers the "fitness" of SMEs in Hungary regarding their EU accession.

2 SMEs and Entrepreneurship in Hungary Under Socialism

Although in Hungary private entrepreneurship lost its major role with the introduction of a centrally planned economic system, different forms of private entrepreneurship co-existed beside state ownership and entrepreneurship within state enterprises during the socialist period. In this regard, one can distinguish between the formal and the grey economy (consisting of the second and the illegal economy), whose "boundaries" frequently changed following political trends of liberalising and restricting private ownership and entrepreneurship (Welter 1996). The formal economy included state enterprises, co-operatives and legalised private businesses such as small family businesses, mainly craft firms. The term second economy refers to any form of unlicensed but tolerated private entrepreneurial activities, including unlicensed activities in the private sector that were not officially recorded, as well as the clandestine use of state property (e.g., raw materials, machines, labour, services) for private business activities (Dallago 1990). It can also be applied to the so-called "parallel circuits" of state firms and co-operatives that were motivated by official enterprises searching for ways to meet planning targets (Kerblay 1977). Finally, during the socialist period the illegal economy was made up of quasi-criminal activities within state enterprises (bribes, theft of resources) and also criminal private activities.

Employment in private enterprises played only a minor role during the first years of socialism in Hungary. In 1949 private employment accounted for 20 per cent of all non-agricultural employment; this share decreased to 3 per cent in 1980 (Kornai 1995). Most private enterprises were nationalised during 1949-1953, in 1958 private craft entrepreneurs had to join production co-operatives (Gabor/Horvath 1987). This was accompanied by a shift from smaller to larger firms. From 1958 to 1968 the share of small firms with less than 100 employees decreased from 28 per cent to 11 per cent, the share of large enterprises with more than 1 000 employees grew from a mere 10 per cent to 37 per cent (Kornai 1995). Moreover, this development went hand in hand with a concentration process through the formation of trusts and associations. At the end of the 1970s there existed 23 trusts consisting of approximately 350 state-owned firms, 3 000 plants and employing 600 000 workers (Grabher 1994). However, entrepreneurship and employment in the second economy still played an important role. Whilst at the end of the 1970s around 5 per cent of the Hungarian workforce worked in the legal private sector, at least an estimated two third of all households earned an additional income in the second economy (Grabher 1994). In an attempt to transform this informal "neighbourhood-based subsistence production" (Grabher 1994) the Hungarian government allowed for new organisational and legal private forms of enterprise.

The first steps towards the (re-)development of private entrepreneurship and businesses in both the formal and second economy occurred from 1968. Central planning and central allocation of resources to firms was abolished almost totally whilst a system of financial (dis-) incentives was introduced as a management instrument for state-owned firms (Laky 1985; Grabher 1994). Although the Hungarian government introduced these reforms to develop price and profit orientation in state firms, they resulted instead in bargaining processes between directors of state-owned enterprises and the state administration which in turn favoured the development of informal networks – the so-called parallel circuits.

Table 2-1: Legal small businesses in Hungary in 1988

	Enterprises	Employees	% full-time	Average membership
Small state plants				
Traditional state firms & co-ops (<300 members)	1 823	307 413	100	169
Small state-owned firms	213	24 829	100	117
Subsidiaries	277	24 079	100	87
Small co-ops	2 126	95 364	100	45
Sub-total	*4 439*	*451 685*		
Partnerships				
Business work partnership (VGMK)	19 120	241 194	0	13
Specialised groups in co-ops	2 336	85 123	25	36
Civil law partnerships (PJT)	2 200	9 289[a]	66	4
Private business partnership (GMK)	11 186	74 795[a]	30	7
Sub-total	*34 842*	*410 401*	*11*	
Independent legal private business				
Craft industry	154 611[b]	215 468[a]	66	1.4
Small retail trade	35 099	59 087[a]	100	2
Sub-total	*189 710*	*274 555*		
Total	**228 991**	**1 136 641**		

a) including family members

b) including part-time licenses and pensioners in work

Source: Laky 1991.

Reforms towards legal private enterprises were more successful on the whole in introducing private entrepreneurship. In 1973 the Hungarian government allowed the creation of joint-ventures, in the late 1970s it liberalised retail trade by renting shops to private entrepreneurs (Bod 1989). During the 1980s legal private entrepreneurship gained momentum (table 2-1) when economic reforms increased the number of employees allowed in small firms and introduced different state and private enterprise organisations such as the totally private business partnership (GMK) consisting of no more than 30 members and 30 employees which were predominately formed in industry, construction and services or the so-called business work partnerships (VGMK). Here, from 1982 onwards, state employees could rent machinery or space from their employer to collectively produce their own products and services. However, these private initiatives eventually became working brigades for state enterprises performing overtime work (Laky 1989). Furthermore, they also reinforced parallel circuits within state enterprises (Bohle 1996).

Although private independent enterprises and partnerships accounted for 98 per cent of all private organisations and already 60 per cent of employment in 1998 (table 2-1), the state and especially large state organisations still played the most important role in the national economy. 97 per cent of all wage earners were still employed in the state sector, only less than 1 per cent of them belonging to small state units (Laky 1991, also for the following figures). Whilst the number of independent self-employed craft and retail entrepreneurs and their employees increased by nearly 100 000 between 1981 and 1988 their total number amounted to only half of that of 1940. In addition, one third of the craft entrepreneurs only worked part-time, in an attempt to earn additional income (table 2-1). The impact of the new partnership forms was also limited: 70 per cent of private business partnerships were working part-time, three quarters had no fixed assets invested in their organisation at all (table 2-1, Laky 1991).

3 Where Do Hungarian Entrepreneurs Come From?

Hungary started the transition process towards a market-based economy already with a considerable number of private businesses, moreover, entrepreneurial behaviour in one form or another never totally lost its importance during socialism. An interesting question in this context concerns the potential of entrepreneurial activities during the socialist period to "breed capitalism" (Kornai 1992). In Hungary – as elsewhere in transformation countries – both state and private entrepreneurship that existed under socialism have provided a "seedbed" for small business activity during the transition period, in both the formal and informal economy. Tibor identifies different groups of contemporary Hungarian entrepreneurs based on their demographic and business characteristics (Tibor 1994): artisans and retailers from the period before 1982 and their offspring, old-new owner-managers from the 1980s, forced entrepreneurs from the early transition period who lost their job due to the restructuring of large enterprises, managers of state-owned enterprises and "old" co-operatives as well as managers of newly established privatised firms, owners/managers of newly established small firms and joint ventures.

Many directors and managers of state-owned enterprises as well as former politicians (the nomenclature) have used their "parallel circuits" to privatise "their" enterprises or to establish new businesses (Dallago 1997; Lageman 1995). The "spontaneous privatisation" that occurred in Hungary in 1988/89 was one such source of nomenclature entrepreneurs (Frydman et al. 1998; Bohle 1996). As soon as the government introduced new laws allowing for the conversion of state enterprises into corporate legal forms, a large number of directors stripped "their" state-owned companies of assets in order to start their own business. Another source is young sons and daughters whose parents were members of the socialist political nomenclature that used their connections to set up new businesses (Tibor 1994).

Formerly independent private enterprises such as the craft and retail trade enterprises continued to exist during the transition period, mainly aiming to contribute to the family income. These entrepreneurs, most of whom are elderly people (Tibor 1994) often experience difficulties in adjusting to the requirements of a market economy, as during socialism they acted on seller markets. Old-new entrepreneurs from the 1980s who are generally educated to university level could be found among the large number of people who (re-)registered new businesses once legislation abolished the legal and administrative barriers to private firms, enabling them to operate on an equal basis with state owned companies (Kuczi and Vajda 1992).

Finally, Hungary had a strong pre-war tradition of private entrepreneurship which resulted in a number of entrepreneurs during the transition period originating from former entrepreneurial families. Pre-war entrepreneurs and their offspring had either been (partly) self-employed in the second economy, or they had often occupied leading positions in state enterprises during the socialist period, i.e. they "parked" their entrepreneurial skills (Szelenyi 1988). This apparently confirms a thesis modelled on Max Weber's research stating that cultural entrepreneurial traditions could be transported via professional positions allowing for autonomous decisions (Welter 1996).

4 The Development of SMEs During the 1990s

When the transformation process started, the number of all enterprises doubled in Hungary within five years (1991-1996). Overall, these developments are due to the upsurge in private and small-scale entrepreneurial activities which immediately followed the introduction of market reforms. Using the number of sole proprietorships as an indicator for newly created SMEs, nearly 650 000 SMEs existed in Hungary in 1998, almost twice the figure for 1990. Hungary had an already considerable level of private entrepreneurship resulting from the previous reforms during the centrally planned period. However, compared to the beginning of the transition process, when small scale privatisation and new market opportunities contributed to an enormous increase in SMEs, the initially rapid growth rate of SMEs has slowed down (table 4-1). The number of SMEs reached its peak in 1995 and has been declining since then although the corresponding growth rates have been decreasing since 1993.

The national enterprise register only paints a very rough picture of the temporal development of the number of SMEs because the regulations regarding registration changed over time. Furthermore, in 1994 the Hungarian Statistical Office introduced new categories for registered companies which render any temporal comparison difficult. To illustrate the development of SMEs, therefore, the share of private entrepreneurs or micro enterprises – measured as the share of sole proprietorships – is taken as a more appropriate indicator. Table 4-1 shows a declining trend with regard to natural persons and self-employed respectively over the past decade (1990-1998). During the same period the share of private companies (legal persons) has been rising. The same applies to growth rates: the growth rate for natural persons is decelerating, while that for legal companies is accelerating. This general trend is partly due to "normal" high market turbulence characteristic of the SME sector, resulting in high rates of market entry and market exit. In Hungary, this overall development goes hand in hand with an overall decreasing share of private legal and natural persons resulting from a shift to limited partnerships as the legal form favoured by small enterprises.

Table 4-1: Development of micro enterprises in Hungary 1990-1998

	Sole proprietorship		Total enterprises
	% of total	Number	Number
1990	96.8	387 340	400 018
1991	92.4	510 459	552 737
1992	91.1	606 207	665 181
1993	82.6	688 843	833 908
1994	80.9	778 036	961 177
1995	78.9	791 496	1 003 624
1996	74.3	745 247	1 002 946
1997	65.8	656 690	998 264
1998	63.2	648 701	1 026 642

Source: Own calculations.

Another reason explaining the declining growth rates for natural persons relates to the changing registration procedures which certainly reduced the number of persons registered "just in case". For example, in the early 1990s a large number of small enterprises simply registered to profit from tax privileges which, however, were only given to firms registered before 1991 (Lageman et al. 1994). A look at data for "dormant"[1] and "operational" firms shows that in 1998 around three quarters of all registered enterprises were operating, only one quarter were dormant (table 4-2). Not surprisingly, legal forms and the actual status of entrepreneurial activities correlate. While around three quarters of sole proprietors are active, the figure rises to around 85 per cent for limited liability companies. This is principally related to the requirements (for example, minimum capital) connected with setting up a limited liability company.

---

1 Dormant firms are those enterprises that are registered but never started their activities or which no longer operate but have not closed down legally.

Table 4-2: Registered and operational entrepreneurial activities in Hungary, 1998

	Registered number	Active number	as % of registered
Sole proprietorship	648 701	485 355	74.8
Unlimited partnership	5 006	4 063	81.2
Limited partnerships	161 857	140 449	86.8
Limited liability companies	157 990	134 107	84.8
Joint stock company	4 251	3 736	88.5
Co-operative	8 230	5 668	68.9
All legal forms	1 026 642	779 470	75.9

Source: Own calculations.

Naturally, the share of registered "dormant" firms will decline during the transition process due to newly introduced strict regulations and a possibly falling optimism regarding entrepreneurial activities. Certificates issued by the chamber of commerce, and social security regulations introduced in 1997-1998, for example, rendered the operation of dormant firms even less lucrative (Tibor 1998). Research by the Rhine-Westphalia Institute for Economic Research estimated the share of Hungarian dormant firms in 1993 to be around 40 per cent (Lageman et al. 1994). In 1996 data published by the Hungarian Statistical Office showed this share amounting to 36 per cent whilst in 1998 the share of "dormant" firms had decreased to 25 per cent. However, in that context a considerable share of micro enterprises still operates on a part-time basis. Table 4-3 indicates that less than half of those self-employed (that is, the registered sole proprietorships) carry out their entrepreneurial activity full time, although this share has been growing continuously since 1994.

Table 4-3: Full- and part-time entrepreneurship in micro enterprises in Hungary 1992-1996 (in per cent)

	Full time	Part time	Pensioners
1992	45.5	42.1[a]	12.4
1993	44.4	43.0	12.6
1994	44.6	42.3	13.1
1995	45.9	40.9	13.2
1996	47.0	39.1	13.8

Source: Own calculations based on Institute for Small Business Development 1997. – [a] defined as second job holder.

5 Structure and Role of SMEs in the Hungarian Economy

Looking at enterprise size, micro enterprises dominate whilst small and medium enterprises are notably underrepresented. Nearly 97 per cent of all operating enterprises classify as micro firms with 10 and less employees, only 3 per cent are small firms employing between 11 and 50 persons and less than 1 per cent are medium firms with 51-300 employees. This overall general tendency towards small and micro enterprises can be observed across all sectors, being particularly pronounced in the tertiary sectors (table 5-1). More than 97 per cent of all enterprises in manufacturing and 99 per cent in trade and services classify as micro and small firms.

Table 5-1: Main sectors of active enterprises in Hungary in 1998

	Manufacturing		Trade, repair		Catering, transport		Total
% vertical	Number	%	Number	%	Number	%	Number
0-10	75 477	91.1	211 517	97.8	89 065	97.9	756 682
11-50 employees	4 929	6.0	4 014	1.9	1 598	1.8	17 096
51-300	1 944	2.4	674	0.3	253	0.3	4 799
More than 300	489	0.6	87	0.0	75	0.1	893
Total number	82 839	100	216 292	100	90 991	100	779 470
% of SMEs horizontal	10.6		27.8		11.7		100

Source: Own calculations (including construction and agriculture).

One obvious reason explaining the overall predominance of micro enterprises is the considerable share of entrepreneurial activities which are carried out as second-job and part-time activities, often in the informal economy (Kornai 1996). A second reason results from the difficulties related to the creation of medium-sized enterprises. The currently existing medium-sized firms are mostly split-offs from large privatised companies. As in Western Europe, greenfield investments in medium-sized firms still tend to be an exception, while the vast majority of start-ups are micro and small firms. The observed size patterns furthermore indicate a rather slow and time-consuming growth process from newly created micro and small firms into medium-sized enterprises. In this context Gabor (1997) even speaks of a "marginalisation" of the small business sector due to the lack of expansion of small firms, the upsurge of part-time business and the large share of hidden and unregistered small businesses. However, even in western economies most SMEs stay small, as Bridges et al. (1998, 122) note: "Once they have started their own business, electricians, plumbers, chimney sweeps and consultants, for instance, rarely grow, and many other one-person businesses are the same: static is the normal state for them."

Looking at the regional distribution of Hungarian SMEs the overall national SME density, calculated as the share of sole proprietors per 1 000 inhabitants, averages out at 45 enterprises per 1 000 inhabitants; this, however, conceals huge differences within the country. Regional disparities in SME density often follow historical spatial patterns. In Hungary, the agglomeration of Budapest and the western (border) regions were historically the earliest developed areas in terms of industrialisation and infrastructure. One can still observe this pattern. SME densities in Budapest and the Western regions are 53 and 48 enterprises per 1 000 inhabitants respectively, whilst SME development lags behind in those north-eastern regions that are predominantly agricultural areas with some highly specialised (former) state industries (Institute for Small Business Development 1997). These latter regions, with patterns of specialisation resulting from the era of central planning (cities with heavy industry combines), but also "old" industrial regions, experience a much slower development of SMEs. Here SME density is far below the Hungarian average, amounting to 35 enterprises per 1 000 inhabitants in Northern Hungary and 38 enterprises per 1 000 inhabitants in the Northern Great Plain.

The sectoral distribution of SMEs in Hungary is, on the whole, still distorted, especially in manufacturing with its rather low number of SMEs. In 1998 the number of SMEs in trade was more than double the number of SMEs in manufacturing. Low entry barriers, in terms of low capital and skill requirements, and a formerly underdeveloped tertiary sector resulted in high numbers of start-ups in trade and services in the first years of transition. Small-scale privatisation played an additional role in creating SMEs in these fields.

Hungarian SMEs contribute to a large extent to economic development although a large share of officially registered SMEs also partly produce in the informal sector (Kornai 1996). In 1998 SMEs officially contributed slightly less than half of the GDP (table 5-2). SMEs' contribution to employment already corresponded to the EU level with a share of more than two thirds (table 5-3). Hungarian micro enterprises contribute more than one third, small firms (10-49 employees) and medium enterprises (50-249 employees) around one third to total employment. Between 1992 and 1998, the contribution of Hungarian SMEs to employment rose by 38 per cent and their contribution to the GDP went up by 16 per cent. Absolute employment figures for SMEs (as opposed to large enterprises) amounted to 2 million (large enterprises 0.9 million) in 1998, compared with 1.4 million (large enterprises 1.3 million) in 1992. Micro enterprises with less than ten employees, in particular, increased their share in employment (+72 per cent), and small and medium enterprises increased their contribution to Hungary's GDP (+30 per cent and +33 per cent respectively).

Table 5-2: Contribution of Hungarian SMEs to GDP 1992-1998 (in per cent)

Enterprise size	1992	1994	1995	1996	1997	1998
Without employees	5.9	4.4	3.3	4.1	3.9	3.3
Micro	10.0	9.0	9.5	10.6	10.3	10.9
Small	10.6	14.1	14.1	13.4	13.0	13.8
Medium	16.2	21.9	22.5	21.7	21.2	21.5
Large	57.3	50.5	50.7	50.3	51.7	50.4

Source: Compiled from Institute for Small Business Development 1996, 1997 and 1999. – data based on tax returns, no data available for 1993.

Table 5-3: Contribution of Hungarian SMEs to employment 1992-1998 (in per cent)

Enterprise size	1992	1994	1995	1996	1997	1998
Micro	21.5	30.4	34.6	34.7	35.5	36.3
Small	9.9	12.4	13.1	13.1	14.2	14.7
Medium	20.5	19.4	19.0	18.5	18.9	19.1
Large	48.2	37.9	33.2	33.7	31.4	29.8

Source: Compiled from Institute for Small Business Development 1996, 1997 and 1999. – data based on tax returns, no data available for 1993.

These figures, however, cover size differences that emerge from the sectoral and size-specific developments outlined above. With respect to employment, micro and small firms experienced a more dynamic development than medium companies, where employment declined from 1992 to 1996. Considering the official contribution of micro firms to GDP, which increased only slightly from 1992 until 1998, the employment growth over the same period allows for the conclusion that most micro enterprises produce in the informal sector. A look at corrected data for the contribution of SMEs to GDP confirms this. Taking into account undeclared revenues, the Statistical Office estimates that in 1997 SMEs' contribution to GDP amounted to nearly 55 per cent, 24 per cent was produced by micro enterprises alone (Institute for Small Business Development 1999).

The conclusion is that, looking at sectors individually, tertiary sectors normally account for the highest share in SME employment and SME output. Considering enterprise sizes, it is the smallest enterprises that contribute most, with micro and small firms in tertiary sectors contributing the highest share. Although these patterns are, at first glance, the result of an initially distorted economic structure, they also resemble SME structures in highly industrialised countries in one particular aspect, i.e. the overall trend towards tertiarisation, and therefore a growing share of services and trade.

One of the reasons explaining increasing employment in SMEs is the decreasing employment possibilities in large companies. In the years 1992-1996, increased employment in micro and small enterprises was accompanied by declining figures for medium and large firms; medium firms have gained ground slightly since 1997 (Institute for Small Business Development 1999). Overall, from 1992-1998 SMEs were apparently able to absorb the major share of the decreasing employment in large enterprises. SMEs contributed 560 thousand employment possibilities whilst employment in large enterprises decreased by 513 thousand.

A different picture emerges with respect to the contribution of Hungarian SMEs to innovation. Direct research and development appears to be extremely low in SMEs. Statistical data – which, however, do not allow any conclusions with respect to enterprise size – show that in 1998, 258 R&D units existed in enterprises employing a total of 6 393 research personnel. 60 per cent of these units were located in manufacturing enterprises, which indicates an overall low share of research and development in Hungarian industry. Oakey (1997) observed that many Hungarian high-technology small firms appear to lead a virtual existence, "mothballing" their employees when there is no work. Moreover, since innovation in socialist countries was mainly pushed by the state, SMEs generally lack the "culture of customer satisfaction" (Oakey 1997, 42) which, however, is one of the main factors contributing to successful innovation.

6 The Legal, Institutional and Political Environment for SMEs in Hungary

Hungary is far advanced in creating a legal and financial institutional frame further enhancing SME development. In fact, Hungary was one of the first countries in Central Europe to create a legal framework for private entrepreneurs and SMEs. Company and tax laws were adopted in the late 1980s, a bankruptcy law was introduced as early as 1986. Already in 1988 the "Unified Entrepreneurship Law" abolished decrees that discriminated against private firms, a year later the Hungarian government introduced the Partnership Law allowing for up to 500 employees in private companies and introducing ownership forms such as joint stock company, limited liability company and the limited company (Laky 1991). The first years of reform saw frequent changes in laws and regulations. For example, the revised version of the bankruptcy law in the early 1990s led to a wave of legal bankruptcies, especially SMEs. The reason was a regulation on compulsory bankruptcy linked to the inability to pay which forced Hungarian firms to declare themselves bankrupt as soon as payment arrears exceeded 90 days, even if their assets still exceeded their debts (Welter 1994). This regulation was abolished quickly because it overloaded the Hungarian courts.

New bankruptcy regulations in 1992 also forced banks to introduce stricter lending policies. Consequently two commercial banks went bankrupt due to non-performing loans (Suzuki 1996). Transformation of the banking sector started already in 1987, when a two-tier bank system was introduced. Nowadays both the financial and legal framework are more or less in place. Whilst tax policy still remains a priority for enterprise development, the current emphasis for the Hungarian government includes bringing legislation and regulations into line with EU standards in preparation for EU accession.

To assist business development the Hungarian government set up chambers of agriculture, commerce and industry and crafts. The first law was passed after lengthy discussions in 1994, introducing obligatory membership. In 1999 the ongoing discussions resulted in a parliamentary resolution to merge the Chamber of Commerce and Industry and the Hungarian Chamber of Crafts and to end compulsory membership from 2001 onwards (Institute for Small Business Development 1999). However, the line between chambers and business associations in Hungary is blurred, impeding successful lobbying activities on behalf of SMEs (OECD 1996). The nowadays largest association, IPOSZ, which emerged as the association of craft enterprises in 1990 from the previous compulsory Chamber of Crafts, aimed unsuccessfully to become the current Chamber of Crafts. IPOSZ claims to be the domestic interest representation of self-employed and micro entrepreneurs in Hungary. The second largest business association is the National Association of Entrepreneurs and Employers (VOSZ). VOSZ developed from the group of SMEs that belonged to the socialist Chamber of Commerce (OECD 1994). Moreover, numerous small associations exist with a few hundred members, although, given their low political significance, these do not adequately represent the interest of SMEs.

Mainly international donors initially were involved in creating a business support infrastructure. In an effort to promote technological changes in SMEs the PHARE programme for example supported the development of incubators, and a national business innovation centre (Oakey 1997). However, success has been modest so far, also due to a modest response from SMEs (Lakalka 1994). A lack of venture and risk capital add to this. Although loans are available, including donor-financed credit schemes for the purchase of production equipment by SMEs high interest rates might impede early stage innovators in realising their ideas.

To encourage regional development of SMEs, PHARE was involved in creating of a network of local enterprise agencies (LEAs) delivering technical assistance and consultancy. These agencies are based on the UK model that has itself been critically reviewed over the past years. They were set up as non-profit agencies through the Hungarian Foundation for Enterprise Promotion (HFEP) which government intended to be the implementing agency for the PHARE programme. However, Gibb and Haas (1996, 213) observed that "the Hungarian experience would indicate that the models used, in so far as they relate to UK LEA experience, are not always appropriate (...)", identifying the sustainability of support structures in Hungary as a critical factor. Although initially successful in supporting SMEs, most centres turned to more profitable clients once EU funding stopped, because central and local governments in Hungary did not take over. That meant that LEAs were forced to become commercial rather quickly. Bateman (2000) refers to the example of an LEA in Eastern Hungary which was established in 1990 and where already in 1991 managers were heavily involved in private entrepreneurial activities to maximise their performance-related income. Consequently LEAs are turning more and more into private business consultants for large enterprises and do not support SMEs any longer.

During the first years of transition Hungarian SME policies could be characterised as a piecemeal approach concentrating on direct support which was channelled through the Hungarian Foundation for Enterprise Promotion. However, the agency apparently restricted its activities to "providing administrative support for the disbursement of Phare and other donor funds" and did not take an active role in designing SME policies (EU 1999, 8). Furthermore, although a special SME department was set up in the Ministry of Industry, Trade and Tourism, its impact on policies relevant for SMEs was limited. The main reasons were a lack of awareness and vision at government level concerning the role and contribution of SMEs as well as their neo-liberal attitude towards SME promotion (Lageman et al. 1994). In order to co-ordinate the various ministries, the Hungarian government established an Enterprise Development Council in 1994. However, Tibor (1998, 243) concludes: "The declared support for enterprises was not concomitant with a coherent economic policy concept or a constructive and consistent effort to develop a suitable institutional framework or to put in place operational control of already existing institutions. For all the ministries and foundations responsibles, it was a period of "anything goes" under the guise of enterprise advancement."

Preparations for the EU accession finally resulted in the development of a national strategy for SME development. In December 1998 the Hungarian government passed a resolution introducing a medium-term strategy for SME development and bundling all support programmes (Ministry of Economic Affairs 1998). As in Western economies, the contributions of SMEs to employment and growth are the underlying rationale of this strategy. The target groups are micro enterprises, most of which are family businesses, small firms employing 10-49 persons, and medium enterprises with up to 250 employees. As of the year 2000, funding is secured by a separate budget item within the central budget (EU & Government of the Republic of Hungary 2000). However, the overall objectives of SME support are not clear-cut. For example, government intends to strengthen existing SMEs and support innovation as well as their professional and technical re-organisation, but it also aims at promoting entrepreneurship of disadvantaged groups. Both aims require different strategies which eventually might result in potential conflicts between social and economic policies in supporting SMEs. Nevertheless, the strategy was a necessary step towards the creation of formal requirements which are necessary when developing a co-ordinated and coherent approach for SME policies.

7 Conclusion: Hungarian SMEs – Fit for Europe?

The development of Hungarian SMEs has been progressing remarkably fast since the beginning of transformation although the rates of start-ups have been slowing down over the past years. A considerable part of entrepreneurial activities is, however, only carried out part-time. In comparison to the EU, enterprise sizes are still distorted in favour of micro companies with the medium enterprise class more or less lacking. This trend could prove critical in the long run regarding the sustainability of the SME sector. Sectoral distribution generally follows the initial transformation pattern, with SMEs dominating in tertiary sectors and low numbers of start-ups in secondary sectors. Compared to the EU, there is still a considerable gap, indicating further possibilities for SME development. Regional patterns still show a distorted structure, with SME clusters in dynamic regions. However, this is a picture also common in European Union member countries.

Piasecki (1992) identified different stages of SME development in transition economies which assist in explaining the Hungarian patterns during late socialism and the transition towards a market economy. The "initial stage of entrepreneurship development" occurred already during the 1980s with the first reforms, whilst the "period of entrepreneurship explosion" was triggered by the elimination of legal barriers such as licenses impeding market entry in the late 1980s and early 1990s, plus niche markets during the early years of transition. The next stage of "market self-regulation" which is characterised by an increasing enterprise turnover and rapidly changing branch structures in the SME sector could be observed from 1993 onwards, when the growth rates of SMEs started declining. Finally, the current state of SMEs in Hungary, i.e., the dominance of trade and service firms and the lack of middle-sized enterprises, would indicate the beginning stage of "restructuring" in SME development which mainly emphasises qualitative changes in the SME sector such as enterprise growth and innovation.

All in all, SMEs made a significant contribution to economic recovery in Hungary. The drop in national economic production and unemployment would have been much higher without the initial start-up boom. Nowadays, Hungarian SMEs account for a major part of national production and employment. However when discussing SMEs' further role in employment the important issue of job quality has to be taken into account. This concerns the type of jobs created by SMEs in terms of working conditions, wages and longer-term perspectives – a question with implications for politics which has also been neglected until recently in Western countries.

Literature

Bateman, M. (2000): Business Support Centres in the Transition Economies – Progress with the wrong Model? Small Enterprise Development 11(2), pp. 50-59.

Bohle, D. (1996): Governance im Spätsozialismus: Die Herausbildung hybrider Koordinationsformen und informeller Vernetzungen in Ungarn und Polen in den achtziger Jahren. WZB-Discussion Paper FS I 96-102, Berlin: WZB.

Bridge, S.; O'Neill, K.; Cromie, S. (1998): Understanding Enterprise, Entrepreneurship & Small Business. Houndsmill, Basingstoke and London: Macmillan Press.

Bod, P. A. (1989): Deregulation and Institution Building. Lessons from the Reform of the Hungarian Public Sector. Jahrbuch der Wirtschaft Osteuropas 13(1), pp. 110-126.

Dallago, B. (1997): The Economic System, Transition and Opportunities for Entrepreneurship. In: OECD (Ed.): Entrepreneurship and SMEs in Transition Economies. The Visegrad Conference. Paris: OECD, pp. 103-124.

Dallago, B. (1990): The Irregular Economy: the "Underground" Economy and the "Black" Labour Market. Aldershot: Dartmouth.

EU (1999): An Evaluation of Phare SME Programmes: Hungary. Final report. Brussels: EU.

EU and Government of the Republic of Hungary (2000): Joint Assessment of the Economic Policy Priorities of the Republic of Hungary. Brussels. http://www.meh.hu/PM/ Dokumentumok/report20000406.htm.

Frydman, R. et al. (1998): Capitalism with a Comrade's Face. Budapest: Central European University Press.

Gabor, I. R. (1997): Too Many, too Small: Small Entrepreneurship in Hungary – Ailing or Prospering? In: Grabher, G.; Stark, D. (Eds.): Restructuring Networks in Post-Socialism: Legacies, Linkages, and Localities. Oxford et. al: Oxford University Press, pp. 158-175.

Gabor, I. R.; Horváth, T. D. (1987): Failure and Retreat in the Hungarian Private Small-Scale Industry. Acta Oeconomica 38(1-2), pp. 133-153.

Gibb, A.; Haas, Z. (1996): Developing Local Support Services for Small Business Development in Central and Eastern Europe – The Donor Challenge. Entrepreneurship & Regional Development 8, pp. 197-216.

Grabher, G. (1994): The Elegance of Incoherence: Institutional Legacies, Privatization and Regional Development in East Germany and Hungary. WZB Discussion Paper FS I 94-103, Berlin: WZB.

Institute for Small Business Development, various years, State of Small and Medium Sized Business in Hungary. Annual Report. Budapest: Institute for Small Business Development.

Kerblay, B. (1977): La société soviétique contemporaine. Paris: Armand Colin.

Kornai, J. (1992): The Affinity between Ownership and Co-ordination Mechanisms: the Common Experience of Reform in Socialist Countries. In: Poznanski, K. Z. (Ed.): Constructing Capitalism. The Reemergence of Civil Society and Liberal Economy in the Post-Communist World. Boulder, CO. et al.: Westview, pp. 97-116.

Kornai, J. (1995): Das sozialistische System. Baden-Baden: Nomos Verlagsgesellschaft.

Kornai, J. (1996): Unterwegs: Essays zur wirtschaftlichen Umgestaltung in Ungarn, Marburg: Metropolis-Verlag.

Kuczi, T.; Vajda, A. (1992): Privatization and the Second Economy. The New Hungarian Quarterly 33, pp. 77-84.

Lageman, B. (1995): Die neuen Unternehmer in Ostmitteleuropa: Herkunft und Rekrutierungsmechanismen. Berichte des Bundesinstituts für ostwissenschaftliche und internationale Studien, 59-1995, Köln: BIOst.

Lageman, B. et al. (1994): Aufbau mittelständischer Strukturen in Polen, Ungarn, der Tschechischen und der Slowakischen Republik. Untersuchungen des Rheinisch-Westfälischen Instituts für Wirtschaftsforschung 11, Essen: RWI.

Lakalka, R. (1994): Incubating Small Entrepreneurial Businesses in Economies in Rransition. Small Enterprise Development 5(3), pp. 13-23.

Laky, T. (1985): Enterprise Business Work Partnership and Enterprise Interest. Acta Oeconomica 34(1-2), pp. 27-49.

Laky, T. (1989): Vanished Myth – Wavering Intentions. (Small Enterprises Revisited). Acta Oeconomica 40(3/4), pp. 285-306.

Laky, T. (1991): Small Business Organization in the Hungarian Economy. In: Henk T. et al. (Eds.): Small-Scale Production Strategies for Industrial Restructuring. London: IT Publications, pp. 244-261.

Ministry of Economic Affairs (1998): Government's Strategy for Supporting Small- and Medium-sized Enterprises. o.O. (Budapest) http://www.gm.hu/english/sme/smestrat.htm.

Oakey, R. P. (1997): High Technology Development in a Transforming Economy: the Case of Hungary. In: OECD (Ed.): Entrepreneurship and SMEs in Transition Economies. The Visegrad Conference, Paris: OECD, pp. 35-50.

OECD (1994): The Emergence of Business Associations and Chambers in the Economies in Transition: Examples from the Czech Republic, Hungary, Poland, and the Slovak Republic. Paris: OECD/CCET.

OECD (1996): Small Business in Transition Economies. Paris: OECD/CCET.

Piasecki, B. (1992): A Comparative Study. In: Piasecki, B. (Ed): Policy on Small and Medium-Sized Enterprises in Central and Eastern European Countries: Survey and Comparative Study. Warsaw, pp. 229-263.

Suzuki, K. (1996): SME Financing in Central European Countries Based on Experiences in Hungary, the Czech Republic and Poland. In: OECD (Ed.): Systems for Financing Newly Emerging Private Enterprises in Transition Economies. Paris: OECD, pp. 17-44.

Szeleny, I. (1988): Socialist Entrepreneurs. Embourgeoisement in Rural Hungary. Madison, WI: University of Wisconsin Press.

Tibor, A. (1994): Entrepreneurs in Hungary '94. In: Pleitner, H.-J. (Ed.): Strukturen und Strategien in Klein- und Mittelunternehmen als Wegbereiter des Aufschwungs. Beiträge zu den "Rencontres de St-Gall" 1994, St. Gallen: Schweizerisches Institut für Gewerbliche Wirtschaft, pp. 63-68.

Tibor, A. (1998): Why do Enterprises Fail in Hungary? A Preliminary Report of an Envisaged Investigation. In: Pleitner, H.-J. (Ed.): Renaissance der KMU in einer globalisierten Wirtschaft. Rencontres de St-Gall 1998. St. Gallen: Verlag KMU HSG, pp. 239-248.

Welter, F. (1994): Bedeutung des Konkursrechts im Transformationsprozess der ostmitteleuropäischen Länder. RWI-Mitteilungen 45(4), pp. 325-344.

Welter, F. (1996): Unternehmer in Osteuropa. Berliner Debatte/Initial, (3), pp. 100-107.

Small and Medium Sized Enterprises in Yugoslavia: A Driving Force in the Catching-Up Process

Djuro Kutlaca

1 Introduction

SMEs[1] are an economic miracle in the Federal Republic of Yugoslavia today – there were four times more in 1998 than in 1990. The "SMEs boom" has some roots in the socio-economic and cultural background as well as in the history of this country. The following contribution describes the development of SMEs in the 20th century in Yugoslavia and tries to identify possibilities for a further development of the SME sector here in the coming years. The paper is organised in five chapters:

- The history of SMEs in Yugoslavia – in this chapter socio-economic conditions for the development of the SME sector are analysed.
- The relevance of SMEs today – changes in the structure of the Yugoslavian economy in the period 1992 – 1997.
- Framework conditions for development of the SME sector in the Federal Republic of Yugoslavia.
- The political environment for development of the SME sector in the Federal Republic of Yugoslavia.
- Final remarks.

---

1 Basic criteria for the division into small, medium and big enterprises are determined by the Accounting Law of the Federal Republic of Yugoslavia and relate to the number of employees, the amount of income and the value of assets (FRY 2000):
- Small enterprises are those that meet at least two of the following criteria: (1) average number of employees not more than 50, (2) annual income less than the equivalent of 8,000 average gross monthly wages in the country and (3) average value of assets (at the beginning and end of the year) less than the equivalent of 6 000 average gross wages in Yugoslavia;
- Medium enterprises are those that met at least two of the requirement in the previous year: (1) average number of employees based on working hours 50 to 250, (2) annual income equivalent to 8 000 to 40 000 average gross monthly wages in Yugoslavia and (3) average value of assets (at the beginning and end of financial year) equivalent to 6 000 to 30 000 average monthly gross wages in Yugoslavia.

2 History of SMEs in Yugoslavia

The history of the development of SMEs can be divided into three periods:

- before 1941 – Kingdom of Yugoslavia (KY);
- between 1945-1992 – Socialist Federal Republic of Yugoslavia (SFRY);
- since 1992 – Federal Republic of Yugoslavia (FRY).

These three periods represent three different socio-economic systems: capitalism (KY), socialism – single party system (SFRY) and socialism – multi-party system (FRY). Changes in the socio-economic system directly imply changes in status, number, impact on economy etc. In this first chapter we will analyse the first two periods.

2.1 SMEs Before 1941

The Kingdom of Yugoslavia was established after the end of the First World War. The economy in the Kingdom of Yugoslavia was practically destroyed during the First World War. Thanks to the predecessor of the Kingdom of Yugoslavia, the Kingdom of Serbia – an ally of countries that won the First World War – the Kingdom of Yugoslavia had to some extent a privileged position regarding credits and other support for reconstruction and building up the country's economy. Yugoslavia's natural resources and its geographical position were also attractive to foreign investors and companies. The socio-economic system was a democratic monarchy with a capitalistic economy.

In the Kingdom of Yugoslavia the main economic activities were: mining, agriculture, forestry, trade and financial services, and some industrial branches: a metal-working industry, a chemical industry, textiles, tanning and clothing, a food industry and a paper industry. A very important economic sector in the Kingdom of Yugoslavia was mining and smelting. The highest average number of employees per enterprise recorded in this sector was 486 (in 1937).

The Kingdom of Yugoslavia, with its capitalistic economic system, was a good environment for entrepreneurship and the development of SMEs as well as other segments of the market economy. However, compared to other countries in Europe, the Kingdom of Yugoslavia was a relatively underdeveloped country. A distribution of factories by size and ownership in the Kingdom of Yugoslavia, available to the author only for the year 1938, is given in table 2.1-1.

Table 2.1-1: Factories in the Kingdom of Yugoslavia – distribution by size and ownership – 1938:

Total number of factories	Size (Number of employees)					Distribution of factories by status of ownership					
	≤ 10	11 - 50	51 - 200	≥ 200	No data on size	Domestic	Foreign	Mostly domestic	Mostly foreign	50% domestic and foreign	No data on ownership
4 257	676	1 341	1 158	1 082	210	3 222	183	346	318	48	140

Source: References SYKY 1929-1940 and SYY 1989.

SMEs in the Kingdom of Yugoslavia were mainly artisan (handicraft) shops (table 2.1-2).

Table 2.1-2: Artisan (handicraft) shops in Kingdom of Yugoslavia

Year	Manufacturing	Services	Total number of shops	Number of employees	Average number of employees per shop
1936	135 152	11 312	146 464	146 464	1.00
1937	138 722	11 868	150 590	274 288	1.82
1938	144 135	11 561	155 696	296 336	1.90
1939	135 152	11 312	162 353	319 662	1.97

Source: Reference SYKY, 1929-1940 and SYY, 1989.

The Artisan sector was an important part of the economy in the Kingdom of Yugoslavia, with 31 per cent of all employees and a share of 8.4 per cent in the gross national product in 1938. In the first part of the 20th century, Yugoslavia was mainly an agricultural country (the share of the agricultural sector in the GNP was 53 per cent in 1923, as compared with only 13.4 per cent for manufacturing and 9.6 per cent for the artisan sector). Before World War Two the structure of the economy changed due to the industrialisation process. In 1938, only 15 years later, the share of manufacturing in the gross national product was much higher (20.3 per cent) and, with the artisan sector mostly engaged in production (91 per cent of all artisan shops were in different industries and only 9 per cent in services in 1938), manufacturing represented one third of the economy during this time (the share of agriculture was now less than a half: 46.5 per cent of the GNP 1938). Industrialisation and private initiative became an important part of the socio-economic image and created an initial stock of technological memory, necessary for the development of the country.

2.2 SMEs Between 1945 and 1992

The Socialist Federal Republic of Yugoslavia (SFRY) was established when the Second World War ended. The economy of the Socialist Federal Republic, as well as the country as a whole – very like the situation in the Kingdom of Yugoslavia following the First World War – had been destroyed during the Second World War.[2]

Thanks to its specific political and geo-strategic position between East (communist) and West (capitalist) blocks, the SFRY as a socialist country benefited from this position through a number of credit lines from the World Bank, the International Monetary Fond etc. for reconstruction and rebuilding of the country's economy. The socio-economic system was socialistic, a single party system, with the economy combining mandatory, planning and self-management principles, i.e. different from the Soviet model, but also without a market driven economy.

The SFRY was still a developing country with companies which were mostly state-owned or publicly-owned. The various industrial branches, agriculture and tourism were mostly developing economic sectors. An employment policy was oriented towards the growth of enterprises – small companies were not "in fashion" (table 2.2-1). Publicly-owned enterprises were obliged by law to hire new employees every year, regardless of their financial results and their actual need for new employees. Companies, especially in manufacturing, became overstaffed compared to the average values for western countries. The share of small firms in the total number of firms decreased strongly between 1965 (50.9 per cent) and 1987 (32.6 per cent), and the number of large firms went up from 17.5 per cent in 1965 to 25.5 per cent in 1987.

The structure of the economy changed completely in Yugoslavia in the period after the Second World War. Rapid industrialisation led in 1952 to a situation where manufacturing had a 48.7 per cent in the GNP and agriculture only a 26.2 per cent share. At the end of this period, in the year 1987, the manufacturing sector had become a very important part of the economy (43.5 per cent of the gross national product). By contrast, the agriculture sector became extremely depressed, declining to only 11 per cent of the GNP. Furthermore an increasing importance of trade can

2 Before the Second World War, the population of Yugoslavia was 15 920 000. Losses in the war were 1 706 000 killed and 2 035 000 wounded, or 23.5 per cent of the pre-war population. Losses in manufacturing amounted to 36.5 per cent of all installations with a total cost of 9.2 billion US$ (calculated for US$ in the year 1946).

be identified during this time (5.7 per cent of GNP in 1952 and 18.5 per cent in 1987).

Table 2.2-1: Distribution of firms by number of employees in the Socialist Federal Republic of Yugoslavia

Year	Total Number of firms	Distribution of firms by number of employees					
		≤ 60 empl.	≤ 60 % of total	60 - 250 empl.	60 - 250 % of total	≥250 empl.	≥250 % of total
1965	14 210	7 236	50.9	4 486	31.6	2 488	17.5
1970	11 100	4 973	44.8	3 582	32.3	2 545	22.9
1975	21 414	7 892	36.9	9 144	42.7	4 378	20.4
1980	27 400	9 509	34.7	12 297	44.9	5 594	20.4
1985	27 791	9 241	33.3	12 132	43.7	6 418	23.1
1987	26 002	8 486	32.6	10 897	41.9	6 619	25.5

Source: Reference SYY, 1989.

As in the Kingdom of Yugoslavia, SMEs were a characteristic form of enterprises in the Socialist Federal Republic, but only in the artisan sector (handicrafts). A decreasing number of firms in this sector during the period 1952-1987 (table 2.2-2) can be seen as a confirmation of the trend in country's economy, where the law of "economies of scale" became relevant, i.e. big firms in public or state ownership were "in fashion". By contrast, firms in the artisan sector were mostly private. This form of ownership was ideologically unacceptable and, therefore, without official organised support (such as credits or funds for starting up, developing and other phases in a firm's life cycle). The SFRY, with its socialistic planned economy, considered private initiative as undesirable. Until the late eighties, private initiative was strictly controlled and even sanctioned. The artisan sector's share in the gross national product started from a very low level (5 per cent in 1952) and decreased to only 4.3 per cent in 1987. The institutional constraints for the development of this sector can be seen as a reference to the ideologically-based fear that the private sector might jeopardise the socialist system. The activities to which private initiative could be applied were determined by law (these were: catering, crafts, transport services and agriculture). The number of employees in a private firm was limited by the same law to five, and the area of private holdings in agriculture was limited to 10 or 20 hectares, depending on the quality of the land. Under such circumstances, there was no motivation for the formation and development of SMEs, or indeed for private initiative at all. The majority of small-scale private enterprises were made up of craft (artisan) workshops and restaurants (plus services in tourism) until the early eighties.

Table 2.2-2: Number of firms and employment in the Artisan Sector (AS) in the Socialist Federal Republic of Yugoslavia

Year	Total number of firms in AS	Total number of em-ployees in AS	Avera-ge no. of em-ployees per firm in AS	No. of publicly owned firms (POF)	No. of em-ployees in POFs	Average no. of em-ployees in POFs	No. of private firms (PFs)	No. of em-ployees in PFs	Avera-ge no. of em-ployees in PFs
1954	160 136	303 774	1.9	4 921	99 473	20.2	155 215	204 301	1.3
1965	116 288	269 569	2.3	3 168	123 921	39.1	113 120	145 648	1.3
1970	144 098	305 079	2.1	2 643	117 642	44.5	141 455	187 437	1.3
1975	138 312	318 392	2.3	2 963	127 097	42.9	135 349	191 295	1.4
1980	132 341	371 547	2.8	1 442	167 107	115.9	130 899	204 440	1.6
1985	155 074	434 771	2.8	1 453	185 002	127.3	153 621	249 769	1.6
1987	166 436	365 426	2.2	1 381	191 097	138.4	165 055	174 329	1.1

Source: Reference SYY 1989.

The social climate changed in the late eighties and new regulations were enacted to encourage an increase in the number of SMEs and sole proprietorship in the private sector. At that time a large economic reform was introduced and accepted by the federal and republic governments together with the communist party's leaders. The transition to a market economy in the SFRY commenced. In 1989 the Federal Assembly adopted the "Law on the Conduct of Business by Personal Labour and Using Assets Owned by Citizens" – a major institutional step towards a market economy, allowing private initiatives and the setting-up of private firms without constraints or ideological rejections. Many citizens used the possibilities offered by this law to register their own firms. However, the number of active enterprises was smaller than the number of actually registered ones because of the difficult operating, social and economic conditions. The adoption of this law was just the first step in creating an institutional framework for economic transition. During this time new entrepreneurs had no idea of how to manage a firm, and were not familiar with concepts of controlling or marketing. The public infrastructure lacked institutions such as colleges for management, marketing and accounting. Agencies for consulting and technology transfer were only subjects of intellectual discussion.

Development of the SME sector was welcomed, but without broad official support for private initiatives. Because of the very high level of the country's foreign debt, economists and politicians planned with money from abroad – for example from expatriate Yugoslavians in former West Germany or Australia. Indeed, it proved possible to make use of private savings and financial support from abroad to relatives in the SFRY as funds for starting-up and developing new SMEs. Unfortunately, the dissolution of the SFRY, wars and other terrible events changed the political and economic picture in this part of Europe and negatively influenced progress in the development of the SME sector in the next, third, Federal Republic of Yugoslavia.

3 The Relevance of SMEs Today – Changes in the Structure of Yugoslavia's Economy in the Period 1992-1999

3.1 Basic Data

The Federal Republic of Yugoslavia (FRY) was established on 27.04.1992, with Serbia and Montenegro as constitutional republics. The socio-economic system is a multi-party democracy, with the economy in transition to a market economy. However, the political and economic blockade since the early 1990s has led to bad conditions, culminating in severe destruction of the infrastructure and industry in 1999. Various economic indicators show a deterioration in the period 1992-1999. The gross domestic product (GDP) in 1996 was 57.5 per cent of the GDP in 1991 (GDP in fixed prices from 1994). The domestic products of the main economic sectors in 1996, compared with 1991, were: manufacturing 54.3 per cent; agriculture and fishing 88.2; civil engineering 43.6 per cent; transport and communication 38.9 per cent; trade 59.9 per cent. A similar situation can be stated for employment. In 1996 the number of people employed was 90.2 per cent of the 1991 figure.[3] However, the situation was not identical in all sectors of the economy: employment in the public sector was only 85.3 per cent compared to 1991, while the private sector showed an increase up to 154 per cent compared to 1991. The socio-economic and political situation improved in 1996-1998. The period of the economic blockade of the country was partly suspended at the end of 1995 and lifted at the beginning of 1996. This resulted in growth of the GDP and an improvement in overall employment figures, but accompanied by continuing transition indicators – a decrease of employment in the public sector and growth in private sector, and a growing share of the private sector's contribution to the GDP (tables 3.1-1 and 3.1-2).

[3] Hidden unemployment was much higher, because of fact that less than half of all industrial firms were active, most of them using only a small part of their installed capacity. The economic infrastructure in the former SFRY was built mainly aiming at exports, and the third Yugoslavia was unable to export because of the blockade and interrupted relationships with former Yugoslavian republics.

Table 3.1-1: Basic data for FRY – population and employment (in thousands of people and percentage share); structure of National Product (per cent of total)

Year	Population (000)	Total employees (000)	Empl Public Sector (000)	Empl Public Sector (%)	Empl Private Sector (000)	Empl Private Sector (%)	Empl Ind. (%)	NP Ind. (%)	Empl Agr. (%)	NP Agr. (%)	Empl Serv. (%)	NP Serv. (%)	Empl Art. (%)	Empl Art. (%)
1992	10 448	2 535	2 328	91.8	207	8.2	50.3	59.0	4.8	17.0	36.0	21.7	6.1	2.9
1993	10 480	2 464	2 243	91.0	221	9.0	49.9	54.2	4.8	23.1	35.7	19.4	6.3	3.1
1994	...[(1)]	2 414	2 178	90.2	236	9.8	49.4	49.4	4.8	23.7	35.5	23.9	6.7	3.0
1995	...[(1)]	2 379	2 114	88.9	265	11.1	48.5	48.0	4.7	23.3	35.3	25.8	7.4	2.9
1996	...[(1)]	2 367	2 079	87.8	288	12.2	47.7	48.3	4.4	22.4	35.6	26.7	7.8	2.7
1997	...[(1)]	2 332	2 014	86.4	318	13.6	46.6	48.4	4.1	22.3	35.6	26.8	8.5	2.4

Legend: **Ind.** – Manufacturing and Mining, Water Works and Supply, Construction, Transport and Communication; **Agr.** – Agriculture, Fishing, Forestry; **Serv.** (services) – Tourism, Public Utilities, Financial Services, Education and Culture, Health and Social Services, Administration; **Art.** – Artisan (Handicrafts); **Empl** – Employees

Note: "In the absence of reliable data for Kosovo and Metohia, data are not available"(SYY 1999).

Source: Reference SYY 1994-1999.

Table 3.1-2: Basic data for FRY – Structure of Gross Domestic Product by ownership (per cent of total)

Year	1988	1989	1990	1991	1992	1993	1994	1995	1996	1997
Public ownership (%)	89.3	89.1	87.4	83.4	78.0	72.2	66.8	64.8	65.5	64.1
Private ownership (%)	10.7	10.9	12.6	16.6	22.0	27.8	33.2	35.2	34.5	35.9
Total (%)	100	100	100	100	100	100	100	100	100	100

Source: Reference SYY 1994-1999.

The main changes in economic structure in the Federal Republic of Yugoslavia, observed in tables 3.1-1 and 3.1-2, are:

- a strong, pervasive trend of growth of the private sector's contribution to the GDP: from 10.7 per cent in 1988 (during SFRY), to 35.9 per cent in 1997;
- a growing share in the GDP of the sectors: agriculture, fishing and forestry and services, a decreasing contribution made by the sectors: manufacturing and mining, water works and supply, construction, transport and communication;

- a decrease in total employment (the figures in table 3.1-1 represent the formally registered number of employees, which is 10 per cent less in 1996 compared with 1991; in reality a further 10 per cent decrease must be assumed to allow for hidden unemployment – workers in factories without or with rather small orders, production etc. compared with firm's capacities);
- an increasing share of employees in the private sector, with more than 50 per cent growth in the number of employees within the 5-year period;
- almost all sub-sectors in the public sector are faced with a decrease of employment due to the economic crisis, political instability and economic blockade. Under these circumstances, the private sector has become the generator of available working places, but not enough to compensate all job losses in the public sector.

3.2 Data on Recently Development of SMEs

The transition of Yugoslavia's economy began in the late 1980s. Reformation of the economy was oriented towards a change in ownership structure with privatisation as a main target, and one result of these reforms was an increasing number of new, mostly private firms. Tables 3.2-1, 3.2-2, 3.2-3, 3.2-4 and 3.2-5 illustrate this strong and pervasive trend of growth of the SME sector, despite all political, economic and other turbulences and wars, the dissolution of the SFRY and the economic and political isolation of the country. The Federal Republic of Yugoslavia witnessed a welcome "boom" of SMEs as a result of private initiative, private funding and the fact that this development was recognised as an officially acceptable way of organising the economy.

Table 3.2-1: Number of firms

Year	Distribution of firms by size									Total number of firms	
	Small firms (1-50 employees)			Medium firms (51-250 employees)			Big firms (> 250 employees)				
	number	growth* (%)	% of total	number	growth* (%)	% of total	number	growth* (%)	% of total	number	growth* (%)
1991	26 923	...	87.2	2 351	...	7.6	1 591	...	5.2	30 865	...
1992	49 697	184.6	92.8	2 367	100.7	4.4	1 509	94.8	2.8	53 573	173.6
1993	52 857	106.4	93.2	2 383	100.7	4.2	1 445	95.8	2.5	56 685	105.8
1994	62 456	118.2	93.5	3 057	128.3	4.6	1 301	90.0	1.9	66 814	117.9
1995	66 426	106.4	94.6	2 692	88.1	3.8	1 092	83.9	1.6	70 210	105.1
1996	69 187	104.2	95.1	2 532	94.1	3.5	995	91.1	1.4	72 714	103.6
1997	70 453	101.8	95.4	2 471	97.6	3.3	934	93.9	1.3	73 858	101.6
1998	71 040	100.8	95.4	2 500	101.2	3.4	913	97.8	1.2	74 453	100.8

Note: *Growth of firms in per cent (previous year = 100, starting year = 1992).

Source: References: Minic and Denda 1998 and SYY 1994-1999.

Table 3.2-2: Number of employees

Year	Number of employees									All firms	
	Small firms (1-50 employees)			Medium firms (51-250 employees)			Big firms (> 250 employees)				
	number	average number	% of total	number	average number	% of total	number	average number	% of total	number	average number
1991	110 193	4.1	6.0	294 210	125.1	16.0	1 435 628	902.3	78.0	1 840 031	59.6
1992	141 769	2.9	8.1	294 690	124.5	16.9	1 304 662	864.6	74.9	1 741 121	32.5
1993	139 716	2.6	8.2	296 058	124.2	17.4	1 267 128	876.9	74.4	1 702 902	30.0
1994	279 816	4.5	15.4	418 519	136.9	23.1	1 114 640	856.8	61.5	1 812 975	27.1
1995	295 963	4.5	17.0	424 397	157.7	24.4	1 016 820	931.2	58.5	1 737 180	24.7
1996	371 126	5.4	21.6	413 227	163.2	24.1	932 789	937.5	54.3	1 717 139	23.6
1997	438 000	6.2	24.9	405 000	163.9	23.0	918 000	982.9	52.1	1 761 000	23.8
1998	441 000	6.2	25.8	394 000	157.6	23.0	876 000	959.5	51.2	1 712 000	23.0

Source: References: Minic and Denda 1998 and SYY 1994-1999.

The SME sector has developed despite all the unfavourable conditions mentioned above. A main reason can be found in the fact that private initiative and private business are much more flexible in finding appropriate solutions for a number of difficulties and obstacles that Yugoslavia's economy has been facing since 1992. The private SME sector is able to compensate a considerable share of missing products and services previously supplied by public sector which is over dimensioned for third Yugoslavia. The public sector, mainly consisting of big firms, is incapable of handling the transition process and is unable to function under the economic blockade. Although the private sector is not greatly favoured by the governing left coalition, economic needs have outweighed ideological conflict, allowing the expansion of private initiatives.

Table 3.2-3: Financial indicators: fixed assets, total revenues, total expenditure, gross gains, gross losses – percentage shares by firm size in total for all firms

Year	Small firms (1-50 employees)					Medium firms (51-250 employees)					Big firms (> 250 employees)				
	FD	TR	TE	GG	GL	FD	TR	TE	GG	GL	FD	TR	TE	GG	GL
1994	10.4	25.0	23.5	46.4	7.1	15.5	14.6	14.8	14.4	16.9	74.1	60.4	61.7	39.2	76.0
1995	8.7	27.5	25.2	41.8	6.5	16.0	15.8	15.0	14.9	7.7	75.3	56.7	59.8	43.3	85.8
1996	10.8	29.2	28.1	36.3	12.5	15.4	16.5	16.4	11.8	12.6	73.8	54.3	55.5	51.9	74.9
1997	12.2	31.2	30.4	38.0	12.8	15.2	15.7	15.8	16.1	12.2	72.6	53.1	53.8	45.9	75.0
1998	10.1	31.5		36.2	11.0	15.6	16.8		21.5	10.8	74.3	51.7		42.3	78.2

Legend: **FD** – Fixed assets; **TR** – Total revenues; **TE** – Total expenditure; **GG** – Gross gains; **GL** – Gross losses.

Source: References: Minic and Denda 1998 and SYY 1994-1999.

Table 3.2-4: Structure of firms by ownership form in FRY – share of different ownership forms within firm size categories (firm size = 100 per cent for observed year)

Year	Small firms		Medium firms		Big firms		All firms	
	Number	per cent	Number	per cent	Number	per cent	Number	per cent
Public ownership								
1996	3 082	4.5	1 208	47.7	454	45.6	4 744	6.5
1997	3 630	5.2	1 177	48.2	419	44.9	5 226	7.1
1998	3 714	5.2	1 161	46.5	403	44.1	5 278	7.1
Private ownership								
1996	61 775	89.3	474	18.7	60	6.0	62 309	85.7
1997	62 492	88.7	423	17.3	54	5.8	62 969	85.3
1998	62 846	88.5	491	19.7	57	6.2	63 394	85.2
Co-operative ownership								
1996	2 223	3.2	108	4.3	9	0.9	2 340	3.2
1997	2 109	3.0	95	3.9	5	0.5	2 209	3.0
1998	2 187	3.1	93	3.7	6	0.7	2 286	3.1
Mixed ownership								
1996	2 113	3.1	743	29.3	472	47.4	3 328	4.6
1997	2 199	3.1	745	30.5	456	48.8	3 400	4.6
1998	2 273	3.2	752	30.1	447	49.0	3 472	4.7

Source: Reference FRY 2000.

Summarising the presented data, one can observe that today, SMEs are relevant in the economy of the Federal Republic of Yugoslavia:

- private entrepreneurship in the FRY is in expansion and more recent data indicate that almost 90 per cent of all firms are SMEs. Considering the number of firms, almost 86 per cent of all firms are private, 7 per cent are in public ownership, 5 per cent in mixed ownership and 3 per cent in a co-operative form of ownership;
- almost all small firms (90 per cent) are in private ownership, and only 20 per cent of medium firms and 6 per cent of big firms are private;
- small and medium firms show an increasing share in total employment. Compared with the time of the SFRY, when big firms were in fashion, this can be seen as an indicative change towards "small is beautiful";
- despite the fact that SMEs show an increase in fixed assets every year, their relative share remains constant (10 per cent belong to small, 15 per cent belong to medium and 75 per cent of all assets belong to large firms);
- SMEs recorded a steady increase in business revenues, generating half of the total revenue in 1998 (32 per cent small and 17 per cent medium sized firms)

compared with 40 per cent in 1994. A similar situation can be stated for business expenditures.

Table 3.2-5: Structure of firms by form of ownership in Federal Republic of Yugoslavia– relative share of different firm size categories in specific forms of ownership

Year	Small firms		Medium firms		Big firms		All firms	
	Number	%	Number	%	Number	%	Number	%
Public ownership								
1996	3 082	65.0	1 208	25.5	454	9.6	4 744	100
1997	3 630	69.5	1 177	22.5	419	8.0	5 226	100
1998	3 714	70.4	1 161	22.0	403	7.6	5 278	100
Private ownership								
1996	61 775	99.1	474	0.8	60	0.1	62 309	100
1997	62 492	99.2	423	0.7	54	0.1	62 969	100
1998	62 846	99.1	491	0.8	57	0.1	63 394	100
Co-operative ownership								
1996	2 223	95.0	108	4.6	9	0.4	2 340	100
1997	2 109	95.5	95	4.3	5	0.2	2 209	100
1998	2 187	95.7	93	4.1	6	0.3	2 286	100
Mixed ownership								
1996	2 113	63.5	743	22.3	472	14.2	3 328	100
1997	2 199	64.7	745	21.9	456	13.4	3 400	100
1998	2 273	65.5	752	21.7	447	12.9	3 472	100

Source: Reference FRY 2000.

Nevertheless, the business indicators are not really satisfactory for SMEs: gross gains show a decrease and gross losses an increase in the period 1994-1998. This is partly because of the privileged position of publicly-owned firms (only 0.1 per cent of big firms are in private ownership and the fact that the infrastructure and institutional framework for the development and functioning of SMEs is undeveloped or inactive in the country. The distribution of SMEs by economic sectors shows that the largest number of small firms is in trade, manufacturing and mining, financial and other services. Medium firms are mostly concentrated in manufacturing and mining, trade, agriculture and fishing. In total, the share of SMEs in business assets and gross capital constituted 30 per cent of the total economy in 1998, about 20 per cent in cumulated losses, about 48 per cent in total operating revenue and 68 per cent in total operating profit (FRY 2000). These shares in business assets, gross capital, operating revenue and financial results are high in agriculture and fishing, civil engineering, trade, tourism, the artisan sector and financial services, and relatively low in manufacturing and mining, forestry and transport and communication. The highest profitability indicators for SMEs in the year 1998 were achieved in forestry, transport and communication and the artisan sector.

One of the reasons for SMEs' flexibility can be recognised in the concentration of SMEs in the service sector, where the use and re-use of working capital is much quicker and the associated business risk is smaller. A more detailed financial analysis of all firms in the country in 1998 showed the following results:

- medium sized firms in the public sector have the worst financial structure,
- almost 90 per cent of all losses are made by big firms,
- small firms with a bad financial position are in mixed and public ownership,
- only small firms in private ownership have positive financial results.

3.3 SMEs and Innovation

An analysis was recently made of the research and development (R&D) sector, which is also in transition and in the process of restructuring (Kutlaca and Lazic 2000). Thus, some light can be shed on future developments in interrelationships between SMEs and R&D, especially regarding the development of new, technology-based SMEs. For the purposes of this paper, we shall analyse data presented in table 3.3-1 (employees in the R&D sector according to national and OECD classification, and distribution of researchers by sectors of performance and fields of science and technology) and figure 3.3-1 (R&D organisations' main activities in the period 1980-1997).

Table 3.3-1: Employees and researchers in Yugoslav' R&D system (Federal Statistical Office – FSO and OECD classification)

Year	Classification	Total number of employees	Researchers	Professional associates	Supporting staff	Others	Researchers G.S.	Researchers B.E.S.	Researchers H.E.S.
1997	FSO	27 194	13 220	2 998	6 798	4 178	26.3%	7.2%	66.5%
1997	OECD-FTE	20 255	7 476	2 199	5 603	4 977	46.4%	12.7%	40.9%

Year	Researchers	NSM	TS	MS	BT	SS	HS	MD
1997	13 220	14.0%	34.1%	13.4%	11.2%	12.8%	13.0%	1.5%

Legend: NSM – Natural Sciences and Mathematics; TS – Technical Sciences and Engineering; MS – Medical Sciences; BT – BioTechnological sciences;
SS – Social Sciences; HS – Humanities; MD – MultiDisciplinary sciences.
FTE – Full Time Equivalent (OECD 1993).

Source: References: FSO 1998; Kutlaca and Lazic 2000.

Figure 3.3-1: Income of Research and Development organisations in Federal Republic of Yugoslavia – share obtained from total (R&D and non R&D) activities registered in the period 1980–1997

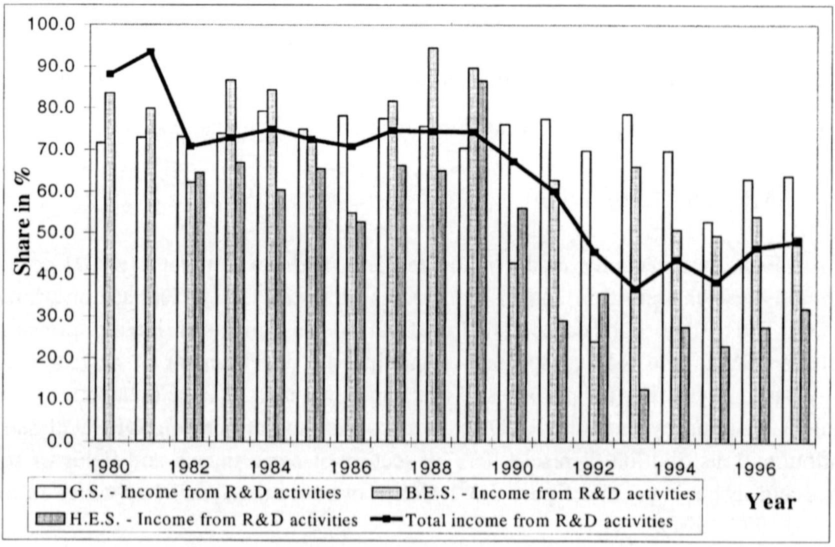

Source: References: FSO 1998; Kutlaca and Lazic 2000.

An analysis of the income structure of R&D organisations, grouped in three sectors according to OECD classification (G.S. – Government Sector; B.E.S. – Business Enterprise Sector; H.E.S. – Higher Education Sector), allows the following conclusions:

- R&D activities were the main activities for all R&D organisations in the period 1980-1989, even R&D organisations in the business enterprise sector made almost 90 per cent of their total income from R&D activities;
- from 1989, all R&D organisations were in some kind of "silent transition", using the R&D infrastructure for non R&D activities: small-scale production, non-R&D services etc. The share of total income from non-R&D activities reached 70-90 per cent in the government sector, 75 per cent in the business enterprise sector and education was practically the sole activity in the higher education sector.

The restructuring process in the R&D sector, not formally conducted by responsible authorities, resulted in a very difficult economic situation. It can be expected that in the future, a certain number of R&D organisations in the government sector and the business enterprise sector will become small or medium size specialised, technology-intensive enterprises; some of them are now exactly this type of firm. Examples of this kind are found in laser technologies, biotechnology, and information technologies, particularly software development and telecommunications.

The total number of employees, as well as the number of Full Time Equivalent (FTE) researchers and the total FTE R&D personnel per thousand labour force in the Federal Republic of Yugoslavia is 6.4 for 1997, which is comparable with the same indicators in developed countries (the overall average for the OECD is 5.5 for 1997; OECD 2000). On the other hand, the employment structure within the R&D system in Yugoslavia is just the opposite of the structure in developed countries: the smallest proportion of researchers is employed in manufacturing (about 13 per cent of the total number are in the business enterprise sector, as compared to 50-70 per cent in developed countries), about 40 per cent are in the higher education sector (compared with 20-30 per cent in developed countries), and over 46 per cent are in the government sector (compared with less than 20 per cent in developed countries). This structure can in itself be regarded as important evidence for the necessary and unavoidable restructuring process in the R&D sector.

Some basic institutions, necessary for the development and support of SMEs, exist in the present infrastructure, such as Chambers of Commerce (federal, republic, regional) and R&D organisations. The number of organisations in the R&D sector in 1997 was as follows:

- Higher Education Sector – 102 faculties;
- Business Enterprise Sector – 63 industrial institutes and R&D units;
- Government Sector – 86 national institutes and laboratories.

However, concerning an infrastructure for the support of SMEs several types of institutions are still missing. First of all, technology transfer organisations and liaison organisations are needed, as well as financial institutions specifically oriented towards supporting SMEs. Initial technology transfers were made due to the fact that some SMEs were established by researchers who left the R&D sector, especially in sectors like software development and telecommunication. But this cannot be seen as organised and stimulated activity. In future, more consulting, assistance in process and product development, marketing and financial services are necessary for SMEs. Some first steps are:

- the establishment of an agency for the transfer of technologies, recently set up in University of Belgrade as a contact point where possible users can contact academics for technologies they need;
- the establishment of an agency for technology transfer, defined as a network of centres for consulting services and technology transfer all around the Republic of Serbia. This agency has just been proposed by the new law on R&D activities in the Republic of Serbia as a common infrastructure which will be developed by

this Ministry and the Republic's Chamber of Commerce. It is still only on paper and does not exist so far.

4 Framework Conditions for Development of the SME Sector in the Federal Republic of Yugoslavia

Besides the political and legislative framework conditions for SMEs and entrepreneurship, which will be discussed in chapter four, the economic and social conditions for the development of a small firm sector in the Federal Republic of Yugoslavia have to be seen in a differentiated way. Thus several aspects are of relevance:

4.1 The Existence of the "Black" Economy and Its Strong Influence

The dissolution of the SFRY, besides other terrible events, gave rise to a very bad economic situation in the Federal Republic of Yugoslavia, resulting in a decrease of all economic activities, very high real and hidden unemployment, and a fall in real GDP and per capita income. The process of transition to a market economy was slowed down and impeded by the privileged position of the public against private sector. The factors mentioned above caused a shifting of the economy to a "black zone": unregistered economic activities without the possibility of tax collection, jeopardising the human and labour rights of people employed in the "black economy", and constituting unfair competition for the legal economy. In 1993, during the strongest international political and economical blockade of FRY, the size of the "black economy" reached more than 50 per cent of the realised GDP. In 1994 a "Programme for monetary reconstruction" was introduced as a basis for the stabilisation of economic conditions in the country. As a consequence, the "black" economy decreased to 40.8 per cent of the real GDP in 1995 and 34.5 per cent in 1997.

Causes for the "black" economy, besides bad political conditions, can be found within the tax system itself and also in the financial sector. The tax system is still "user oriented" – more than 60 per cent of the GDP has to be distributed to a number of users (social security and welfare, health services, education, culture, R&D sector, public administration and other public payments), compared to 30-40 per cent in OECD countries (OECD 2000). This made conditions difficult for tax payers and caused a shift towards the "black" (i.e. non-tax paying) economy. The financial sector itself is also one of the causes for the existence of the "black" economy – most of the payments are handled outside legal financial channels (partly because of the financial blockade of the country, and partly because of the very high level of internal debts, making the banks insolvent) and this further reinforces the operation of the "black" market.

All in all, conditions can be said to be difficult for entrepreneurship and the development of SMEs. As a consequence, a number of SMEs have unregistered workers and "parallel" accounting just to avoid big taxes; they realise financial transactions in the best possible way – which is, usually, the worst way for society and good only for the SME owners. Privatisation and restructuring of enterprises and financial institutions, and speeding up the transition to a market economy, are necessary factors to destroy the "black" economy and strengthen the development of the SME sector and the economy as a whole.

4.2 Perspectives of Future Economic Development of the Country

SMEs could be a strong driving force for the Federal Republic of Yugoslavia to catch up in technological and economic development. SMEs acting within the country as subcontractors or affiliated firms for big foreign companies are a source of technology transfer, but also for the transfer of management, marketing and other "best" working practices, useful for other economic aspects in the country, too. However, under the present political and economic blockade of the country it is very difficult to make prognoses for future economic development. Therefore the only foreseeable and realistic assumption is still the possible and necessary development of business connections between domestic private SMEs and foreign partners in all sectors of the economy.

4.3 Development of a Financial Infrastructure to Support Development of the SME Sector in the Federal Republic of Yugoslavia

During the 1990s some initial steps were taken in the financial sector to support business start-ups and particularly SMEs. This action was a response to increasing unemployment and hidden unemployment (many enterprises were using less than 30-40 per cent of their capacities because of the economic isolation of the country). Special institutions were responsible for this support (in both constituting republics), namely:

- The Republic Office for the Labour Market, and
- The Republic Development Fund.

These two institutions have financed a number of training programmes for employees wishing to establish their own businesses, and for prospective employees of SMEs. Up to now these are the only available funds to which SMEs can apply for financial support.

Besides the various institutions mentioned above, generally speaking, government programmes and supporting institutions and infrastructure are either just being organised or are due to be established. In the absence of financial institutions dedicated to the support of SMEs, the main sources for start-up and business capital are personal savings, assets and money borrowed from relatives and friends (most of them emigrants). The taxation system is still not encouraging investment in production and business, and the capital market is underdeveloped (FRY 2000). This is also an area for necessary framework improvements which need to be made in order to facilitate the development of SMEs sector.

5 The Political Environment for SMEs in the Federal Republic of Yugoslavia

Some initial steps have been made, both at the federal level and at the level of the republics, to support SMEs in the Federal Republic of Yugoslavia. At the federal level, the "Programme of Advancement of the Institutional, Organisational, Financial and Technical Conditions for the Development of Small and Medium Enterprises" was adopted by the Federal Government at its 134th session of 18 May 2000. The Programme consists of the following three parts:

- analysis of the present status in the field of development of SMEs in the Federal Republic of Yugoslavia;
- strategy and policy for fostering SMEs in the Federal Republic of Yugoslavia;
- proposed institutional infrastructure for the support of SMEs in the country.

The main findings of this analysis coincide with the analysis given in previous chapters. The strategy and policy proposed by this programme are based on the presumption of the development of a market economy system. The programme has a target, which is to form as many new SMEs as possible throughout the country every year, while supporting the development and consolidating the business of existing SMEs. In order to achieve this target, the programme has defined measures aiming to accelerate adjustment of the economic system and adapt economic and development policies to the needs of SMEs, as follows (FRY 2000):

- Creation of macroeconomic conditions for the unhindered and rapid development of SMEs (i.e. creation of a favourable climate for the efficiency of business and the economic system; a sound economic policy geared to inflation control; and a taxation and credit policy which would encourage investment in business and especially in SMEs).
- Formation of an institution specialised in SME development – a so-called "SME Agency" – as a Federal public enterprise with the purpose of
  - introducing appropriate policy for the regulation and fostering of SMEs;
  - preparing special supportive programmes and participating in their implementation;

- evaluating opportunities for the development of small-scale industries and identifying the main problems of the SME sector;
- making recommendations to the government and other authorities on SME development programmes and projects to be financed;
- organising a consultant network and training programmes for entrepreneurs and SME employees.

Other institutions which it is proposed to establish are:

- an SME Development Centre,
- a network of regional and local business centres.

- The assistance of government agencies in raising funds for the financing of SME development programmes, i.e. it has been suggested that a special "SME Development Programme Financing, Deposit, Insurance and Guarantee Fund" should be established in the framework of the YU GARANT Bank in which the Federal Government is the majority shareholder.
- The creation of entrepreneurial potential, i.e. by giving priority and special treatment to an entrepreneur ready to go into business and take the risk associated with investment decisions.
- Collection of relevant statistics relating to the SME sector.
- Special forms of assistance to SMEs given on the basis of special programmes, i.e. developing suitable methods of operation and business development such as: (a) franchising, (b) leasing, (c) risk capital, (d) "sub-supplier" arrangements between big and small firms, (e) business incubators.

Several other federal laws have been adopted as a part of an institutional framework for a new market economy, which will also foster the development of the SME sector:

- the aw on foreign investment (introduced in 1994, improved in 1996);
- the aw on privatisation and ownership changes (introduced in former SFRY 1989; in Montenegro 1992, improvements in 1994, 1996; in FRY 1996, improvements in 1997, 1998, 1999; in Serbia 1997);
- the law on enterprises (introduced in 1996, improvements in 1997, 1998, 1999).

While the next actions at the federal level need to be organised, and the adopted measures realised, a number of activities are in progress at the republic level. The Government of the Republic of Serbia has adopted (04.05.1999) during the war (24.03.-10.06.1999) the "Socio-Economic Programme for Employment and Reconstruction of the Enterprises Destroyed During the Aggression Against Yugoslavia" which is based on the development of small and medium sized firms. This programme, supported by the Law on Solidarity of 16.07.1999, is addressed to workers primarily employed in destroyed enterprises. Since its introduction more than

14 000 people have found employment. Almost all of these are practically self-employed, setting-up small firms, or employed by other SMEs on programmes defined by the Special Expert Working Group established under the Ministry for Science and Technology of the Republic of Serbia. In January 2000, the Expert Group defined (MNT, 2000a):

- a catalogue of 2 304 business programmes;
- a catalogue of 644 ideas – "How to make a successful business";
- a catalogue of 689 business programmes (completed programmes i.e. technologies, products, services for establishing new business, new firms) addressed to SMEs in 23 different sectors and technologies (agriculture and food industry, machine tools industry, textiles, wood industry, mining, recycling, equipment for medicine and health services, electrical tools and equipment, civil construction, chemical industry etc.);
- 204 business programmes (programmes i.e. technologies, products or services for establishing new business, new firms) are in developing phase;
- 11 strategic development programmes, and
- a number of documents which could help entrepreneurs in starting-up and developing businesses (basic laws and other regulative documents, together with instructions, comments and useful information (MNT 2000b); examples of business plans; models for setting up new plants, workshops etc.).

Synchronised with this action, the Republic Assembly has adopted the "Law on Private Entrepreneurship" and the Republic Chamber of Commerce, together with the Republic Ministry for Science and Technology, has established a "Technology Brokerage Point", i.e. they collect only results but without demands for new technologies, a computerised data base on results from the R&D sector that are ready to be transferred into production and business from selected technologies: information technologies, energy technologies, new materials, biotechnologies, revitalisation of existing production technologies, genetic engineering. Once a year in autumn, this technology brokerage point and other related activities and results are presented at the "Fair of new technologies: fair as a part of the network between science, technology and production – NovoTex". All these activities are directed towards a new phase of expert group function in the future – setting up a better general environment (general in the sense that it considers the economy as a whole rather than continuing to focus on individual firms that have been destroyed) and improving conditions for the development of SMEs.

6 Final Remarks

Summarising the results, two general conclusions can be made: first, that SMEs are not a myth but a reality in the Federal Republic of Yugoslavia. They constitute a serious part of the economy in terms of absolute numbers, workforce and the generating of revenue. By contributing to the gross domestic product, they contribute to changing the country's economic structure and building a market economy. Secondly, the creation and development of the SME sector is mostly the result of a struggle for survival, rather than the result of organised, supported action sponsored by authorities at all levels. It has become possible to question and modify this second conclusion thanks to the activities organised by the federal government and both republic governments in the last two years and addressed to the SME sector. These activities are a result of the broadly adopted opinion that SMEs represent an opportunity, a realistic solution and a driving force for Yugoslavia's economy to "catch up". This opinion could be regarded as a renaissance of the socio-economic and cultural status of private entrepreneurship as it used to be established in the Kingdom of Yugoslavia (but was subsequently pushed aside and abandoned in the SFRY). It must also be considered as an essential component of the economic restructuring of the Federal Republic of Yugoslavia.

7 Conclusion

Due to revision procedure, this article is in finishing phase after revolutionary political changes in FR of Yugoslavia. New government could be represent with two main characteristics in everyday life in the country: democracy (in politics) and market (in economy). Therefore, we are ready to foresee the following future for SMEs in Federal Republic of Yugoslavia:

- SMEs will be no longer unwilling and forced but desirable alternatives for Yugoslav' economy with private incentives and ownership including foreign investors and entrepreneurs from abroad, as favourable source for start-up and business life in new, market economy;
- small firms could expect at least equal treatment with other companies. If some discrimination will be institutionalised, this must be some privileged business conditions for small firms in favour;
- from the country's technological development point of view, SMEs should expect some special treatment in case when they are technology or R&D intensive. Also, this technology intensive SMEs could rise as result of restructuring process in R&D system;
- promotion of innovation activities in SMEs must be subject of technological and industrial politics in country. These politics should be created having in mind

best practice in EU and OECD member countries considering transfer and diffusion of technologies and SMEs role in these processes.

We hope that future under new democratic circumstances is better of for SMEs and economy and society in Federal Republic of Yugoslavia.

Literature

FRY (2000): SMEs Development Programme. Federal Republic of Yugoslavia – Federal Government, Belgrade.

FSO (1998): R&D organisations. Statistical bulletins, Federal Statistical Office, Belgrade.

Kutlaca, D.; Lazic, M. (2000): R&D System in the Federal Republic of Yugoslavia. In: Matejic, V. (Ed.): Technology, Culture and Development – Experiences and Presumptions for Good Scientific, Technological and Developmental Policy in FR of Yugoslavia. Conference proceeding: Mihajlo Pupin Institute, Science and Technology Policy Research Centre, Belgrade, pp. 103-125.

Minic, J.; Denda, A. (1998, Eds.): How to Support SMEs in Yugoslavia. European Movement in Serbia. Institute of Economic Sciences, Ekonomska Politika, Konrad Adenauer Stiftung, Belgrade.

MNT (2000a): Business Programmes for SMEs. Ministry for Science and Technology of Republic of Serbia, Belgrade.

MNT (2000b): Possibilities for Foreign Investment. Ministry for Science and Technology of Republic of Serbia, Belgrade.

OECD (1993): The Measurement of Scientific and Technical Activities, Proposed Standard Practice for Surveys of Research and Experimental Development – Frascati Manual 1993, Paris.

OECD (2000): OECD in Figures 2000 edition – Statistics of the Member Countries, Paris.

SYKY (1929-1940): Statistical Yearbook of Kingdom of Yugoslavia: 1929; 1930; 1931; 1932; 1933-1934; 1935-1936; 1937; 1938-1939; 1940. General State Statistical Office, Belgrade.

SYY (1994-1999): Statistical Yearbook of Yugoslavia: 1994; 1995; 1996; 1997; 1998; 1999. Federal Statistical Office, Belgrade.

SYY (1989): Statistical Yearbook of Yugoslavia 1918-1988. Federal Statistical Office, Belgrade.

SME Development in the Republic of Slovenia

Viljenka Godina

1 The State of SMEs in Slovenia at the Dawn of the 21st Century

Some fifteen years ago, European institutions started to discuss the role of entrepreneurship as a push for further development of national economies, particularly in line with the formation of new small and medium-sized enterprises (SMEs), promotion of their faster growth and active employment policy. Researchers (e.g. Reynolds/Hay/Camp 1999 found a strong correlation between the economic success of national economies, enterprises, economic and employment growth rates and the awareness of the role of SME and entrepreneurship in a society).

1.1 Slovene SMEs – an Overview

In Slovenia, at the beginning of the 1990s, the SME sector started to play a key role in the dynamic growth of the national economy. After 1989, when a liberal "Enterprise Law" came into force, Slovenia boasted a very high birth rate of small businesses, which resulted in thousands of new micro and small enterprises. After 1995, the small business formation slowed down, but the SME sector has continued to strengthen its place in the national economy by increasing its contribution to the national product and employment.

The recent SME development trends are best illustrated by the analysis of changes in active population (table 1.1-1).

As shown in table 1.1-1, the SME sector increased significantly during the last decade. The proportion of employment in SMEs of all categories (farmers, sole proprietors, micro, small and medium-sized enterprises) increased from 32 per cent to 46 per cent. The fastest growth of employment was recorded in the production and service sector (35 per cent to 62 per cent), mainly due to a significant development shown in micro and small enterprises, while medium-sized enterprises reduced their staff (by some 5 per cent points).

Table 1.1-1: Active population in Slovenia 1989 – 1998

Categories of Employed	Number		Percentage	
	1989	1998	1989	1998
Self-employed in agriculture	40 000	41 012	4.2	4.7
Sole proprietors & employed by sole proprietors	51 146	121 499	5.4	13.8
Employed in micro enterprises	1 102	58 023	0.1	6.6
Employed in small enterprises	19 109	54 537	2.0	6.2
Employed in medium-sized enterprises	187 511	127 544	19.8	14.5
Employed in large enterprises	489 271	218 505	51.8	24.8
Employed in other organisations	122 997	132 569	13.0	15.1
Registered unemployed	33 796	126 079	3.6	14.3
TOTAL	**944 932**	**879 768**	**100**	**100**

Source: Ministry of Small Business and Tourism of the Republic of Slovenia, 2000.

The employment in large companies decreased by over 50 per cent. The SME sector replaced about one third of redundancies by jobs created in newly established businesses and contributed to major structural changes in the national economy in terms of the number of enterprises. The figures for 1998 are shown in table 1.1-2.

Table 1.1-2: Enterprises by size and employment in business sector, Slovenia 1998

Enterprises by Size	Enterprises		Employment	
	Number	Share (%)	Number	Share (%)
Sole proprietors	64 845	63.3	121 499	20.9
Micro enterprises	33 157	32.4	58 023	10.0
Small enterprises	2 778	2.7	54 573	9.4
Medium-sized enterprises	1 293	1.3	127 544	22.0
Large enterprises	348	0.3	218 505	37.7
TOTAL	**102 421**	**100**	**580 144**	**100**

Source: Ministry of Small Business and Tourism of the Republic of Slovenia, 2000.

A fast growth of the SME sector was accompanied by significant changes in the structure of the sectors. Before the 1990s, the manufacturing sector used to employ almost 60 per cent of the total workforce and produce over one-half of the gross domestic product. At the end of the 1990s, the manufacturing sector was still strong, but the economy was already dominated by the service sectors. A few figures are presented in table 1.1-3.

Table 1.1-3: Enterprises and employment by sectors, Slovenia, 1998

Sectors	Enterprises		Employment	
	Number	Share(%)	Number	Share(%)
Agriculture, hunting, forestry	879	0.86	5 786	1.95
Fishing	47	0.05	128	0.04
Mining	164	0.16	1 407	0.47
Manufacturing	19 768	19.37	105 114	35.42
Power, gas & water supply	288	0.28	4 164	1.40
Construction	11 003	10.78	32 530	10.96
Trade, motor vehicle repair	24 958	24.45	60 252	20.30
Catering	6 071	5.95	18 013	6.07
Transport, warehouse, communication	10 509	10.30	13 813	4.66
Financial intermediaries	423	0.41	1 471	0.15
Real estate, rental, business services	15 518	15.20	33 960	11.44
Education	645	0.63	1 408	0.48
Health & social care	705	0.69	8 435	2.84
Other public, common and pers. services	4 068	3.99	7 513	2.53
Unknown[1]	7 021	6.88	2 762	0.93
TOTAL	**102 677**	**100**	**296 756**	**100**

Source: Faculty of Business and Economics of the University of Maribor, 1999.

According to the figures, in 1998 SMEs were the most numerous in trade and motor vehicle repair (almost one fourth of all SMEs). The sector contributed over 20 per cent to total SME employment. The manufacturing sector, representing one fifth of all SMEs, still created over one third of all jobs. The real estate, rental and business service sector represented 15 per cent of all SMEs and contributed over 11 per cent to total SME employment. It was followed by construction, which contributed about 11 per cent. Transport, warehouses and communication services were well represented regarding the number of enterprises, but their contribution to total SME em-

[1] The table includes figures for sole proprietors. Their sectors do not correspond to those used for legal entities.

ployment lagged behind. Agriculture, hunting, forestry and fishing were of minor importance in the SME sector and in the whole economy as well.

A comparison between employment and turnover, presented in table 1.1-4, shows some significant differences between sectors. Manufacturing, boasting the highest proportion of jobs, created slightly over one quarter of the total turnover. A similar situation was found in construction, catering and in some less important sectors. In 1998, trade and motor vehicle repairs was the most successful sector, achieving almost 39 per cent of the total turnover of SMEs. The proportions of turnover contributed by transport, warehouses and communication and financial intermediaries slightly exceed their contribution to the total employment.

Table 1.1-4: Turnover and gross value added by sectors, Slovenia, 1998

Sectors	Employment		Turnover (Mill SIT[2])	
	Number	Share(%)	Amount	Index
Agriculture, hunting, forestry	5 786	1.95	54 797	1.27
Fishing	128	0.04	1 731	0.04
Mining	1 407	0.47	14 650	0.34
Manufacturing	105 114	35.42	1 139 809	26.37
Power, gas & water supply	4 164	1.40	41 719	0.97
Construction	32 530	10.96	301 210	6.97
Trade, motor vehicles repair	60 252	20.30	1 675 282	38.76
Catering	18 013	6.07	115 076	2.66
Transport, warehouse, communication	13 813	4.66	220 534	5.10
Financial intermediaries	1 471	0.15	75 892	1.76
Real estate, rental, business services	33 960	11.44	520 915	12.05
Education	1 408	0.48	10 000	0.23
Health & social care	8 435	2.84	42 692	0.98
Other public, common and pers. services	7 513	2.53	60 399	1.40
Unknown[3]	2 762	0.93	47 313	1.10
TOTAL	**296 756**	**100**	**4 322 019**	**100**

Source: Faculty of Business and Economics of the University of Maribor, 1999.

2 Slovene Tolars (1 € = 213.252 SIT)

3 The table includes figures for sole proprietors. Their sectors do not correspond to those used for legal entities.

1.2 Slovene and European SMEs – a Comparison

In terms of size of enterprises Slovenia has reached the proportion of SMEs in the developed European countries. The SME sector represents 99.7 per cent of the total number of enterprises operating in the business sector. Micro enterprises (companies and sole proprietors) absolutely predominate (95.7 per cent of all enterprises). Small enterprises represent 2.7 per cent and medium-sized 1.3 per cent of all enterprises. The number of large companies accounted for only 0.3 per cent of all enterprises in 1998 (table 1.1-2).

In employment the situation is significantly different. The majority of the workforce is still employed in large companies (almost 38 per cent). Medium-sized companies employ around one fifth of the total workforce, while sole proprietors, micro and small enterprises contribute about 40 per cent to total employment in Slovenia.

According to these figures, the Slovene SME sector is lagging behind the developed European countries. Table 1.2-1 contains some figures presented for developed European countries and Slovenia.

Table 1.2-1: Proportion of enterprises and employment in Europe and Slovenia, 1996

Area / Country	Small and Medium Sized Enterprises				Large Enterpr.	Total
	Micro	Small	Medium	Total		
Proportion of Enterprises in Total Number of Enterprises (in %)						
Europe – 19[4]	92.0	6.0	0.9	99.8	0.2	100
Non-EU countries	88.7	9.3	1.7	99.7	0.3	100
Slovenia	**94.8**	**3.7**	**1.2**	**99.7**	**0.3**	**100**
Employed in SME – Proportion in Total Employment (in %)						
Europe – 19	33	19	14	66	34	100
Non-EU countries	26	22	20	69	31	100
Slovenia[5]	**37**		**15**	**52**	**48**	**100**

Source: Faculty of Business and Economics of the University of Maribor, 1999.

As shown in table 1.2-1, the Slovene SME sector employs some two thirds of the average number of the population employed in the European SMEs. Significant

4 European countries included in the European Observatory for SMEs (Rebernik et.al. 1999).

5 Data available from Slovene sources are not directly comparable to data comprised in the European Observatory for SMEs, since data for sole proprietors are not divided by size of enterprises.

differences appear in the sectors of micro and small enterprises, while the employment in Slovene medium-sized enterprises is only slightly over the European average. The proportion of employees in large companies substantially exceeds the European average.

Selected differences between the Slovene and European SME sectors are additionally illustrated in table 1.2-2.

Table 1.2-2: Selected indicators of the Slovene economy compared to the EU, 1997

Indicators		Small and Medium Sized Enterprises: Small Enterprises: Entr.& Sole Prop.	Small and Medium Sized Enterprises: Small Enterprises: Sole Propriet.	Small and Medium Sized Enterprises: Medium Sized	Small and Medium Sized Enterprises: Total SME	Large Enterprises	Total Enterprises
Number[6] of Enterprises (in thousands)	SLO[7]	99	64	1,5	100	0.87	101
	EU	18 390		170	18 560	40 000	18 600
Number of Employees (in thousands)	SLO	212	105	83	245	270	515
	EU	58 110		15 070	73 180	38 220	111 400
Average size of enterprises	SLO	2.1	1.6	56.5	2.4	310.9	5.1
	EU	3.0		89.0	4.0	956.0	6.0
Annual sales (in million EUR)	SLO	0.11	9.67	3.58	0.16	24.18	0.36
	EU	0.36		16.00	0.50	175.00	0.80
Value added per employee	SLO	10 566	6 815	16 366	12 198	19 838	15 920
	EU	33 600		50 000	35 000	55 000	40 000
Labour costs as % of value added	SLO	61	46	73	66	66	66
	EU	40		60	52	53	53
Profitability[8] (%)	SLO	39	54	27	34	34	34
	EU	60		40	48	47	47

Source: Faculty of Business and Economics of the University of Maribor, 1999.

6 Slovene data on number of companies are not entirely comparable to European Observatory standards: calculations for sole proprietors and specific industries cannot be made.

7 Slovenia.

8 Difference between Value Added (VA) and labour costs (including salaries of self-employed) as a percentage of VA.

Compared to the SMEs operating in Europe, the Slovene SME sector is lagging substantially behind. The average value added per employee in a European SME is EUR 35 000 while the Slovene SMEs achieve only EUR 12 200. Similar discrepancies can also be found in other features: an average Slovene enterprise achieves approximately 45 per cent of the average European sales, while the average sales of a Slovene SME achieves only 32 per cent of the average sales of the European SME.

The share of labour costs in value added in Slovene SMEs is about 27 per cent higher than in Europe and SMEs' profitability in Slovenia averages out at less than three quarters of the average profitability of European SMEs.

The structure of the Slovene SME sector by industries does not significantly differ from the European one: construction, trade, catering, financial intermediaries, education, real estate, rental and business services are in the domain of SMEs. Employment is still concentrated in large companies operating in mining, manufacturing, power, gas and water supply, transport, warehouse and communications.

The Slovene SME sector is involved rather closely in co-operation with European partners. The highest share of co-operation is shown in sub-contracting, supply, marketing and distribution. Other forms of co-operation, such as licenses, franchising, joint research and development (R&D) and joint ventures are less developed, which shows that current forms of co-operation can be considered as short-term rather than long-term relations. As expected, micro enterprises and enterprises without employees are not likely to be involved in international co-operation.

1.3 Main Weaknesses of the Slovene SME Sector

Slovenia has overcome the first SME and entrepreneurship development wave started at the beginning of the 1990s. This was the time of extremely high enterprise birth rates and intensive developments, particularly in the service sector, but mainly in retail, trade etc.

The current state of the SME sector shows some maturity concerning the number of small enterprises in the society, which has achieved the proportions of developed economies. At the same time, it is lagging behind its more developed neighbours: the sales, size and value added of an average Slovene SME are substantially below the European average.

The main weaknesses of the current Slovene SME sector and its promotion infrastructure are:

- a low business birth rate during recent years,
- an absence of fast growing SMEs,

- a relatively small number of high-tech and high value-added enterprises,
- SMEs are not strongly oriented to world markets, particularly not with long-term forms of co-operation; this situation is linked with a lack of managerial skills, in particular for international operations, and poor language skills,
- insufficient awareness of the need for co-operation and partnership among Slovene SMEs,
- insufficient business infrastructure, especially business premises for expansion (expensive, difficult to get and of inadequate quality),
- concentration of entrepreneurial activities in developed areas,
- an insufficient supply of organised venture capital and seed money,
- inadequate remuneration for highly skilled personnel,
- bureaucracy (red tape) at all levels and in all fields,
- a rather strong "grey economy".

Following the examples of the developed countries, Slovenia established quite early the foundations for public promotion schemes aimed at ensuring a faster growth of the SME sector.

2 Public Support for SME Development

As mentioned earlier, the SME sector achieved high growth rates in the period after Slovenia declared independence, practically on the basis of its own strengths and skills in a very hostile environment (restructuring and downsizing, shrunk markets, extremely expensive loans etc.). The introduction of a friendly legal and business environment followed with a substantial delay. It is well known that in terms of competitiveness, SMEs are in a less favourable position compared to large companies. Governments should bridge this weakness by introducing an appropriate legal framework and a favourable and supportive business environment. This task can only be implemented through a co-ordinated and harmonised action with the involvement of all government departments, local authorities and SME promotion institutions.

Quite early on, Slovenia introduced several instruments for the promotion of new enterprise formation. Most of these instruments were developed at the beginning of the 1990s under the pressure of a high unemployment rate and as a consequence, they were focused on the promotion of self-employment. A few instruments and schemes for the promotion of growing businesses were also developed at that time, such as customised training courses and advisory and counselling services. Some of them were occasionally supplied at subsidised prices. A public financial support for

SMEs – a national public SME guarantee and loan fund – was established in 1993. Since 1992 the municipalities have also implemented various local financial schemes, such as subsidised loans directly from local budgets or subsidising of commercial interest rates for loans provided by commercial banks.

Unfortunately, such diverse promotion schemes were not sufficiently co-ordinated among different stakeholders at a national level, were not linked to local support schemes, did not always match specific needs of different target groups of SMEs and entrepreneurs and, which was perhaps their main weakness, they were not provided over a long period. Insufficient national budget available for such schemes, unstable public financing and a one-year-based budgetary expenditure represented a great obstacle to the introduction of more ambitious projects that would need a longer period for preparation and implementation. All the projects had to be planned and accomplished within one year, taking into account also great delays in public tendering and selection procedures. After the budgetary year was finished, there was no guarantee that a specific scheme would attract any further public finance for launching and implementation, even if the programme development was financed by public money and foreseen for potential subsidising. It can be assumed that the results were sub-optimal.

A more systematic designing and co-ordination effort for public SME promotion schemes started towards the end of the 1990s, based on co-ordination between the government departments responsible for the development of SMEs (four ministries: economy, small business, economic relations and development and science and technology) and national public institutions (such as the National Employment Service, Small Business Development Centre, Small Business Development Fund, Slovene Development Corporation etc.). At the beginning of 2001, the government was restructured – three ministries were merged and the technology department of the Ministry of Science and Technology joined the new Ministry of Economy. It is assumed that this merging will improve the co-ordination at the national level. At the same time, as the former independent Ministry of Small Business and Tourism, responsible for the development of micro and small businesses, has joined the new Ministry of Economy, the SME sector might have weaker support than previously.

2.1 Strategy of SME and Entrepreneurship Development

Some time ago the former Ministry of Small Business and Tourism prepared a new strategic document on the development of SMEs and entrepreneurship. The document was submitted to the Government of the Republic of Slovenia for approval. It analyses the state of the SME sector and public promotion schemes currently in place in Slovenia and recommends measures and actions to be taken to improve the support environment and promotion system. The recommendations are fully in line with the recommendations of the European institutions. Slovenia has successfully concluded the adoption of Acquis Comunnitaire for the Chapter 16 – SMEs and has already approved several regulations in order to harmonise the related Slovene legal system with the Acquis. The strategic document represents a framework for the implementation of the relevant promotion schemes aimed at ensuring a faster development of the SME sector, including adoption of some examples of "best practice" implemented in the EU Member States.

The document set seven goals for SME and entrepreneurship promotion including measures and activities intended to improve and support the orientation of entrepreneurs' behaviour and operations on the improvement of competitiveness:

- Systematic support for the development of entrepreneurship in order to increase the number of dynamic, innovative enterprises with a growth potential and high value added, which includes:
  - support for risk taking,
  - promotion of entrepreneurship and development of entrepreneurial culture,
  - development of a dynamic and friendly business environment that will enable growth and facilitate innovation,
  - promotion of local and regional development initiatives,
  - promotion of the development of micro enterprises;
- co-ordination and active participation in the EU promotion programmes for SMEs;
- promotion of co-operation between SMEs operating in Slovenia and foreign partners (internationalisation, "Europeanisation" of enterprises);
- introducing new methods of co-ordination: benchmarking, statistics observation and exchange of experience;
- facilitation of SMEs' transition into the information and internet society;
- protection of the environment by environmentally friendly industries;
- support for specific target groups.

There is, however, an array of measures and instruments recommended to facilitate the achievement of each strategic goal. These, for example, include a systematic approach to changing values and the development of the entrepreneurial culture, which is considered to be of special importance since Slovenia has a rather weak entrepreneurial tradition, different societal rules and the Slovenes are not considered particularly entrepreneurial; there are weaknesses found in the state administration and the media do not treat SMEs in a sufficiently professional manner.

The development of a dynamic and favourable business support environment includes several recommendations, such as reduction of administrative obstacles and burdens, development of premises and related infrastructure, improvement of tax and financial environment and access to financial resources, development of information network for enterprises, support for research and technology development, development of quality and technical standards, support for innovation and facilitation of regional and local development initiatives. The measures combine professional support (provision of customised information, advice, consulting and training), awareness campaigns, support for the development of networks (innovation networks) and institutional building (introduction of innovation in enterprises) with public financial support for specific assignments, such as joint research, access to modern technologies, innovation etc.

2.2 "Anti-Bureaucratic Programme"

This programme deserves special attention. The Anti-bureaucratic Programme is a comprehensive and detailed list and analysis of obstacles hindering the formation and operation of enterprises by regulation and administrative procedures at national and local levels.[9] The programme was developed by an interdisciplinary group of experts as a joint effort of several ministries, public institutions and organisations. It includes a variety of measures focused on a simplification and harmonisation of laws, regulations and administrative procedures, aimed at the reduction of overlaps, time and costs linked with the implementation of regulations in the day-to-day operation of the SMEs. The programme has identified the examples of "best practice" implemented in the European Member States with the purpose of reducing "red tape". It also includes the development of simple, transparent and equalised administrative procedures at local levels, the provision of informative material that would help the entrepreneurs to find their way through administrative requirements and procedures, "one-stop" advice shops and other relevant forms of advice, awareness-raising among officials and training courses for civil servants dealing with entrepreneurs. The programme was completed in April 2000 and submitted to several administrative units and entrepreneurs' associations for comments and suggestions. The document is regarded as a government programme and will be formally approved by the government. The implementation will take several years of co-ordination and harmonisation and a clear commitment of all government departments involved. We believe that the document is probably one of the best-structured materials recently drafted in the area of the SME support.

---

9 Slovenia has not yet established regions as administrative entities. For the purpose of planning and programming of regional development measures and instruments, Slovenia has adopted the so called "statistical regions". Inside these, a great variety of interest networks, formal or informal, are envisaged. The administration tasks will be defined by the Law on Provinces (currently in parliamentary procedure).

2.3 New Forms of Inter-Enterprise Co-Operation and Information Society

The support for inter-enterprise co-operation will be focused on clustering and networking aimed at the promotion of joint R&D activities, development of high quality products and services and joint activities linked with attracting foreign markets. A very important issue will be the promotion of sub-contracting relations between SMEs and large companies. Liberalisation of trade will require a substantial investment by SMEs in the attraction of foreign markets and a significant improvement of the related skills – for entrepreneurs and their staff.

The development and promotion of the information society was ranked very high among the goals for the entire economy. Recently, the government established a new ministry responsible for information and communication technologies. SMEs should be encouraged to develop the e-trade, which will be promoted through the development of relevant legislation and standards. The information society has created new job opportunities (such as home-based business and IT-business) – a comprehensive project has been launched recently and new ones are to be developed and launched in the near future.

Environment protection and support for environmentally-friendly technologies has been recognised as one of the potentially highly interesting areas. As in the EU, special programmes are designed to train entrepreneurs and personnel in SMEs to fulfil the demanding standards.

2.4 European SME Support Programmes

The area of European programmes focused on the promotion of SMEs and entrepreneurship is considered to be very important. Several projects have already been implemented under European programmes, such as: the concept of an SME support network, local development partnerships, development of a supportive environment, the concept of "voucher" system for subsidised advisory and consulting services for SMEs, development and implementation of a pilot regional Human Resource Development Fund, support concepts for specific target groups etc. During the pre-accession period, Slovenia stresses the importance of co-ordination of the promotion programmes with the purpose of channelling them to the implementation of key issues for a faster growth of SMEs and entrepreneuship, namely the preparation of SMEs for opportunities and potential difficulties associated with full EU membership, introduction of the EU quality standards and transfer of knowledge and practical solutions from EU Member States.

The implementation of activities related to the third strategic goal – introduction of new methods of co-ordination – requires permanent research and monitoring of the sector and its features – a basis of the European Observatory for SMEs. It should be underlined that since the beginning of the 1990s, almost no research has been commissioned in the field of SMEs. Meanwhile, statistical monitoring of the SME population has changed and current statistic data do enable in-depth analysis of the sector.

3 Conclusion

The majority of the promotion programmes for SMEs have already been drafted or developed and launched, many of them based on examples of best practice transferred under European programmes and bilateral co-operation. Slovenia should now explore the possibilities of developing an advanced system of public promotion programmes for SMEs, based on co-ordination between the government departments, public institutions, local authorities and regional and local development agencies.

The network of these institutions is currently under development and is considered as the key to improving the efficiency of public SME promotion schemes. Based on the Law on Regional Development introduced in 1999, Slovenia is introducing a systematic approach to project plann ing and programming at the local, regional and national levels, through identification of problems and gaps, public – private partnerships for joint development issues and interests, systematic development of customised support measures and instruments for specific areas, along with a systematic monitoring of project implementation and evaluation of results. Based on a combination of "bottom-up" and approaches, it is expected that the network of SME support institutions, based on regional and local SME development centres established a few years ago, will take over the majority of SME promotion assignments at local and regional levels. Most of the regional SME development centres will obtain the status of regional development agencies. They will provide access to information, advice and well-established links to the relevant national SME development institutions including foreign partners.

It is expected that the information from local areas gathered by the network will provide a sound basis for the development and design of government programmes and, at the same time, a feedback from the local levels which will help the government to evaluate its programmes and measures.

Literature

Glas, M.; Pšeničny, V. (2000): Podjetništvo – izziv za 21. Stoletje (entrepreneurship – a Challenge for the 21st Century), GEA College, Ljubljana.

Tomanič-Vidovič, M.; Marovt, A.; Vahčič, A.; Glas, M.; Drnovšek, M.; Rus, M. (2000): Strategija razvoja malih in srednjih podjetij in podjetništva v Sloveniji (Development Strategy on SME and Entrepreneurship in Slovenia), working material. Ministry of Small Business and Tourism of the Republic of Slovenia, Maribor.

Ministry of Small Business and Tourism, Ministry of Labour, Family and Social Affairs (2000, Ed.): Antibirokratski program v okviru Akcijskega programa zaposlovanja v Sloveniji za leti 2000 in 2001 (Anti-Bureaucratic Programme under the Action Employment Programme in Slovenia for 2000 and 2001), Maribor.

Rebernik, M.; Knez-Riedl, J.; Močnik, D.; Rus, M.; Širec, K.; Primec, A.; Sovinc, B.; Godina, V.; Veingerl, Ž.; Zastavnikovič, Z.; Štrukelj, T.; Hauptman, L. (1999): Zasnova modela zbiranja, analiziranja in vključevanja podatkov o slovenskem malem gospodarstvu v "The European Observatory for SMEs (Draft Concept on Selection, Analysis and Inclusion of Data on Slovene SMEs in the European Observatory for SMEs), Faculty of Business and Economics of the University of Maribor.

Reynolds, D. P.; Hay, M.; Camp, S. M. (1999): Global Entrepreneurship Monitor. Ewing Marion Kaufman Foundation, Babson College, London Business School.

Small Business and Entrepreneurship in Romania

Ioan Piturescu

1 Introduction

Romania, like other former communist countries, is in the situation of reinforcing the SME sector. After many years of a rigidly centralised economy, the result has been a disappearance of any entrepreneurial spirit. In this context, rapid development of the SME sector represents a priority in the complex process of transition, not only for the general reasons which sustain this sector in the developed countries, but also for other specific reasons, as follows:

- the need to supply jobs for the labour force previously employed in the state sector;
- the need to promote increased adaptability to market demands;
- acceleration of the decentralisation process;
- promoting the creation of a "middle stratum" of people;
- the need to reinforce the economic basis of political pluralism.

2 History of Small and Medium Sized Enterprises

While the fast development of the SME sector represents a priority direction of reform for all countries in transition to a market economy, the necessity holds true especially in the case of Romania. Among all other CEECs, Romania has been known as the most centralised political and economic system with a very reduced private sector. It is important to mention that during the past ten years, Romania had chosen democracy as a way of political organisation, and has been relatively successful in creating institutions and organisations to promote a market-oriented economy. As in most countries which were previously under the communist regime, ownership of assets was communal for all people in the hand of the state. Consequently individual wealth was minimal, and at the beginning of the reform period potential entrepreneurs started from a very low personal asset base. It is interesting to note, however, that opportunities after liberalisation of markets were so vast and numerous that entrepreneurship, as a logical consequence, had very good chances of success. In addition entrepreneurship in Romania is regarded as crucial, in order to manage successfully the structural and social changes in the process of transition from centrally planned to market economy.

Like many other transition countries, Romania was – and still is – faced with the challenge of developing coherent and creative policies which are appropriate for its turbulent environment and its needs. The environment even in the early to mid 'nineties was characterised by galloping inflation, cripplingly high interest rates, factories full of obsolete machinery and a serious general shortage of financial resources. While these circumstances would have discouraged any western entrepreneur, the case of Romania adds some new insights into investigation on the generation and development of small firms and entrepreneurship.

3 Relevance of the SME Sector Today

For Romania, small and medium enterprises are the only source of new jobs. Looking at the present structure of the Romanian economy, the private sector of SMEs constitutes a remarkable presence with special contributions to sustaining the state budget and developing the economy; however, it has modest results considering the Romanian potential and when comparing it to its homologue from developed countries. Although at the end of the nineties more than 97 per cent of all 313 689 Romanian enterprises had less than 50 employees,[1] they cannot be regarded as agents of industrial change in general. Despite some progress the economic impacts, even in the outgoing nineties, are not satisfying at all. Most of these entrepreneurial firms exhibit a low economic potential, having an extremely modest turnover of less than US$ 10 000 per year.

The data presented in the following table (table 3-1) concerning the distribution of firms by ownership nevertheless offer an impressive view of the considerable place occupied by private SMEs in the Romanian economy.

An analysis of the dates reveals the fact that the larger firms in Romania are, the more they are equipped with state capital and – especially in the case of medium-sized and large enterprises, with both state and private capital.

In Romania, starting from 1990, a rapid process of setting-up took place: organisation and development of enterprises, owners and managers creating a large number of SMEs.

1 Numbers are from 1998, see tables 6a-d.

Table 3-1: Distribution of firms by ownership (in 1996, in per cent)

Firms	Total SMEs	Micro	Small	Medium	Large
Employment	(0-249)	(0-9)	(10-49)	(50-249)	≥250
Private capital	97.4	99.3	91.1	50.0	24.9
State-owned	0.3	0.1	0.9	6.7	7.6
Both state and private capital	2.3	0.6	0.8	43.3	67.5
TOTAL	100	100	100	100	100

Source: "The private Sector of Small and Medium Sized Enterprises in Romania – Annual Report 1997" – Chamber of Commerce and Industry of Romania and Municipality of Bucharest National Trade Register Office and The CRIMM Foundation.

Now we can state that there are two stages in the development of the Romanian SME sector:

- A stage of qualitative and quantitative increase of SMEs, making a substantial contribution to the economic and social life of the country, which continued until mid-1995.
- A stage of stagnation or more specifically a regression of SME dynamics, from 1995 to the present day (table 3-2).

Table 3-2: Dynamics of the number of SMEs (1991-1999)

No	Year	Number of SMEs registered monthly	Total number of SMEs registered yearly
1	1991	7 988	95 856
2	1992	11 142	137 456
3	1993	9 752	117 078
4	1994	11 141	137 445
5	1995	5 416	65 479
6	1996	5 169	62 089
7	1997	4 638	55 663
8	1998	5 322	63 869
9	1999	5 700	17 100

Source: National Commission for Statistics.

The dynamics of the SME sector are the result of many causes and specific conditions, as follows:

- the absence of this sector before 1990;
- legislative particularities regarding the functioning and mode of organisation of SMEs;
- the restructuring of state enterprises and the rhythm of privatisation.

In addition, many small and medium enterprises have developed their activity only in the period in which they have some fiscal facilities. After this period, the shareholders have preferred to found other businesses with a view to continuing to benefit from these facilities without eliminating the old ones. In this way, they have tried to avoid the measures provided by law.

3.1 Activities by Sectors of Industry

Considering SME structure by sectors of activity, one can observe great heterogeneity. The majority of firms have shown a tendency to engage in several types of activity. Not surprising is the predominance of SMEs in the sector of trade (72 per cent), followed by SMEs in the field of services (~14 per cent), in the manufacturing sector (~10 per cent) and, in last place, the construction sector, which is surprising considering that it is potentially an economically attractive sector. This structure reflects an important degree of economic indecisiveness, indicating an absence of business plans and an uncertain approach regarding what field of activity to adopt. These characteristics reflect the incipient stage of the development of entrepreneurial phenomena and also the entrepreneurs' degree of maturity. Once firms become functional, i.e. once they are operating in a more product-oriented way, they choose in most cases a single field of activity. Relevant from this point of view is the information offered by the National Commission of Statistics concerning the distribution of SMEs by activity sectors, in the period 1996-1997 (tables 3.1-1a/b), which indicates the absolute predominance of SMEs from the trade and services fields; these two sectors together represent around 86 per cent of all SMEs in the national economy.

Table 3.1-1a: Distribution of SMEs by size classes and sectors of activity (absolute number of enterprises), 1996 and 1997

Size / Sector	Manufacturing		Construction		Trade		Services		Total	
	1996	1997	1996	1997	1996	1997	1996	1997	1996	1997
Micro (0-9)	23 508	26 003	3 812	5 873	216 406	215 189	42 309	40 144	286 035	287 209
Small (10-49)	5 317	6 400	1 938	2 234	8 154	9 417	2 751	3 159	18 160	21 210
Medium (50-249)	2 012	2 347	934	1 025	1 253	1 273	1 060	1 119	5 259	5 764
Total	**30 837**	**34 750**	**6 684**	**9 132**	**225 813**	**225 879**	**46 120**	**44 422**	**309 454**	**314 183**

Source: Romanian Statistical Annual, 1998.

Table 3.1-1b: Distribution of SMEs by size classes and sectors of activity (number of enterprises in per cent), 1996 and 1997

Size / Sector	Manufacturing		Construction		Trade		Services		Total	
	1996	1997	1996	1997	1996	1997	1996	1997	1996	1997
Micro (0-9)	76.23	74.83	57.03	64.31	95.83	95.27	91.74	90.37	92.43	91.41
Small (10-49)	17.24	18.42	29.00	24.46	3.61	4.17	5.96	7.11	5.87	6.75
Medium (50-249)	6.53	6.75	13.97	11.23	0.65	0.56	2.30	2.52	1.70	1.85
% of all SMEs	**9.96**	**11.06**	**2.16**	**2.91**	**72.97**	**71.89**	**14.90**	**14.14**	**100**	**100**

Source: Romanian Statistical Annual, 1998.

The data presented in the tables above evidence a number of changes realised in 1997 as compared to 1996:

- a decrease in the overall percentage share of micro enterprises and an increase in the overall percentage share of small and medium sized SMEs by 1.02 per cent can be observed. This results from the much more accentuated dynamics of SMEs (change from 1997 to 1998 = + 14.7 per cent, table 3-2);
- the most important changes were registered in two key sectors of the economy: manufacturing and construction. The share of micro enterprises in the manufacturing sector decreased by 1.4 per cent in 1997 compared to 1996, and at the same time the share of small and medium sized enterprises in the same sector went up by 1.18 per cent and 0.22 per cent respectively. In the construction sector an opposite evolution is observed: here the share of micro enterprises increased by 7.27 per cent in 1997 compared to 1996, whereas the shares of small and medium sized enterprises decreased by 4.54 per cent and 2.74 per cent respectively;
- the changes in the trade sector and in the service sector show some elasticity.

3.2 SMEs and Employment

Concerning the distribution of employees by sectors of activity, it should be noted that even for micro enterprises/entrepreneurial firms, trade and service are the dominant areas of operation. Data of the National Commission for Statistics, used in the study "Evolution of the private sector in Romania in 1997", show that in private SMEs

- at the end of 1997 an occupied population of 3 156 000 persons is registered in the agriculture sector, representing nearly 95 per cent of the total employed in this field;
- the population employed in the manufacturing sector at the end of 1997 amounted to 727 000 (29.7 per cent of the total employed in this field);
- at the end of 1997, 293 000 persons were working in the construction sector (66.7 per cent of the total occupied population in this field);
- in the service sector at the end of 1997, the occupied population was 1 003 000 persons (36.5 per cent of the total employed in this field).

However, the employment shares reveal the fact that micro enterprises are less important than their larger counterparts, because micro enterprises represent 91.4 per cent of the total number of active SMEs in 1997, but account for just 38.1 per cent of the total number of employees. And although medium sized enterprises represent only 1.8 per cent of the total number of SMEs, they comprise 31.7 per cent of the total number of employees occupied in SMEs. While there is already a shift towards the number of private micro enterprises, the new jobs generated seem less numerous.

3.3 Innovation and Technology Transfer

Transition to a market economy requires restructuring in all sectors, and the whole of industry, as a very complex system, is most affected. The long way from a centralised economy to a market-oriented economy implies innovation-related issues that will need to be addressed and dealt with. It is obvious that the restructuring of industry in a country like Romania will be difficult to imagine without huge innovation costs related to new products, technological updating, quality assurance, adaptation to world standards, market-oriented marketing. The local infrastructure of research and development (R&D) should play a crucial role in this restructuring. Nevertheless Romania faces two sources of problems: on the one hand – lack of funds for R&D activity and difficulties in transferring the R&D results to industry; on the other hand – the struggle of a barely surviving economy to get off the ground.

The Romanian economy is passing from a protected economy to an open market-oriented economy, which means putting local producers to compete with foreign products in a free market. In order to become competitive, it is necessary to assimilate and use modern technology. However, lack of appropriate finance still dissuades researchers from attempting to exploit their inventions, and hampers the entrepreneurs who could transfer research results to new regions and sectors.

The potential for creating new high-quality jobs is thought to be concentrated in emerging high-technology sectors and the innovative, dynamic and rapidly growing small and medium-sized enterprises which characterise them. Long-term economic difficulties and rising unemployment in Romania have focused attention on the importance of innovation and technological progress for business competitiveness, sustainable growth and job creation. To deal more effectively with all these aspects, the following areas are targeted for future integrated innovation policy:

- promoting a real culture of innovation: focusing initially on education and training, but also provoking a greater awareness and introducing more efficient procedures in business and public authorities;
- setting up a favourable environment for innovation: through improved protection of intellectual property rights (IPR), streamlined administrative procedures and additional finance;
- creating stronger links between research and innovation: both at national level and at regional and local level, via the mobilisation of EU resources and tools such as structural funds and international co-operation agreements.

It is well known in Romania that, in order to perform this role, small and medium enterprises cannot act self-sufficiently. By their nature they have a light structure and cannot have in-house availability of all the skills and functions that they require. They depend, not only on outsourcing and subcontracting, but also on a range of technical and support services that they have to procure from outside. Small and medium enterprises constitute the demand, rather than the supply, of industrial RTD. For this demand to be actively satisfied, it seems essential firstly to strengthen its absorptive capacity for technology through the availability and quality of the partners and intermediaries, and secondly to encourage their participation in co-operative and collaborative research. The reality, however, as the following tables show, is not a favourable situation for innovative SMEs:

Tables 3.3-1a–c present the main indicators characterising research and development units, by sectors of execution:

- enterprise sector,
- government sector,
- higher education sector.

The tables 3.3-1a-c and the following tables 3.3-2a-c show a general tendency: not the numbers of institutions in the R&D sphere, but the numbers of employees, are reduced. However, a differentiated view exhibits growing private R&D activities within the enterprise sector. This allows some specifications concerning innovative SMEs.

Table 3.3-1a: Main indicators for research and development units, by sectors of execution (Units (number) – end of year)

	1994	1995	1996	1997
Enterprise sector	452	454	455	496
Government sector	105	120	122	109
Higher education sector	34	41	39	40
Total	**591**	**615**	**616**	**645**

Source: National Commission for Statistics Romanian Statistical Yearbook, 1998.

Table 3.3-1b: Main indicators for research and development units, by sectors of execution (Employees – number – end of year)

	1994	1995	1996	1997
Enterprise sector	90 272	78 308	77 882	68 702
Government sector	24 091	23 487	21 351	18 493
Higher education sector	2 683	3 400	4 952	5 627
Total	**117 046**	**105 195**	**104 185**	**92 822**

Source: National Commission for Statistics Romanian Statistical Yearbook, 1998.

Table 3.3-1c: Main indicators from research and development units, by sectors of execution (Average number of employees per unit)

	1994	1995	1996	1997
Overall average	**198**	**171**	**169**	**144**
Enterprise sector	200	172	171	139
Government sector	229	196	175	170
Higher education sector	79	83	127	141

Source: National Commission for Statistics Romanian Statistical Yearbook, 1998.

The number of the R&D units remains approximately the same between 1994 and 1997, without important changes. What can be registered is a slight increase in 1997 (645 units) compared to 1996 (616 units). A characteristic over the whole period 1994-1997 is the majority weight of research and development units in the enterprise sector (77 per cent of all R&D units in 1997). Compared with the number of the employees, which show a drastical reduction (-24 per cent since 1994) the enterprise sector has lost its dominance (Average number of employees per unit).

Table 3.3-2a: Main indicators for research and development units, by sectors of execution and types of ownership (Units – number – end of year)

	1996			1997		
	Type of ownership			Type of ownership		
	Public	Mixed	Private	Public	Mixed	Private
Enterprise sector	388	13	54	397	53	46
Government sector	122	-	-	109	-	-
Higher education sector	36	-	3	37	-	3
Total	**546**	**13**	**57**	543	**53**	**49**

Source: National Commission for Statistics Romanian Statistical Yearbook, 1998.

Table 3.3-2b: Main indicators for research and development units, by sectors of execution and types of ownership (Employees -number – end of year)

	1996			1997		
	Type of ownership			Type of ownership		
	Public	Mixed	Private	Public	Mixed	Private
Enterprise sector	72 813	2 457	2 612	58 849	6 916	2 937
Government sector	21 351	-	-	18 493	-	-
Higher education sector	4 727	-	225	5 558	-	69
Total	**98 891**	**2 457**	**2 837**	**82 900**	**6 916**	**3 006**

Source: National Commission for Statistics Romanian Statistical Yearbook, 1998.

Table 3.3-2c: Main indicators for research and development units, by execution sectors and by type of ownership (Average number of employees per unit)

	1996			1997		
	Type of ownership			Type of ownership		
	Public	Mixed	Private	Public	Mixed	Private
Enterprise sector	188	189	48	148	130	64
Government sector	175	-	-	170	-	-
Higher education sector	131	-	75	150	-	23
Total	**181**	**189**	**50**	**153**	**130**	**61**

Source: National Commission for Statistics Romanian Statistical Yearbook, 1998.

A differentiation by type of ownership however, exhibits that within enterprise sector especially mixed and even private R&D units gain employment while public units have registered a considerable loss. The shift from public to mixed and private R&D units is an indicator for the commercialisation of the technology transfer process within the innovation system.

The restructuring process is still crucial and influenced by the economics situation. Therefore innovative SMEs are still a minority and only 3 per cent of the total number of employees in all SMEs work in the domain of R&D.

There is a need for a continuous campaign to inform SMEs about research schemes – both directly and through an extensive network of intermediaries, so that they can maintain close links with key industrial and academic contacts. The characteristic of modern economies facing international competition, the strong link between innovation, growth and employment is generally accepted within Romania. And although innovation is primarily seen within the responsibility of individual companies, governments have to optimise the general conditions for innovation, in particular the legal and administrative environment. Here, much needs to be done in the near future.

4 Framework Conditions for the SME Sector in Romania

The present environment is characterised by some elements that are specific to the transition period. Some of these support the development of the SME sector. Thus the market economy orientation which has materialised from the fast creation of an institutional and legislative framework, although it could be improved, does not offer favourable premises for putting the principles and rules of market economy into practice. At the same time, the drawing up of some development strategies for the SME sector, and also the implementation of some legislative, economic and institutional measures, have as a result supported small and medium sized private enterprises.

The main actions have been:

- elaborating development policies for the SME sector and co-ordinating the national programmes in order to achieve the goals;
- finalising and reinforcing the institutional framework for the development of the SME sector;
- developing an institutional system for consultancy services, assistance and information;
- creating an informational system to support the SMEs sector;
- initiating and putting in practice the regional development programmes;
- providing financial assistance for the SME sector;
- building a positive attitude regarding the SME sector;
- developing some training programme for human resources;
- supporting and intensifying contacts between Romanian and foreign SMEs.

However, the proposed strategies are neither linked with specified intermediate steps nor is provision made for the necessary resources to achieve the stated goals. Nor are the responsible institutions and organisations specified. Furthermore, beside these positive factors, there are also elements with negative effects in the situation in Romania which slow down the development of SMEs. Thus the deep economic and political instability induces uncertainty, inhibiting the development of the entrepreneurial spirit.

4.1 The Institutional Framework

The most important actions to support the creation and reinforcing of an institutional framework for supporting the SME sector include, on one hand, efforts directed towards setting up governmental and non-governmental institutions with specific competencies and, on the other hand, those concerned with the development of stimulative national and international programmes.

At government level a succession of organisations has been created, with the specific purpose of elaborating strategies for small and medium enterprise, putting into practice the programmes for implementing them and in initiating legislative projects etc., as follows:

- an organisational unit was set up for the promotion of small and medium enterprises, with the goal of organising promotion actions for SMEs. Initially these activities were performed within the framework of the National Agency for Privatisation, were then temporarily taken over by the Romanian Development Agency, were subsequently re-transferred to the National Agency for Privatisation, took place for a period in the framework of the Council for Reform and are now performed by the Agency for SMEs;
- included among the other competencies of ministers are institutions which support the SME sector and create a competitive business environment: ministries and institutions which are involved with various aspects of SMEs are the Ministry of Labour and Social Protection, the Ministry of Industry and Commerce, the Ministry of Research and Technology, the National Committee for Statistics, the Chambers of Commerce and Industry etc.

At non-government level, a great number of organisations and institutions have been founded which are involved in the field of small and medium enterprises. These institutions have various organisational forms depending on their profile and their aims. Three of the most important are:

- the CRIMM Foundation (Romanian Centre for Small and Medium Enterprises) which has acted since 1993 as an organ for implementing programmes (especially PHARE), as a supplier of technical assistance, and as main consultant and initiator of proposals in the field of development of small and medium sized private enterprises;
- the Romanian Fund of Credits Guarantee (FRGC) founded in 1993 with the dual aim of supporting entrepreneurs in the conception and elaboration of business plans, and partially assuming the repayment risk for requested credits (maximum 70 per cent of the total amount of the credit);

- ARD-PNUD Centre (Romanian Development Agency – United Nations Development Programme) was founded in 1991 with PNUD and governmental logistic and financial support, with the general objective of supporting private entrepreneurs by free consultancy.

In addition, there are centres for the development of SMEs, such as the Balcanic Co-operation Centre for small and medium sized enterprises; agencies for local development, entrepreneurs' associations such as the National Council of Small and Medium Sized Private Enterprises from Romania, the National Union of Romanian Employers' Associations, the Entrepreneurs Counselling Council: institutions for the development of private entrepreneurs and support in obtaining special premises or workshops, such as the Technological and Business Incubator Centre Bucharest (CITAF) or pilot business incubators created – with CRIMM support – in Braila, Miercurea-Ciuc, Sibiu and Timisoara; business consultancy centres; professional training and guidance institutions; and finally banking institutions such as the Bank for Small Industry and Private Initiative (MINDBANK) specialising in small and medium sized private enterprises, and other banks which provide banking services for small and medium enterprises (Romanian Development Bank, Ion Tiriac Bank, Romanian Commercial Bank).

4.2 The Legislative Framework

The transition from a centralised economy to a market economy has involved radical transformations from the legislative point of view. A part of this new legislative structure is represented by the settlement regarding the establishing and functioning of SMEs. Although this is incomplete and sometimes confusing, especially with regard to fiscal and commercial aspects, it at least provides a legitimating framework, if not a stimulating one. Thus these primary authoritative acts regarding SMEs have been complemented by specific legislation for SMEs, especially after 1992. In the period 1990-1992, with one exception (Decree 54 from 1990), no other settlement specifically targeted the SME sector. Subsequently, a series of legislative measures were adopted which reflected a change in attitude regarding small and medium sized enterprises.

The Governmental Ruling No. 25 from August 1993 gave the first legal definition of categories of SMEs, depending on number of employees and turnover (natural person and family associations, small sized enterprises with 5-25 employees, medium sized enterprises with 26-200 employees). This ruling also settled the systems of facilities and advantages for SMEs. The necessary resources were made up from the amount approved yearly by the State Budget Law, from private contributions and foreign economic assistance. At the same time, the ruling provided the legal framework for setting up representative associations for SMEs as legal entities and using a simple procedure, with flexible conditions. Through these associations SMEs are able to amplify their own representative strength, report to other entities, benefit from better co-ordination and mutually support each other in achieving their own objectives. Although the ruling has many good points, it must be noted that it also has a high level of generality, with insufficiently definite elements which are open to interpretation (for example: "access to resources without any discrimination, to materials and basic services offered by commercial societies and state owned societies").

A series of economic and financial facilities for SMEs were stipulated by the Governmental Order No. 805 from 1994. Thus, for investments, SMEs could benefit from credits of up to 80 per cent of the project value (maximum 50 million Lei with a "grace period" of 6 months) at an interest rate of half the BNR reference interest. In the absence of covering guarantees, the Romanian Credit Guarantee Fund for Private Entrepreneurs could guarantee these credits. The approval procedures for granting financial support, which are relatively complex, and also the amount of funding involved (which has become useless for entrepreneurs because it has not been brought up to date) represent significant limitations of this ruling. The Governmental Order No. 20 from January 30 1998, regarding risk capital funds, suggested using these funds as institutional instruments for supporting businesses which do not involve a high risk. Also called development funds, they represent an alternative to methods of finance which are more difficult for SMEs to access, such as bank credits or the capital market. The main characteristic of these funds, which have structures with exclusive private ownership, is the fact that the creditors do not require guarantees when sharing the business risk with the owners of the financed enterprises. From the moment when the fund becomes the associate of a business with a high level of risk, it has the right to supervise how the business is run, with a view to reducing the investment risk and can also provide consultancy.

In July 1999, the Romanian Parliament unanimously approved the "Law No. 133/1999, regarding the stimulation of private entrepreneurs for the creation and development of small and medium sized private enterprises". This law stipulates the general framework for SME policy, including setting up the National Agency for Small and Medium Sized Enterprises. The law deals with the setting up and development of SMEs and provides special measures for their development, including improving the business environment, access to premises and professional training, finance schemes, etc. At the moment this law is being partially applied, because further amendments, very important stipulations for the SME sector (articles 15, 22-27) were suspended by Government Orders in December 1999.

4.3 Support Programmes for SMEs

As well as the organisations and institutions relevant to SMEs, a series of programmes were developed, starting in 1990, which have made a substantial contribution to supporting the SME sector and finding modern, efficient and realistic solutions:

- The PHARE Programme for the development of the SME sector in Romania, financed by the European Union: this has a budget of 10 million ECU (2.7 million ECU for CRIMM and SME consultancy centres; 1.5 million ECU for the creation of a favourable environment for small and medium enterprises; 4.8 million ECU for pilot projects; 1 million ECU for PMU – Project Management Unit).
- The PHARE Programme for small and medium enterprises and regional development (FIDEL) for the period 1996-1997, with the following components: government policies for the development of SMEs (0.75 million ECU), the fund for supporting local development initiatives (6 million ECU), informing, training and consultancy activities (2.8 million ECU), financial instruments for small and medium enterprises (8 million ECU).
- The programme initiated by "Corpul Pacii" ("Peace Organism"), a USA governmental agency – in collaboration with the Romanian Development Agency, with a view to providing the necessary assistance for local Chambers of Industry and Commerce and other organisations involved in supporting SMEs.
- Programmes with the goal of developing the entrepreneurial spirit: the "Economic and Managerial Training" Programme developed by USAID (USA Agency for International Development), which aims to train personnel from the National Agency for Privatisation and the counsellors from the programmes financed by PNUD and USAID in the field of consultancy for entrepreneurs; the "Good Morning Romania" Programme initiated by USAID with a view to informing people regarding privatisation issues and stimulating entrepreneurial spirit.

In 1999, two programmes supporting SMEs (Governmental Ruling No. 788 from 1998 and Governmental Ruling No. 789 from 1998) were developed which provided for the allocation of small grants without reimbursement. These two programmes, co-ordinated by National Agency for Small and Medium Sized Enterprises, are financed by funds from the state budget.

5 Conclusion

In summary, it can be concluded that despite economic reform, small and medium enterprises in Romania are still confronted with a series of obstacles which, in view of the economic and political instability, lead to uncertainty and to inhibition of the entrepreneurial spirit.

The main barriers arise from the following aspects:

- Legislative constraints:

- the co-existence of authoritative documents belonging to different legislative systems (the system existing until 1948, the system of the socialist period and the system which came into existence in 1989) generate ambiguities and are not in concordance;
- the frequent changes in legislation, the elaboration of authoritative documents which are subject to interpretation, and their deficient application, also have a negative impact on small and medium enterprises – SMEs are known to have a limited capacity for assimilating new legislative conditions. At the same time, this situation does not stimulate potential entrepreneurs, but rather creates an image of inaccessibility of the business field.

- Fiscal constraints:
  - at present, small and medium enterprises bear an excessive tax burden, in the sense that taxation is the same for all sectors of activity and for all sizes. This situation leads to SMEs becoming undercapitalised, making it impossible for them to invest.
- Institutional constraints:
  - the absence of an integrated institutional framework based on collaboration and co-operation between the institutions and organisations involved in supporting the SME sector, as well as the large number of these institutions, and the overlapping of their functions and responsibilities, generate confusion among entrepreneurs.
- Financial and banking constraints:
  - although the state has taken a series of measures with a view to encouraging financial credits for SMEs, the absence of financing for these is still one of the major obstacles to the development of these firms. The large instalments of bank interest repayments and their fluctuation make this modality of financing uninteresting; entrepreneurs are forced to rely on their own resources, which are very modest;
  - on the other hand, even the banks are not interested in co-operating with small and medium enterprises because of the very high financing costs. These costs are generated by administrative expenses and expenses for gathering information;
  - the existing banking system is not adapted to the financing of small and medium enterprises.

We consider that setting up a favourable institutional framework for small and medium enterprises constitutes a complex process which ought to commence at the beginning of the transition process. Experience shows that clear competencies and responsibilities for these institutions have to be settled in order to avoid duplications and confusions and to delimit the area for action. Nevertheless, the Romanian government is not in a position either to guarantee favourable framework conditions for SMEs, or to counterbalance unfavourable conditions by financial measures. Today, the view which is taken as a current guideline is that the most important way of supporting small and medium enterprises is to encourage the business environment and the general development of the economy.

Table 5-1a: Structure of enterprises in Romania by selected activity sectors and by size classes (Absolute numbers of enterprises)

	TOTAL	<50	50-250	>250
Energy and water industries	369	92	135	142
Industries mainly based on production of intermediate goods (excluding energy, water and motor vehicles)	12 575	11 381	701	493
Motor vehicle industry	197	130	25	42
Industries mainly based on production of equipment goods (excluding motor vehicle industry)	3 713	3 196	363	254
Industries mainly based on production of consumer durables (excluding motor vehicle industry)	1 929	1 608	207	114
Agricultural and food industries (excluding manufacture of grain mill products, manufacture of starches and starch products, manufacture of prepared fodder)	83 216	82 557	450	209
Industries mainly based on production of consumer nondurables, other than agricultural and food	11 628	10 394	861	373
TOTAL	**313 689**	**305 315**	**6 035**	**2 339**

Source: Economic Activity Units, National Commission for Statistics, 2000.

Table 5-1b: Structure of enterprises in Romania by selected activity sectors and by size classes (Percentage of total number of enterprises)

	<50	50-250	>250
Energy and water industries	24.93	36.59	38.48
Industries mainly oriented to production of intermediate goods (excluding energy, water and motor vehicles)	90.50	5.57	3.93
Motor vehicle industry	65.99	12.69	21.32
Industries mainly based on production of equipment goods (excluding motor vehicle industry)	86.08	7.08	6.48
Industries mainly based on production of consumer durables (excluding motor vehicle industry)	83.36	10.73	5.91
Agricultural and food industries (excluding manufacture of grain mill products, manufacture of starches and starch products, manufacture of prepared fodder)	92.61	5.05	2.34
Industries mainly based on production of consumer nondurables, other than agricultural and food	89.39	7.40	3.21
TOTAL	**97.33**	**1.92**	**0.75**

Source: Economic Activity Units, National Commission for Statistics, 2000.

Table 5-1c: Structure of enterprises in Romania by selected activity sectors and by size classes (Numbers of employees)

	TOTAL	<50	50-250	>250
Energy and water industries	391 003	1 371	16 952	372 680
Industries mainly based on production of intermediate goods (excluding energy, water and motor vehicles)	721 556	67 512	79 245	574 799
Motor vehicle industry	89 221	1 515	3 335	84 371
Industries mainly based on production of equipment goods (excluding motor vehicle industry)	397 772	22 173	28 972	346 627
Industries mainly based on production of consumer durables (excluding motor vehicle industry)	142 799	11 191	31 929	99 679
Agricultural and food industries (excluding manufacture of grain mill products, manufacture of starches and starch products, manufacture of prepared fodder)	226 544	46 110	47 112	133 322
Industries mainly based on production of consumer nondurables, other than agricultural and food	452 569	55 397	110 573	286 599
TOTAL	**4 167 012**	**905 236**	**670 922**	**2 590 854**

Source: Economic Activity Units, National Commission for Statistics, 2000.

Table 5-1d: Structure of enterprises in Romania by selected activity sectors and by size classes (Percentage shares of employees)

	<50	**50-250**	**>250**
Energy and water industries	0.35	4.34	95.31
Industries mainly based on production of intermediate goods (excluding energy, water and motor vehicles)	9.36	10.98	79.66
Motor vehicle industry	1.70	3.74	94.56
Industries mainly based on production of equipment goods (excluding motor vehicle industry)	5.57	7.28	87.15
Industries mainly based on production of consumer durables (excluding motor vehicle industry)	7.84	22.36	69.80
Agricultural and food industries (excluding manufacture of grain mill products, manufacture of starches and starch products, manufacture of prepared fodder)	20.35	20.80	58.85
Industries mainly based on production of consumer nondurables, other than agricultural and food	12.24	24.43	63.33
TOTAL	**21.72**	**16.10**	**62.18**

Source: Economic Activity Units, National Commission for Statistics, 2000.

Supporting Innovation Through Institution Building in Central and Eastern Europe: Between Visions and Realities

Slavo Radosevic, Günter H. Walter

1 Introduction

After 10 years of transformation and recovery the economies of the most of CEECs, including Russia, are recording positive growth rates. If this growth is to continue it will require, beside physical and human capital investments, new and further institution building. This has been obvious throughout the whole transition period in areas of macroeconomic policy, privatisation and other areas of establishing market economy. However, institution building for innovation was not given equal importance. Yet, growth literature tells us that the long-term growth and its sustainability in CEECs will rest not only on competitive markets but also on the emergence of systems of support to innovation.

The research on determinants of growth in transition economies shows that development in CEECs has been so far primarily dependent on initial conditions and transition specific variables, like privatisation, liberalisation and structural reforms in banking, trade, legal system, etc. (Berg et al. 1999; Fischer et al. 1998) CEECs that have been more successful in transformation, like Poland and Slovenia, are recovering faster and have surpassed their 1989 GDP levels. For the future any advantages within the endogenous resources such as physical and human capital that these economies have are conditional upon the existence of institutions and developed networks which may turn this conditional advantage into a real absolute advantage. This is especially important because the co-ordination between actors in policy, economy, science and on the different levels, e.g. the local, regional, national level and international level, is decisive for restructuring and innovation based growth. Good opportunity to do so are economies, areas and locations with short distances between the actors, close contacts, mutual interests, limited resources and the greater capacity for collective action, e.g. in so called locational economies that means regions of very large countries (Russia) and small national economies (Slovenia).

One of the major difficulties in transformation of CEECs economies is co-ordination. Physical and human capital determinants of growth can produce modernisation only if complemented by institutions which operate as network co-ordinators or organisers, e.g. innovation centres and innovation agencies: These entities should also align "their" networks to other local, regional, national and global networks. Co-ordination within a network and the intersection between different networks is specific to every single case and involves a variety of hindering or enabling governance factors. An extensive literature has shown that the more successful locations have a co-ordinated structure of governance (Braczyk et al. 1998). The strong level of co-ordination appears to be giving them the ability to reproduce themselves as successful economies. At lower levels of economic development and/or declining industries, the networks are fragmented and separated. This demonstrates the importance of programmes that can improve networking.

Small firms are often the most important actors of innovation networks (Koschatzky et al. 1996) Experiences has shown that a healthy core of innovative small and medium sized enterprises (SMEs) could induce growth in other companies and in a whole region or country (Herden 1992). However, the process of building up networks needs much time. Therefore, some state authorities supported these efforts by establishing innovation centres or other bodies to enforce, complement or enlarge these activities.

It is from this point of view that we approach to the issue of institution building for innovation in CEECs. This perspective belongs to framework developed within the innovation oriented policy which is concerned with building knowledge networks, learning mechanisms and social capital (Morgan 1996; Braczyk et al. 1998).

In this paper we apply this perspective in the context of the CEECs economies. The novelty of our applicative work is the emphasis on institutions which are founded or initiated by local, regional, national or international bodies and are intended to operate as network organisers. Rather than focusing on linkages as such we think that it is the agent that primarily determine the extent and quality of networking and linkages. So far, the emphasis of policy was on linkages and networks while at least partly neglecting the role of this kind of agents that able to enhance networking. In the CEECs the role of network entrepreneurs or organisers is extremely important given the poor existing locational networking and weak actors, both public agencies and enterprises and the limited time to catch up with the west.

In the empirical part we provide evidence on issues involved in building and operation of the whole range of private, public private and joint efforts to support the establishing and operating of innovation oriented networks. We analyse four regional innovation centres[1] in Russia and the national Slovenian Innovation Agency

---

[1] For definition of different terms see also Heering in this volume.

(SIA). Our objectives are (1) to evaluate these cases of institution building for enhancing innovation networks in CEECs and analyse problems involved, and (2) to contribute to policy analysis based on these cases in both theoretical and policy terms.

In section 2 we introduce the basic theoretical or conceptual perspective on the problem of institution building for innovation. In the third section we describe the issue of innovation centres and agencies as instruments of policy. In section four we provide the empirical evidence on policy attempts to support innovation through the SIA and innovation centres in Russia. Although the cases that we present come from the two very different economies we show in the fourth section that the lack of success in both cases can be ascribed to common factors which contain more general lessons. In the last section we reinterpret the empirical cases in more general terms and develop management (policy) implications.

2 Network Organisers in Innovation Process

Innovation is a collective process requiring an interaction of large number of actors. The chain link innovation model has become the major metaphor and framework for much of thinking within the economics of innovation as well as the basis for policy making. This understanding of technical change has led to extensive policy attempts and theorising that try to support networking. Based on this conceptual thinking scholars have recently started to conceptualise innovation systems as spaces where intensive interactive learning activities are taking place (Lundval et al. 1992; Nelson 1993; Brazyk et al. 1998).

At regional level this conceptual understanding of the innovation process has been subsequently transformed into programmes like the Regional Innovation Strategies and the Regional Innovations and Technology Transfers Strategies of the EU. The emphasis is on the interaction between demand and supply as the most significant factors in innovation. The policy tries to enhance the quality of the linkages and the presence of synergies.

However, supporting networks is not a panacea. In conceptual terms, we think that this framework needs to be complemented with the following two aspects. First, if support for networking is to be effective than we have to take into account the power and control structure of networks. Second, beside the networking the equal emphasis should be given to potential network organisers or organisations that can promote network linkages or align their interests to external interests.

Especially in CEECs, given the scale of their restructuring problems we may expect that many of existing networks are so called status quo networks. When institutions and institutional rules are undeveloped any change is more risky as it is simply not regulated. Change generates resistance from still existing informal relations and status quo behaviour. If we are to understand how networking could be effective in such a situation an understanding of the strategies of individual actors and content of networking is indispensable. As Bennet and Krebs (1994) point out that in some cases networks may be essential to bring together the agents required to act jointly if an activity is to succeed. In other cases a network lever reluctant agents into action. In yet other cases, a network could limit the negative influence of some agents (who may be either inside or outside the network). Thus, a given network does not imply that all agents are equally important; often only one agent is the key animator of development.

This suggests that the structure of a kind of leadership is the crucial determinant of networks and that the formation of networks is highly dependent on the attitude to change of leadership. Identical networks can function positively or negatively for economic or other performance according to what is communicated (Fine 1999). This aspect of the problem is tackled by Grabher and Stark (1997) who observe network ambiguity in the post-socialist context so that the same network can be a source of strong performance or of stagnation.

The policy issue is under what preconditions could these problems be resolved and change generating networks be built? First, networks can be accountable if they are formalised or institutionalised. This suggests that the policy should try to make the existing informal networks transparent and accountable. Second, as Dornisch (1999) points out, networks in the post-socialist context are primarily tools employed by organisations and individuals. If this is so, than it is the internal organisational preconditions and the network external societal framework conditions like effective legal system, which will make networks accountable. Therefore it is not networks per se that causes problems but the weakness of organisations and in the environment.

Third, how network organisers can be supported is an indispensable complement to the issue of how innovation in general can be supported. This aspect often is neglected in policy because it reflects situation of countries where public or private organisations are able to mobilise resources for change. In the CEECs, actors are faced with large financial and knowledge constraints and poor institutional support, i.e. they are able to mobilise resources for restructuring on a very limited scale. In this case, there are limits to networking of actors that are weak, e.g. with limited resources for restructuring.

The process of creation of networks is highly non-linear and is dependent on the emergence of network organisers. Its non-linearity comes from initially high fixed costs which, after a critical mass of understanding and consensus is reached, may generate a collective learning process with increasing returns. However, it is also a risky effort as each of potential beneficiaries may want to have advantages for entering into the network but is not able or willing to incur upfront costs (time, funding, image, etc.) (Kuznetsov 1997).

This becomes much less of a problem as the network expands. The value of the network membership increases as more mutual benefits are available through networks, and as access to new potential co-operation partners, new suppliers, new customers becomes easier. The main issue is how to generate a critical mass of supply (new services) and demand for services (clients) and this within a rather short time span? There are two options:

- First option, network may develop through the provision of activities of organisations which can gradually generate profits by providing collective services. For example, organisations may be established as initiatives which offer initially "first aid" services (business plans, accounting, etc.) and than gradually move into more network relevant and complex services like business partnering, venturing, projects co-operation, etc. This is the case of successful operating entities.
- Second option, networking may be initiated by organisations that are willing or in the position to contribute to the organisational costs of networking, most often through public programmes or as governmental agencies that provide information to potential customers or consultancy on governmental complex subjects, e.g. technology based state R&D support programmes which should enforce co-operative R&D between industry and science (Walter/Bross 1997). In some cases they could also administer these programmes. In longer term, both kind of institutions can and often must take over network organiser's functions. Policy can support these efforts by seed-funding the network, by partly financing start-up operations and equipment and also by subsidising network relevant industrial R&D programmes such as joint or contract research. If all the different R&D supporting institutions and programmes work together additional synergy effects can be expected.

A problem in both cases is the development of networking functions. In the first case the networking services are mainly supplied through the process of development of market based services. In the second case these services are supplied through publicly supported programmes. In both cases, the major problem is the relevance of services for a diverse potential of partners. Only organisations that are able to provide the necessary variety of networking functions can operate as network organisers. These organisations must be able to connect different agents into joint efforts and to fulfil functions like:

- Support of innovation activities by making use of contacts with players in research and economy etc.;

- identification and organisation of exchange of specific capabilities of existing and potential network actors, particularly of funds and banks, and business advisory organisations (e.g. management, marketing and market research);
- together with business sector, elaboration of co-operative strategies such as qualified division of labour between large enterprises and SMEs, between SMEs themselves, between firms and R&D institutes etc.;
- assistance of the science sector to provide demand oriented (counselling and advisory) services to industry, especially to identify technologies with market potential and facilitate the detection of the demand for research results;
- taking over activities that are not provided by the market (venture funding, real estate development).

Additionally network organiser should be able to connect "their" networks to other networks at the same level or at different levels (national or global) by organising exchange of information or making the network resources available to other networks.

In this paper we confine ourselves on two types of organisations – innovation centres and innovation agencies – which operate as providers of network relevant services and which hence have potential to become network organisers.

3 Innovation Centres and Innovation Agencies as Networking Agents

From the mid to late 1970s onwards, at least within (West) Europe, there has been a general trend towards increased autonomy at different levels, especially with respect to regional economic and industrial development. A number of agencies were created and new initiatives were stimulated. In each of the OECD countries there has been significant increases in the number of agencies designed to encourage technological development especially at a local level of e.g. German federal states – "Bundesländer" or at small economy level e.g. Austria/Finland (see also Steiner`s contribution in this volume). During the 1980s this trend intensified specifically with respect to policies, which marked a dramatic shift from the old exogenous policies of the 1960s to the strongly endogenous policies of the 1980s and 1990s. But still most of these initiatives are highly dependent on public subsidy. The most marked trend was the creation and enhancement of co-operative technology initiatives such as innovations centres and innovation agencies. As a result of these initiatives in many western countries we find today a complex web of interface organisations and mechanisms for the encouragement of innovation.

Contrary to this, after 10 years of transition, no coherent policy agenda on innovation has been set in many CEECs. The impression is that CEECs are still in the process of learning and defining these policies within a discourse that is still dominated by transition issues. The severely constrained financial resources of CEECs explain only in part the low treatment of this kind of policies. We believe that the problem is deeper and is of a conceptual nature, for instance, a question of how to couple transition policies to policies that explicitly address growth[2].

Innovation centres, science parks, technology transfer units at universities and research institutes, free economic zones, incubators, economic development agencies have been established in all CEECs in at least a few places. Many of these efforts have been undertaken with international assistance. In terms of our conceptual framework outlined in previous section this is basically a kind of support to potential network organisers and to network alignment. However, the results of these policies fall short of objectives. Although we have not come across a comprehensive review of all these initiatives there is enough evidence to suggest that their effects and results are not very encouraging (Walter 2001; Webster 1996; SQW 1994, Heering in this volume). Often they are initiated through foreign assistance programmes and operate successfully only as long as foreign assistance is in place. As Smith (1998) points out foreign supported programmes have involved piecemeal attempts to construct an entrepreneurial local governments in the sphere of innovative development.

It is essential that the public sector and here especially the policy concentrates on its core areas and accepts a division of labour between private and public bodies. The policy ought to delegate tasks to non-governmental bodies but has to be responsible for the co-operation and co-ordination. In particular, the state should regard itself as a moderator between different societal groups.

In developed market economies semi-public and private organisations, which provide information and consultancy and administer governmental programmes, are given adequate freedom of action but ultimately are accountable to the state for their actions and their results. Organisations of this kind that fulfil specific tasks for the state, according to certain rules and procedures are the so-called agencies. They can be characterised according to the level of responsibilities and tasks that they are appointed to undertake. This ranges from providing information and consultancy for the state to administrating or even managing state programmes etc.

It is important that the activities of the state and of the agencies are confined to roles assigned to them; for instance, government should not interfere in the day-to-day

2 For discussion on the relationship between transition and growth-oriented policies in the post-socialist context see Radosevic (1997).

running of agencies. Sticking to this principle enhances the transparency and reliability of governmental decisions and actions.

Innovation agencies are bodies to support the development and marketing of new products and production processes by providing

- technical and economic information services and consultancy;
- financial incentives;
- mediation of R&D contracts and co-operation;
- provide access to innovation industry and science and visa versa.

An innovation agency is a private, public or semi-public institution and receives public funding for operational costs supporting the state to implement policy and/or profit from services for economy and science.

The task of an innovation is to provide consultation, planning, assessment, monitoring, steering and success monitoring of the state's support measures. Innovation agencies must have access to the necessary technological and economic expertise, e.g. through networks. The tasks, agencies take on for policy are bound by guidelines. Basically, three types of such innovation agencies are to be distinguished:

- consulting agencies providing information and consultancy;
- innovation agencies providing organisation and administration support for industrial innovation activities (organiser agency). Their tasks generally include carrying out and administering state programmes. They also make suggestions and recommendations to the state (e.g. the so-called "Projektträger", the R&D project organisers in Germany or within the European Commission – the Technical Assistance Units);
- innovation agencies providing management support for industrial innovation activities, with a (general or partial) right to make decisions on funding.

The legal relationship between innovation agencies and the government usually is regulated by agreements. Besides administrating public R&D support programmes innovation agencies do own research on their subjects or provide market relevant services. Both activities are possibilities to raise own funding.

4 Setting Up Innovation Centres and an Innovation Agency: Russia and Slovenia Compared

In CEECs, the issue of innovation and networking has received an extensive international support. Models of innovation centres and innovation agencies have been transferred into CEECs in attempt to foster restructuring and develop new sources of growth. However, given the undeveloped market and missing innovation policy much less demand than expected is articulated for services from enterprises. Experiences in supporting institutions like agencies and centres are faced with significant difficulties in their implementation.

In CEECs, innovation centres and innovation agencies are most often established with the following objectives in mind:

- Contribution to innovation based economic development by mediating contacts and co-operation and by thus connecting this development to job creation, diversification of economy or in networking by linking organisations from different sectors.
- Forming new networks for exchange and providing assistance in diversification of economy.
- Identification of potential technologies for commercialisation as the real commercial scientific potential in CEECs is often unknown due to a lack of technical and legal information of sufficient quality for the assessment of the market potential of specific technologies.
- Enforcement of entrepreneurship in SMEs as in CEECs have been previously dominated by large firms. The support of small firms to enables them to work openly in economy.
- Property venture/real estate development as poorly-functioning property markets often force firms to come up with unusual ways of utilising external fixed assets.

To sum up: Innovation centres and innovation agencies are organisations designed to support the development and marketing of new products and production processes by providing technical and economic information services and consultancy, mediation of R&D contracts and co-operation or administer and manage state provided R&D and innovation oriented financial means. Centres and agencies could be private, public or semi-public institutions and receive public funding to implement policy and/or profit from services by earning money on the market.

We may expect the following elements to be difficult if implementing innovation centres and innovation agencies:

First, due to the lack of private sector service institutions innovation centres and agencies might have a broader spectrum of activities than in the West. However, this could make them unable to provide more specialised services and meet firm demands for innovation support.

Second, innovation centres and agencies are expected to experience difficulties in finding financial resources for funding their activities.

Third, the process of bringing together different actors absorbed a great deal of staff time and expenditure and increased set up costs.

A success of innovation support activities could only be expected if they are able to bring customers for their services and be funded (at least partly) from the market. Innovation centres and innovation agencies are also institutions that can take over tasks from public bodies in order to support specific groups of customers, e.g. technology based SMEs that are chosen by the state to play an important role in the society or economy. Especially innovation agencies are usually founded to support state organs in implementing and proceeding innovation policy tasks.

But both institutions usually are not successful if they are not able to build up networks or to be integrated into them. Therefore, they often have to operate as network organisers, which is difficult task in CEECs where many preconditions for successful networking are not in place.

4.1 Russia: Innovation Centres as Sources of New Growth and Networking[3]

In the early 1990s, Russian R&D policy started to support organisations such as innovation centres and technoparks. In the meantime, more than 50 technoparks and innovation-centres exist in Russia.

In 1995, partly as a result of the government resolution no. 360/1995[4], regions have been encouraged to form own institutions in the area of R&D and innovation policy. In 1997, in the subjects of the Russian Federation, there were 15 Scientific-Co-ordination Councils, and 10 Scientific and Scientific-Co-ordinative Centres (Pletnev 1997).

Innovation centres are expected to provide a good nurturing environment for the large number of small innovative business that are growing out of the old system of state-run science. They are expected to help to rebuild the decentralised research and industry networks, by keeping and augmenting the research and economic base in the regions.

The commercialisation of new technologies through industrial utilisation of R&D results e.g., by R&D spin offs were considered as important to this objective. Innovation centres should reduce uncertainty that NTBFs face and thereby increase

3 This section draws on Radosevic and Dranev (1999).

4 Decision of the Russian government of April 17, 1995, no. 360 'About state support for development of science and S&T development'.

chance of firms' survival and growth by providing innovation services (consultancy, information transfer, market research).

The analysis of demand for innovation services in four Russian regions studied (Radosevic/Dranev 1999) shows that (1) this innovation services segment of the market especially for the SMEs and NTBFs is very limited as the market is mainly confined on "first aid" business services (e.g. business plans) (2) there are signs of a gradual shift from services induced primarily by problems in the business environment (accounting and tax services) towards technology market and investment related services.

Innovation centres in Russia supported by EU programmes show steps that have been taken, as well as the variety of problems which hinder this realisation (table 4.1-1). In this section we evaluate their role by pointing to several issues which are important for understanding the main function of innovation centres being an agent which facilitates the innovation process.

Table 4.1-1 Innovation centers – vision and reality

	Vision	**Reality**
Objectives	(Regional) Innovative development	No acceptance, status quo,weak organisation
Strategies	Long-term technology Competitiveness	Short-term needs of potential customers
Services	Innovation Orientation	Traditional
Target groups	New technology based firms	A variety of SMEs
Financing	By customers	External support and income from services

4.1.1 The Objectives of the Russian Innovation Centres

Founders and initiators of innovation centres usually determine their objectives as reflections of the policy context in which they operate. The experience suggests a need for stakeholders to clarify objectives from the outset already at an early stage in order to avoid frictions between different interests and, just as important, to facilitate the evaluation of innovation centres. In the case of the Russian innovation centres a problem of too many objectives has been strongly present. This problem is exacerbated by the two not always compatible objectives of innovation centres.

The first are tasks initiators of the innovation centres have in mind when they found such organisations, in Russia this was the support to a specific group of firms, especially to technology based companies. These firms are expected to diversify the economy and generate new growth opportunities especially when operating within a network and by co-operating often with R&D institutes in high tech fields. Such joint efforts of firms and institutes are seen as a way to preserve the existing R&D.

The second is to be self-financed in short- or medium-term and to act as a commercial organisation which has to satisfy the current demand. The duality of first and second objectives is obvious. For employees of innovation centres, the different objectives means building an autonomous commercial organisation that has to survive on shallow and cash-stripped markets, and thus has to go wherever the demand is. However, they have at the same time to fulfil a public role to support SMEs, especially NTBFs.

The process of setting up innovation centres that are expected to be self-financed in a short or medium-term is a business venture in itself. Only when faced with the realities of demand can an innovation centre team try to define its best strategic profile. In this process the support of initiators and founders of the innovations centres, a good communication with them or even their involvement to a certain extent is essential. This requires also commitment on the side of founders and initiators as well as clear criteria on which innovation centres will be evaluated. In Russia it seems that there are too many and too unclearly defined objectives which stakeholders want to achieve while at the same time not being able to commit enough resources. The lack of clarity regarding the objectives makes it very difficult to assess whether the innovation centres have fulfilled their objectives or not.

4.1.2 The Gap Between the Existing and Wanted Demand

The main distinctive feature of innovation centres when compared to market oriented innovative business support services providers should be that they serve a specific segment – that of NTBFs. These firms are expected to have specific problems in growth which distinguish them from other firms. Technology based firms usually develop technologies which are not proven and whose markets are not yet certain. This makes assistance more complicated as it must include besides a strong technical evaluation component and an assessment of often very specialised and narrow markets.

If we take into account the current structure of demand for consultancy services in Russia, it is clear that the great bulk of demand is for general business `first aid` consultancy activities. It is difficult to build a real innovation centre mainly focused on support to the very small group of the often financially weak technology based firms that also has to survive in the market for consultancy services.

In order to be of help for such a peculiar group of companies as NTBFs any assistance of innovation centres must be much more specific in technology and market. This means having an understanding of very specific market, and being able to organise the technical evaluation of the feasibility of the technology. In that case centres need to strengthen their capabilities in technology audit and technology innovation management. This could be overcome by developing a strong network of technical experts attached to innovation centres. Russian centres analysed have not yet done that because this is a major investment which cannot be realised with the day to day activities of search for contracts as the centres are very much forced to be engaged in earning own resources.

One solution for the centres is to specialise in specific technologies. This would allow the accumulation of expertise in limited areas and understanding of specific markets and technologies. The activities of Tomsk innovation centre in establishing the biotechnology industrial parks may lead in this direction (Radosevic/Dranev 1999).

4.1.3 Difficulties in Supporting Only Technology Based Firms

Innovation centres in Russia primarily were meant by their founders and initiators to support a population of NTBFs. However, due to the limited demand for such services and the difficulties when catering only for NTBFs, innovation centres are likely to develop into organisations providing a general business consultancy.

Experiences in Russia show that the most successful of the newly founded firms and SMEs are those with proven technologies which try to serve known, most often, domestic markets. Successful firms seem to be those from whom market and technology risks are low. Contrary to this, technology-based firms operate on not yet tested markets with new, not yet proven technologies where development and marketing costs largely surpass their resources.

In current Russian circumstances, the provision of business services, be it business plan or assistance in registering a company, is usually the only activity which can generate income for innovation centres. A specific assistance to technology-based firms, which can be of use to them, requires specific expertise for which it is unlikely to be self-financed. So, initiators and founders of a centre must be able and ready to put sufficient resources into the centre so that it can carry out such activities for a limited group of companies which are financially weak and able to pay only a fraction of full price for these services. Otherwise, it is very likely that innovation centres will develop into consulting organisations where the attribute ‘technology’ or ‘innovation’ will lose its content.

4.1.4 Tasks of Innovation Centres: Market Driven Consulting Firm or Provision of Public Support to NTBFs?

In the Russian centres we could observe the conflicting interests of initiators and founders and the realities of current demand for consulting services. These tensions could be defined as a dilemma between innovation centres being market-driven consulting entity, or as public body which take care of technology firms and their partners in their innovative activities, possibly R&D institutes.

In their pure forms, these activities could be organisationally separate in two different types of organisations: consulting firms and public organisation. On the one hand, the advantage of this solution is that there are no additional complications as public and commercial activities are kept separate. On the other hand, the problem with this "pure" solution is that the major opportunity – to assist firms to commercialise R&D technologies – may be lost. Consultancy firms may, in the end, do little about this kind of technologies while a public organisation may turn into one more layer of administration with limited relevance for enterprises.

The whole rationale of innovation centres is that they undertake some public functions, like promotion of innovation policy activities and earn own money by operating on the market that means also to contribute to solve the basic problems of firms. In the current activities of innovation centres the relationship between these two functions of the centre are not harmonised.

In successful innovation centres, the services offered to individual firms are clearly specified and have an individualised price. The relationship is usually formalised through a contract. In this case it must be expected that the innovation centre are not doing any publicly relevant tasks like supporting firms and activity connected to this, e.g. monitoring of firms to identify potential customers for their innovative services. Yet, at a time, the founders and initiators of innovation centres are rightly expecting that centres operate in the public interest and that they have to contribute financially to these activities.

If centres are to operate by combining commercial and public functions than their public functions and market should be also formalised in an approved programme of activities. This programme can then serve as a basis for the evaluation of the centre's work in its public function as well as for the basis of market funding. The current situation in Russia creates misunderstandings which may undermine the whole initial rationale for setting up innovation centres.

4.2 Slovenian Innovation Agency as Promoter of Innovation Linkages and Restructuring

In the framework of the techno-scientific co-operation between Slovenia and the EU, the European Commission supports the establishment of the SIA as an institution to efficiently execute R&D programmes, elaborate new programmes and accelerate the building up of innovative networks. The development of the SIA concept was directed towards potentials of growing technology based industries and the still underdeveloped SME sector.

The concept for developing the Slovenian innovation support infrastructure through the SIA combined a bottom-up and top-down approach. On the one hand, decentralised activities like the acquisition of know-how and industrial networking were supported. On the other hand, funding was provided centrally to guarantee easy access to all potential users. The SIA network for innovation support therefore included the following structural elements:

- SIA as a central point of the network and – by handling the administration of R&D programmes from ministries – with techno-economic competence and numerous contacts to suppliers and users of innovation services. As necessary resources for action, SIA required access to innovation support funds and should use gained expertise in administering programmes to optimise existing schemes and elaborating new programmes if necessary and demanded by public and private bodies.
- Sectoral transfer and advisory units, e.g. in public teaching and research institutions, and in technology departments of chambers of economy and crafts, and in branch associations that co-operated with SIA within the network thus having better access to funding programmes for their clients. Units such as technology centres and associations have specialist emphasis, depending on the organisation to which they are attached, in order to provide services that are complementary at a national level. In this sector, particularly detailed expert information should be available which could be used by the other network partners.
- Contact offices, to provide users in the different parts of Slovenia with demand-oriented information, advice and funding, to contact and activate demand. These partners of SIA as the sectoral and advisory units (the Small Business and Development Centres) should co-operate with SIA within the network. In this way they would have good access to innovation programmes of ministries and could act as demand oriented mediators between SIA and their customer. Being situated close to the firms they were also able to provide intensive and personal support and project monitoring for their clients. These offices should be already existing or be attached to existing industrial and technology-related institutions (e.g. economic promotion agencies, technology centres). For them, proximity to the users of their innovation services is essential.

Thus in the long term a three-tier innovative network should be formed by SIA as a network organiser (figure 4.2-1). All levels should be permanently inter-linked by being involved in supporting innovative firms and managing public R&D programmes – thus making use of the wide service spectrum. Network management and access to public financial innovation support was performed by the SIA acting as the network's centre point. Via the network partners industry should be able to articulate the specific needs in different branches and size ranges.

Figure 4.2-1: Network and co-operation

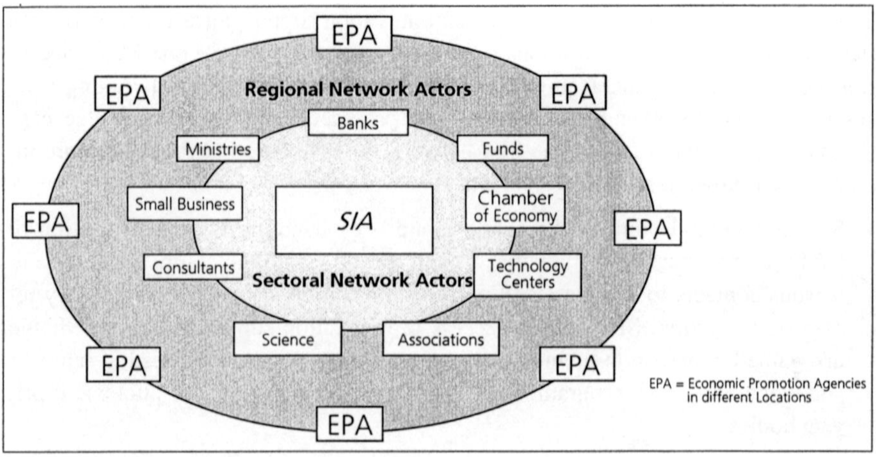

At a later stage, to complement the structure, other institutions could be integrated into the network, e.g. when financing industrial development projects, funds and credit institutions have to rely on technical consulting and then they can make use of the specific expert competences of the network. The SIA innovation network, with its broad spectrum of services and its complex structure of participants, could only be realised in long term.

The set-up of the SIA was based on strong participation of Slovenian R&D institutes, e.g. they seconded scientists as managers and employees to SIA in part time jobs. After the start-up phase supported by the EU in 1997 and beginning of 1998 (especially the payment for the SIA employees), the SIA was to be run by Slovenian experts. For implementation of the SIA it was necessary to have an intensive dialogue-oriented consulting provided by EU consultants, who promoted communication and co-operation between the main actors of policy, industry and science.

SIA should be established in stages and start as a co-ordinating unit for public bodies that support industrial innovation and fulfil administrative tasks of funding programmes, beginning with the support of the operational management of a small subsidy programme on behalf of the Ministry of Science and Technology. These activities should be pilot or demonstration projects in co-operation with industrial firms and R&D institutes. The subjects of these projects were defined in a way that always a cluster of Slovenian firms could see problem solvings which are also relevant for their purpose, e.g. by joint research projects in pre-competitive fields for high tech firms, low budget modernisation of production lines etc. However, these demonstration projects were never realised.

SIA started working in autumn 1997, as a unit within the subdivision for Technology and Innovation of the Slovenian Ministry of Science and Technology. SIA received staff training in Slovenia and in EU countries and the staff of the SIA visited companies, ministries and other possible network actors. SIA also organised events in relation to EU access of Slovenia and elaborated a business plan for its future work in which SIA claimed 30 Mio DM to be transferred from the public budget to full responsibility of SIA.

Later in 1998, SIA activities stopped or were partly integrated into the usual administrative work of the ministry. The employees of SIA moves to new or their previous jobs. Reasons for this development were legal problems. The law of science and technology, which also contained regulations on setting up agencies was delayed in Slovenian Parliament. Today, SIA is no longer acting in network coordination. However, a continuation of the activities can be expected in the near future, based on a new law on science and technology in Slovenia as regulations on independent agencies also are a part of this law (Kalin 1999).

5 Conclusions

In both cases, innovation centres in Russia and innovation agency in Slovenia, some of the objectives have been achieved. Innovation centres and agency were set up. Some of the innovation centres continue to offer services to clients until today. The innovation agency operated for some time after the support of the EU ended in March 1998. However, their networking objectives, e.g. to cover high costs for networking of individual firms, to reach a critical mass and consensus driven actions have not been very successful in both cases. Why? The core problem in both cases is – how to undertake collective action or the (in)ability of people to work together in groups and organisations towards a common purpose in environments with undeveloped institutions. Collective action always starts as a specific activity which then diffuses into other sectors and becomes generalised. In the case of the SIA, pilot or demonstration projects to solve specific problems of the different types of Slovenian companies should be the action to start with. Financially supported by the Slovenian Ministry of Science and Technology, a diffusion of the best practice should come about through demonstration effects. In case of Russia, the lack of consensus on which activities require public support and which should be financed by clients led to very piecemeal results. In both cases, the first steps were not clearly articulated and well implemented. This is partly the result of implementation gap but also is due to conceptual weaknesses as we will argue later on.

As pointed out by Morgan (1995), the main objective of the technology policy exercises is to develop a innovation process, in which stakeholders are enjoined to define a commonly agreed, bottom up strategy. The cases of institution building in Russia and Slovenia show that there are conceptual and implementation weaknesses. The final gap between objectives and outcomes is due to several problems specific to institution building in CEECs and to few factors which are of general nature, i.e. relevant to other regions as well.

First, the establishment of institutions like centres and agencies required long-term funding and commitment. The 1-3 year time span within which the initiatives in Russia, or the one and a half year period the SIA was funded by EU cannot ensure long-term viability of such new organisations and create network organisers in the environment with weak leadership and status quo attitudes. Once innovation centres are left without support they were too weak to survive on their own or to retain their initial strategic objectives. When faced with a cut in subsidies or uncertainties of future existence (as in the Slovenian case) or with uncertainties and weak local demand (as in Russia) they were forced to abandon their original networking functions. They turned to activities which enable them to raise money from the market (Russia) or as in Slovenia, the employees left SIA because they could find more promising jobs elsewhere. Organisations that do not have long-term policy support have difficulties to develop and embody themselves within the economy. Policy has to recognise the long-term nature of institution building and gear funding mechanisms to the nature of this process.

Second, institutional building for innovation support most often does not represent the response of the locality to their problems. They are no more than a transfer of western models to CEECs which do not solve the main constraint – lack of collective action, which is implicit in institutions like the Russian innovation centres or SIA. In bringing new institutions into an environment with scarce resources and organisations with their own vested interests and agendas it is not surprising that such organisations do not operate as sources of growth and network organisers. The failure or success of new organisations does not depend so much on their own efforts as on whether networks in which they operate are status quo or pro change.

Third, the support failed as the programmes emphasise the new institutions rather than the new functions. This is partly due to the logic of international technical assistance where sponsors prefer to be in full control during the project by establishing 'greenfield' institutions rather than dealing with the messy and complicated world of existing institutions. Networking or bridging functions are supported through new stand-alone organisations, like innovation centres, and agencies rather than as a part of the existing entities, universities, R&D organisations, and industrial associations. What is needed is support for the bridging or networking functions not as a stand-alone function but more as a complementary function of existing institutions. In this latter case, networking functions should be supported as a way to better understand the client/customer needs and requirements of the existing organisations. In this way some of the organisations supported may turn into important network organisers for the economy by expanding their existing networks. New stand-alone organisations usually operate in the transfer of simple and general information like marketing and technical information, rather than firm- or sector-specific information and knowledge. Thus they do not address the main constraints to the innovation process. Hence, policy should support new functions and programmes, which if successful can lead to the creation of new organisations, rather than supporting new stand-alone organisations.

Fourth, the structure of existing political, knowledge and production networks should be taken into account if networking is to be successful. Institutionalisation of change through new "organisations" will not ensure change which requires 'institutionalisation of new patterns of behaviour'. Indeed, new organisations in Russia and Slovenia are created but the institutionalisation of new patterns of behaviour in innovation remains limited. Stakeholders with different interests, time horizons, funding modes etc. make unlikely that new organisations will become agents of change.

In summary, network organisers cannot be created from outside the locality or in top – down manner but they have to be embodied in the existing structure. As a result, innovation centres and agencies remain isolated from or marginal to the local economy and are merely surrogates of modernisation. Instead of setting up organisations from outside it might be more sensible to support the existing potential network entrepreneurs in concrete projects through which they can than create new, more dynamic public-private learning networks.

So far, our discussion suggests that we are not overly optimistic regarding the prospects of innovation centres and agencies to operate as sources of growth and innovation, especially if set up through programmes outside the local context. Given huge needs for supporting networking functions, of a variety of organisations, enterprises and universities we consider setting up stand alone centres and agencies as not being a priority. However, it would be misleading to conclude that such organisations do not have rationale. Based on good practice in this area (Shapira 1997) and on the positive experiences in setting up innovation centres and agencies. In the next section we address several issues that should be taken into account when implementing similar initiatives in the future.

6 Policy Reasons

Define objectives and mission from the outset: Innovation centres and agencies are organisational forms which by themselves do not have in advance clearly specified different objectives and missions. They can accommodate a variety of functions that have to be specified from the outset. A clearly defined strategic profile of the centre/agency is the good guarantee for avoiding expensive mistakes and delays later on. Defined objectives and mission accepted by stakeholders should be a first precondition for support and not the end of the process of setting up of innovation centres and agencies.

Recruit entrepreneurially oriented managers and interdisciplinary personnel: Innovation centres and agencies are as much a public policy initiatives as they are business ventures. This requires recruitment of entrepreneurial managers who have experience of communicating with both the public and commercial sector. The quality of working team is a very important feature of successful innovation centres and agencies. It is thus important for centres and agencies to start by finding and employing people whose qualifications (techno-scientific or techno-economic) and other abilities make them suitable. For example, they should have distinguished themselves in their previous jobs by their quick grasp of complex matters, their receptivity for interdisciplinary learning and their analytical and creative abilities in finding – and implementing – solutions to problems. People of this kind can probably acquire the skills and qualifications required for innovation centres and agencies through "learning by doing" in the longer term.

Focus on "cluster-based" technologies: The qualified support for technology based innovation requires a focus on technology in its business and market context. This could be possible if centres and agencies focus on "cluster-based" technologies and on services which are needed to cater for technologically-related firms rather than a set of unrelated enterprises. Whenever possible, preference should be given to those centres or agencies which will be focused on specific technological areas. This also could acquire own R&D which is relevant for the region or country they are responsible for.

Assist to enterprises according to "needs and fits": The support to such a peculiar firm group as technology based firms cannot be confined only to those who are able to pay for their services. If innovation centres and agencies are to serve public functions than they should be helped, either by programmes or through service price subsidies, to cater for those entrepreneurs and firms who are promising but not yet able to pay. The same should be done for specific services that could not be paid totally. Successful innovation centres and agencies have to develop a portfolio of different clients according to several criteria.

Tailor and leverage different types of services: The portfolio of services should be short term oriented and as long term strategies develop also tap latent demand for complex consultancy and innovation services. To be an agent of innovation a centre or agency has to be pro-active, especially in offering strategic technology-based services and networking activities. Some of the services can be fully covered by clients while some other cannot or not in their full cost. The founders and initiators of centres and agencies should agree on the portfolio of these services and on modes of their pricing and funding.

Build on local and international linkages: Innovation centres and innovation agencies which are not sources of contacts and nodes of networks cannot fulfil their role to support actions by providing know how. This is a mayor problem, the market-driven innovation centres which may eventually be transformed into business consultancy firms. Innovation centres and agencies have to build on the linkages developed during their set up but they also have to be assisted in developing new links.

Diversify sources of finance: The more networked innovation centres and agencies and other innovation supporting entities are, the more likely it is that they will exploit emerging opportunities. The final proof of this is the diversified portfolio of sources of finance. In the business plan and in the annual programmes of activities specific targets should be set in this respect.

Share experience: Innovation centres and innovation agencies should share often the experiences of their work with technoparks or business incubators etc. This is the best mechanism for transferring knowledge and in making short-cuts. Policy should initiate a regular annual forum for these organisations where not only domestic but also foreign experiences can be shared.

Introduce evaluation mechanisms: Without systematic evaluation it is impossible to find out whether objectives have been achieved. A good evaluation helps in redefining the objectives. The regular, independent evaluation of innovation centre/agency activities should be introduced by founders and initiators.

Literature

Braczyk, H.-J.; Cooke, Ph.; Heidenreich, M. (1998, Eds.): Regional Innovation Systems. London: UCL Press Limited.

Bennet, J. R.; Krebs, G. (1994): Local Economic Development Partnerships: An analysis of Policy Networks in EC-LEDA Local Employment Development Strategies. Regional Studies, vol. 28.2., pp. 119-140.

Berg, A.; Borensztein, E. R.; Sahay, R.; Zettelmeyer, J. (1999): The Evolution of Output in Transition Economies – Explaining the Differences, IMF Working Paper WP/99/73.

Fine, B. (1999): The Developmental State is Dead – Long Live Social Capital. Development and Change, 30, pp. 1-19.

Fischer, S.; Sahay, R.; Vegh, C. (1998): From Transition to Market – Evidence and Growth Prospects, IMF Working Paper WP/98/52.

Grabher, G.; David S. (1997, Eds.): Restructuring Networks: Legacies, Linkages and Localities in Postsocialism. London: Oxford University Press.

Herden, R. (1992): Technologieorientierte Außenbeziehungen im betrieblichen Innovationsmanagement, Heidelberg: Physica.

Kalin, T. (1999): Future Institutional Changes in Research Environment in Slovenia: For Better or for Worse. Paper presented on the 4th Semmering Science & Technology Forum: Institutional Changes: Efficiency and Effectiveness, The Interdisciplinary Centre for Comparative Research in the Social Sciences (ICCR), Vienna, 3-5 December 1999.

Koschatzky, K.; Frenkel, A.; Walter, G.H.; Shefer, D. (1996): Regional Concentration and Dynamics of Fast Growing Industries in Germany and Israel. In: Koschatzky, K.; Shefer, D. (Eds.): Spatial Diffusion of Industrial Innovation and Regional Development. Annual Report on Completion of the Second Year of Research under Support of the German-Israel Foundation Grant for 1996, Haifa and Karlsruhe.

Kuznetsov, Y. (1997): Can Private-public Collaboration Solve Mexican Growth Riddle? Concept of Social Capital in Growth Theory, World Bank, mimeograph.

Morgan, K. (1996): The Learning Region: Institutions, Innovation and Regional Renewal. Regional Studies, 31, 5, pp. 491-503.

Lundvall, B.-A. (1992, Ed.): National Systems of Innovation – Towards a Theory of Innovation and Interactive Learning. London: Pinter Publishers.

Nelson, R. (1993, Ed.): National Systems of Innovation: A Comparative Analysis, New York/Oxford: Oxford University Press.

Radosevic, S. (1997): Strategic Policies for Growth in Post-Socialism: Theory and Evidence based on Baltic States. Economic Systems, 21, No 2, pp. 165-96.

Radosevic, S.; Dranev, J. N. (1999): Regional S&T and Innovation Policy and Innovation Centres as its Instruments in the Four Russian Regions: Novosibirsk, Tomsk, Samara and Zelenograd, EC TACIS Project: 'S&T Development in the Russian Market Economy', Nauka, Moscow, pp.72. (published in Russian).

Shapira, P. (1997): Support to New Technology-based Firms in Russia: An Overview. OECD, mimeograph.

Smith, A. (1998): Reconstructing the Regional Economy. Industrial Transformation and Regional Development in Slovakia, Cheltenham: Edward Elgar.

SQW (Segal Quince Wicksted Limited) (1994): Survey of the Innovation Infrastructure in Central and Eastern Europe. A Report to SPRINT, EC-DGXII.

Webster, A. (1996, Ed.): Building New Bases for Innovation: The Transformation of the R&D System in Post-Socialist States. Anglya Polytechnic University, Cambridge.

Walter, G. H.; Bross, U. (1997): Promoting Technology Development in Slovenia by International Co-operation. Presented on the Second Annual Conference on Promotion of Technological Development. Portoroz, Slovenia.

Walter, G. H. (1999): Innovation Agencies: Their Role in Science, Technology and Innovation Policy. In: Pejovnik, S.; Komac, M. (Eds.): FORUM BLED, Science and Technology Investment. Priority in the Development Strategy of the Nation. Ljubljana: Ministry of Science and Technology, pp. 89-95.

Walter, G. H. (2001): Implementation of Innovation Networks in Transition in Central and Eastern European Countries – Slovenia as an Example. In: Koschatzky, K.; Kulicke, M.; Zenker, A. (Eds.): Innovation Networks – Concepts and Challenges in the European Perspective, Heidelberg: Physica, pp. 111-126.

Entrepreneurship, Innovation and Small Firms: A Case for Technology Centres and Science Parks in the Transition Process?

Walter Heering

1 Introduction

Eastern reform countries formerly under the influence of the Soviet Union apparently now have all concluded the first phase of the transition process and have entered a second stage (Stern 1998; EBRD 1998). In the first phase priority was laid on macroeconomic stabilisation and on privatisation of state enterprises. Depending on initial conditions as well as design and persistence of the chosen transition policy, there are large differences between countries with regard to success. Generally, the further East one looks, the slower the transition process and the larger the transition problems. Especially, the Czech Republic, Hungary and Poland seem to be quite advanced, while Russia and other countries of the CIS still show poor performance. It is now becoming clear that further progress, even in the macroeconomic field, needs support from more microeconomic measures. All countries, although to a different degree, lack appropriate institutional environments to provide proper incentives for market-oriented economic activity. In particular, there is now widespread disillusionment concerning the results of privatisation, which left serious problems of enterprises' restructuring unsolved and created some fairly new problems too. Emphasis on privatisation of existing state-owned enterprises has often diverted attention away from establishing of new firms, which is at least as important. Based on empirical research during 1997/98 in Hungary, Poland and Russia,[1] the following remarks consider the role of industrial parks, science parks, innovation centres and the like[2] as one of the possible instruments to deal with

1 See Heering/Pfirrmann/Schroeder 1198. The interpretation given here as well as remaining errors are due exclusively to the author.

2 In the literature there is some terminological variety all amounting roughly to the same thing. The only relevant distinction in the sequel is between business incubators with no specific technological demand, and technology parks ("technoparks"), which support firms' foundation in technological advanced activities. I speak of "science parks" ("innovation centres") if reference is made to the latter idea, and simply of "parks" ("centres") if the former concept is meant.

those problems at the enterprise level, especially in fostering the foundation of innovative small and medium-sized firms, on which some hope for improving competitiveness of the economies rests.

2 Industrial Policy in Transition Countries

Recently the overall disappointing results of privatisation have led to political measures dedicated to stimulating endogenous potential for entrepreneurship and economic development. Assimilating more recent debates in western countries, the particular hope is to foster the emergence of SMEs with a bias to advanced technology in order to strengthen the competitive power of the national economy. In most transition countries a fairly respectable pool of technological competence seems to be left at universities and in other state-managed research units as a heritage of the former innovation system. It might thus be possible – or so the hope goes – to induce a significant portion of this staff to build up new firms, thus providing the means to overcome the technological backwardness of those economies. Since those persons do not, as a rule, posses the suitable know-how to manage a firm, it seems quite plausible to connect the technological know-how to external managerial facilities. One way such a symbiosis can be envisaged is by establishing a park or a centre where newly founded enterprise settle down; this arrangement may give rise to synergetic effects between the firms and would have the enormous advantage, particularly relevant to transition countries, of being able to provide for entrepreneurial infrastructures which are otherwise not easy to access.

Basically, this is the simple idea of a technopark or an innovation centre, a concept developed some years ago in the West, already applied in some developing countries and more recently spreading into the East. The concept has been under attack from western scientists and practitioners: in particular, it is said to entail a somewhat mechanical, "linear" conception of industrial innovation, and it implies significant subsidising of firms selected by some administration, which seems unfair to outsiders and is possibly inefficient with regard to market priorities; it may even lead to some degree of "ivory towerism" on part of the insiders which is certainly detrimental to the intention (Oakey 1985). In the meantime several empirical studies have been performed to assess the impact of those parks and centres; the overall results are not very encouraging (for a synopsis see Heering/Pfirrmann/Schroeder 1998). These criticisms notwithstanding, more important to our present concern is the question whether the premises of the western model fit the present state of transition countries sufficiently to make success likely. A priori, of course, deviations in both directions can occur: The basis for an implementation of the idea may not exist or be weakly developed in those countries. On the other hand, the case for implementing the concept may even be stronger there. Our empirical findings in three reform countries, Hungary, Poland and Russia, suggest a differentiated and pragmatic answer: while broadly there seems to be little evidence for the thesis that scientists or researchers are a serious potential for innovative SMEs in the three countries, it cannot be neglected that parks or centres fulfil a highly useful function in forming new enterprises, innovative or otherwise. The reason for this divided answer refers to the hybrid intention of the concept itself: although it is a device generated as a reaction to specific growth obstacles in developed western countries during the eighties, thus stressing the technological orientation of the firms under question, it also contains the general idea of a specific area in which industrial agglomeration may take place. This ambiguity is also reflected by the different types of parks and centres, which the empirical research has been able as well as forced to identify (for a short overview see Heering/Pfirrmann/Schroeder 1998).

To be sure, in most transition countries meanwhile there exists a very large sector of small and smallest firms, sometimes partly as a result of modest reforms undertaken already in the eighties. The remarkable nominal figures concerning the share of the private economy is one indicator (for 1997 see Heering/Pfirrmann/Schroeder 1998, see also the country studies in the preceding chapters). In Hungary the fraction of small firms with up to ten employees amounts to 97 per cent and firms with up to fifty employees constitute 99 per cent; in Poland, too, 99 per cent of all firms have fifty or less employees. In Russia the fraction of SMEs is about 42 per cent. However, if one looks beyond the purely numerical dimension, the main shortcomings become clear: the great bulk of those firms is concentrated in trade and services; 75 per cent in Poland, 60 per cent in Russia (Heering/Pfirrmann/ Schroeder 1998). Thus the small economy seems to be overloaded with redistributional rather than proper productive activities (Batstone/Westhead 1996). Moreover, most firms operate on a "family base"; 75 per cent of all Hungarian businesses do not employ staff, compared to 50 per cent on average in the European Union (HMEA 2000a). Experiences in developed as well as underdeveloped countries suggest that this is presumably not the appropriate structure to enhance economic progress. Many factors are responsible for this state of affairs, but the evidence provides a prima facie argument for the view that simply to release the legal restrictions for entering economic activities is not sufficient and may even make things worse rather than better. Some additional political measures seem to be in order.

While industrial policy in developed countries is still theoretically controversial, although generally practised, there seems now to be little doubt that there is a strong case in favour of it in the CEEC.[3] The most striking argument against it, implying that by undertaking such a policy the state usurps knowledge which only the market mechanism can provide, simply loses much of its persuasiveness in the absence or

---

3 It is sometimes argued that "new growth theories" and "theories of strategic trade" have led to a revised perspective on industrial policy, giving it a fresh and solid foundation. On closer inspection, however, this view is doubtful; what remains in the end is the old-fashioned advice that the state should take care of the building and qualification of human capital and of non-market R&D-activities, measures which can be founded on nearly any approach whatsoever (Siebert/Rauscher 1995).

serious weakness of regular markets. Of course, the government taking responsibility in these issues under such conditions is no guarantee of success, but in any case the range of alternatives is extremely narrow. Poor performance of markets and weakly developed market institutions (bearing in mind in particular the lack of functioning capital markets[4]) generate high costs of entering markets especially for smaller domestic firms, which are further compounded by administrative barriers to setting up new firms. Establishing a park or centre where newcomers may settle down more easily, where the technical infrastructure is on average better than elsewhere and which may deliver some of the most urgent managerial, marketing and legal know-how, is in these circumstances very likely to serve a basic function for the emergence of new firms. If these initiatives are undertaken by the government, this provides (to some degree at least) a binding commitment on its part not to interfere with the development of the new business sector; this will in particular be true if the programmes are sponsored by foreign agents. It is, however, questionable whether the state could – or should – do more than to perform such a neutral subsidiary policy; in particular, experience warns against stipulating too many and too ambitious preconditions for firms to enter the area.

3 Parks and Centres in Hungary, Poland and Russia

In Hungary so-called technology parks were founded already in the mid eighties; this development was initiated by the discussion on technology transfer and innovation in western industrial countries. The parks at that time, however, turned out as a complete flop. Some still exist, but they lack relevance and have rather a bad reputation; the best-known is perhaps INNOTECH at the technical university of Budapest.

In the second half of the nineties the debate flared up again, now pushed by the Ministry for Industry and Trade. In 1996 a law was passed introducing the term "industrial park" as an official title to be applied on a yearly base. The acknowledgement as an industrial park provides several organisational, logistical and financial benefits for firms which settle in the area. In 1997, twenty-eight industrial parks had been acknowledged; meanwhile some 112 are operating or will shortly be in operation (HMEA 2000a). The number of firms within these parks (measured from the date of acknowledgement) has increased by 272, the number of employees by 34 000 (HMEA 2000b). Originally, the concept was closely linked to the pro-

4 Recent empirical work on SMEs in transition countries lends support to the thesis that lack of funds ranks among the three most important obstacles, compared to its far less damaging impact on western SMEs (Pissarides 1998). However, other findings from a broad sample of manufacturing SMEs in Poland, Romania, the Slovakian Republic, Russia and the Ukraine suggest that lack of finance may only be of secondary relevance compared to insecurity of property rights, which primarily seems to influence investment decisions and thus the demand for, rather than the supply of, funds (Johnson/McMillan/Woodruff 1999 and Heering/Pfirrmann in this volume).

motion of technological innovation, but this claim mostly proved unrealisable. There are other, and sometimes more ambitious, centres in Hungary outside the programme fostering industrial parks, mainly founded on a local or regional base; however, the claims very seldom tally with reality: according to an official of the National Committee for Technological Development (OMFB) in 1998 there were roughly forty parks and centres in Hungary operating or in preparation, of which at most ten qualify as technoparks in the proper sense.

Discussions on technoparks and business incubators in Poland also date back at least to the second half of the eighties, although the first centre for innovation and entrepreneurship in Posen was founded not earlier than 1989 (Matusiak 1995; Matusiak/Zasiadly/Krukowski/Lavelle 1996). The original focus, however, was not on the promotion of technological innovation but rather on generally fostering economic development and the founding of new enterprises. Since 1990 three phases of Polish approaches to parks and centres can be distinguished: between 1990 and 1992 there was some support of the innovative activities of SMEs. Between 1993 and 1995 the emphasis shifted to combating unemployment. From 1996 onwards, the main interest lies on local aspects of economic performance, structural change and the transfer of technology.

Currently about fifty-five parks and centres are operating in Poland; among them are at least forty-nine which are pure incubators, that is, they have no technological claim whatsoever. The development is just at its beginning, an perceptible influence on regional or even local development does not exist, and there is a still high dependence on public funds. Also, the pressure for the park to earn its own funds has frequently undermined original existing orientations towards technology-based enterprises.

In Russia the corresponding discussion started no earlier than the beginning of the nineties. The first round in the founding of innovation centres and science parks was dominated by universities, later other units from the military-industrial complex and big state-owned firms joined the movement (Sitter 1995; Batstone/Westhead 1996; Radosevic/Walter in this volume). During our research there were presumed to be about twenty-eight technoparks operating. Some of the firms working there were equipped with high-tech know-how concerning military projects or conversion from military to civil applications. Their products were not well suited to domestic (not to speak of regional or local) needs, nor do they meet the standards of export markets. This finding gives support to the opinion "that much of the technology does not appear to have been designed with particular customer groups in mind and it is difficult to see how much of it will ever reach commercialisation" (Batstone/Westhead 1996, 87).

Looking at the experiences from three transition countries, there is certainly a wide range of variation between countries as well as between parks/centres in one country. Broadly speaking, and not very surprisingly, the differences seem to be highest in Russia and lowest in Hungary. However, there also are some quite common features, which we may summarise as follows (the table at the end of the section gives a synoptic overview on our qualitative findings):

The employment and other economic effects of the parks and centres are, hitherto at least, almost negligible; this is true even if attention is restricted to regional or local levels. The industrial parks in Hungary differ sharply from this picture, presumably due to their early switching to another philosophy as well as to the fact of massive support by the central government.

Technological levels within the parks and centres are more or less diffuse, sometimes quite remarkable if measured by domestic standards. On the whole there is, however, no evidence that firms within these units are more innovative than outsiders. In addition, there seems to be no systematic technology transfer between the firms and properly located research units, either with respect to products or processes or with regard to human capital. As a matter of fact, scientists and researchers in transition countries not infrequently seem to found their own firms, but like all other founders in those countries they mostly choose sectors of activity quite distant from high-tech sectors.[5]

As a rule, parks and centres in transition countries depend heavily on public support, especially public funds. Most parks and centres are linked to complex networks of clients with the same or similar interests. Those networks serve not least as media to acquire financial support from internal, often also from external sources. As has been reported to us, competition in parks/centres and their firms is frequently is directed much more towards the raising and distribution of funds than to product markets. Although funds are without doubt necessary to fulfil the defined purposes, those activities often give the impression of pure rent-seeking. It should be borne in mind that this was exactly the ruling pattern of activities under the old regimes. There also existed several networks which had basically the same objective: to gather and redistribute resources according to well established loyalty channels. Indeed, it would be quite astonishing if those trained capacities were to have vanished over night, all the more as the institutional and cultural environment certainly did not change that fast.

Everywhere, however, it is emphasised that one of the main motives for firms to settle within the area of a park or centre lies in the offer of material and technical infrastructure as well as several consultant services at favourable tariffs. It seems that this is in fact the most crucial single reason in favour of such units.

---

5 It may, however, be that academics regard those activities simply as an interlude to accumulate the capital required, not easy to get from capital markets, to start a more ambitious business (Batstone/Westhead 1996, 86).

Table 3-1: Synopsis: Impacts of parks/centres in Hungary, Poland and Russia

Level of Investigation	Criterion	HU	PL	RU
Micro: Firms in Parks/Centres	Direct Employment Effects	3	1	1
	Level of Technology and Innovation	2	2	3-
	Technology Transfer Activities	1	0	1
	Improvement of Infrastructure	3	1	2
	Concentration of Subsidies	2	2	2
	Relations to International Networks	3-	3	3
Mezzo: Regional Impacts	Contribution to regional GDP	3-	0	0
	Number of Innovations and Patents (compared to Regional Level)	1	1	1
	Regional Birth Rate (New Firms)	2	0	0
	Fraction of Innovative Firms	1	0	0
	Indirect Employment Effects	0	0	0
	Relations to Regional Networks	3-	2	3
Macro: Impacts on National Economy	Competitiveness on Global Markets	1-2	0	1
	Number of Innovations and Patents (compared to National Level)	0	0	0
	Number of SMEs	3	0	0
	Brain-Drain-Effects	0	0	0

HU = Hungary; PL = Poland; RU = Russia; 0 = Very Low; 1 = Low; 2 = Medium; 3- = Partly High; 3 = High

Source: Heering/Pfirrmann/Schroeder 1998, 149.

4 Interpreting the Empirical Results

The findings reported in the preceding section are sobering, at least if compared to the more ambitious conjectures and if confronted with the picture of the relevant scene which is conveyed to outsiders often with remarkable professionality. In this section I try to give an interpretation of the results.

To start with let me give a short analytical assessment of the concept of science parks and innovation centres. Conceptually, the idea is based at least on the following five ideas: 1. The idea of industrial agglomeration being favourable to economic development. 2. The idea of reducing barriers to market entry. 3. The idea of SMEs as promoters of innovation, flexibility and growth. 4. The idea of technology transfer between producers and researchers, which may take either the form of spillover or of transfer of human capital and/or technological information. 5. The idea of synergetic effects between different firms or between firms and research units. While the first three points deal with business incubation in general, and especially with improving the conditions for SMEs, the fourth and fifth focus on advanced technology.

There is a good deal of rationale in this conception, but it also entails some fairly naive elements, in particular with respect to the latter two ideas. The relevant issue is, however, whether any of these ideas give reason for policy measure, and of what sort if any. The concept of technology transfer is based on the presumption that there are always sufficient inventions produced by scientific research which only await commercialisation. If the latter does not happen, there must be barriers which need to be overcome by some (presumably governmental) agency. Such a linear model of innovation is surely overly simplified. Synergy, on the other hand, will naturally arise to some degree during the co-operation of people with different capabilities, but such effects are mostly non-intentional, that is, they cannot be (re)produced ad libitum. Nothing in this story per se legitimates any sort of public intervention. According to well-established economic principles, governmental intervention into market processes should only be undertaken if there are serious market failures which otherwise cannot be resolved, and which the state is able to address at reasonable costs. The main reasons for such failures are strong externalities (including "public goods" aspects), the existence of a natural monopoly, lack of adaptability of the market and asymmetric information between market parties (Fritsch/Wein/Ewers 1993). We should at least check whether some of these problems apply to the present case. There is certainly a public goods problem in the creation of inventions (Schroeder/Fuhrmann/Heering 1991). But there seems to be little that a science park or innovation centre can do about it. And it is even more unclear that any of the other aspects intervene, without considering whether parks or centres could provide an effective remedy to potential defects. At any rate, the only further candidate is the asymmetry of information, and while this phenomenon surely is a factor relevant to inventions (and rightly so), it is again questionable whether it can legitimate public interference. These caveats are equally relevant to transition countries. There may be a case for technology transfer here, but in my opinion the simple model of science parks etc. is badly suited to the specific conditions, as I shall explain below.

There also may be externalities with regard to the first three of the above-mentioned ideas, but it is doubtful why those should not be internalised by purely private initiatives. Quite successful parks and centres, for example, have been founded spontaneously by private actors. That does not mean, of course, that public agents are not able to establish successful arrangements, but only that success seems to occur largely at random, that is, it cannot be staged at will. This is exactly what the diverse empirical studies seem to suggest. All in all, those arguments should levy some scepticism on the constructivistic philosophy of science parks, at least for developed countries.

Nevertheless the case in transition countries may be altogether different. But here we have to identify very thoroughly the relevant issues in which they may differ. There is, I believe, a rather good point for parks and centres as a medium for improving the comparative conditions which domestic new firms face and which are not the last unintended consequences of the chosen variant of transition. Consider the case of Hungary, the government of which seems to have a particularly clear understanding of the situation (HMEA 2000a). During the first phase of transition the government took an extremely liberal approach, in particular decidedly abstinent with regard to specific industrial policy measures; it primarily relied on private initiatives coming from foreign investors. This policy has been extraordinarily successful; Hungary was able to attract the highest rates of foreign direct investment of all Eastern transition countries: in 1989-97 investment per capita amounted to 1,52 thousand USD, while the Czech Republic received 730 USD, Estonia 560 USD, Slovenia 540 USD, Latvia 520 USD; Poland got 220 USD, and Russia only 70 USD (Heering/Pfirrmann/Schroeder 1998). There cannot be much doubt that foreign engagement was one of the main impacts for the overall transition progress in its first phase.

However, the Hungarian success also had its price: For quite understandable reasons foreign investors not only favoured specific sectors, in particular energy, finance and the chemical industry, but also specific regions; almost one half of all foreign investment flowed into the conurbation around Budapest. As a result there was a strong asymmetry in development with regard to sectors as well as regions, leading to extreme differentials in welfare positions. Moreover, despite the strong dynamic of newly-founded firms, in the second half of the nineties a process of re-concentration set in – also due, to a high degree, to the impact of powerful foreign enterprises. Finally, domestic R&D-capacities almost completely broke down, not only because of the break in the system, but also because foreign firms were extremely hesitant to employ domestic R&D-staff, who on average did not fit their demands well.

The Hungarian government reacted to these undesirable trends with an fairly intelligent dual strategy: it subsidised foreign enterprises which decided to hire domestic R&D-personnel; the expectation was that those persons should be adapted to their new task by qualification and training internal to the firms. And the government designed its industrial park programme to combat the other defects. Industrial parks, from this perspective, can mainly be interpreted as an attempt to regain the balance of economic take-off chances for domestic entrepreneurs which was almost necessarily lost during the first period of transformation. The impression that the programme is apparently rather successful underlines the rationale of the strategy.

While Hungarian industrial parks, in this context, may be seen as a legitimate measure of industrial policy to correct self-made malformations, they are not dedicated to specific economic activities; in particular, no special weight is given to supporting the implementation of advanced technology, although such is, of course, not excluded. The latter idea was, as in the other countries, originally contemplated, but as elsewhere turned out not to be very promising. I suppose that this is due to the general deficiencies of the concept of science parks, as well as to specific conditions for R&D-activities found in more or less all transition countries, which render the conception even less appropriate. Basically, I think, three aspects deserve attention:

Under the regime of central planning, R&D was by and large extremely inefficient. There were certainly some well-known technological high-lights, especially in the Soviet Union, but these centred primarily upon military and space technology. Put systemically, this means that highly specialised researchers were working on predetermined tasks with respect to pre-defined goals. To be sure, similarly specialised research areas can be found in almost all advanced countries, but under market conditions there has always existed a sufficient body of firms and market oriented scientists to be able to adapt many of the respective results to market demand. In socialist countries there was no counterpart for this adaptation process. Apparently the traditional pattern of research activities seems effectively to endure. The fact that many of the more advanced products reported by managers and firms from science parks in Russia and elsewhere, neither fit the need of domestic nor of foreign markets, clearly supports to this guess. If it proves correct, then the basic premise of the science park concept, that there are sufficient marketable inventions from the old R&D-staff, simply lacks realism. What is reported from Russian science parks, and which is presumably also true elsewhere, is that academics take the opportunity to work within those areas not primarily to develop commercialisable products, but to get access to additional public funding for further research (Batestone/Westhead 1996). It is doubtful whether this research is actually in need and should be publicly supported.

Furthermore, the incentives for academic researchers to found their own technology- based firms are rather bad. On the one hand, research units generally foster any form of market-oriented side-activities by their members. Thus there are opportunities to gain higher income, while staying within the unit. Of course, the entrance into pure business may promise much higher rewards, but at the obvious cost of being also highly risky under present circumstances. If academics, on the other hand, actually decide to leave their work, they will rather choose to emigrate or to take an offer from foreign firms or to look for a job within an administration.

Finally, adverse incentives exist also for universities and other public research units as well as for the management of parks. The former have an interest in binding academics with marketable ideas, since these ideas are sources of additional funds. They are therefore ready to give support to side activities of their staff, but tend to refuse support for any form of spill-over. In addition, the fact that patents are still ascribed to research units rather than to individual researchers functions as an effective barrier to potential founders of innovative firms out of those research units. Managers of parks, on the other hand, have to earn money and may even have to made profits by renting business areas, leasing technical equipment, selling services and so on to the firms in the park. If tariffs are fixed irrespective of the specifics of the firms, managers will maximise the certainty of a steady monetary inflow. However, acquiring innovative firms which are less liquid, have lower sales proceeds over a longer time period and carry a larger market risk than non-innovative but solvent enterprises, will prove extremely risky and must often lead to a preference for more traditional activities. The situation would be different if tariffs could be adapted to specific risks, but given asymmetric information about firm's economic prospects and given the capital restrictions which small innovative firms necessarily face, this would probably not be workable. The problem may be solved by public provision of venture capital, but this measure is independent of the concept of science parks.

All these three factors interfere with the general problems implied by the concept of science parks or innovation centres. In sum, there cannot be much hope that they may prove helpful in starting up a new dynamic of innovation in transition countries; at least for the present that seems rather improbable. As the case of Hungary shows, however, abandoning those expectations does not make the general park-idea useless, if more modestly and more pragmatically designed.

5 Concluding Remarks

The time period which has elapsed since the first parks/centres were established in the three countries under investigation is certainly much too short to draw a final conclusion. However, the overall impression we have gained from our work is that in any case the original idea of setting up a new base for industrial innovations in some of the transition countries, by linking together technological know-how from the old R&D-systems and market-oriented competence in technoparks and innovation centres, has hardly anywhere been achieved. In this sense the expectations of western consultants and observers, as well as the hopes of domestic activists, have to a great extent been disappointed and destroyed. Taking a sober-minded view, this does not come as a very big surprise given the fact that even testing the idea in the West led to controversial results, and the idea now was to be implemented in a completely different environment in the East. One political message from all this seems to be quite clear: sometimes less would really be more! Although it makes good sense to build up parks and centres in transition countries as one of several means to support the founding of new firms and to foster regional development in an environment which at present is extremely unfavourable to both, such initiatives lose much of their sense if the claim associated with them is too ambitious and correspondingly the standards for participation are too restrictive. In particular, the original emphasis given to the promotion of highly innovative SMEs is far away from the mark. Moreover, the more open the parks/centres are to outsiders with respect to actors as well as activities, the smaller is the chance of the units becoming essentially "closed shops". In any case, what is required is a more pragmatic rather than a dogmatic approach. The Hungarian government seems to have learned this lesson quite quickly.

Literature

Batstone, S.; Westhead, P. (1996): The Development of Science Parks and New Technology-Based Firms in Russia. In: Brezinski, H.; Fritsch, M. (Eds.): The Economic Impact of New Firms in Post-Socialist Countries. Bottom-up Transformation in Eastern Europe. Cheltenham – Brookfield: Edward Elgar, pp. 72-93.

EBRD (1998): European Bank for Reconstruction and Development; Enterprise Performance and Growth. Transition Report Update April 1998; London.

Fritsch, M.; Wein, T.; Ewers, H. J. (1993): Marktversagen und Wirtschaftspolitik. Mikroökonomische Grundlagen staatlichen Handelns. München: Vahlen.

Heering, W.; Pfirrmann, O.; Schroeder, K. (1998): Technologie- und Gründerzentren in Mittel- und Osteuropa. Überarbeiteter Endbericht der Arbeitsgruppe EXIS^{3}T zum Forschungsprojekt "Technologie- und Gründerzentren in Mittel- und Osteuropa als Instrument einer wettbewerbsorientierten Strukturpolitik". APT-Paper 2/98,Center of Research on Policy and Technolgy/Free University of Berlin.

HMEA (2000a): Hungarian Ministry of Economic Affairs; Széchenyi Plan. A National Development Plan, First Draft.

HMEA (2000b): Ungarisches Ministerium für Wirtschaft, Industrieparks.

Johnson, S.; McMillan, J.; Woodruff, C. (1999): Property Rights, Finance and Entrepreneurship. EBRD Working Paper no. 43. European Bank for Reconstruction and Development.

Matusiak, K. B. (1995): Technologie- und Gründerzentren in Polen – Fünfjährige Erfahrungen und Entwicklungsperspektiven. In: Groß, B.; Zasiadly, K. (Eds.): Technologie- und Gründerzentren in Polen. Berlin: Weidler, pp. 23-44.

Matusiak, K. B.; Zasiadly, K.; Krukowski, K.; Lavelle, J. (1996): Business Incubators. Warsaw.

Oakey, R. (1985): British University Science Parks and High Technology Small Firms: A Comment on the Potential for Sustained Economic Growth. International Small Business Journal, 4, pp. 58-67.

Pissarides, F. (1998): Is Lack of Funds the Main Obstacle to Growth? The EBRD's Experience with Small and Medium-Sized Business in Central and Eastern Europe, EBRD Working Paper no. 33, European Bank for Reconstruction and Development.

Schroeder, K.; Fuhrmann, F. U.; Heering, W. (1991): Wissens- und Technologietransfer. Bedeutung und Perspektive einer regionalen technologiepolitischen Strategie am Beispiel Berlins. Berlin: Duncker und Humblot.

Siebert, H.; Rauscher, M. (1995): Außenhandelstheorie. In: Berthold, N. (Ed.): Allgemeine Wirtschaftstheorie – Neuere Entwicklungen. München: Vahlen, pp. 251-265.

Sitter, W. (1995): Perestroika und Innovation. Stuttgart u. a.: G. Fischer.

Stern, N. (1998): The Future of the Economic Transition. EBRD Working Paper no. 30, European Bank for Reconstruction and Development.

Regional Innovation Capacities and Economic Transition: The Example of West Transdanubia

Emmanuel Muller, Andrea Zenker, Tibor Dőry

1 Introduction

In the literature devoted to interrelations between innovative firms and economic transition, only little attention has been paid to the influence of regional determinants. In line with the current academic and political debates on the role of regions for competitiveness and economic development, the aim of this paper is to provide some insights on innovation activities from a regional perspective. The investigation deals primarily with a Hungarian region: West Transdanubia. More precisely, the analysis focuses on firm behaviours and characteristics with regards to innovation and co-operation, determining remarkable facts on an empirical basis. This in turn enables a typology of regional firms to be established which may be helpful for innovation policy in West Transdanubia. The paper is organised as follows. The first section reviews the background of the analysis, addressing the concept of innovation systems and economic changes from a regional perspective. The second section, concentrating on manufacturing firms, contrasts innovation and co-operation patterns in West Transdanubia with two other central European regions (Saxony and Slovenia) allowing the introduction of comparative elements into the investigation. The third section examines the innovation and co-operation activities of manufacturing and business service firms in West Transdanubia. Finally, concluding comments explore policy implications, insisting notably on the current and future importance of regional innovation capacities.

2 Systems of Innovation, Regional Learning and Economic Transition: The Background of the Investigation

To address the issue of innovation, especially from a regional perspective, implies considering multiple aspects relating notably to the diffusion of knowledge within networks and systems. Crucial in this respect are new combinations of knowledge that lead to innovations (Lundvall 1992; European Commission 2000) as well as the interactive and systemic character of innovations (for instance Lundvall 1992;

Cooke 1998). Pointing to knowledge and learning as fundamental prerequisites for innovation, Lundvall (1992) emphasises the interactive character of learning and refers to the specific institutional and cultural context in which it takes place. This leads notably to a consideration of the regional dimension of learning activities. Concerning innovation phenomena, systems may be defined as "complexes of elements or components, which mutually condition and constrain one another, so that the whole complex works together, with some reasonably clearly defined overall function" (Edquist 1997, 13). Following Freeman (1987) and Lundvall (1988, 1992), abundant literature can be found relating to national innovation systems (NIS). The regional innovation system (RIS) takes the innovation system concept on the national level and adapts it to the sub-national one, referring notably to specific characteristics and emphasising phenomena such as internal cohesion and identity (Cooke et al. 1996; Cooke 1998).[1] Focusing on the interactions of its elements in the production, diffusion and use of new knowledge (Lundvall 1992), the innovation system approach highlights why certain regions (and a fortiori some countries) are more innovative than others and tries to deliver the underlying arguments for these developments.

Referring for instance to the arguments developed by Lawson and Lorenz (1999), the processes underlying regional collective learning can be examined along three central ideas: firstly, the overall attitude towards innovation within a region, which relies on the concept of a regional innovation culture. A lack of innovation culture in a region results in the development of regional inertia, meaning that firms face resistance when trying to introduce, use and diffuse new knowledge.[2] Secondly, the resources potentially available within a region in terms of knowledge bases and possible knowledge combination: these constitute the regional innovation potential. Learning, with respect to innovation, appears to be a path-dependent and cumulative process. The search for, and access to, new knowledge which becomes incorporated into the regional firms' routines enables the introduction of innovations (which are mostly incremental and may – exceptionally – be radical). Finally, the willingness of regional actors to have an open attitude towards knowledge sharing, and their ability to exchange ideas on innovative topics, constitute the aptitude to build up regional innovation networks. The existence of a "common language" or, more generally, of a regionally-rooted (business) culture explains how such networks may resolve the problems of co-ordination/competition which inevitably arise when knowledge on innovative topics is shared. As a consequence, it is par-

1 An alternative perception, which can be found in the literature but is not retained here, should be briefly evoked. It is also possible to define a region from an economic perspective, for instance with the help of the 'industrial clusters' approach given by Porter (1990). From this point of view, the industrial cluster may be seen as the sum of all the economic actors contributing directly to the dominant production process of the considered region.

2 To a certain extent, it is possible here to link up with the GREMI (Groupe de Recherche Européen sur les Milieux Innovateurs) approach related to "innovative milieux" (for instance Perrin, 1990; Maillat/Perrin, 1992).

ticularly important to consider the systemic aspect of regional innovation in the light of cultural, historical, social and political conditions: "Accordingly, the future development of every region is largely predetermined by its technological, economic, cultural, political and social history. In our context, regionally rooted technological competence plays an exceptional role. Here, regionally developed "assets", which may be embedded in densely woven networks of interactive and exchange relationships, must be comprehended as the key to understanding regional problems and regional capacity for taking action, as they are a central precondition for regional capacity for action". (Braczyk/Heidenreich 1998, 416). Considering the policy implications of regional learning in terms of innovation support, the hypothesis is nowadays widespread that the nature and frequency of interactions between actors significantly influence regional development, because the actors learn from and with each other. Nevertheless, no unique way to foster regional innovation capacities and to ensure the competitive advantage of regional firms can be established. This probably constitutes one of the main policy challenges for European regions in economic transition, such as West Transdanubia.

Concluding from the theoretical overview, the establishment and support of a functioning regional innovation system – including a favourable innovation culture, identification of the regional innovation potential and support of innovation networks – can be considered as an important element in a successful regional development strategy. In this context, the introduction of innovation-related initiatives would be a means to promote the conditions for sustainable knowledge-based economic development on a regional level. Integrating regional actors and building interrelationships between them would be a first step towards a regional innovation culture.

The socio-political and economic context of innovation in the West Transdanubian region has been characterised by fundamental changes during the last few years. The transition process of the Hungarian economy and society began exactly ten years ago, and every part of this system underwent fundamental change. The country's regional structure and its spatial, economic and societal structures followed the transition too, and they precisely reflected the step-by-step altering of the socialist political-economic system and the fast development of the new system. The effects were very spectacular both at a regional and local level, and led to shifts of former relationships and spatial functions. The main characteristics of the transition are the following (Rechnitzer 2000):

- The reduction of state ownership through the dynamic expansion of private ownership, partly through privatisation, partly with the help of foreign and internal capital and their rapid expansion throughout the country.
- The establishment of institutions of the market economy, the reinforcement and real functioning of all laws and organisations guaranteeing the freedom of enter-

prises, the security of private ownership and the equality of values for all participants in the economy.

- The dramatic evolution of the former economic structure, notably the dramatic expansion of the service sector compared to agriculture and industry.

Like other Hungarian regions, West Transdanubia faced extensive and rapid changes in society, economy and in institutional frameworks. These changes have taken place within a short period of time, i.e. particularly since the political transformation in the early 1990s and the process of reform towards a market economy. The West Transdanubian Region is one of the seven regional development, planning and statistical regions created under the recent national legislation. The regional territorial units conform with the EU classification at NUTS II level.[3] The region is subdivided into the three counties of Győr-Moson-Sopron, Vas and Zala (figure 2-1).

As well as the fundamental changes which were brought about by political transformation – for instance, changes in the ownership structure – the opening up of borders and markets has resulted in greater exposure of the region to globalisation trends. In general, the effects of globalisation can be both positive and negative for regions and sub-regions. The balance of positive and negative effects depends on many factors, but crucially, on the capacity of individual regions to adapt to change, and to take advantage of broader trends. This includes, in particular, the capacity to access new technologies, new types of industries and employment, and to attract mobile investment in new sectors. The latter is increasingly less dependent on low wage factors and more on overall competitiveness of regions in terms of location, the quality of the infrastructure (basic and institutional infrastructure including education, training, R&D facilities etc.) and transport connections, level of education and skills in the labour force, dynamism in the regional economy etc. Its geographic location makes West Transdanubia an interface for the breaking down of barriers with the EU. It is also forging new relationships with adjacent regions in other Central European countries, notably in Slovenia and Slovakia. West Transdanubia has been a centre of dynamic development linked, inter alia, to achieving high levels of foreign investment and new industrial development.

---

3 The region covers an area of 11 182 sq. km and has a population of approximately 992 000 inhabitants.

Figure 2-1: The region of West Transdanubia

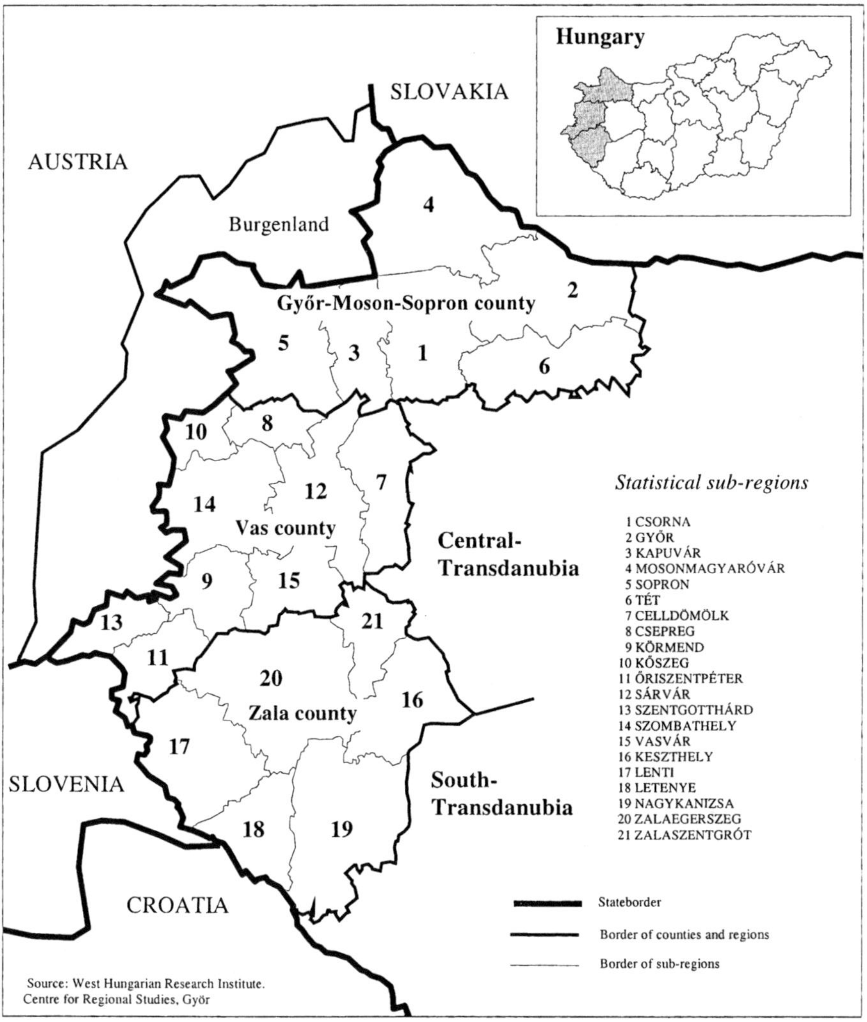

Nevertheless, considering the situation in West Transdanubia in comparison with the Hungarian national average (table 2-1), even if the region is characterised by high-level industrial production and GDP (per capita), innovation and R&D efforts appear as rather weak. Especially when comparing the region's situation with the Hungarian average, it is obvious that the share of regional workplaces provided by industrial companies, as well as the per capita value of industrial production, are above the average, whereas the relevance of the service sector and the proportion of research and development units per 10 000 inhabitants lie below the Hungarian average. Especially indicators referring to R&D in the region are very weak in the Hungarian context: gross expenditure on research and development (GERD), the proportion of scientists and engineers per 10 000 inhabitants and the amount of R&D expenditure per 1 000 inhabitants are less than 50 per cent in relation to the national average. These first indications point to a relative high importance of the industrial sector, but at the same time relatively low regional activities in the fields of research and development. These facts may reveal strengths in the (industrial) production system, but they also indicate weaknesses in the region's innovation system which could be a threat for the future. However, this broad comparison is not in itself sufficient to explain the complex phenomena relating to the region; thus a more detailed investigation at the level of firms is presented in the second and third sections of the paper.

Table 2-1: Some basic statistical indicators for the West Transdanubia region

Indicators	West- Trans-danubia1997	Relation to the national average (%)
Proportion of active earners in agriculture (%)	7.4	92.5
Proportion of active earners in industry (%)	39.6	147.8
Proportion of active earners in services (%)	53.0	81.3
Foreign direct investment per capita in 1 000 HUF*	185.4	92.1
Value of industrial production per capita, in 1 000 HUF*	941.0	231.8
GDP per capita, in 1 000 HUF*	885.0	105.2
R&D units per 10 000 inhabitants	1.4	82.4
R&D expenditure per 1 000 inhabitants, in million HUF*	2.3	36.2
GERD (% of GDP)	0.33	44.6
Scientists and engineers per 10 000 inhabitants	4.4	40.0

*1 EURO= ~239 HUF (Hungarian Forint)

Source: Central Statistical Office, Budapest.

3 Characterising Innovation and Co-Operation Patterns in West Transdanubia with the Help of an Interregional Comparison

This section explores the situation in West Transdanubia on the basis of an interregional comparison. The investigation of firm samples from Saxony and Slovenia allows similarities and differences to be pictured, reflecting region-specific innovation-related characteristics and behaviours (figure 3-1). In fact, since the three areas correspond to different national contexts in economic transition, the hypothesis can be formed that firms follow different trajectories, notably in terms of innovation and co-operation patterns.

Figure 3-1: The three regions at a glance: Saxony, Slovenia and West Transdanubia

The information used for comparison is from the European Regional Innovation Survey (ERIS) database as well as the innovation survey in West-Transdanubien that will be described in the following section.[4] The interregional comparison, fo-

4 The ERIS, investigating innovation and co-operation characteristics of manufacturing and service firms as well as research institutions was conducted by a multidisciplinary research team of economic geographers and regional economists in Germany supported by research counterparts in Austria, France, Netherlands, Slovenia, Spain, Sweden and the United Kingdom. This joint research project was granted by the Deutsche Forschungsgemeinschaft and involved conjointly the

cusing on manufacturing firms with at least 10 employees[5], considers the key indicators shown in table 3-1. Besides the size of the firms, firms' propensity to export, to innovate, to invest in R&D and to co-operate with different partners (Knowledge Intensive Business Services – KIBS, other firms, universities and research organisations) are considered.

Table 3-1: Key variables used for the interregional comparison

Variables	Labels
Firm size	1: Small (less than 100 employees) 2: Medium (between 100 and 499 employees) 3: Large (500 and more employees)
Export orientation	1: Weak (less than 5% of sales) 2: Medium (between 5 and 50% of sales) 3: High (more than 50% of sales)
Propensity to innovate	1: Performance of innovation and/or development 2: No innovation/development
R&D intensity	1: Weak (less than 3.5% of sales) 2: Medium (between 3.5 and 8.5% of sales) 3: High (more than 8.5% of sales)
Innovation-related co-operations with other manufacturing firms	1: Co-operation with other firms 2: No co-operation
Innovation-related co-operations with knowledge-intensive business services	1: Co-operation with KIBS 2: No co-operation
Innovation-related co-operations with universities or research organisations	1: Co-operation with universities or research organisations 2: No co-operation

The comparative analysis considers proportions (i.e. statistical frequencies) which are displayed in the following synopsis (figure 3-2 and appendix 1). Interpreting these results, divergent patterns can be identified. In comparison with the other two samples, manufacturing firms in Saxony can be characterised as being mainly small firms, less export-oriented but presenting higher rates in terms of innovation and R&D investments. The Slovenian sample contains a higher proportion of medium-sized and large manufacturers than the German one. Slovenian firms display high export rates (exports mainly to EU countries) but appear to be less innovative and

Department of Economic Geography at the University of Hannover, the Department of Economic and Social Geography at the University of Cologne, the Faculty of Economics and Business Administration of the Technical University Bergakademie Freiberg and the Fraunhofer ISI in Karlsruhe.

5 The respective sizes of the samples are: (i) Saxony: n=920; (ii) Slovenia n=398; and (iii) West Transdanubia: n=72.

less R&D intensive than firms in Saxony. In the case of Slovenia, co-operation patterns (with firms, KIBS and research organisations) are similar to the ones observed for the East German sample, though weaker. Turning to West Transdanubian manufacturing firms, a weaker propensity to innovate and to invest in R&D (compared to the two other samples) can be observed. In parallel to this, frequencies of co-operation with other actors appear relatively low. Finally, the proportion of large firms is higher in West Transdanubia, and the propensity to export is higher in West Transdanubia than in Saxony, but lower than in the case of Slovenia.

The interregional comparison shows specific characteristics of each of the samples that may be summarised as follows: the analysis reveals differences in the size structure of manufacturing firms in Saxony, Slovenia and West Transdanubia. The differences in export shares might reflect firms' competitiveness as well as the importance of the domestic market: in Saxony, only 7.2 per cent of the sample firms reported high export shares whereas 46.5 per cent of the Slovenian and 25 per cent of the West Transdanubian firms can be described as firms with high export ratios. It can be assumed that the German market plays an important role for East German firms, whereas the Slovenian market is assumed to absorb only a limited share of national firms' production. Thus Slovenian manufacturers tend to export their products. West Transdanubia shows a rather "mixed" structure with nearly 60 per cent of firms with weak export shares and 25 per cent of firms with high export rates, so that a clear pattern cannot be detected. The indications related to research and development as well as to innovation activities are striking, showing very high innovation rates for Saxony and nearly as high shares for Slovenia, but lower innovation rates for West Transdanubia. Furthermore, high innovation performances in Saxony are accompanied by a relatively high proportion of high-tech firms (i.e. firms investing significantly in terms of R&D expenditure). In contrast, the high innovation rates of Slovenian firms are not reflected in a similar propensity to invest in R&D. West Transdanubia's small proportion of innovators is accompanied by a weak R&D intensity. Finally, with regard to firms' co-operation patterns with other firms, research institutions and knowledge-intensive business services, manufacturers in Saxony show the highest co-operation rates. West Transdanubian firms show a very low inclinations to co-operate, the highest share of co-operations being with other firms. It may be assumed that, independently of the context of economic transition, co-operations with KIBS and research institutions appear to be a strong discriminating factor and illustrate the existence of region-specific features.

Figure 3-2: Synopsis of regional characteristics

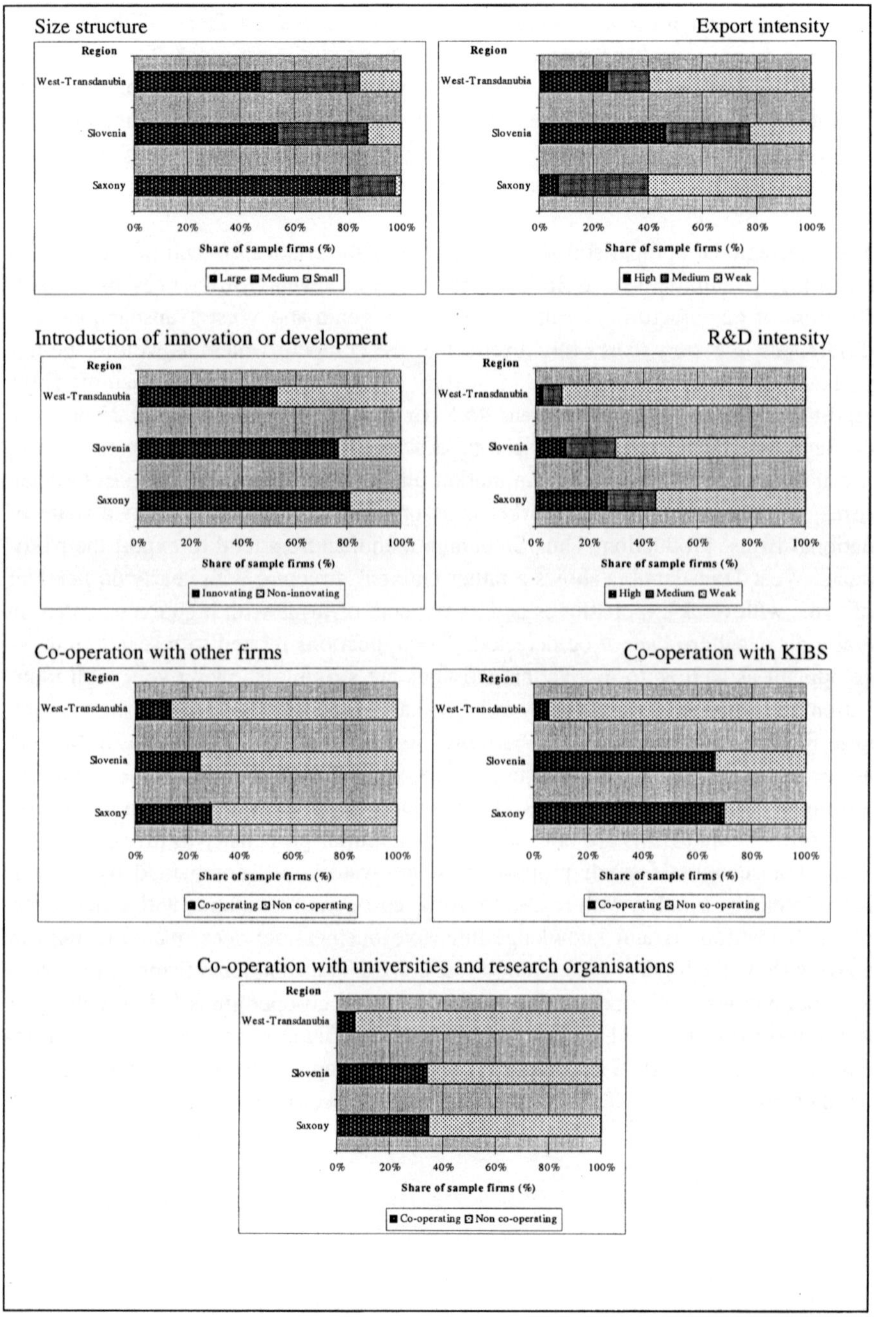

These findings reflect different strategies for catching-up: Saxonian firms try to achieve competitiveness by high innovation rates, whereas Slovenian manufacturers show high export and innovation rates and are characterised by a relatively small share of high-tech firms. West Transdanubian firms are characterised by low innovation rates and low levels of internal and external knowledge acquisition. This suggests that a functioning regional innovation system, based on endogenous innovation potentials and on an appropriate innovation culture, still needs to mature in West Transdanubia.

4 A Regional Analysis of Innovation Behaviours

The following analysis of West Transdanubian firms' innovation and interaction characteristics is based on an innovation survey performed recently by the West Hungarian Research Institute.[6] The survey aims at providing a deeper understanding of aspects related to innovation activities in West Transdanubia. These results may help to define strategic programmes for initiating better innovation conditions and more innovations in the region. Since innovation policy measures should focus on the specific needs and demands of regional firms, a typology of regional firms is proposed, based on the survey results.

As table 4-1 shows, the database contains firms belonging to the manufacturing, services and building trade sectors. The sample comprises 117 firms with more than 10 employees, which corresponds to a response rate of 8.4 per cent. The overall surveyed population of regional firms consisted of 1 401 firms, more than 50 per cent of which belong to the manufacturing sector. 27.3 per cent of the firm population are service companies whereas 18.3 per cent belong to the construction sector. Comparing the sample structure with the population in terms of sectoral distribution, it is obvious that manufacturing firms are over-represented, whereas firms in the service and building trade sectors are under-represented, introducing a slight bias in the analysis.

---

6 In the frame of the "Strategic Innovations Programme", the West Hungarian Research Institute, Centre for Regional Studies, Hungarian Academy of Sciences carried out a postal innovation survey in the region West Transdanubia in 1999/2000. The regional firms were identified with the help of the Chamber of Commerce. The questionnaire focused on aspects like research and development, innovation, forms and contents of co-operations and EU accession. The methodology of the investigation was developed in co-operation with the Fraunhofer ISI supported by the German Federal Ministry of Education and Research (Walter/Zenker/Muller 2000).

Table 4-1: Sectoral distribution of the sample

	Population of regional firms (n)[1]	Population (%)	Sample firms (n)[1]	Sample (%)
Manufacturing	762	54.4	74	63.2
Construction	256	18.3	18	15.4
Services	383	27.3	25	21.4
Total	**1 401**	**100**	**117**	**100**

1: Firms with 10 and more employees

Source: County Statistical Yearbooks 1999. Central Statistical Office, Budapest.

Referring to innovation activities, it can be stated that 51 firms reported the performance of innovations and/or further developments of existing products or services. This corresponds to 43.6 per cent of firms in the sample. Firms in the manufacturing sector display the highest share of innovations (52.8 per cent) whereas less than one third of construction and service sector firms innovated (31.6 per cent and 26.9 per cent respectively; figure 4-1).

Figure 4-1: Innovating firms in the manufacturing, building trade and service sectors

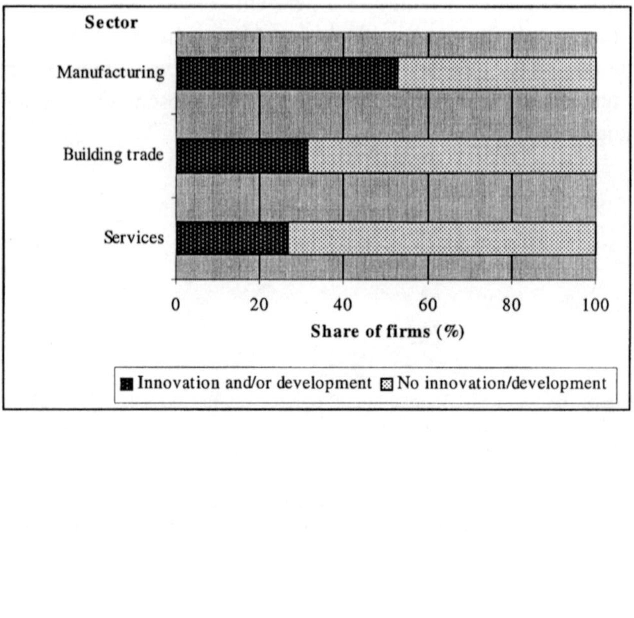

Regarding innovation activities according to firm size, it is noticeable that firms with 100 to 500 employees showed higher innovation rates both than smaller firms and very large firms in the sample. 64.7 per cent of firms with 100 to 199 employees had introduced innovations or further developments, whereas 73.3 per cent of firms with 200 to 499 employees had innovated (figure 4-2).

Figure 4-2: Relationship between innovation and size

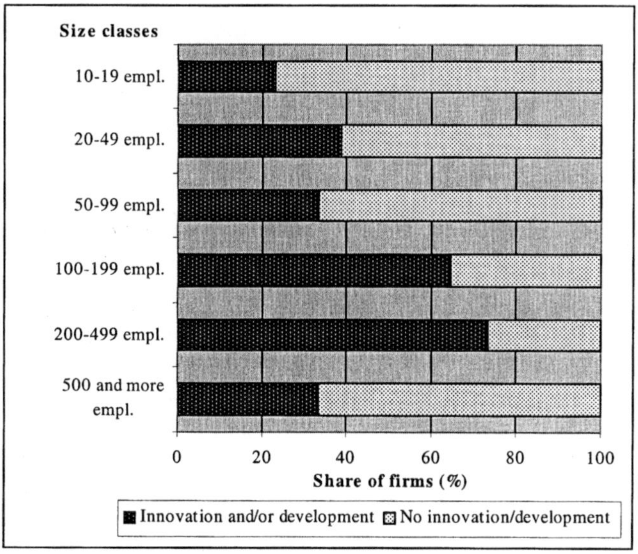

The following multiple correspondence analysis provides a typology of regional firms which may contribute to the design of targeted measures to support specific firm groups according to their characteristics. The innovation and co-operation characteristics of the sample firms are investigated according to similarities and associations. This type of analysis detects structures or patterns in the relationships between variables, by presenting these relationships along a few dimensions. The variables are merely inspected for their categorical information, i.e. the affiliation of the objects to categories. Thus, a multiple correspondence analysis is concerned with non-linear relationships in categorical data. One of the results consists of a graphical output presenting the different categories and their association to each other. Objects of the same category are plotted in near neighbourhood whereas objects of different categories are plotted far apart.[7]

7 The variables included in the multiple correspondence analysis are detailed in appendix 2.

Figure 4-3: Graphical output of the multiple correspondence analysis

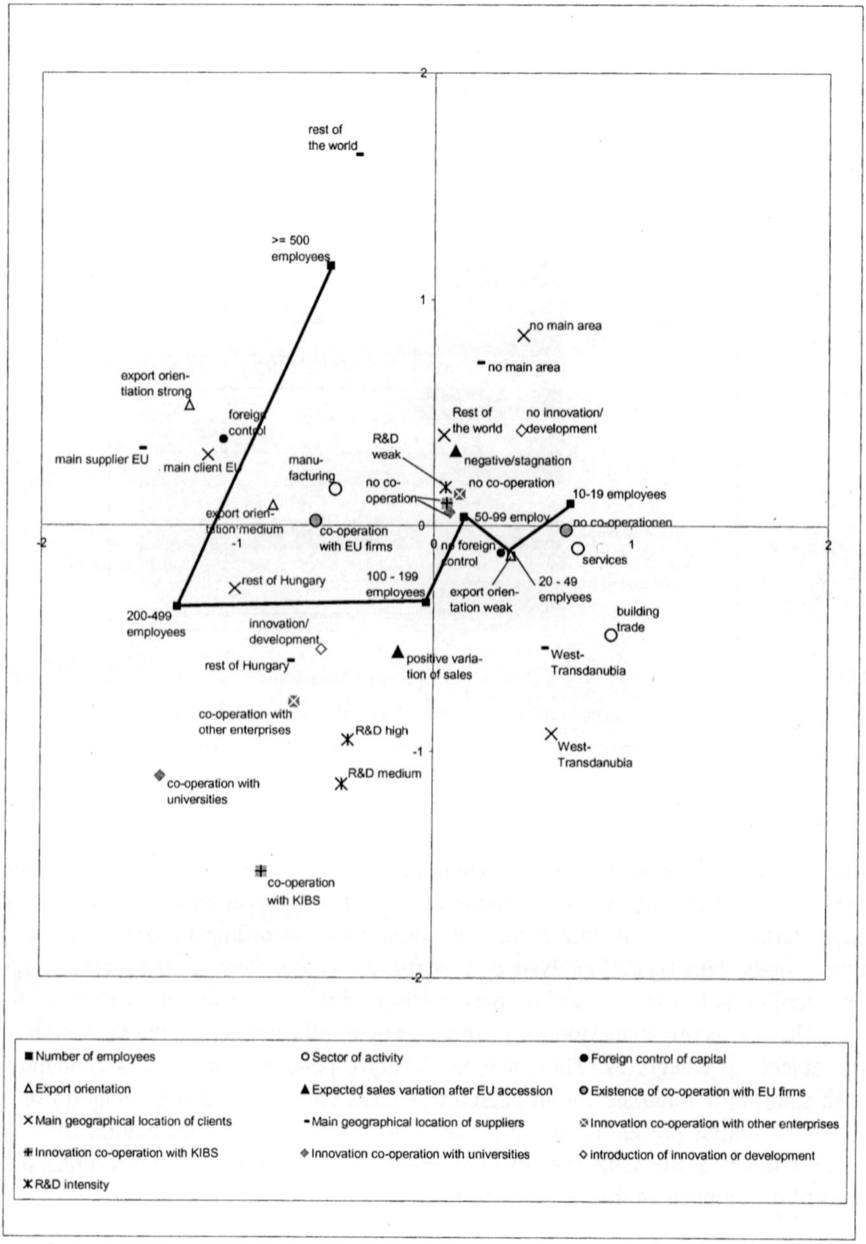

The graphical output of the multiple correspondence analysis is presented in figure 4-3. The eigenvalues are 0.2767 for the first dimension and 0.1704 for the second, which indicates that not all the information is presented in the first two dimensions.[8] Variables like the geographical distribution of suppliers and clients (GEO_SUP, GEO_CL), firms' export orientation (EXPORT), their sector of activity (ACTIVITY), and already existing co-operations with firms from the European Union (EU_COOP) are the main discriminators on the first dimension. This suggests that the first dimension is mainly characterised by production characteristics of the sample firms, contrasting firms whose linkages with suppliers and clients are oriented outside the region (rest of Hungary, EU; cf. the western part of the plot) to firms with intraregional and mixed relationships (West Transdanubia, no main area; cf. the eastern part of the plot). The western part also presents medium and strong export orientations, i.e. more than 5 per cent of firms' sales, whereas the eastern part contains the category "weak export orientation", i.e. firms that do not export or whose exports constitute less than 5 per cent of their sales. Finally, the category "co-operation with EU firms" is plotted on the western part, whereas the category "no co-operation with EU firms" is associated to the variable categories on the eastern part of the graph.

The second dimension is mainly based on the categories of the variables GEO_CL and GEO_SUP, opposing firms with supplier and client linkages without main location and with locations the European Union or in other countries to those that are situated in Hungary, including West Transdanubia. Innovation and/or development activities are discriminating on both dimensions; the innovation category is plotted in the south-west part, whereas the non-innovating/developing category can be found in the north-east. The category "weak R&D intensity" (i.e. internal research and development activities equivalent to less than 3.5 per cent of the firm's turnover) is plotted in the northern part. Contrary to this, medium and high intensities are plotted in the southern part of the graph.

Considering innovation behaviour, it appears that the category "innovation and/or development" is associated: (i) with linkages to suppliers and clients located in the rest of Hungary; (ii) with innovation co-operations with other enterprises; and (iii) with R&D expenditure higher than 3.5 per cent of turnover. Moreover, firms between 100 and 499 employees seem to be more innovative than smaller or very large ones. Innovation-related co-operations with universities, research organisations and knowledge-intensive business services, as well as existing co-operations with firms located in the European Union, tend to be associated with innovative rather than non-innovative behaviours. Finally, innovative firms express more positive expectations concerning Hungary's accession to the European Union: the category "positive variation expected" tends to be associated with the innovation category, whereas negative expectations or stagnation are plotted close to the non-innovation category.

---

8 The discrimination measures of the multiple correspondence analysis on dimensions 1 and 2 are displayed in appendix 3.

Aiming at a typology of regional firms, the output of the multiple correspondence analysis indicates a first group whose characteristics are plotted in the north-western part. Firms in this group are characterised by a high share of foreign capital and more than 50 per cent of their sales are exports. Their supplier and client linkages are mainly abroad. These characteristics are associated with the large size classes of the sample. The second group can be described as being composed of innovating firms with client and supplier linkages mainly within the Hungarian market. Further characteristics are innovation co-operations with other enterprises, a positive assessment of the EU accession and a (comparatively) high level of R&D expenditure. The size categories 100 to 199 employees and 200 to 499 employees are plotted relatively close to the innovation category. A third group of firms reveals characteristics that are plotted in the eastern part of figure 4-3: mainly the absence of innovation and co-operation. In this part, the non-innovation category as well as the non-co-operation categories are plotted. Additionally, firms in this group show weak export activities and they perform little or no R&D. These categories are associated with the smaller size classes, i.e. less than 100 employees. The capital of these firms is not in foreign hands and these firms are rather sceptical concerning the effects of EU accession.

To summarise, the analysis reveals three different types of regional firms: (i) relatively large ones with a strong business focus on foreign markets and high export shares that are mainly governed by headquarters outside the region, (ii) innovative and relatively co-operative firms oriented towards the Hungarian market and performing internal R&D, and (iii) firms that neither innovate nor co-operate.

5 Conclusion

Summing up, it is probably too early to speak of a well-established innovation system in West Transdanubia. In fact, only a limited share of firms seem to consider innovation-related activities as being decisive for competitiveness. Comparing West Transdanubia with other central European regions (Saxony and Slovenia), it appears clearly that even if fundamental changes have been undergone, further improvements are essential. In the region, the co-operation structure has proved to be relatively weak and innovation networks seem to be quite limited. In order to improve this situation and to support the development of an innovation system in West Transdanubia, the general innovation culture and performance of regional firms could be enhanced by specific innovation policy measures. The typology of regional firms presented in the paper may provide a framework for the conception of policy measures. The establishment and support of production networks integrating foreign firms and regional suppliers could be one starting point. Firms that already introduced innovations show that they gained innovation experience. Further support of their activities can lead them to continuous innovative activity. Non-innovators might be supported either by helping them to start innovative activities or by focusing on experimental development in these firms. The fact that neither high-tech firms nor business service firms could be distinguished in the sample indicates that these two firm types lack in the region. Specific programmes could deliver supportive measures for those firms to be founded and interrelated to the other agents in the regional economy. Innovation policy measures arising form these examples should of course be embedded in an overall conception of regional innovation development. Regional innovation strategies can valorise endogenous resources (e.g. knowledge gathered in sectors with a long tradition in the region), give incentives for firms to introduce innovations, and enhance existing innovation activities. This is corroborated by recent research results which suggest that regional learning is of crucial importance in increasing firms' knowledge bases, improving their competitiveness and their ability to be included in networks. To be successful, such strategies must be embedded in a vision built on a broad regional participation. Facing the particular context of economic transition and future EU accession, and heightening the awareness of innovation, constitute important steps towards a sustainable regional development for West Transdanubia.

Literature

Braczyk, H. J.; Heidenreich, M. (1998): Regional Governance Structures in a Globalized World. In: Braczyk, H. J.; Cooke, P.; Heidenreich, M. (1998) (Eds.): Regional Innovation Systems – The Role of Governance in a Globalized World. London: UCL Press, pp. 414-440.

Cooke, P. (1998): Origins of the Concept. In: Braczyk, H. J.; Cooke, P.; Heidenreich, M. (1998, Eds.): Regional Innovation Systems – The Role of Governance in a Globalized World. London: UCL Press, pp. 2-25.

Cooke, P.; Boekholt, P.; Schall, N.; Schienstock, G. (1996): Regional Innovation Systems: Concepts, Analysis and Typology. Paper presented at the EU-RESTPOR Conference "Global Comparison of Regional RTD and Innovation Strategies for Development and Cohesion". Brussels, 19-21 September.

Edquist, C. (1997, Ed.): Systems of Innovation. Technologies, Institutions and Organizations. London: Pinter Publishers.

European Commission (2000, Ed.): Innovation Policy in a Knowledge-based Economy. A MERIT Study Commissioned by the European Commission, Enterprise Directorate-General, EUR 17023.

Freeman, C. (1987): Technology Policy and Economic Performance: Lessons from Japan. London: Pinter Publishers.

Lawson, C.; Lorenz, E. (1999): Collective Learning, Tacit Knowledge and Regional Innovation Capacities. Regional Studies 33, pp. 305-317.

Lundvall, B.-Å. (1988): Innovation as an Interactive Process: From User-Producer Interaction to the National System of Innovation. In: Dosi, G.; Freeman, C.; Nelson, R.; Silverberg, G.; Soete, L. (1988, Eds.): Technical Change and Economic Theory. London: Pinter Publishers, pp. 349-369.

Lundvall, B.-Å. (1992): Introduction. In: Lundvall, B.-Å. (Ed.): National Systems of Innovation. Towards a Theory of Innovation and Interactive Learning. London: Pinter Publishers, pp. 1-19.

Maillat, D.; Perrin, J.-C. (1992, Eds.): Entreprises innovatrices et développement territorial. Neuchâtel: EDES.

Porter, M.E. (1990): The Competitive Advantage of Nations. New York: Free Press.

Perrin, J.-C. (1990): Organisation Industrielle: La composante territoriale. Revue d'Economie Industrielle 51, pp. 276-303.

Rechnitzer, J. (2000): The Features of the Transition Hungary's Regional System. Discussion Papers no. 32, Centre for Regional Studies of the Hungarian Academy of Sciences, Pécs.

Walter, G. H.; Zenker, A.; Muller, E. (2000): Entwicklung eines Indikatorensystems zur Potenzialanalyse von Forschung und Innovation in Ungarn. Innovationsorientierte Unternehmenstypologie und technologiepolitische Maßnahmen für Westransdanubien. Working Paper, Fraunhofer ISI. Karlsruhe.

Appendix 1: Synopsis of regional characteristics

Regions / Indicators	Saxony (n=920)		Slovenia (n=398)		WTD (n=72)	
Firm size structure	Small:	80.9%	Small:	53.7%	Small:	47.2%
	Medium:	16.7%	Medium:	33.9%	Medium:	37.5%
	Large:	2.3%	Large:	12.3%	Large:	15.3%
Export intensity	High:	7.2%	High:	46.5%	High:	25.0%
	Medium:	32.7%	Medium:	30.9%	Medium:	15.3%
	Weak:	60.1%	Weak:	22.6%	Weak:	59.7%
Introduction of innovation or development	Innovating:	81.1%	Innovating:	76.6%	Innovating:	52.8%
	Non-innovating:	18.9%	Non-innovating:	23.4%	Non-innovating:	47.2%
R&D intensity	High:	26.5%	High:	11.1%	High:	2.8%
	Medium:	18.2%	Medium:	18.6%	Medium:	6.9%
	Weak:	55.3%	Weak:	70.4%	Weak:	90.3%
Co-operation with other firms	Co-operating:	29.6%	Co-operating:	25.1%	Co-operating:	13.8%
	Non-co-operating:	70.4%	Non-co-operating:	74.9%	Non-co-operating:	86.2%
Co-operation with KIBS	Co-operating:	70.2%	Co-operating:	66.8%	Co-operating:	5.6%
	Non-co-operating:	29.8%	Non-co-operating:	33.2%	Non-co-operating:	94.4%
Co-operation with universities and research organisations	Co-operating:	34.8%	Co-operating:	33.9%	Co-operating:	6.9%
	Non-co-operating:	65.2%	Non-co-operating:	66.1%	Non-co-operating:	93.1%

Appendix 2: Variables included in the multiple correspondence analysis

Variables	Labels
SIZE (Number of employees)	1: 10-19 employees 2: 20-49 employees 3: 50-99 employees 4: 100-199 employees 5: 200-499 employees 6: 500 and more employees
ACTIVITY (Sector of activity)	1: Manufacturing 2: Construction 3: Services
FOREIGNC (Foreign control of the capital)	1: Foreign control (participation >50% of capital) 2: No foreign control
EXPORT (Export orientation)	1: Weak (less than 5% of sales) 2: Medium (between 5 and 50% of sales) 3: High (more than 50% of sales)
INNOV (Innovation and/or further development during the preceding 3 years)	1: Performance of innovation and/or development 2: No innovation/development
RD_INT (R&D intensity)	1: Weak (less than 3.5% of sales) 2: Medium (between 3.5 and 8.5% of sales) 3: High (more than 8.5% of sales)
COOP_ENT (Innovation-related co-operations with other firms)	1: Co-operation with other firms 2: No co-operation
COOP_KIB (Innovation-related co-operations with knowledge-intensive business services)	1: Co-operation with KIBS 2: No co-operation
COOP_UNI (Innovation-related co-operations with universities or research organisations)	1: Co-operation with universities or research organisations 2: No co-operation
GEO_CL (Main location of clients)	1: No main location 2: West Transdanubia 3: Rest of Hungary 4: European Union 5: Rest of the world
GEO_SUP (Main location of suppliers)	1: No main location 2: West Transdanubia 3: Rest of Hungary 4: European Union 5: Rest of the world
EU_SALES (Expected sales variation after EU accession)	1: Positive expectation 2: Negative expectation or no changes
EU_COOP (Existing co-operations with EU firms)	1: Co-operations with EU firms 2: No co-operation

Appendix 3: Discrimination measures of the multiple correspondence analysis

Variables	Dimension 1	Dimension 2
ACTIVITY	0.405	0.056
COOP_ENT	0.092	0.110
COOP_KIB	0.048	0.148
COOP_UNI	0.104	0.066
EU_COOP	0.404	0.000
EU_SALES	0.019	0.182
EXPORT	0.433	0.058
FOREIGNC	0.363	0.046
GEO_CL	0.575	0.544
GEO_SUP	0.517	0.369
INNO_DEV	0.255	0.231
RD_INT	0.028	0.227
SIZE	0.355	0.176

From Old to New, from Big to Small? – Transformation of Firm Behaviour in Declining Regions in West and East

Michael Steiner

1 Introduction

The paper explores changes in firm behaviour in old industrial areas in the West and draws parallels to declining regions in Central and Eastern Europe. It argues that the support for firm foundation and for small and medium-sized enterprises has to consider their embeddedness in a regional context. Strategic policy orientations are presented and lessons for transformation processes drawn.

A starting point of transformation in Central and Eastern Europe was the fact that these countries were dominated by an "oversized" industry, characterised by nationalised big firms with a soft budget constraint by means of generous credits from nationalised banks, a restricted market orientation and a limited degree of competition from the world market (see e.g. Döhrn/Heilemann 1992; Brenton et al. 1997; Welfens 1997). The adaptation problems of firms in this context seemed very similar to those in old industrial areas in the western countries one or two decades ago.

This paper starts with the hypothesis that the experience of firms in such old industrial areas (OIAs) and the attempts at reconversion in the last ten to twenty years can serve as an example for transformation processes; it can also be regarded as an argument for countries in transition to strengthen their regional dimension of economic policy and to concentrate on firm foundation and support for SMEs and to create a (material and immaterial) infrastructure to support co-operative forms of entrepreneurship. This implies that the strategies for firm foundation and for SMEs cannot be developed in isolation and that the specific local milieu and the regional embeddedness of firms have to be taken in consideration when dealing with questions of firm support in the process of transformation.

In the following, theoretical interpretations for reasons of stagnation in OIAs in the western economies will be given. Then some empirical evidence will be collected to show some common features of regional concentration of industrial decline both in the West and the East. A design for policy strategies and instruments will then be presented. Finally, some conclusions for firm support in the transitional countries will be suggested.

2 Theoretical Aspects of OIAs and the Behaviour of Their Industries and Firms

A first and necessary step of theory based knowledge creation consisted in the important insight that the problems of these areas were specific in kind and not just a transient feature of general economic development accidentally scattered in space. Several explanations were put forward that focussed on some of the specificities of these areas and tried to explain the changing (and declining) fortunes of their (mostly large and nationalised) firms.

- The "structural" approach tried to explain the decline in terms of the composition of its sectors. Indeed it was very tempting to explain the decline in terms of "structure", particularly if the economy of the unit under scrutiny was characterised by monostructure. It basically meant interpreting the regional decline in terms of the decline of the dominating industries and firms.

  Yet this approach suffers from two essential shortcomings: the first is the rather weak theoretical content; the second shortcoming is that countless studies undertaken were unable to show the dominant influence of the structural component (Steiner 1990). This is not to suggest that the "structural" explanation must be dismissed completely, but it means that the decline of OIAs cannot be explained exclusively in terms of structure in the traditional sense of sectoral compositions.

- The "sclerosis approaches" went a step further. This is an expression going back to Kindleberger (1978), sometimes also known – more technically – as the "blockage of endogenous renewability" (Geldner 1983). The basic assumption here is that adaptive mechanisms do not work any more and that behavioural potentials of the firms in OIAs have been reduced. The external conditions for "entrepreneurial alertness" (a notion introduced by Kirzner (1980) in the tradition of Schumpeter) have deteriorated, the subjective element of entrepreneurial behaviour has been negatively influenced by objective preconditions (the "entrepreneurial climate").

- These approaches have been taken up and integrated in a systematic way in a cyclical-evolutionary interpretation of regional development and spatial concentration of sectors and industries. It combines Vernon's (1966) and Hirsch's (1967) contribution to a product cycle in international trade with evolutionary theories of economic change (Nelson/Winter 1982) and "Austrian" interpretations of the creative function of the market. The main elements of this interpretation can be summarised by the following points (Steiner 1990): the endogenous ability to renew was blocked; if firms in market economies perform well, they demonstrate a behaviour in which they get rid of ageing products and create new ones – this process did not work in old industrial areas. Is it possible to avoid this – can old industrial areas get young again, can regions in transforming countries pick up the impetus of the transformation process?

3 Stylised Facts and Examples in East and West

Old industrial areas show some surprisingly consistent features if one takes into consideration indicators that point to the ability to adapt, to be flexible and open for change: they are dominated by a few large-scale enterprises, they reveal a strong monostructure, they have a low (labour) productivity and low productivity growth, a one-sided qualification of the labour force accompanied by above-average wages, and a low turnover in firm foundation and in the closure rate of firms. In addition, their decision-making units are not located in the region itself (their headquarters are mostly outside) and hence they are hardly able to develop entrepreneurial behaviour; they show a low female participation rate and a high duration of unemployment (once a person gets unemployed the chances of getting re-employed are rather low).

A long list of empirical studies may be quoted in support of the consistency of these common features among "western" regions (Steiner 1990a, 1999).

All these examples – stretching from US regions and agglomerations to the old centres of European industrial activity – give evidence supporting the hypothesis that these industrial centres are homogenous, and therefore a specific type of region with low adaptability, inflexible patterns of behaviour and insufficient ways of mastering change. The indicators used to support this interpretation point to a restricted use of endogenous resources, a lack of entrepreneurial initiative and a domination of large organisations with a strong tendency to vertical integration and a resulting misbalance between large and small firms, leading to a lack of co-operation and network formation.

Yet change is, and was, possible: Several of the formerly "old" regions have experienced a renaissance and a revival.[1] However, the question must be asked: how ap-

---

[1] Examples are to be found in and around the industrial centre of Glasgow, in the "Automation Alley" between Detroit and Ann Arbour (The Economist 1987, April 11), in the iron and ore manufacturing region of northern Styria (Geldner 1998), in the coal mining region in Belgium's province of Limburg (Baeten et al. 1999). The core of the (in detail quite diverse) strategies of reconversion consisted in splitting up large enterprises, re-introducing decision making units (and power) into the region, in supporting and developing the endogenous potential and connecting it in cooperative alliances within and outside the region.

plicable is this interpretation to the state of industrial centres and their prospects of reconversion in "eastern" countries?

Examples of this kind do exist and give evidence of the dangers associated with the absence of an adequate policy response. These examples are not as consistent and systematic and – for obvious reasons – do not cover a time span as long as in most studies about regions in the US and in Western Europe. But there are several examples that may serve as evidence for the typical problems of adaptation, of lack of entrepreneurialism and of the missing balance between small and large firms – problems which are certainly reinforced by the historical legacy of the former economic order.

An outstanding example of the difficulties connected with transformation and integration into new markets is Zaporizhzhya in the Ukraine, which, as a major industrial centre with almost 1 million inhabitants, was firmly integrated in the Soviet planning economy (Zon 1998). By 1997 the disruption of these ties had caused a decline of about 60-70 per cent in industrial production. Zaporizhzhya was relying on heavy industry, whose orders came predominantly from the military: of the total industrial workforce, 55 per cent were employed in machine building and metal processing, 16 per cent in heavy metallurgy and 7 per cent in the electro-energy sector. These sectors were dominated by large enterprises often having a monopoly position within their sector. The share of finished products was low, with few consumer goods produced in the area. There were hardly any ties between these large enterprises and the regional economy, with most inputs coming from outside and most products being exported. Consequently there was a low level of regional coherence and embeddedness.

An attempt at reorientation led rather to a negative development in isolation whose reasons are listed by Zon (615): especially in the first phase till 1994, the main problem of enterprises was their difficulty in finding suppliers; the transaction costs of dealing with former partners across the borders became prohibitively expensive; many contracts were "one-off" agreements; trade with the developed market economies became marginalised; import competition nevertheless led to a disruption of existing supply chains; new linkages with foreign partners were usually not strong and were confined to exchange. All this led to a regression into "backward" activities and to a reversion to primitive forms of economic activity. Altogether it was an economic "involution" instead of an evolution.

A contrasting example of integrated and embedded inward investment is the co-operation of Volkswagen and Skoda in the Czech Republic; the majority of the inward investment in the automobile industry has been in the Skoda works in Mlada Boleslav and its associated plants (Pawlinek/Smith 1998). The main strategy here consisted in building on an indigenous supplier network and transforming it into new supplier systems. The former networks that existed under state socialism were utilised but transformed according to the needs of the new investor. The starting point was certainly the long tradition of automobile production in the area, with strong traditions of skill and relatively independent innovation. Part of the transformation strategy was to encourage Czech suppliers to form joint ventures with western companies. On the one hand, this meant that the low-cost but skilled labour could still be used; on the other, it meant that the quality could be improved and the technological know how of the West transferred. This resulted in the fact that 70 per cent of VW-Skoda's purchase of components and 60 per cent of materials are derived from Czech-located producers.

This process of transformation of the former networks did have its ambiguities, such as segmentation of the labour force and strategic insourcing of foreign key components. Yet overall in the case of this Czech region it was rather a case of "offensive restructuring" with a conservation and enrichment of skills, rising wages, an upgrading of productivity and important levels of co-operation and regional and institutional embedding.

Maribor and the surrounding region of Podravska is an example of the fact that it is not always the "Far East" where industrial centres in crisis are to be found. This region in Slovenia – bordering on Austria and the west of Hungary – reveals problems (at least compared to other regions in Slovenia) similar to those in more remote areas (Koman 2000):

- its industry is dominated by basic metals, textiles, machinery and equipment – sectors with heavy losses up to 1999;
- this industry is marked by an inefficient vertical integration where many services are still part of the large enterprises;
- productivity – as gross value added per employee – is below average;
- to this situation is added a specific kind of ownership: 60 per cent of the shares are in the hands of internal owners and only 40 per cent in the hands of external owners; this is combined with a continuing political control leading to a strong lobby of large enterprises, local and regional politicians and trade unions favouring the old industrial structure;
- there is – despite the reorganisations since 1990 – a strong, unresponsive central control of most institutions: educational institutions, banks, research institutes, funding and industrial associations;
- the percentage of small and medium sized firms is significantly below average, suffering from unequal forms of co-operation with the large firms;
- entrepreneurial activities – as expressed in the number of enterprises per 1 000 inhabitants – are consequently below average too.

Yet there are early indicators of change:

- productivity – also compared to the national average – is improving;
- the rate of unemployment is declining;
- the service sector is expanding, the share of the traditional manufacturing sectors has drastically decreased;
- there is a considerable number of spin-offs and new start-ups.

These examples in the transitional countries show that cases do exist that are quite similar to old industrial areas in the West with regard to the geographical concentration of individual sectors and their specific firm behaviour. Besides the general problems of transformation – creating and adapting (to) the new rules of a market economy – they have to solve their additional problems of regional industrial decline.

4 Strategies and Instruments in Support of Reconversion

The problems of old industrial centres and their firms, both in the West and in the East, call for a design of policy strategies and instruments. Economists who strongly believe in the allocative power of markets may object to this (in their view) misplaced task of policy. Yet history has proven that rejuvenating OIAs is possible and that this process of rejuvenation was definitely (and positively) influenced by policy. Economic policy was necessary and in many cases successful – not in the form of subsidies and public ownership, but by: improving infrastructure, creating access to various kinds of information, a differentiated form of social policy, the support of new firm creation, deregulation, an induced change of mentality.

With hindsight, these policy experiences can be presented as stylised steps of strategies and instruments; they can be seen as an attempt to change the institutional framework and supply it with new incentive structures for entrepreneurial activities, firm foundation and network oriented co-operation. From the perspective of the start of the process, it was certainly also a process of trial and error. Some of these steps – exemplified by the process of restructuring the old industrial area of Upper Styria (Steiermark) with its heavy concentration of iron and steel production – will be outlined in the following. This process started in the 1970s with – as yet – little knowledge or experience as to how such a strategy should be designed; at that time (without the knowledge and interpretation of some 20-30 years later) it certainly was a process of trial and error.

4.1 Concentration

The dominant strategy during the 1960s, 1970s and early 1980s was the search for economies of scale through vertical and horizontal integration. This centralisation process was accompanied by a concentration of headquarter functions outside the region, plants in Upper Styria came under "external" control. In most cases, planning, R&D and marketing/distribution functions, i.e. those responsible for the monitoring of markets and technology, were lost. Moreover, not only the steel-producing industry but also the steel trade became the subject of mergers.

Mergers and concentration therefore constituted a first step. Yet the capability for structural change decreased, since nearly every merger was accompanied by a reduction of independent suppliers. All preconditions for success, e.g. impartiality, independence etc., had been disregarded. This strategy was founded on an uncritical belief in the advantages of large-scale enterprises and technological economies of scale. In conjunction with mergers, the decision-making process also changed and this had consequences for firm strategy: after management had left the region and been centralised in headquarters outside it, ownership changed to "permissive" public ownership, no emphasis was put on productivity, and salaries rose to above-average levels in relation to other regions.

4.2 Deconcentration

The strategies of mergers, vertical and horizontal integration to deal with crises were abandoned during the second half of the 1980s – decentralisation was the next step.

In 1986, a new executive board in the nationalised steel group comprising the largest steel manufactures in Austria launched an extensive analysis of the organisational and operative structures of the group. Only one year later, the whole company was split up into four independent legal corporations with a management that was shifted back into the region.

After experiments regarding product range during the concentration phase in the 1970s and 1980s, the focus was put back on the group's core competences rather than on a wide product range with low competitive advantages. In 1993, the parent company of the main and dominant steel firms in Upper Styria concentrated on only three core divisions: flat product division (focussing on rolled steel products and surface treated flat steel products with several patented applications), long product division (rails, wires, steel pipes) and the sales division.

Those partly privatised and reorganised enterprises regained some decision-making functions in the process of decentralisation within the group. Yet this restructuring led to the closure of several of the former spin-offs and resulted in substantial unemployment.

4.3 Improvement of Infrastructure

These steps toward deconcentration were accompanied by a gradual improvement of the infrastructure:

- Regarding traffic infrastructure, road and rail projects had been speeded up during the 1980s: for better regional "incoming" and "outgoing", the accelerated construction of a motorway leading to the North brought lasting improvement for Upper Styria.
- In the south-eastern direction, the centre of Graz and the state of Slovenia were connected by a motorway as well.
- Speedways mainly along the river valleys Mur and Mürz brought an important East – West connection between the metal-processing centres in Upper Styria. Another speedway brought access towards the agglomeration of Vienna.
- Rail infrastructure projects included improvements for higher speed and capacities and a double-tracked extension. A further project, the "Semmering Tunnel", connecting Upper Styria with Lower Austria for higher speed and freight capacity, is still in preparation.

In addition, and even more important, institutions were created to support the spin-offs, the newly founded firms and the existing small and medium sized enterprises, and a broad net of research and technological infrastructure was installed.

The first of these enterprise support institutions were already installed during the second half of the 1980s:

- The "Technology-Transfer-Centre Leoben (TTZ)" – a co-operation of several institutions such as the regionally based Montan University and an applied research institution – was founded in 1986 with the intention of implementing environmentally-oriented technologies as a promising regional promotion for endogenous firms. Innovative foundations of SMEs in the metal, electronic, mechanical engineering and plastics industries generated a strong demand for technological and management consultancy. The TTZ reacted and reoriented itself to meet the SMEs' demand, focusing on an advisory board for technology and management for existing and newly-founded enterprises, with the goal of modernising economic structures in Upper Styria. The centre's work focuses on technology transfer and management advice for SMEs. TTZ also initiates project co-ordination between enterprises and research institutions.
- The "Business Incubator Kapfenberg" was founded in 1989. Since then two or three enterprises have joined every year; the "Technology Centre Kapfenberg"

was established in 1993 with production halls for qualified young enterprises. Focal points were new materials, laser technology and industrial installations to continue with the tradition of metal processing and mechanical engineering in Kapfenberg. Future projects include customised industrial installations for automation and control systems.

- The "Technology Centre Niklasdorf", founded in 1989, now consists of a technology park, a vocational institution of the Chamber of Commerce and a laser centre. In the late 1990s it included twelve enterprises plus another five which are externally located. Focal points are new materials and electronic data-processing, now complemented by laser technology. The key characteristics of the centre are consultation, assistance and infrastructure services as well as modern teaching in conjunction with the vocational institution. Besides knowledge transfer, the centre puts emphasis on motivation and contacts.
- The "A.i.Z. Unternehmerzentrum Zeltweg", an entrepreneurial centre founded in 1989, consists of 16 enterprises with over 90 employees. It offers management and finance consulting and focuses on environmental technology and production-oriented services. Currently there are plans for further technological orientation and development towards a technology and innovation centre.
- The emphasis of the "Joanneum Research Laser Centre Leoben", founded in 1988, is on the industrial application of laser technology. Process and production systems are adopted in co-operation with the customers.

Although the importance of these institutions is hard to evaluate directly, institutions became especially successful as soon as their activities were oriented towards regional enterprises with their specific demand and capacities. Further success indicators are the strong demand for institutions providing qualification and vocational training, as well as the need for additional motivated key players within these institutions.

The great number of facilities called for a more co-ordinated division of labour. A stronger co-operation and networking of these institutions was therefore proposed and new institutions to improve the information flows were created.
As a step towards a reorganisation of the economic development policy in the early 1990s, the "Styrian Industrial Promotion Agency" (Steirische Wirtschaftsförderungsgesellschaft – SFG) was founded in 1991. It acts as an independent, semi-public regional development agency, owned, controlled and financed by the provincial government. Together with its subsidiary Innofinanz, it not only plans, builds and supports technology and entrepreneur centres in Styria, but also acts as a service agency, supporting innovative activities, and providing direct financial incentives including seed capital, subsidies for project costs, new start-up premiums and consultancy. Further tasks are in the area of support for the start-up of new firms, firms in the phase of growth, technology transfer, attraction of investment and training.

Besides this new agency, various additional intermediary organisations such as the decentralised and semi-privatised "Labour Market Service" (formerly centrally organised and run as a public institution with civil servants), and the vocational institution of the Chamber of Commerce, have refocused their activities on a regional level.

In addition, there are now several public, semi-public and private intermediary organisations active on a regional level such as the "ÖAR" (organisation for endogenous regional development), "BFI" (training institute of the Chamber of Labour, operating several branches in Upper Styria) and the "ITF" (Innovation & Technology Fund).

In order to enhance co-operation, including the aspects of information, education and consulting activities, institutions such as the "Austrian Information Centre for Co-operation", the "BIT" (International research and technology co-operations) and the "APS" (Co-operation between Universities and Enterprises) were founded; since 1995, the first year of Austria's EU membership, an additional institution for the organisation and management of knowledge transfer – regional management offices – have been installed, with the special task of supporting the structural fund programmes of the European Commission.

4.4 Support and Creation of Co-Operation and Networks

A further step to improve the situation in this region was to create "territorial networks" and "competence clusters" as a tool to improve locational quality. Styria, as the region with the most urgent problems of OIAs in Austria, was the first region to pursue deliberately a cluster strategy of this kind. It was partly a strategy to create and support a new, albeit in some respects complementary, automobile cluster in the southern part of the region in addition to the old declining concentration of steel manufacturing in the northern part of the country. This action was appropriate as some firms – a few of them even in dominant niches – already existed, but there was no network linking them, and an automotive cluster is a good customer for steel and steel products. The promotion was quite successful. A network was formed between previously unconnected firms, partly situated in the old industrial area. The existing firms expanded, co-operation and specialisation increased, and foreign investment was attracted.

Yet the explicit aim of this cluster philosophy was more than a replacement and support of the old cluster: it was meant to aim at empowering entrepreneurs. By that we mean their ability to use global competition as an opportunity. To put it even more clearly: We would like to see ineffective mechanisms of protection replaced by "upgrading" and entrepreneurial fitness. In achieving this goal, we regard the cluster philosophy, already a fixed element of the Styrian subsidy policy, to be a most appropriate instrument" (original quotation from H. Paierl, regional minister for Economic Policy of Styria, 1997).

This "cluster philosophy", which is especially pronounced in Styria, is gaining an impetus of its own. Different forms of co-operation and networks are emerging also in other sectors.

Of special interest were projects relating to learning activities in the clusters and networks. This is all the more important because the decline of Upper Styria was to a large degree caused by an inability to learn new forms of behaviour and the preservation of old ones. The attempts to develop a culture of learning among SMEs may be also interpreted as a regional process of "unlearning" old habits (something that is harder than learning new ones). Therefore, SME clusters create positive spill-over for the region as a whole, and effectively demonstrate the importance of joint learning.

4.5 Toward a Regional Innovation System

A further step – the last so far – in the process of reconversion of this old industrial area is the attempt to integrate it into the combined strategies and instruments of a national and regional innovation system. Innovation is now understood to be an iterative interaction between a wide range of actors including research organisations, firms, policy providers and the market.

These activities for Upper Styria are now strongly embedded in a general strategy to "upgrade" Styria's economy by means of an explicitly technology and innovation oriented policy. The "Styrian Technology Policy Concept", elaborated by Joanneum Research, a regional applied research institution (Steiner et al. 1996), proposed three main strategies: co-operation; absorption and diffusion; quality and qualification.

5 Lessons to Be Drawn?

The experience of OIAs in the West suggests that such regions can grow old and petrify even under the general conditions of a market economy: the firms in these areas tend to become inflexible and, in the worst cases, unable to adapt to the new environment. Different theoretical answers (not quite incompatible) have been given: why this happens, why OIAs cannot adapt to new conditions; why they cannot develop new products, why they cannot adapt their skills; why their old specialisation no longer meets a demand. In this sense they can serve as examples of why – and how – market processes under certain conditions are not able to prevent ageing and petrification.

To overcome these deficiencies, a well designed change of institutional framework with new incentive structures became necessary. It is in this sense that OIAs, and regional and industrial/technology policy oriented towards them, can serve as an example for processes of transformation – this policy with its strategies and instruments should be interpreted as creating institutions that accommodate change, in times of insufficient incentives for endogenous improvement. These steps were certainly a process of trial and error: the phase of concentration at the beginning was certainly an error; the steps in the 1980s to decentralise and to foster spin-offs seemed very small at the beginning and were rather ad hoc measures, without a strategy as yet to combine those institutions into a network for entrepreneurial support; the endogenous approach was ridiculed as being too "alternative" for the big nationalised corporations with an international orientation. It took a long time till the new policy institutions learned to deal with their new tasks; to begin with, the cluster approach was criticised as a dangerous new specialisation. Yet altogether all these single steps led to a change in mentality, to a feeling of the involved agents – managers, workers and politicians alike – that behaviour and attitudes had to be changed.

In this sense they can also be used as examples of support policy for firms in the industrial regions of the transitional countries. Most of these countries have mastered the most difficult part of the transformation period: they have adopted the essential institutions of a market economy with a corresponding legal system and most of the economic freedoms (of trade, of capital, of services, more or less of labour). Some of these institutions still need further reforms (banks, for example), some were ill-conceived (there were evident problems with privatisation processes), some need further refinement (e.g. capital markets, legal procedures in case of insolvency). Yet the basic mechanisms of a market economy do apply and are working. There are still problems of adjustment, of mental reservations, of still ongoing processes of learning and adapting: there are certainly also differences in the standard of living, different levels of productivity, differences in the degree of competitiveness. Nevertheless: these economies have to a large degree working market economies where all the rules associated with a market economy apply – in this respect they are not different. Consequently, processes of change that happen in market economies – even in our specific case of insufficient change as found in OIAs – can also be applied to problems of adjustment in the by now transformed former transition economies.

Moreover a specific policy focused on the regionally concentrated problems of firms remains necessary in these countries too and calls for a well designed mixture of institutions giving the right incentives, passing on the relevant information and allowing for the necessary time. The strategies adopted in the West may serve as an example of what kind of instruments, infrastructure and institutions may be applied, but not as a rigorous template for imitations. The sequence of policy measures has its own logic and dynamics following the specificities of the region and its history. Nevertheless this experience is comparable for similar areas insofar as it points to the underlying problems of retarded adaptation, of a lack of information, to necessary changes in mentality. It also underlines the time-span necessary for reconversion: the time needed is not due predominantly to the techno-economic implementation of strategies and instruments – for this maybe half the time might have been sufficient –, the difficulty was one of convincing the people involved – politicians, but even more the ones affected by this policy – that a change of strategy was necessary, that new instruments had to be applied which were costly for some of them. It also meant convincing people that the costs are evident in the short term and that benefits will only accrue in the long run. Difficulties in the reconversion of OIAs then become part of a general problem of political governance: a generally short period for political legitimisation, a long one for processes of economic and social recovery – a problem which is especially evident in the process of transformation.

Literature

Baeten, G.; Swyngedouw, E.; Albrechts, L. (1999): Politics, Institutions and Regional Restructuring Processes: From Managed Growth to Planned Fragmentation in the Reconversion of Belgium's Last Coal Mining Region. Regional Studies 33, pp. 247-258.

Brenton, P.; Gros, D.; Vandille, G. (1997): Output Decline and Recovery in the Transition Economies. Causes and Social Consequences, 5, pp. 113-130.

Döhrn, R.; Heilemann, U. (1992): Zur allokativen Dimension: Sektorale Entwicklungsperspektiven für Ungarn, Polen und die CSFR. In: Wirtschaftsreformen in Mittel- und Osteuropa, Beiheft zur Konjunkturpolitik. Heft 40, Berlin, pp. 51-69.

The Economist (1987): Automation Alley, April 11, p. 15.

Geldner, N. (1983): Der Problemfall alter Industriegebiete. In: Realisierung des österreichischen Raumordnungskonzeptes, Schriftenreihe Raumplanung für Österreich.

Geldner, N. (1998): Erfolgreicher Strukturwandel in der Steiermark. WIFO Monatsberichte, 3, Vienna, pp. 167-172.

Hirsch, S. (1967): Location of Industry and International Competitiveness. Oxford: Clarendon Press.

Kindleberger, Ch. P. (1978): The Aging Economy. WA 114(3), pp. 407-421.

Kirzner, J. M. (1980): The Primacy of Entrepreneurial Discovery. In: Institute of Economic Affairs (Ed.). The Prime Mover of Process, London: IEA readings, 23.

Koman, K. (2000): Transformation of Podravska Region. Institute for Economic Research, Ljubljana: mimeograph.

Nelson, R.; Winter, S. (1982): An Evolutionary Theory of Economic Change., Cambridge: Harvard University Press.

Paierl, H. (1997): Competence Clusters. Graz: Leykam.

Pawlinek, P.; Smith, A. (1998): Internationalization and Embeddedness in East-Central European Transition: The Contrasting Geographies of Inward Investment in the Czech and Slovak Republics. Regional Studies, 32, pp. 619-638.

Steiner, M. (1990): How Different are Regions? An Evolutionary Approach to Regional Inequality. In: Peschel, K. (Ed.): Infrastructure and the Space-Economy. Berlin: Springer, pp. 294-316.

Steiner, M. (1990a): Regionale Ungleichheit. Wien/Köln: Böhlau.

Steiner, M., (1999): Institutional Change in Old Industrial Areas. Lessons for Industrial Policy in the Transformation Process. Proceedings of the 4th Trilateral Conference, CERGE-EI, Prague, 1999, pp. 155-189.

Steiner, M.; Jud, T.; Pöschl, A.; Sturn, D.; Gundrum, U.; Walter, G. H. (1996): Technologiepolitisches Konzept Steiermark. Graz: Leykam.

Vernon, R. (1966): International Investment and International Trade in the Product Cycle. Quarterly Journal of Economics, 80(2), pp. 190-207.

Welfens, P. J. J. (1997): Osteuropäische Transformation, EU-Integrationsdynamik und Perspektiven der Osterweiterung. In: Cassel, D. (Ed.): Europäische Integration als ordnungspolitische Gestaltungsaufgabe. Schriften des Vereines für Sozialpolitik, Band 260, Berlin: Duncker&Humblot.

Zon, H. v. (1998): The Mismanaged Integration of Zaporizhzhya with the World Economy: Implications for Regional Development in Peripheral Regions. In: Regional Studies, vol. 32, 1998, pp. 607-618.

Possible Strategies and Policy Steps for an Innovation Oriented Modernisation

Günter H. Walter

1 On Technology and Innovation Policy for CEECs

Industrialisation and technology within large production complexes had been a key component of Central and Eastern Europe's economic performance throughout the post World War II period. Nearly all countries within the area of influence of the former USSR had developed a science and technology (S&T) system similar to the Soviet pattern. This system had three elements: an Academy of Sciences for the leading researchers, and often highest priority for public funding, industrial or branch research institutions as a technology base for industry, and universities for education. Research institutions were not treated as autonomous entities but were controlled by respective ministries. As a result of the collapse of the socialist system, the links between industry and the S&T system disappeared (Bitzer 1998). With the beginning of the transition period, however, reforms and restructuring of both the S&T system and the industry sector led to considerable losses in the research potentials of all CEECs. The main negative tendencies were a declining gross expenditure on R&D and a decreasing number of R&D personnel, sometimes leading to a brain drain, i.e. either an external (for the country) or internal (for industry) loss of scientists and workers. While these often drastic changes are described perfectly elsewhere[1] the question arose of how to achieve industrial restructuring. Many concepts by policy makers and consultancies were offered to CEECs. However, all of them were rooted in the structures of the industrialised countries of the western hemisphere, and very often they were simply adopted by the CEEC authorities, taking the effectiveness of these technology and innovation policies for granted. Today, additional hurdles apart from the problem of financial means are created by the fact that existing and planned technology and innovation policies in the CEECs are not regarded in their entirety and are only evaluated for their specific effects in initiating and realising innovation activities in the different groups of enterprises. Moreover, many concepts are still in their infancies.

---

1 In this context we are not able to present a complete bibliography of all contributions to the topic of science and technology within transitional societies. Thus we refer to Dyker/Radosevic (1999), Radosevic/Auriol (1999), Bitzer (1998), Mayntz et al. (1995) and Dyker (1994).

Given the importance of technology and innovation for economic development and international competitiveness, it seems crucial to rethink past strategies. This contribution deals with focussing current technology and innovation policies on the specific effects to be achieved in strengthening companies, especially small and medium sized enterprises (SMEs), in their different ways of realising innovation. The following builds largely on knowledge accumulated in supporting CEECs by assistance (Walter 2001) in the conception and realisation of modern research, technology, innovation and regional policies. The article exemplifies the main elements of this point of a specific innovation policy support approach followed by information that has been implemented so far will be presented for selected countries such as Slovenia, the Czech Republic, Hungary and Latvia.

2 Main Characteristics of a Specific Innovation Support Approach

Relevant societal actors in policy, economy and science should have a common point of view of the situation of their countries and their future needs, and of ways to develop strategies for structural changes. This transformation and modernisation can be achieved by developing innovative behaviour and defining a vision in terms of measures. This seems to be necessary in order to reach a common goal and to identify priority fields and promising strategic fields of modernisation for future activities. A central aim is to increase the innovation and adaptation capabilities of already existing enterprises, institutions, and to attract experts. Additionally, CEECs have a strong need to be connected by transnational and global networking to development outside the country and globally.

Development of Innovative Attitudes and Elaboration of Visions

The nature of individual thoughts and actions, the lifestyle and working style, the existing status of training and education of the (working) population, 'entrepreneurial spirit', institutional modes of behaviour – in other words, the cultural frame conditions – are factors which influence modernisation. Thus access to know-how, familiarity in handling skills and the readiness and ability to use them are important for the innovative capability of CEECs. Approaches and visions should take into consideration the possibility of transforming the "common culture" into a "common technology culture". Such developments and visions generally usually ensure a positive public opinion about innovations. Policy measures to achieve these goals would be efforts such as the foundation of innovation-oriented associations, coordination of promotion programmes, exchange of experiences of the different societal actors, implementation of regulations favourable to innovation etc. (Walter 1997).

Mobilising Endogenous Resources

The main goal for modernisation is to make the existing potentials favourable to industrial restructuring (see Kandil/Walter in this volume). Specific effects of modernisation are to be achieved by different instruments of technology and innovation policy (Meyer-Krahmer 1989).

- Increasing existing innovation potentials and adaptation capability of existing but not yet innovative companies and already innovative firms.

  It is possible for existing firms which have not been innovative so far to engage in relevant activities. Sufficient availability of information and knowledge for these enterprises can create an awareness of innovations among the firm's decision-makers, thus clarifying the risks for the firm associated with innovations, and enabling them to be dealt with. Experience has shown that this can be supported by innovation consultancy by attempting to positively influence the interactions of objective and informal mechanisms in industrial activities. Already-existing and innovative industry can be motivated to expand or strengthen their innovative efforts by providing public funding for R&D (Meyer-Krahmer et al. 1984).

- Increasing innovation potentials and adaptation capability by founding new technology-based companies.

  Modernisation needs dynamic driving forces. One possibility to generate dynamism is to stimulate the founding of technology-based firms. To support these activities usually needs expensive financial programmes combined with techno-economic consultancy, services and infrastructures such as technology and incubator centres etc. Another approach measure concerns the creation of regulatory conditions for industrial and other establishments which help to support founding activities – both formally and informally – for employees of these institutions wishing to found their own firm. Support might consist in paid or unpaid leave, an agreed guarantee of re-employment in case of failure of the new enterprise, and the right to make use of certain results of the firm or institution either free of charge, or at low cost.

- Increasing innovation potentials and adaptation capabilities by attracting innovative mobile firms from abroad.

  Besides motivating firms to innovate and stimulating new firm foundations, another possibility for modernisation is to attract innovative, mobile firms, institutions and also experts from abroad, by providing conditions for innovation and particularly innovation-supportive services. That means equipping the country with relevant R&D institutions, e.g. by enlarging the fields of activities of existing entities or getting institutions, or branch institutes of organisations, to locate there. Another way of ameliorating innovation conditions is to increase the opportunities for contacts and exchanges with R&D institutions by the transfer of personnel, and by creating opportunities for industry to make use of scientific apparatus and equipment at low cost. Additional strategies that can be used to attract firms are to specialise the "classic" industrial promotion measures, by e.g. providing industrial sites for use by enterprises active in priority technology fields' and by providing other good and societal framework conditions.

Besides these effects to be achieved with the help of technology and innovation support, it is necessary to create a broad innovation-based networking in production and service. All relevant capacities have to co-operate closely, according to their capabilities. A precondition for achieving these developments is to integrate various different institutions so that the network is able to provide the necessary services of consultancy, moderation and co-ordination, and financing. Policy may support the foundation of co-ordinating institutions for such networks but in the long term, they must be able to cover their own costs at least partly from the market (see Radosevic/Walter in this volume). This would appear to be possible provided that, on the one hand, the institutions can offer services that a sufficient number of firms are able and willing to pay for (services close to the market for daily business such as bookkeeping, marketing, legal consultancy) and, on the other hand, they offer state-supported innovation services for a very specific group of firms eligible for public support, such as new firms or small companies which have high dynamic growth potentials but are unable to cover all their costs at present.

International Integration and Networking

Besides mobilising endogenous resources, it is necessary to integrate CEECs more strongly into global techno-economic development. This aspect particularly concerns the international exchange of information (for instance, technology and innovation policy may support setting up new service institutions, extending the fields of activity of existing ones). Possibilities for creating contacts and co-operations with institutions outside the country should be offered by institutes such as advisory and information centres, industrial associations etc. It is particularly important for SMEs and newly-founded firms to have access to advice and information that is specifically suited to this target group and adapted to their requirements.

Besides the acquisition of information, another necessity for CEECs is to raise funds from outside the country for innovation financing. This is possible by integrating the country's expertise into funds or equity capital societies and providing residual financing for international support programmes. There may also be a necessity for the setting up (or specialising) of more national, regional or local institutions (such as funds) in order to co-operate with relevant international institutes.

Another form of such activities is international co-operation projects. In order to participate in these, the CEECs themselves have to make their knowledge and experience available, also internationally, possibly via specific service enterprises or agreements. This aspect is important, since an innovative country also has to make substantial contributions of its own in international co-operation if it is to be recognised as an equal partner in the global exchange of information.

3 Overview of the Specific Innovation Support Approach in Individual CEECs

Successful technology and innovation policies give support for co-ordinating and mobilising the endogenous resources of a country and connect national innovative capabilities globally, e.g. by motivating already existing firms to start or enlarge their innovative efforts, stimulating the foundation of new technology-based firms, attracting innovative firms, R&D institutions and experts from abroad, and taking part in the global exchange of information and financing.

Basically, technology and innovation policy in various CEECs already tries to take these factors into consideration, as is demonstrated by the following examples of Slovenia, the Czech Republic, Hungary and Latvia and also by the various country studies.

Slovenia

Among the institutional policy measures introduced by Slovenia, the foundation (Bross/Walter 1999) of the (former) Ministry of Science and Technology (MST) in 1991 was of pre-eminent importance for technology and innovation policy until the end of 2000.[2] The MST included all functions in the domain of policy-setting and management of the R&D system (including preparing and implementing the policy and programmes, defining the procedures and making selections), and it acquired the necessary capabilities such as knowledge relevant to policy planning (foresight), management and evaluation of support instruments (Ministerium für Wissenschaft und Technologie 2000).

Besides dealing with the institutional promotion of R&D in the universities, in national research institutes and in other institutes, the MST was responsible for the financial support of industry in the generating of new technologies and in the application of new types of products and production processes, and consultancy-based innovation services. As well as institutional support for R&D establishments in the field of (specific purpose) basic and applied research, Slovenia established the following funding and consultancy instruments and institutions:

2 The sector for technology of the former MST is now part of the Ministry of Economic Affairs.

- Industrial technology projects in the pre-competitive phase and in areas close to the market are subsidised (up to the realisation of a prototype), with special bonuses for using the endogenous resources of the country, e.g. in co-operations (in order to support contract and co-operative R&D by institutes).
- Furthermore, financial support schemes to facilitate the new employment also in industry of junior researchers have been introduced as a specific incentive for intensifying R&D ("young researchers" programme).
- Financial help is also provided for R&D equipment.
- In the field of consultancy, the establishment of technology parks and technology centres is supported. Subsidies to technology centres and technology parks have partially covered start-up costs, operating costs and costs for expansion. Know-how transfer offices at research institutes and universities also receive public funding.
- Information and documentation institutes such as the Academic and Research Network of Slovenia and Institute of Information Sciences are subsidised (support for start up, temporarily running costs, services, upgrading of an online supply of various databases necessary for science and technology, including information on services and products in Slovenia and the establishing of a reference database for such domestic and foreign data).
- Development of bilateral and multilateral strategic alliances is supported and special conditions are provided for access to international R&D such as EU-Action Plans and EUREKA.
- Protection of industrial and intellectual property, for instance by the Slovenian Intellectual Property Office, is also within the field of public responsibility.

The legal system of Slovenia is being further improved in the sense of creating a more direct impact on the promotion of technology and innovation development. Thus there are fiscal incentives for development within the framework of tax and customs legislation. A number of incentives have also been introduced for investments in know-how and development by independent commercial and financial entities and persons. By extension, the role of individual ministries in defining and implementing more innovatively targeted programmes and encouraging of economic and technological development is to be expected.

Taking an overall view, it becomes visible that promotion measures have been introduced in Slovenia for the support of the relevant factors to build up innovative attitudes, mobilise endogenous resources and integrate the country into international technology development.

A contribution to the mobilisation of endogenous resources is made by subsidy programmes for technologies and innovations and by measures enhancing the quality of personnel (young researchers programme). All these contribute to achieving better conditions for the creation of firm-internal innovation capabilities, and thus also help to attain an improvement in co-operation in the form of external contract research. Specific measures for the promotion of firm foundations are not planned; however, newly-founded firms are also able to participate in the existing programmes.

From the viewpoint of providing good conditions in order to enable a country to attract new firms to locate there, there is support for a high national scientific level and for technology and incubator centres and technology transfer. Also efforts are apparent to build up an adequate patent organisation and improve the framework conditions for innovations.

A contribution to the integration of Slovenia into global development is made by the support of information systems and by international and bilateral co-operation programmes with all the leading industrialised countries. Bilateral programmes strengthen the exchange of information and promote co-operation. Slovenia's participation in international possibilities for acquiring capital and financing takes place, e.g. via its EUREKA membership and its access to the Fifth Framework Programme of the EU.

However, the realisation and relative weighting are open to question. Public discussion between all relevant societal actors about new methods such as foresight or about promotion of the innovation society, measures for the improvement of 'firm founder' mentality, decisions on the co-ordination of the individual promotion measures in the ministries, are in some cases still in their initial stages. The processes have not advanced as far as could have been expected, in view of the length of time they have been in existence (since 1991). Also, public expenditure for technology and innovation support in Slovenia is low when compared to science and research policy efforts.

Czech Republic

Since 1992 government financing of R&D and innovation has included tools for financing public research, and for institutional R&D promotion, as well as project financing in R&D institutes and companies (Bross/Walter 1999). Project-bound financial support is approved as a donation if it is of public interest, or given as a loan if only firms can appropriate the results. Important institutions in charge of financing R&D and technology are the Ministry of Education, Youth and Sport, the Grant Agency of the Czech Republic and the Ministry of Industry and Commerce. This arrangement provides a good institutional base available for developing an innovation society.

Promotion instruments (Ministorstvo Ykolství, Mládeže a Tělovýcheovy, 1999) especially for innovative SMEs are subsidies, loan guarantees, and interest-reduced loans. The following activities can be funded: technical and innovative development, qualification measures for personnel, consulting, industrial co-operation, the acquisition, processing and distribution of information, employment creation, cross-border co-operation, participation in technology exhibitions and fairs.

A specific programme for SMEs provides access to long term investment loans with favourable conditions. The programme is also available for increasing the (technological) export capacity of SMEs by the use of modern technology. For the foundation and growth of small enterprises, a subsidy for interest rates for bank loans is provided, together with a consultancy and information service. Another grant programme for consultancy services helped SMEs to qualify the companies for other financial support programmes. Under another programme, companies can apply for loans and grants for the improvement of their current technology level in order to introduce new materials and new technologies in general, but especially for information technology (grants and loans for part of the project costs). There is also support for the establishing, development and maintenance of science and technology parks linked with R&D institutions and occupied by innovative companies.

In charge of international co-operation is the Ministry of Education, Youth and Sport. This ministry also acts as an interface for those who wish to access programmes of the EU etc.

This short overview shows that the Czech Republic currently provides a variety of technology and innovation promotion measures intended to support the country in the development of innovative attitudes, to mobilise endogenous resources, and for integration into international technology development. However, the financial promotion for R&D, technology and innovation in SMEs is rather low as the budget for technology-based SMEs accounts for only a few percent of the total promotion budget for R&D.

Hungary

By setting up the National Committee for Technological Development (OMFB).[3] Hungary has secured important politico-administrative prerequisites for a successful innovation and technology policy and for the development of innovative attitudes within society. With the aim of creating a societal and institutional basis for an innovative economy, Hungary is also making efforts, in co-operation with state institutions and self-administering organs of the economy (Subvention Funds, National

---

3 In the year 2000 the OMFB has been transformed into the Innovation Research Department of the Ministry of Education.

Patent Office), to improve especially their own qualifications, e.g. by the use of new methods such as audits and foresight (Bross et al. 1998), and to contribute to co-operative thinking within the entrepreneurial sector (Ministerium für Wirtschaft 2000).

Incentives come from measures to regulate the innovative activities of firms, and associated tax reductions. This aim is also served by the creation of technology markets and the setting up of an Advisory Committee on the technological development of enterprises and of a Development Agency. For technology and innovation policy in a narrower sense, for the mobilisation of endogenous resources and the strengthening of innovation activities – especially in existing firms – a support system has been developed and introduced, consisting of grants, credits, guarantees and interests subsidy schemes for R&D, technology and innovation projects, but also for innovation consultancy. The same aim is targeted by programmes especially to support SMEs' R&D and their innovation activities on a national and regional level. The most important element in the mobilisation of innovative resources is co-operation: inter-firm, between large Hungarian and international firms and small enterprises, in order to intensify local supply and collaboration between enterprises and research institutions in the development of new products and production procedures. To promote co-operation, Hungary has introduced other instruments such as the Regional Innovation programme and measures supporting small firms when introducing quality systems, on condition that these meet standards high enough to enable them to engage in technological co-operations with large enterprises. Hungary also makes support available to firm founders (e.g. capital endowment funds) and for the promotion of micro enterprises. In addition, in some Hungarian regions there are measures relating to the Venture Capital market.

Hungary enhanced the country's attractiveness for investments by enterprises thinking of locating there was to put in place an innovation-oriented infrastructure (advisory services, consulting, co-ordination, financing). Hungary supports the development of technology and incubator centres, industrial parks and foundations (endowment funds) also in decentral locations and via appropriate umbrella organisations (see also Heering in this volume).

The aims of integrating Hungary into international technology development and acquiring information and foreign capital, are served by measures such as adapting Hungarian promotion programmes to tie in with EU standards, subsidising and qualifying enterprises for participation in EU programmes. On a general level, the high degree of societal consensus regarding Hungary's joining the EU is a positive factor. Hungary has also contracted R&D bilateral agreements with all leading technology nations world-wide.

Efforts towards Hungary's informational integration into the global information exchange include measures to support the world-wide exploitation of Hungarian patents and the EURO Information Centres. Companies are supported if they present their new products at international fairs or if they try to register Hungarian patents abroad.

Hungary possesses an comprehensive repertoire of instruments for the support of innovative modernisation efforts, and possibilities to co-ordinate these measures through the different existing institutions. The existing programmes and institutions in fact cover those areas which are regarded as important for modernisation (positive attitude of the actors, mobilisation of innovations and the country's involvement in international technology competition).

Latvia

Latvia, one of three Baltic states, is one of the smaller CEECs. In contrast to other Central and Eastern European countries, Latvian science and technology infrastructure had been developed along similar lines to the Soviet pattern, without regarding the history of the research institutions prior to World War II. They became an integral part of the USSR science and technology system. However, the research infrastructure has been taking shape over the last 100 years and has not just starting to develop (Kristapsons/Tjunina 1995).

An important step at the beginning of 1989/90 was to reform the system of funding for science from the state budget. This policy decision created a system of funding in which the total science budget is divided into separate grants given to particular R&D and technology projects. In 1992/93, Latvia established the concept of technology centres, science parks and business incubators as a vehicle to promote innovation, and especially new technology-based firms. Also a market oriented research programme was introduced.

Several types of institutions, like university research centres, state institutions and other organisations are among Latvia's pro-innovative structures. The ministries in charge of technology policy are the Ministry of Education and Science, the Ministry of Economy, and the Ministry of Environment and Regional Development.

Currently, the policy towards R&D and innovation comprises elements such as:

- Strengthening national R&D potentials, i.e. unification of state research institutions and universities with the aim of supporting modernisation.
- Definition of national R&D priorities: these are organic chemistry, biomedicine and pharmacy, material sciences, information technology, forestry and wood sciences and electronics.

- Creation of research centres of national significance, oriented towards criteria such as the extent of international collaboration in R&D and the degree of innovation of expected results.
- Renewal and strengthening of the staff of researchers, i.e. recruitment of gifted young specialists for research and teaching at universities.

Latvian government support for technology and innovation exhibits a strong orientation towards fundamental and applied research projects, while market oriented research projects and projects commissioned by state institutions play a minor role.

Nevertheless a large spectrum of support measures is available to SMEs and entrepreneurs working in technological areas. The measures consist of R&D contracts, (either by direct support or indirect via tax reduction). Latvia supports SMEs through technology centres, science parks and business incubators, and information centres providing business advisory services as well as access to international co-operation projects in R&D, for instance in EUREKA (Stabulnieks 1999).

Evaluations that have been made show several weaknesses so far. For example, there is minor participation of SMEs in the market oriented research programme, due to a high participation of state research institutes. Furthermore, SMEs at technology centres develop slowly and the service offered by these centres is often not accepted due to a too small turnover of the tenants. In many firms, especially the small ones, the importance of the innovation process had not yet been understood. However, the case of Latvian technology centres and science parks shows also that many researchers have used the opportunity to create their own firms and have established co-operations world wide. Thus new firm foundation activities such as technology transfer by spin-off from research institutions can be regarded as mainly successful.

As a conclusion, the Latvian government has established a science and technology infrastructure, but lacks money. The national innovation system is still in its infancy (Berg-Andersson 1998). What has been established so far is a well functioning market oriented research programme and a strong innovation support structure comprising technology centres, science parks, and information centres.

4 Conclusion

This paper has presented an approach that has been developed to enhance existing technology and innovation policies. When these policies were adopted by CEEC authorities, they often did not take into account the specific characteristics and capabilities of the target group firms. Specific modernisation strategies have been developed for different CEECs. With the aim of strengthening and creating competences in economic policy and technology. They are built on the assumption that relevant societal actors in policy, economy and science should have a common point of view on the country's situation, its future needs, and ways of developing strategies for structural changes. Following this view, modernisation can be achieved by defining a vision in terms of measures. This vision is necessary in order to attain a common goal and to identify priority fields and promising strategic fields of modernisation for future activities. Examples of goals are, for instance: to increase the innovation capability of already existing firms; to encourage the founding of new firms; and to attract enterprises, institutions and experts into the country. In addition, the countries needs to be connected by transnational and global networking to development and globally.

The conference "Industrial Transformation in Central and Eastern Europe – The Role of Innovative Small Firms in the Manufacturing Sector" was also devoted to presentations describing policies measures. Here representatives from Albania, Croatia, the Czech Republic, Hungary, Latvia, Poland, Romania, Slovenia and Yugoslavia described their experience and gave up-to-date information on their technology and innovation policies towards small and entrepreneurial firms. Their contributions aimed to describe a cross-section of the activities, programmes and institutions concerned with new technology based firms and innovating firms, the experience gained and the progress achieved. Up to now a comprehensive assessment of the effectiveness and efficiency of the strategies applied cannot be made; nor can the information given claim to provide a complete picture of all science, technology and innovation-oriented policies. However, concrete experiences in the countries themselves allow the conclusion that a strategy which relies on the analysis of specific target groups is often more readily accepted by the economic actors than the adoption of innovation strategies from abroad, which may require many adjustments in order to key in with the specific transformation conditions and the establishing of a market economy.

Literature

Berg-Andersson, B. (1998): Comparative Evaluation of Science & Technology Policies in Lithuania, Latvia and Estonia. In: Industrial Restructuring and Economic Recovery in the Baltic Countries – Lithuania, Latvia and Estonia. Final Project Report. Deutsches Institut für Wirtschaftsforschung (Ed.), Berlin.

Bitzer, B. (1998): Demand-oriented S&T policies or Alternative Strategy for Post Socialist Countries – An Industrial Economic Analysis. mimeograph.

Bross, U.; Walter, G. H. (1999): Development Prospects of the Czech Venture Capital Market. Stuttgart: Fraunhofer IRB.

Bross, U.; Inzelt, A.; Reiß, T. (1998): Bio-Technology Audit in Hungary – Guidelines, Implementation, Results. Heidelberg, New York: Physica.

Bross, U.; Walter, G. H. (2000): Socio-Economic Analysis of North Rhine Westphalia. Working Paper Firms and Region no. R2/2000. Karlsruhe: Fraunhofer ISI.

Dyker, D. A. (1994, Ed.): Problems of Science and Technology Policy in Countries of Transition. Economic Systems 18 (special issue).

Dyker, D. A.; Radosevic, S. (1999, Eds.): Innovation and Structural Change in Post-Socialist Countries: A Quantitative Approach. Dordrecht et al.: Kluwer.

Kristapsons, J.; Tjunina, E. (1995): Changes in Latvia's Science Indicators in the Transformation Period, Research Evaluation 5, pp.151-160.

Mayntz, R.; Schimank, U.; Weingart, P. (1995, Eds.): Transformation mittel- und osteuropäischer Wissenssysteme. Opladen: Westdeutscher Verlag.

Meyer-Krahmer, F.; Dittschar-Bischoff, R.; Gundrum, U., Kuntze, U., Gielow, G.; Krist, H.; Walter, G.H.: Erfassung regionaler Innovationsdefizite. In: Schriftenreihe des Bundesministeriums für Raumordnung, Bauwesen und Städtebau, Heft 06.954. Bonn 1984.

Meyer-Krahmer, F. (1989): Der Einfluß staatlicher Technologiepolitik auf industrielle Innovation. Baden-Baden: Nomos.

Ministerium für Wissenschaft und Technologie (2000, Ed.): Bericht 1997-2000. Ljubljana.

Ministerium für Wirtschaft (2000, Ed.): Széchenyi Plan – Nationaler Entwicklungsplan. Budapest.

Ministorstvo Ykolství, Mládeže a Tēlovýcheovy (1999, Ed.): Průvodce 1999: Systémem Státni Podpory Výzkumu a Vývoje v České Republice (Führer durch die staatliche Forschungsförderung der Tschechischen Republik). Prague.

Radosevic, S.; Auriol, L. (1999): Patterns of Restructuring in Research, Development and Innovation Activities in Central and Eastern European Countries: Analysis based on S&T Indicators, Research Policy 28.

Stabulnieks, J. (1999): Presentation at Baltic Dynamics Conference, June 12-14, 1999, Tallinn (Estonia).

Walter, G. H. (2001): Implementation of a Network based Innovation Policy in Central and Eastern European Countries – Slovenia as an Example. In: Koschatzky, K.; Kulicke, M.; Zenker, A. (Eds.): Innovation Networks – Concepts and Challenges in the European Perspective. Heidelberg: Physica, pp. 111-126.

Walter, G. H.(1997): Emergence and Development of Regional Technology Policy in Germany – The Technology Region of Karlsruhe. Presentation on the Conference "Technology Assessment, Strategy, Forecasting and Regional Policy". May on 29th, 1997, Haifa, Israel: mimeograph.

Summary and Outlook

Oliver Pfirrmann

1 Detailed and Overall Results

In this last chapter we will summarise the main results of the contributions presented, draw some conclusions for policy, and dare to include a critical outlook on future issues. Here we compare traditional as well as the latest findings of certain research disciplines with recent developments in the countries under investigation. We have found no general confirmation regarding our theses drawn from the existing literature in the introductory chapter. The situation is still diverse, as is the matter of the investigation itself. Moreover, the picture on SMEs, especially in manufacturing, their role for economic restructuring and their innovative capacity in in our country studies seems less promising than expected. It would be misleading if the following were to be regarded as suggestions as to how the situation may be improved. Rather, the observations are intended to generate further discussion by emphasising issues that have received insufficient attention especially in the context of transformation in Central and Eastern Europe. Although the issues discussed may lead to the impression that more research is needed, they are far from constituting a research agenda. Indeed, as long as detailed research in western industrialised countries on topics like entrepreneurship remains incomplete there will be no lessons that can be simply transferred from West to East. We hope that an intensive consideration of the questions outlined will at least help to avoid pitfalls along the way to a market economy.

Whereas investigations at the beginning of the transformation process suggested that small firms played an almost insignificant role in economic activity throughout CEECS (Acs/Audretsch 1993), the preceding country studies have shown that the relevance of small firms and entrepreneurship has grown remarkably. There are still risks in simply interpreting national registers because they are comprised of active firms, partially privatised firms, part-time enterprises as well as "dormant" firms.[1] During the last decade, however, a shift in industry away from the large collective combines within central planning power towards small enterprise and decentralised

[1] Dormant firms can be characterised as "only registered without having started their activities or [...] already no longer operating without having officially closed down." (Welter 1997, 5).

economic activity has become visible. From the empirical material presented here one can conclude that there is a tendency towards a "left skewed" firm size distribution which is similar to countries of the western hemisphere. And, as Audretsch has pointed out in his contribution, the persistence of an asymmetric firm-size distribution biased towards small-scale enterprises reflects the continuing process of the entry of new firms into industries, and not necessarily the permanence of such small and sub-optimal enterprises over the long run. Although the overall difference between East and West is still obvious, there are some facts referring to this tendency which need to be summarised.

SMEs account for the majority of firms, and a significantly large share of employment and value added. For example Matusiak for Poland, Welter for Hungary, or Kutlaca for Yugoslavia underline that SMEs' share of GDP grew constantly during the nineties. However, since the beginning of the transformation process the growth of the private sector, in particular SMEs, has always been emphasised as considerable or phenomenal (Levitsky 1996). Now it seems that the growth rates have declined, a consolidation of the small firm sector is taking effect. Employment in the small firm sector is becoming more and more important in contrast to employment in large firms (Godina). Nevertheless, employment shares rise from an initially low level. Here the examples of Romania (Piturescu) and Russia (Kovaleva) show that employment in small firms is low at present, even micro enterprises generate less numerous jobs than medium sized enterprises, but in some branches, like construction and services, the share of small business employees in total employment exceeds this overall figure. The analysis provided by Kovaleva underlines that simple statistics often underestimate the relevance of small firms because of job solutions that are outside the traditional employment relationship, due to the often complex framework conditions. The picture, however, is rendered still more complex because many people involved in self-employment become so after facing a situation in the transformation economy that cannot offer them formal employment.

The propensity of small firms towards innovation in CEECs is relatively unimportant. Moreover, SMEs have not been found to play either a relevant complementary role or a substitutional role in the process of technological change. Here the overall picture is that the greatest capacity for innovations is still shown by larger firms with a relatively stable financial position and diversified economic activities (Kovaleva, Muller/Zenker/Dőry). In order to perform R&D, many small firms depend on outsourcing and subcontracting. Here SMEs' needs are often confronted with a struggling R&D infrastructure characterised by a lack of funds and difficulties in transferring scientific results to industry (Piturescu, Kutlaca). Most entrepreneurs compete by means of their still relatively cheap workforce and their ability to find market niches, and with regard to the Hungarian (Welter) and Polish (Matusiak) example, they often lack the culture of customer satisfaction. Nevertheless, stocktaking of the current situation does not suggest that innovation in Central and Eastern European small firms is just wishful thinking. Although high technology small firms are still a minority in the SME sector, the Polish example also emphasises that at present these few companies represent the economy's modern segment and have potentials to become a source of considerable innovative activity.

What has been overrated recently is the role of SMEs in promoting the ability of countries to improve their international competitiveness. Whereas in industrialised countries of the West, networks of innovative small and large firms do exist, nothing similar could be stated for any of the individual countries studies of CEECs. The majority of small firms in CEECs operate outside the manufacturing sector, in markets with low entry barriers. Only a few serve as high value added suppliers for large firms or are active through newly created niches on global markets. Thus, the small firm sector is far from becoming an important part of the system of technology production and assimilation in Central and Eastern Europe. At least the comparative investigation of Muller, Zenker and Dőry permits the hope that within a network of co-operations between firms, knowledge-based suppliers, universities and research organisations, innovation activities may be enhanced. Today, taking into account the massive distortions within the sector of science and technology, this seems little more than a vision.

It would be a misnomer to view small firms and entrepreneurship as the only vehicles of economic growth and employment within CEECs. Indeed, high technology small firms are a new and rare phenomenon in Central and Eastern Europe. The majority of small firms in those countries have little in common with the typical Schumpeterian entrepreneurial firm. They still operate today with limited human and capital resources and are confronted with insufficient framework conditions for their business. The country studies have carefully attempted to document the role of small firms across a well-defined spectrum of issues, and in particular to identify the manner in which there economic activity has evolved in the past decade. Thus, by stressing again the issues defined in the introductory chapter and used as a guideline, we arrive at a more pragmatic view of the small firm sector.

The identification of sectors of industry where SMEs do play an important role in Central and Eastern Europe shows that it is still the trade, repair and service sectors which are predominantly relevant. In manufacturing, SMEs still constitute only a small share of economic activity. In some cases they are assisted by production-oriented service companies, for example from the computer industry. The contributions in this book that deal with individual countries provide little evidence for an early Schumpeterian view that small firms are the key actors for new industries, emerging as an result of "creative destruction". Moreover, the majority of small firms have trading or craft functions in traditional markets, rather than acting in new markets that have emerged as a result of privatisation. Even though a few country studies like Poland or Slovenia, refer to some innovative activities of small firms, we have to accept that these countries, and a few others, are more highly developed economically than most CEECs. Here the European integration – has achieved different economic and political incentives. It would appear obvious that a certain state of economic development is necessary in order to carry out innovative activities. Wherever these conditions do not seem to be fulfilled, there is either no basis, or at most a poor basis, for the existence of innovative SMEs. While at the heart of conventional wisdom it has been stated that innovation fosters economic growth, our temporarily conclusions are more far-reaching: in CEECs, a comprehensive framework for a supportive business environment has to be put in place, covering the following aspects: taxation, property rights, clear and reliable rules for market actors, financial and institutionally-based support involving government policies, the creation of capital markets and business support organisations. And it is essential that support institutions should work effectively together. Otherwise innovative small firms and entrepreneurship will fail to develop.

We thus turn to a description and investigation of institutional factors influencing the economic environment of the small firm sector. Analyses in the countries under investigation show that privatisation and liberalisation have created a climate favourable to entrepreneurial business activity along market economy principles. According to Heering and Pfirrmann in this volume, privatisation per se does not solve the entrepreneurial problem. Privatisation is only a necessary step and is far from being sufficient for an efficiently functioning market system. A lack of trust concerning the new political and institutional system apparently emerges as the pivotal element of the whole transformation process. Beyond a supportive macroeconomic environment, and irrespective of whether small firms belong to the manufacturing or service sector, they need to satisfy their concrete demands for technological know-how from a co-operative infrastructure (universities, research labs), financial support from banks, or investment companies. Here imperfect framework conditions for market operations, for instance regarding the security of property rights as well as other elements of the legal and institutional system, mean that a system of institutions and rules has not yet been constituted which is acceptable to the majority of economic actors. The implementation of a productive order of this kind is still incomplete in all transitional societies and therefore hampers the development of the small firm sector.

The policy chapter contributed by Walter has made clear that many schemes for SMEs do exist, which follow the approach of western programmes fairly closely. Taking into account the initial situation, with virtually no institutional or governmental support for small firms or entrepreneurship, it is remarkable how much has been implemented so far. It is also recognisable, however, that many countries try to develop their own innovation support system, resting on the former science and technology structures adopted during the predominance of the Soviet Union. What is interesting to note is that many support measures focus on entrepreneurship and/or entrepreneurial activities within an existing firm. Here the spectrum in CEECs ranges from financial subsidies to motivational measures encouraging firms to innovate. The Russian example provided by Kovaleva shows a differentiated framework of measures by state, regional and local authorities dealing with support for small business. Also countries like Romania and Yugoslavia are making efforts to create a supportive framework consisting of specific legislation for SMEs and SME support programmes. Therefore it seems that with initial help from institutions like EBRD, IWF, the World Bank and EU programmes like PHARE and TACIS, important steps have been carried out. Although the implementation process could be improved. As Audretsch/Steiner and Radosevic/Walter argue, the regional level seems a promising way to complement insufficient macroeconomic by industrial policies. In particular the regional dimension of the transformation process – a long neglected dimension – shows that endogenous potential, i.e. small firms, can be supported most effectively within the regional environment. Welter's conclusion in her country study for Hungary can be regarded as generally applicable: most countries are far advanced in creating a support framework that can further enhance SME development. The present situation in many CEECs exhibits several problems and underlines the fact that simple transfer and implementation without consideration of a country's specific situation and traditions is often not appropriate.

Beyond the general problem of the fine tuning of policy measures (Hughes/Hare 1991) it is has become clear that to launch support schemes like micro credits or start-up loans is not sufficient; corresponding mechanisms like tax structures appropriate for SMEs also have to be worked out on the governmental side.[2] A mismatch also occurs if support measures are not embedded in the existing structures, as Radosevic/Walter argue, or seem to be to over-ambitious with regard to the existing industry structure, as stated by Heering. The example of innovation centres and agencies that remain isolated from or marginal to the local economy, and are merely surrogates for modernisation, provides strong confirmation for their theses. The lack of co-ordination is not necessarily to be compensated by broadening the activities and programmes, but rather by intensifying existing ones and focusing them more strongly on the needs of SMEs within industry. One promising approach is to bring together all relevant actors within networks. Muller, Zenker and Dőry support the assumption that CEECs policy-makers are better off if they support the existing innovative firm potential in concrete projects through which they can than create new, more dynamic public-private learning networks, rather than setting up organisations from outside.

Above all, the translation from wishful political thinking to concrete economic support often fails, mainly due to lack of finance. Thus a discussion of strategic options for Central and Eastern European countries leads to the fundamental question: how large is the gap between formal declaration of responsibility for new firms and ac-

---

2 A good example was provided by Russian government in the late 1990s, when turnover instead of profits became the object of taxation and the equity base of potential applicants was dramatically influenced.

ceptance of market competition on the one hand, and the financial margin for political inspired support activities on the other hand?

To summarise the results of the country studies: one cannot ignore the growing economic relevance of small firms for Central and Eastern Europe. They fulfil important tasks for a successful economic and political development. It is, however, clear that much of the work on the restructuring of post-socialist countries had – and still has – a lot to do with macroeconomic issues. But – as the other chapters have pointed out – this level has to be complemented by policies taking into account structural aspects like firm size, sectors of industry and the regional dimension. As Acs et al. point out in their volume (1999,31), "...there is a strong connection between changes that occur at the microlevel and macroeconomic performance... " The country studies have provided additional examples of this relationship. On the macroeconomic level a policy framework is reproduced along western lines that helps small firms grow, but all too often inappropriate tax structures as well as an ineffective administration results in inadequate framework conditions. This situation gives rise to budget constraints which prevent the implementation of constructive policies for SMEs. Furthermore these factors heavily influence the options to launch public support programmes for small firms and entrepreneurship. Viewed from a bottom-up perspective the mass of small firms create production and employment which are, on an aggregate level, indispensable for any macroeconomic policy. They are not the only vehicles of economic growth and employment, however they are an important and promising group of economic actors on the way to transform central planned economies into decentralised market economies.

More and more it becomes clear that ineffectiveness and inefficiencies of public policy can be traced back to a neglect of social and historical traditions. While the structural change in countries of the West occurred within a well-developed, relatively stable and broadly accepted legal and institutional framework, this has first to be established in the East. It would be astonishing, however, if CEECs were able to create a market economy not taking into account the cultural context of their small firm sector. Whereas western economies have had a differentiated support structure at their disposal for decades and policy-makers have needed a great deal of time to arrive at a better understanding of the nature of small business, the eastern economies lacks this experience.

In general it seems that the mechanisms of microeconomic regeneration within CEECs are as yet not fully understood. As Brezinski et al. (1998, 9) pointed out, following a microeconomic approach to the process of transformation demonstrates the limits of neo-classical formalisms and emphasises that other directions than mainstream economic thinking, for instance an institutional and evolutionary view, may provide a productive approach for both research and policy. However, neither a purely institutional approach, asking how different paths of extrication from state socialism shape different possibilities of transformation (Stark 1994), nor a western-determined evolutionary economic perception alone, seems to offer a sufficient explanation. We therefore prefer to rest on an interdisciplinary view – a view that emphasises the historical and social aspects of transformation as well as the political aspects, instead of applying theories which ignore or neglect those considerations in the development of theories and policy recommendations.

2 An Attempt to Look Beyond the Issues Under Discussion

Despite a bulk of literature on small firms and entrepreneurship, even the emergence, functioning and effects of Central and Eastern European entrepreneurship is little more than a "terra incognita". In important areas such as economic development, the existing conceptions of entrepreneurship are not well integrated into theory. As Suarez-Villa (1989, 8) who cites the earlier contribution of Baumol (1968): "The theoretical firm is entrepreneurless – the Prince of Denmark has been expunged from the discussion of Hamlet". Without doubt entrepreneurship constitutes the seedbed for an industrial structure with competitive small and large firms. But what determines the growth process of entrepreneurial firms, and are there any economic lessons to be learned?

Because entrepreneurial activity is of great importance in the processes of economic growth and development, there are no theories and models that can simply be transferred from the West to the East. When western economists sought to explain the success of those economies which had managed to grow significantly compared to those which had remained relatively stagnant, it was found difficult to do so without taking into consideration certain differences with regard to the economic, social and historical development of each country (Baumol 1990; Foreman-Peck/Minoglou 2000; Klep 1994; Siebert 1993). Based on experience from industrialised countries of the western hemisphere, much has been said about conditions that support and hinder small firms. In contrast, investigation has focused less on the person who generates a small firm and operates in the centre of its economic activity. When entrepreneurship is examined it is unsurprising that most authors naturally tend to fall into one distinct camp, Schumpeter. For example, from an early Schumpeterian point of view, small, newly-established firms are the key actors for new industries that emerge as an result of "creative destruction". Building upon the Schumpeterian tradition authors like Acs and Audretsch (1993) argue from an evolutionary economic view that small firms make a significant entrepreneurial contribution, in the sense that they are a source of considerable innovative activity. In addition, they view small firms, and especially innovative SMEs, as promoters of market turbulence which also provide a mechanism for regeneration. But isn't the perpetual emphasis on the innovative capacity of small firms and entrepreneurship misleading especially when we look at the results of the country studies of this volume?

Yet a closer look into the literature on entrepreneurship reminds us of other distinct aspects of entrepreneurial activity. These are for example the functions of arbitrageur, co-ordinator, organiser of economic resources, contractor, and risk bearer (Hérbert/Link 1988). And many of these aspects have been little investigated, even in neo-classical theory. Following the view of Schultz, the entrepreneur is "a stranger in general equilibrium theory" (1975, 833). Thus, research on entrepreneurship becomes a fine example of the crucial scientific problem of perceiving quality changes by observing quantities. Schumpeter dealt with this topic precisely, leaving the mainstream quantitative neo-classical economics for the field of what he called "The Circular Flow of Economic Life as Conditioned by Given Circumstances" (1934, 61). However, it is not only the mainstream view of an economic system's tendency towards an equilibrium position which appears rather unrealistic in transitional countries. Even Schumpeter's view becomes problematic when characterising post-socialist entrepreneurial activities. While early contributions about Russian society have pointed out that their emphasis was upon the redistribution rather than the creation of wealth (Ardishvili/Cardozo 1993), Heering's contribution in this volume shows that despite an infrastructure of incubators to help high-tech start-ups, many natural scientists and engineers in Russia and Poland engage in activities that are outside their technical expertise. They work as traders or salesmen, or in some cases they are unemployed.

Baumol (1990) has pointed out that the variation in the productive contribution of a society's entrepreneurial activities is greater than the variation in the total supply of entrepreneurs between societies. This implies that policy can influence the allocation of entrepreneurship more effectively than it can influence its supply. Supply is regarded as being inelastic. According to this view, policy options either generate unproductive, rent-seeking entrepreneurs, or productive ones who help the economy to grow effectively. Whereas for some researchers this view proves to be to radical (Tyson et al. 1994) others emphasise that economic conditions in some CEECs, for instance Russia or Albania, promote unproductive entrepreneurship and rent seeking in a certain magnitude (Huber/Wörgötter 1998). In any case, however, the market allocation of technical and business knowledge rarely seems effective for CEECs and a major challenge for post-socialist policy makers is to create structures that channel into productive uses the entrepreneurial potential that is already available to their economies.

From our viewpoint it appears necessary to question the model of optimal market allocation, and as outlined above seek other explanations apart from economic ones that will help us to understand entrepreneurial activities in Central and Eastern Europe.

3 Contributions of Non-Economic Theories Revisited

In general it seems easy to explain entrepreneurial activity by purely economic arguments. There are, for instance, approaches which view the entrepreneur as a special type of opportunist who has a strong ability to act upon dynamics in the economy. In this case, entrepreneurship can simply be regarded as a function of economic development itself (Casson 1990). Others view entrepreneurship as the preference for taking risks, which enables an entrepreneur to undertake ventures, not necessarily innovations, that others are unwilling to attempt (Ronen 1983). Each of these ways of defining entrepreneurship – and there are several more, chronicled for example by Herbert and Link (1988) – can be traced back to the issue of the pursued opportunity. In virtually all examples the opportunity is profit. Baumol (1990), for instance, centred his analysis on profit motivation as the driving force for the establishment and growth of business activity variety. Referring to some historical examples, however, he concluded similarly to Suarez Villa (1989) that his own approach does not fully explain the phenomenon of the entrepreneur. Indeed Casson (1999, 45) noted that economists who have taken research on entrepreneurship seriously have been those who have viewed the economy as being socially embedded.

Thus the question arises what characteristics precisely stifle or encourage successful entrepreneurship and the supply of entrepreneurs? This leads us to contributions based on sociological, historical as well as political theories. Samuelson (1964) showed in his early analysis that fundamental psychological or cultural drives are often associated with entrepreneurial vigour. Thus reasons for our concern about regarding entrepreneurship as a simple economic matter can be found in theory as well as in historical evidence. Since a traditional maximising approach focuses on what firm owners or managers routinely do, on a day-to-day basis within accepted rules, resourcebased and technical constraints, such a view cannot accommodate the entrepreneurial function, which is specifically oriented towards changes in the ends and means of production. Focusing on entrepreneurship implies, almost by definition, a behavioural rather than a maximising theory of organisational behaviour (Young 1990). Furthermore, as Supple (1997) has shown in his synthesis of pre-industrial entrepreneurship, the non-economic context, e.g. anti-entrepreneurial values and norms in society, can be of great importance too. They are often at the heart of a strong mechanism suppressing the supply of entrepreneurship.

Thus, by leaving the baselines of traditional economic theory, especially the micro-economic foundations of the entrepreneurial supply and demand functions, issues come into view which are, in our view, better explained by other disciplines. Indeed, research on entrepreneurship, which is seen by many as the prime mover of human action, initiative and innovation (Kirzner 1973 and 1980; Klep 1994), offers a broad spectrum for scientists beyond economic theory and even beyond mainstream economics. Resting on the writings of Karl Marx, Alfred Weber and Joseph Schumpeter and their scholars leads to a more profound and useful view on entrepreneurship. The sociological tradition which has grown out of the writings of Marx and Weber was dominated by the claim to explain how the bourgeoisie could have emerged from a corporate system and a religiously preoccupied feudal society. Though differing in emphasis, their accounts overlapped. Whereas Marx stressed more "material" factors, like technical change and the expansion of production and trade, Weber discussed changes in the value systems of individuals and groups. The German historical school, mainly represented by one of its protagonists, Werner Sombart, as well as the Austrian school with authors like Ludwig von Mises or Israel Kirzner, have stressed the dynamic role of entrepreneurship within economic systems. While their background was that of economists, their exceptional contribution to economic theory was based on borrowings from sociology, psychology and history – disciplines which also offer rich insights into entrepreneurship. Let us start by reviewing contributions from social science and history.

Prior to Baumol's approach development theorists like McClelland (1955 and 1961) emphasised that there are systematic variations in the supply elasticity of entrepreneurial effort across social groups found in complex societies, and these variations are understandable in general terms, given a detailed grasp of the social matrices that the actors come from and operate in. The Polish example provided by Matusiak (in this volume), for instance, has shown that the desire to improve their own financial situation is the leading motive for Polish entrepreneurs. But the motive is twofold: on the one hand, it can be used as explanation for expecting extraordinary profits. On the other hand, it rests on a desire to stabilise ones own position compared to ones former existence as an employee, or compared to the present alternative: becoming unemployed. Suarez-Villa (1989) outlined the importance of non-material aspects and rewards such as achievement motivation or status in promoting entrepreneurial action. Similarly to the various roles played by entrepreneurs, their reasons for operating on markets are often influenced by motives more significant than profits or material reasons, even when country-specific aspects are taken into account.[3]

Klep and Cauwenberghe (1994) offer an interesting collection of studies on the role of the state in promoting, protecting, correcting or discouraging entrepreneurship. This view emphasises the interweaving of both actors which has evolved over the centuries. For example Samsonowicz (1994) shows, in the context of the city of Gdansk in the fifteenth century, how in the relatively autonomous sphere some important innovations were made through the use of public authority. Another, more ambiguous example is provided by Fursenko (1994), which stresses the role of unfavourable framework conditions for entrepreneurs imposed by state agencies and traditional élites in Russia in the late nineteenth century. Also the example of Hungary (Pach 1994) in the sixteenth and seventeenth centuries refers to an incentive

3 Here we refer to several empirical studies on motives of entrepreneurship in Europe and the US as well as the Asian region, such as Casson (1990), Ronen (1983) and Schak (1994).

structure for entrepreneurs which did not lead to a continuation over generations as merchants, for example, but often ended in a position within the ranks of aristocracy. Thus social prestige, status and security were perceived as more attractive than personal prosperity. While these examples stem from a historical perspective, their implications are in some cases useful for present investigations into CEECs transformation process.

It seems, not only from the view of traditional social scientists, that an over-accentuation of the transformation process as an economic process has led to a neglecting of the historical and social heritage of each country in Central and Eastern Europe. Following the main thesis provided by Kandil and Walter in this volume, a certain degree of consensus in society has to be created on the specific needs, the ranking in time and priorities of the final outcome of the transformation process. In order to be successful new élites are needed, and they can be found among the "practitioners", e.g. among managers or innovators engaged in entrepreneurial activities. According to this view, transformation has be complemented by education and qualification – here specifically education of these new élites. Consequently entrepreneurs perform more than a production function; they are social beings with different expectations, incentives and preferences, their decisions relate to society in various ways, and they operate in different ways within economic systems. As outlined in the country studies above, establishing a firm requires multiple skills and resources. Beyond the specific product knowledge financial, personal and, last but not least, social resources are needed. Not all of these belong to the basic equipment of a potential entrepreneur. Firm-specific resources are often provided by the entrepreneurial environment. But specific knowledge has to be acquired either by learning routines or by qualification activities. In any case, particularly in CEECs, the availability of resources and specific knowledge cannot be taken for granted. Therefore appropriate investment in education and training may be regarded as a determinant of entrepreneurship. As Foreman-Peck and Minoglou (2000) point out, in a simpler technological and institutional environment, essential human capital and information sources are likely to have been supplied informally more often. A spell abroad to gain business experience in other countries, foreign origins, or a father already in business, might provide the ability to identify unique profit opportunities. Therefore, beyond an economic view, thinking on entrepreneurship is concerned with the social and psychological origins of the actors themselves, sometimes rooted in historical aspects of societies' development.

Again by interpreting Schumpeter, this time as expressed in his later work Capitalism, Socialism and Democracy (1942), another issue comes into view which is not purely economic related. Here we rely upon a more political view, i.e. how and whether entrepreneurship can contribute to carrying the burden in transitional countries' path to democracy. In addressing the political role of small firms and entrepreneurship, we are asking about their the stabilising force within capitalistic systems. Schumpeter's view on the prevailing power of socialism rested on the extinction of the entrepreneurial class, while at the same time large firms and bureaucracy gained more and more importance. Today, CEECs have to go the other way round. That is, they have to replace central economic planning by individual planning, and reduce the power of the larger collective combines through private firms.

In some cases the former power of the combines has not been completely restricted, in others it has been transformed into a new monopoly. Major problems occur through the chronically deficient and unproductive large firms which are still managed by the state. They are one of the central obstacles on the way to a market economy. The option of closing these state-owned firms is often rejected because of the effects on labour markets and the politically motivated fear of losing the next election – a phenomenon that is well know in western democracies too. Instead, the preferred option in CEECs is reform, either within the state's responsibility or by privatisation. However, in many cases these firms are poor candidates for market viability. In either case (state-organised reform or privatisation) the aim is to restructure these former large combines to compete on international markets. This has happened very often in branches such as energy or transportation. And these are industrial sectors which allow high profits compared to other sectors. In addition, an imperfect institutional pattern of the political and economic system in transition economies has sometimes generated a status of non-equilibrium in the power system, which influences the formation of motives and behaviour of economic and state agents. Non-equilibration of the power system shows itself on the one hand in the absence (or weakness) of market system-forming power sources like competition, legal power of the state, consumer power and, on the other hand, in the surplus of economic (market), administrative, management, and other power sources (Heering/Pfirrmann in this volume). The dominant agents, i.e. large firms, their management and proprietors respectively are then able to set up their own rules and to violate those that are necessary for a functioning market economy (Dementiev 2000). As a consequence large firms are favoured, at the expense of small firms and entrepreneurs. Examples are loans and credits, trade licenses, and distribution of land. In contrast, small firms and entrepreneurs often face administrative hindrances of various kinds, corruption and bribery. The latter have become a big problem in those CEECs where inexperienced market regulators were not – and still are not – able to police markets that are moving quickly and without apparent reason. In addition, the illegal role carried out by entrepreneurs often leads the impression that rent-seeking is the only game. However, investigation into the reasons behind a "racket economy" of this kind again reveals the relevance of mainly non-economic factors. The presence or absence of factors like the withdrawal of the state from law enforcement, weak societal organisations, or a moral vacuum are often important in explaining why economic reforms tend to fail (Fish 1998).

The political implication of these monopolies is obvious, for example, in Russia as well as other countries in particular from the former Soviet Union and crucial for their development: if monopoly in the words of Schumpeter (1942) means arteriosclerosis on the way to a capitalistic system, then more small firms and entrepreneurs are needed to bring the transitional countries into a state of health where a "self responsible" continuation is assured without the fear of falling back onto the former path of socialism. This task cannot be fulfilled by the class of technical entrepreneurs, artisans, retailers and managers. As outlined by Kandil and Walter (in this volume), new élites are required. They ought act as a strong political group, and as an important element of democratic stabilisation.

4 Concluding Remarks – Are Certain Models of Entrepreneurship Needed?

Defining entrepreneurship in the Central and Eastern European context is a crucial task, which remains vital for an understanding of economic transformation and democratic development. To choose the definition of entrepreneurship most appropriate to the Central and Eastern European context, it is necessary to bear in mind the entrepreneurial origins, skills and incentive structures that will be needed to complete a successful transformation to a market economy. In economies characterised by highly imperfect markets and substantial distortions, the conventional neo-classical assumption of self-combining factors of production is particularly unrealistic. Furthermore, what is neglected by mainstream theory is the socio-cultural establishment as well as the stabilising role of entrepreneurship, not only as a factor that moves markets towards equilibrium, but also as a political force in democratic societies.

Based on comparative historic analysis, Supple (1977) launched the issue of "national models of entrepreneurship", showing the functional fit of entrepreneurship, economic conditions and political as well socio-cultural institutions and values. While this view argues towards the need for a fundamental investigation into all dimensions of entrepreneurship and its environment, we must conclude that the present circumstances do not allow an adequate assessment and evaluation within the context of transformation. While the creative entrepreneur is always linked to dynamics in an economy, and thus considered as a function of economic development itself, we believe that trials aiming at a quantification of the benefits of entrepreneurial activity execute the second step before the first one, i.e. expecting results before an effective framework has been established. Moreover it seems that an integrated perception of entrepreneurship, taking into account contributions from

- sociological and psychological research,
- historical analyses, and
- political science

would appear to be a prerequisite for understanding the relationship between entrepreneurship and economic development, as well as for the formulation of policy recommendations for the transition countries.

The outlined discussion has made clear that economists mainly regard entrepreneurship as a distinct form of economic activity. But there are others who have not examined entrepreneurship from a purely economic viewpoint. We have mentioned above the limitations of a purely economics-driven perception of the transformation processes in CEECs, stating that there are no theories or models that can simply be transferred from the West to the East. If asked to define entrepreneurship, or at least to describe the object of investigation, we would not really be less satisfied with conventional definitions or new syntheses[4] based on a purely economic position. However, we are as yet only in the position to shed some light on aspects that may be largely viewed as a response to the shortcomings of traditional definitions offered by economists.

It is assumed that the Central and Eastern European economies will have a great need for the combinatory and market-supplementing skills of entrepreneurs. What should have become clear is that entrepreneurship is more than a function of economic development itself. To regard it as such would narrow our view and inhibit the perception of other important factors that influence entrepreneurially-based growth. In contrast, we question the view that in economies in transformation, it is specifically national models of entrepreneurship that are relevant, rather than specific cross-national patterns of entrepreneurship. The latter can be regarded as a compromise to supplement the shortcomings of "cut-and-dried" definitions of entrepreneurship by drawing on different scientific disciplines. We are aware of the incompleteness of our argumentation; however, at least we are able to propose three further issues that may act as a guideline for further investigation: The first of these is the question of the origins of an entrepreneur. The second, closely intertwined with the first, is the issue of the behaviours and characteristics which constitute entrepreneurship. The third question, an area which also appears to have been little investigated, regards the dynamic interaction of endogenous and exogenous determinants in the development of small firms, and especially the relationship between entrepreneurial firms and the state. The challenge now is to elaborate an integrative conceptual framework which considers all the issues mentioned above, and adapt it to the process of transformation in Central and Eastern Europe. Until this task is fulfilled government will not, from our point of view, be able to launch effective, efficient mechanisms and support measures aiming to provide an environment which will foster the success and viability of small firms and entrepreneurship.

---

4 See for example the contribution made by Hérbert and Link (1988).

Literature

Acs, Z. J.; Audretsch, D. B. (1993): Conclusion. In: Acs, Z. J.; Audretsch, D.B. (Eds.): Small Firms and Entrepreneurship: an East – West Perspective. Cambridge, MA: Cambridge University Press, pp.227-232.

Acs, Z. J.; Carlsson, B.; Karlsson, C. (1999): The Linkages among Entrepreneurship, SMEs and the Macroeconomy. In: Acs, Z. J.; Carlsson, B.; Karlsson, C. (Eds.): Entrepreneurship, Small and Medium-Sized Enterprises and the Macroeconomy. Cambridge, MA: Cambridge University Press, pp.3-42.

Ardishvili, A.; Cardozo, R. (1993): Socio-Political Structure of a Society as a Determinant of Entrepreneurial Behaviour: The Case of Post-Communist Russia. Paper presented at the Third Annual Global Conference of Entrepreneurship Research, Lyon, March 8-10th, mimeograph.

Baumol, W. J. (1968): Entrepreneurship in Economic Theory. American Economic Review 58 (2), pp.64-98.

Baumol, W. J. (1990): Entrepreneurship: Productive, Unproductive, and Destructive. Journal of Political Economy 98 (5), pp.893-921.

Brezinski, H.; Franck, E.; Fritsch, M. (1998): Introduction. In: Brezinski, H.; Franck, E.; Fritsch, M. (Eds.): The Microeconomics of Transformation and Growth. Cheltenham: Edward Elgar, pp.1-14.

Casson, M. (1990, Ed.): Entrepreneurship. Aldershot: Edward Elgar.

Casson, M. (1999): Entrepreneurship and the Theory of the Firm in Entrepreneurship. In: Acs, Z. J.; Carlsson, B.; Karlsson, C. (Eds.): Small and Medium-Sized Enterprises and the Macroeconomy. Cambridge, MA: Cambridge University Press, pp.45-78.

Dementiev, V. V. (2000): Transitional Economy as the System of Unbalanced Power. Paper presented at the annual EAEPE conference in Berlin, November 2.-4th, mimeograph.

Foreman-Peck, J.; Pepelasis Minoglou, I. (2000): Entrepreneurship and Convergence. Greek Businessmen in the later Nineteenth Century. Paper presented at the annual EAEPE conference in Berlin, November 2.-4th, mimeograph.

Fish, S. M. (1998): The Roots and Remedies for Russia's Racket Economy. In: Cohen, S. S.; Schwartz, A. (Eds.): The Tunnel at the End of the Light: Privatisation, Business, Networks, and Economic Transformation in Russia. University of California at Berkeley, pp.86-138.

Fursenko, A. A. (1994): Public and Private Affairs of K.A. Skal'kovskii (as seen from his personal papers). In: Klep, P.; Cauwenberghe, E. V. (Eds.): Entrepreneurship and the Transformation of the Economy. Leuven: Leuven University Press, pp. 267-274.

Hérbert, R. F.; Link, A. N. (1988): The Entrepreneur. New York: Praeger.

Hughes, G.; Hare, P. G. (1992): Industrial Policy and Restructuring in Eastern Europe. Oxford Review of Economic Policy 8, pp. 42-104.

Huber, P.; Wörgötter, A. (1998): Political Survival or Entrepreneurial Development? Observations on Russian Business Networks. In: Cohen, S. S.; Schwartz, A. (Eds.): The Tunnel at the End of the Light: Privatisation, Business, Networks, and Economic Transformation in Russia. University of California at Berkeley, pp.51-65.

McClelland, D. C. (1955, Ed.): Studies in Motivation. New York: Appleton-Century Crafts.

McClelland, D. C. (1961): The Achieving Society. Princeton, NJ: Van Nostrand.

Kirzner, I.. (1973): Competition and Entrepreneurship. Chicago: The University of Chicago Press.

Kirzner, I.. (1980): The Primacy of Entrepreneurial Discovery. In: The Institute of Economic Affairs (Ed.): The Prime Mover of Progress. The Entrepreneur in Capitalism and Socialism, pp.3-26.

Klep, P. (1994): Entrepreneurship and the Transformation of the Economy: an Introduction. In: Klep, P.; Cauwenberghe, E. V. (Eds.): Entrepreneurship and the Transformation of the Economy. Leuven: Leuven University Press, pp. 59-82.

Klep, P.; Cauwenberghe, E.V. (1994, Eds.): Entrepreneurship and the Transformation of the Economy, Leuven: Leuven University Press.

Pach, Z. P. (1994): Embourgeoisement or Ennoblissement? The Problem of the Lack of Capital in Hungary (Sixteenth and Seventeenth Centuries). In: Klep, P.; Cauwenberghe, E. V. (Eds.): Entrepreneurship and the Transformation of the Economy. Leuven: Leuven University Press, pp. 165-172.

Ronen, J. (1983, Ed.): Entrepreneurship. Lexington, MA: D.C. Heath and Company.

Samuelson, K. (1964): Religion and Economic Action. New York: Harper Row.

Samsonowicz, H. (1994): New Financial Institutions in Gdansk in the Fifteenth Century. In: Klep, P.; Cauwenberghe, E. V. (Eds.): Entrepreneurship and the Transformation of the Economy. Leuven: Leuven University Press, pp. 229-234.

Schak, D. (1994): Entrepreneurship, Economic Growth and Social Change: the Transformation of Southern China, Griffith University. Australia-Asia Paper No.71, Griffith (Queensland).

Schultz, T. W. (1975): The Value of the Ability to Deal with Disequilibria. Journal of Economic Literature 13, pp.827-846.

Schumpeter, J. A. (1934): The Theory of economic development, Cambridge, MA: Harvard University Press.

Schumpeter, J. A. (1942): Capitalism, Socialism and Democracy. New York: Harper Row (dt.: Kapitalismus, Sozialismus und Demokratie, 6.Auflage, Tübingen: Francke).

Siebert, H. (1993): Preface. In: Siebert, H. (Ed.): Economic Growth in the World Economy. Tübingen: Mohr, pp. V-VIII.

Stark, D. (1994): Recombinant Property in East European Capitalism (quoted by D. Bohle 1999: Der Pfad in die Abhängigkeit, Discussion Paper FS I 99-103, Wissenschaftszentrum Berlin für Sozialforschung, Berlin).

Suarez-Villa, L. (1989): The Evolution of Regional Economics, Entrepreneurship and Macroeconomic Change. New York: Praeger.

Supple, B. (1977): The Nature of Enterprise. In: Cambridge Economic History of Europe, vol. V, chap. VI, Cambridge.

Tyson, L. D.; Petrin, T.; Rogers, H. (1994): Promoting Entrepreneurship in Eastern Europe. Small Business Economics 6, pp.165-184.

Young, D. R. (1990): Entrepreneurship and the Behavior of Nonprofit Organsization: Elements of a Theory. In: Casson, M. (Ed.): Entrepreneurship. Aldershot: Edward Elgar, pp. 161-184.

Contributors

David B. Audretsch, Ameritech Chair of Economic Development and Director of the Institute for Development Strategies at Indiana University. Research Fellowships at the Centre for Economic Policy Research (London) and the Wissenschaftszentrum (Berlin); consultant of the World Bank, National Academy of Sciences, U.S. State Department, United States Federal Trade Commission, General Accounting Office and International Trade Commission, United Nations, Commission of the European Union, the European Parliament, the OECD, Member of the Advisory Board to a number of international research and policy institutes; research fields: links between entrepreneurship, government policy, innovation, economic development and global competitiveness. Founder and editor of the journal: Small Business Economics: An International Journal.

Tibor Dőry, PhD in regional economics, Research Fellow at the West Hungarian Research Institute, Centre of Regional Studies of the Hungarian Academy of Sciences in Győr; graduated in mechanical engineering at the Technical University Budapest, diploma in finance and accounting at the College of Finance and Accountancy in Budapest; research and consulting experience focuses on regional economic development strategies, cross-border development, strategic innovation programmes and regional foresight exercises.

Viljenka Godina, Director of the Economic Institute Maribor, Slovenia, member of the CityCouncil and member of the Slovene Government Working Group for the Adoption of Acquis Communitaire; co-chair of the Central European Initiative Working Group on SMEs and member of national and international working groups dealing with SME issues; her expertise includes research, consulting and development of customised training courses for entrepreneurs and development of SME promotion programmes.

Walter Heering, senior lecturer at University of Brighton, assistant professor at the Free University of Berlin, Department of Political Science; Doctorate in economics and degree in economics at the Free University, research fellow at the Center of Labour Economics and the Center of Research on Policy and Technology; research in micro- and macro-economics; specialisation areas: employment and qualification, firm theory, money and finance, transformation of Eastern Germany.

Fuad Kandil, Professor at the Interfacultative Institute for Applied Studies of Culture and Society at the University of Karlsruhe (TH); doctorate in political sciences and in sociology, graduated in engineering from the Technical University of Darmstadt in 1964; studied economics and social sciences at the Rheinisch-Westfälische Technische Hochschule Aachen, University of Cologne and University of Karlsruhe (TH); research and special interests focus on the sociology of developing countries, tradition and modernity, Muslim minorities in Europe, trans-cultural communication, multiculturalism, industrial modernisation, small enterprises.

Natalia Kovaleva, leading researcher at the Centre for Science Research and Statistics, Moscow, PhD in science (economics). Professional interests: education and science; economics, statistics and sociology. Previous professional background: the USSR State-Plan Economic Research Institute and All-Russian Public Opinion Research Centre.

Krzysztof B. Matusiak works at the Institute of Economics, University of Lodz. PhD in economics, expert of the World Bank in entrepreneurship, advisor and consultant in governmental, regional and local institutions, former vice-president of the Polish Business and Innovation Association in Poland; his research activities include theory and practice of entrepreneurship, innovative processes, technology transfer and forms of regional development support.

Duro Kutlaca, head of the Science and Technology Policy Research Center, Belgrade; PhD in organisational sciences, research associate at Mihajlo Pupin Institute, visiting researcher to Fraunhofer ISI and visiting fellow at Science and Technology Policy Research Unit, University of Sussex, United Kingdom, former member of (National Experts for Science and Technology Indicator) group at OECD; his scientific disciplines: operations research; information theory; organisation and management in research and development.

Emmanuel Muller, researcher at the Fraunhofer ISI and member of the Bureau d'Economie Théorique et Appliquée (BETA) at the University Louis Pasteur (ULP), Strasbourg, lecturer at the Department of Economics, ULP; European PhD in economics, graduated in management, postgraduate degree in international financial management. Research stays at the Technical University of Budapest, National Institute of Scientific Research, Montreal, University College, London; current research activities: regional development and innovation strategies, innovation processes in SMEs and knowledge-intensive business services, knowledge economics.

Oliver Pfirrmann, founder and leading member of the expert and consultancy group EXIS^{3}T at the Free University of Berlin, Center of Research on Policy and Technology; Doctorate in Economics and Social Science at the Free University of Berlin and degree in political science; research fellow at the Fraunhofer ISI and consultant at the VDI/VDE-Informationstechnik, Berlin Teltow. Main areas of research: small firms and entrepreneurship, technology policy, development and diffusion of new technologies, regional development.

Ioan Piturescu, President of the National Institute of SMEs, Vice-President of the National Council of Small and Medium-Sized Private Enterprises in Romania, director of Technology and Business Incubator Center, scientific research degree; former head of the Information and Automation Department of the Mechanical Engineering and Research Institute, Bucharest.

Slavo Radosevic, lecturer at the School of Slavonic and East European Studies, University College London, Senior Research Fellow at the Science and Technology Policy Research Unit, University of Sussex, United Kingdom, consultant for UNIDO, World Bank, OECD, and the European Commission, former researcher at the Institute of Economics Zagreb, Federal Under-Secretary for Development in the last ex-Yugoslav Government; research interests: science, technology and industrial change in CEECs.

Michael Steiner, Professor at the Department of Economics, University of Graz; Head of the Institute for Technology and Regional Policy, Joanneum Research, Graz; Expert of the German Ministry for Education and Research, European Commission, OECD; studies in Law, Economics and Sociology at the University of Graz, the University of Miami/Ohio, and the Faculté Internationale du Droit Comparé (Strasbourg); visiting professor at the University of Glasgow; University of Kent (Canterbury); University of Bacconi (Milano); University of Klagenfurt; University of Pécs.

Günter Hans Walter, project co-ordinator and research scientist at the Fraunhofer ISI and lecturer at the Interfacultative Institute for Applied Studies of Culture and Society at the University of Karlsruhe (TH); Dr. phil. (Political Sciences), Free University of Berlin, diploma in Business Engineering, University of Karlsruhe (TH), professional qualification in industrial management; current research activities: regional innovation and technology policy, technology transfer, modernisation of CEECs.

Friederike Welter, scientific consultant at the Rheinisch-Westfälisches Institut für Wirtschaftsforschung in Essen, working group "Craft and SMEs", Doctorate and Masters Degree in economics; specialisation areas: policy for SMEs, small firms and entrepreneurship in transformation countries, entrepreneurship research.

Andrea Zenker, scientist at the Fraunhofer ISI; diploma in Geography, technical assistant at the Lower Saxony Forest Tree Breeding Station; studied Geography and Modern Languages at the University of Gießen and l'Université de Besançon, consultant for Desktop Mapping at Graphical Information Technology Consulting; current research activities: regional science, regional innovation strategies, methodology in innovation research, knowledge economics.

Printing: Strauss GmbH, Mörlenbach
Binding: Schäffer, Grünstadt

Lightning Source UK Ltd.
Milton Keynes UK
09 January 2010

148343UK00003B/64/A

9 783790 814675